An Ode to Joy

Erica Brown • Shira Weiss
Editors

An Ode to Joy

Judaism and Happiness in the Thought of Rabbi Lord Jonathan Sacks and Beyond

Editors
Erica Brown
Yeshiva University
New York, NY, USA

Shira Weiss
Yeshiva University
New York, NY, USA

ISBN 978-3-031-28228-7   ISBN 978-3-031-28229-4   (eBook)
https://doi.org/10.1007/978-3-031-28229-4

© The Editor(s) (if applicable) and The Author(s), under exclusive licence to Springer Nature Switzerland AG 2023

This work is subject to copyright. All rights are solely and exclusively licensed by the Publisher, whether the whole or part of the material is concerned, specifically the rights of translation, reprinting, reuse of illustrations, recitation, broadcasting, reproduction on microfilms or in any other physical way, and transmission or information storage and retrieval, electronic adaptation, computer software, or by similar or dissimilar methodology now known or hereafter developed.

The use of general descriptive names, registered names, trademarks, service marks, etc. in this publication does not imply, even in the absence of a specific statement, that such names are exempt from the relevant protective laws and regulations and therefore free for general use.

The publisher, the authors, and the editors are safe to assume that the advice and information in this book are believed to be true and accurate at the date of publication. Neither the publisher nor the authors or the editors give a warranty, expressed or implied, with respect to the material contained herein or for any errors or omissions that may have been made. The publisher remains neutral with regard to jurisdictional claims in published maps and institutional affiliations.

This Palgrave Macmillan imprint is published by the registered company Springer Nature Switzerland AG.
The registered company address is: Gewerbestrasse 11, 6330 Cham, Switzerland

Paper in this product is recyclable.

Foreword: This is the Day God Has Made, Let Us Celebrate and Rejoice in It

Of the many topics which my father Rabbi Sacks *z"l* explored and expounded in his lifetime, it is interesting to me—and would I think have been to him as well—that it is his teachings on the subject of joy which strike a particular chord with so many, and which merit a volume of reflections such as this.

Because joy was not something which came easily to Rabbi Sacks. He was, instead, highly attuned to the pain of the world, the "music in the minor key" he said that he sensed in the world, even as a child. By his own admission, had some of the circumstances of his life been different—in particular had he not met and married my mother—he may have been overwhelmed by the sadness of life.

Perhaps that is precisely why joy was a topic he took very seriously indeed. Joy could not be taken for granted. It was not, for Rabbi Sacks, simply an emotion—something which came, and left, fleetingly; which one either felt or did not feel at any given moment. It was rather something to be worked at, learned, and earned. Nor was joy the absence of pain, the opposite of sadness, something to be found by overcoming or erasing the bad parts of life. Instead, joy had to coexist with sadness, each making space for the other, shedding new perspective on the other. Above all, for Rabbi Sacks, joy was active—something we could create through how we lived. The task was to work out how. And for that task, as for so many others, he wanted to know what Jewish text and tradition had to say, and how he could shed new light onto its teachings.

Others far more expert than I respond to that question in the chapters that follow. I would simply add three small lessons in joy which he taught through how he lived.

Firstly, joy can be created when you pay attention to the details. Whether the particular expression in the eyes of a grandchild's photograph, the successful pursuit of the perfect pencil or white shirt collar, or a single exquisite note in a symphony, his unbounded enthusiasm for the details was infectious. Don't assume joy is to be found only in the grand or noble things in life. Stop, pay attention to the tiny points of perfection in front of you, and don't waste a drop.

Secondly, joy will always, ultimately, be made with others. Joy, he taught, is something we create when we share what we have. When we open ourselves up to others, when we work with others, learn from others. Joy is created not simply with the people we love, but also from the chance encounters, the people who teach us or challenge us, the strangers we can turn into friends. We can't do it alone, and sometimes we all need reminders of that.

And thirdly, joy is a skill which takes practice. Rabbi Sacks studied and taught about joy, but he also worked at it throughout his life. Because joy is not something we just wait to be lucky enough to find—it is something we have to take responsibility for.

My heartfelt thanks go to those who conceived of, curated, edited, and contributed to this book, which will help to give the topic of joy the focus and the seriousness which Rabbi Sacks knew it merited. In particular to Erica Brown and her team at the Sacks-Herenstein Center for Values and Leadership, and the Herenstein family and Yeshiva University community for their vision and dedication to the values my father lived and taught. In their merit, and in his memory, may we each get a little better each day at the holy task of creating joy. Because "*This* is the day God has made, let us celebrate and rejoice in it." It is not over a distant horizon; it is something we can do today.

London, UK   Gila Sacks

Foreword: Building Bridges

Rabbi Jonathan Sacks was the consummate bridge builder. He bridged the humanities and the sciences, the ancient and the modern, never missing an opportunity to share stories—from the Torah and from Greek mythology—while at the same time possessing a voracious appetite for latest research in psychology and neuroscience. In his sermons Rabbi Sacks brought these worlds together, seamlessly, naturally.

Rabbi Sacks created bridges within the Jewish communities, appealing to the orthodox and the reformed, the ultraorthodox and the unidentified—who often identified a little bit more after encountering his wisdom. He created bridges with other religions, often meeting with Christian and Muslim clerics, to discuss our common past and the potential of a bright future. Professor Ed Husain, author of *The House of Islam* described Rabbi Sacks as "a towering intellectual figure with a command across faiths, philosophy, history and public policy."

I had been an admirer of Rabbi Sacks for years before first meeting him in person, on a flight from Tel Aviv to London. I could hardly believe my good fortune, when I realized that we were seated next to each other, and the next five hours and thirty minutes passed in a blink of an eye. Time flies when you're having fun—and it flies exceedingly fast when you're in the presence of one of the great minds and hearts to grace our global village.

In the Jewish tradition, names are not considered a random collection of letters and sounds assigned to a particular person. Rather, names define our essence, guide us towards our destiny, are a reflection of our soul. The word for soul in Hebrew is Neshama (נשמה). The middle two letters, shin

(ש) and mem (מ) spell Shem, which means "name." In his essay "Judaism and the Power of Names" Yeshiva University Professor Rabbi Benjamin Blech writes about the midrash that tells us that when we leave this world and face the judgment of our creator, "one of the most powerful questions we will be asked at the outset is, What is your name—and did you live up to it?"

Yonatan, Rabbi Sack's first name in Hebrew, comprises two words—Yo (God) and Natan (Given). God has given. Yes, Rabbi Yonatan Sacks is God's gift to us. But there's more. The word "natan" (meaning given or "to give") is unusual in that it is a palindrome, which means that it can be read left to right or right to left. In our conversation on that flight the Rabbi and I talked about the word *natan* in the context of the research on happiness. Studies by psychologists Ed O'Brien, Sonja Lyubormirsky, and others demonstrate that one of the most powerful ways to increase our own happiness is through giving, because when we give (natan) we are given (natan) right back. It is through giving, argued Rabbi Sacks, that we bridge between Martin Buber's I and Thou, between my own happiness and that of others.

Rabbi Yonatan Sacks lived up to his name, bridging among religions, disciplines, and people. I hope we can live up to Rabbi Sacks' vision of a world with a myriad of bridges connecting us together.

Centenary UniversityTal Ben-Shahar
Hackettstown, NJ, USA

Acknowledgments

The Rabbi Lord Jonathan Sacks-Herenstein Center for Values and Leadership at Yeshiva University was founded by Terri and Andrew Herenstein to disseminate and integrate the teachings of Rabbi Sacks within the ethos of Yeshiva University's core values and to develop future leaders. The Herensteins' generous gift has enabled this anthology, among the many other academic, communal, educational, and literary initiatives of the Sacks-Herenstein Center. We dedicate this book to Terri and Andrew with our most profound gratitude for making all of this possible. Your warmth, your depth, and your leadership are a model for us all. You have brought honor to a great man and to a great institution.

We would also like to acknowledge all of the Sacks family members and those who worked directly with Rabbi Sacks for their contributions and thank the many academics, educators, and artists who, by expounding on joy in its myriad dimensions and in a variety of Jewish disciplines, will hopefully expand the joy of the reader. The Sacks-Herenstein Center is also privileged to consult with the Rabbi Sacks Legacy Trust in the UK on our shared work. Special thanks to Rabbi Dr. Ari Berman, President of Yeshiva University, for his dedication to making the Sacks-Herenstein Center a reality. To our wonderful family, friends, and colleagues, thank you for being a source of daily happiness and reminding us why the work matters.

Contents

1	**Introduction** Erica Brown and Shira Weiss	1
Part I	**Personal Reflections: Rabbi Sacks and Joy**	5
2	**Rabbi Sacks and Joy: A Personal Reflection** Alan Sacks	7
3	**Joy as Challenge: Personal Reflections on Working with Rabbi Sacks** Dan Sacker	13
4	**Beethoven's Last Sonata** Joanna Benarroch	21
5	**The Language of the Soul** Shim Craimer	25

Part II Joy in the Bible   33

6 "What Good Is That?" Happiness and the Emotional
   Range of Ecclesiastes   35
   Erica Brown

7 Joy to Shushan: The Book of Esther's Radical Cocktail of
   Happiness   43
   Stuart W. Halpern

8 Odes to Joy in Sonnets and Psalms   49
   Shaina Trapedo

9 Flowing with Joy   59
   Raphael Zarum

10 Joy and Trembling   65
    Alex Israel

Part III Joy in Rabbinic Literature   75

11 Reflections on the Human Experience of Joy   77
    Jacob J. Schacter

12 All for the Best: Rabbi Akiva's Theodicy of Joy   83
    Gila Fine

13 Inclusive Joy: On Maimonides' Definition of Meaningful
    Happiness   91
    Ari Berman

14 Show Me Those Pearly Whites: Divine and Human Smiling   97
    Elana Stein Hain

15 Bright Yellow Judaism   103
    Chaim Strauchler

16	*Simha Shel Mitzvah*: The Commandment of Joy, or the Joy of a Commandment? Sara Tillinger Wolkenfeld	109
17	Finding Happiness in the Transience of Sukkot Joseph Dweck	119

Part IV Joy in Legal Thought 125

18	Law's Joy: Celebrating the Study and Practice of Law Michael A. Helfand and Chaim Saiman	127
19	Joy as a Legal Metaphor Suzanne Last Stone	133
20	Emotion, Connection, and Motion: Deploying Positive and Negative Emotions in Conflict Resolution Michelle Greenberg-Kobrin	139

Part V Joy in Jewish Philosophy and Kabbalah 145

21	Happiness and Joy: Rabbi Sacks' Dialogue of Athens and Jerusalem Hava Tirosh-Samuelson	147
22	Crescas and Rabbi Sacks on Happiness and Joy Samuel Lebens	159
23	Standing Before God in Joy and Fear Shira Weiss	169
24	Joys, Oys, and the Pursuit of Happiness Daniel Rynhold	175

25 Affirming Life in Joy Across the Divinity Divide: Rabbi
    Jonathan Sacks and Friedrich Nietzsche   183
    Michael J. Harris

26 Sacks on Sisyphus and Soloveitchik: From Myth to
    Meaning   191
    Dov Lerner

27 "I Will Tell You How Once They Were Joyous": On the
    Joy of the Baal Shem Tov's Hasidim and of R. Nahman of
    Bratslav   197
    Biti Roi

Part VI   Joy in Jewish History and Modernity   209

28 Happy Alone or Happy Together? R. Jonathan Sacks,
    Contemporary Culture, and the Promise of Hope   211
    Jonathan D. Sarna

29 Joy and Judaism at the Battle of Bunker Hill   217
    Ari Lamm

30 Joy in the Interfaith Encounter   225
    Malka Z. Simkovich

Part VII   Joy in Hebrew Literature and Prayer   231

31 Joy, Sorrow, and Emotional Equilibrium in Agnon   233
    Jeffrey Saks

32 The Joy of Ordinary Living   243
    Yael Ziegler

33 Celebrating the Good Through the *Sheheheyanu* Blessing   249
    Johnny Solomon

Part VIII Joy in the Arts — 255

34 *Ashrei Yoshvei Veitekha*: Joy in the Ancient Synagogue — 257
Steven Fine

35 The Music Beneath the Noise: Faith and Joy in the Writings of Rabbi Sacks — 267
Meir Soloveichik

36 Expressing the Inexpressible: Rabbi Sacks on Music and the Search for a Religious Aesthetic — 273
Harris Bor

Part IX Joy in Psychology and Human Agency — 287

37 Agency in the Bible: Humans Wrestling with God — 289
Martin Seligman, Noah Love, and Philip Maymin

38 Serve God with Joy (and Self-Actualization): Positive Psychology and the Thought of Rabbi Sacks — 299
Tamra Wright

39 Joy Stick: Judaism, Video Games, and the Pursuit of Happiness — 311
Liel Leibovitz

40 Rabbi Sacks' Psychology of Individual and Collective Well-Being — 317
Eli Gottlieb

41 Becoming Whole: The Positive Value of Negative Emotions — 327
Marc Eichenbaum

Part X Joy in Jewish Education 335

42 Positive Psychology and Jewish Wisdom in the Classroom: A Synergic Effect 337
Mordechai Schiffman

43 The Jewish Value of Joy and Positive Education 345
Daniel Rose

44 Joy and Parenting: Partners or Paradox? 355
Rona Milch Novick

45 Building the Joyful Classroom 367
Jeremy Bruce

46 Three Paths to Joy: *Noble Sacrifice, Inner Peace, and Covenantal Community* 375
Benji Levy

Index 383

Notes on Contributors

Joanna Benarroch has been involved in the Jewish community for almost 30 years, working with many communal organizations, synagogue bodies, community professionals and individuals and is a qualified accountant. She joined the Office of the Chief Rabbi in 1997—working for Rabbi Sacks for 23 years. As executive director, Benarroch had responsibility for running a very busy, high profile, public office with multi-faceted roles, managing a wonderful team and supporting Rabbi Sacks in his day-to-day activities. When Rabbi Sacks stepped down as Chief Rabbi in 2013, Benarroch transitioned to jointly run his private office. Since Rabbi Sacks' passing in November 2020, she, as chief executive, has established the Rabbi Sacks Legacy to continue to perpetuate and promote Rabbi Sacks' values and teachings.

Tal Ben-Shahar is an author and lecturer. He taught two of the largest classes in Harvard University's history: "Positive Psychology" and "The Psychology of Leadership." His books have been translated into more than 30 languages, and have appeared on best-seller lists around the world. His latest books are *Happiness Studies* and *Happier, No Matter What*. Ben-Shahar consults and lectures to executives in multi-national corporations, the general public, and at-risk populations. The topics he lectures on include leadership, education, ethics, politics, happiness, self-esteem, resilience, goal setting, and mindfulness. He is the co-founder and chief learning officer of The Happiness Studies Academy and Potentialife. In 2022 Ben-Shahar designed and launched the world's first master's degree in Happiness Studies in collaboration with Centenary University. An avid sportsman, Ben-Shahar won the US Intercollegiate and Israeli National squash championships. He holds his PhD in Organizational Behavior and BA in Philosophy and Psychology from Harvard University.

Ari Berman is Yeshiva University's (YU) fifth President and has authored *The Final Exam* and published articles in *Forbes*, *Newsweek*, and *The Wall Street Journal*. Previously, he was Senior Rabbi of The Jewish Center in New York City, an instructor of Talmud at Yeshiva College and Herzog College, served on the executive council at Herzog College, and is a former chief executive of Hechal Shlomo, the Center of Jewish Heritage in Jerusalem. Rabbi Berman holds his BA from Yeshiva College, his MA in Medieval Jewish Philosophy from the Bernard Revel Graduate School of Jewish Studies, and his rabbinical ordination from the Rabbi Isaac Elchanan Theological Seminary. He holds his PhD in Jewish Thought from the Hebrew University of Jerusalem. His studies also included two years of learning at Yeshivat Har Etzion in Israel.

Harris Bor is an English barrister (trial advocate) specializing in international arbitration and commercial litigation, a lecturer and research fellow at the London School of Jewish Studies, and a rabbinic scholar with the Montefiore Endowment, London. His areas of interest include Jewish intellectual history and thought, and contemporary religion. He has written in both the legal and religion fields, including most recently the book *Staying Human: A Jewish Theology for the Age of Artificial Intelligence* (2021). Bor is an adviser to *AI and Faith*, a US cross-spectrum consortium of faith communities and academic institutions and contributor to the course *AI Ethics: Global Perspectives* offered by The Governance Lab at New York University's Tandon School of Engineering. He holds Master of Laws in International and Comparative Dispute Resolution from Queen Mary, University of London, and a PhD in Theology from Cambridge University.

Erica Brown is the Vice Provost for Values and Leadership at Yeshiva University and the founding Director of its Rabbi Lord Jonathan Sacks-Herenstein Center for Values and Leadership. She previously served as the director of the Mayberg Center for Jewish Education and Leadership and Associate Professor of Curriculum and Pedagogy at The George Washington University. Brown was a Jerusalem Fellow, an Avi Chai Fellow, the recipient of the 2009 Covenant Award, and is a faculty member of the Wexner Foundation. She has written or co-authored 15 books on the Hebrew Bible, spirituality, and leadership and her work has been published in the *New York Times*, *The Atlantic*, *Tablet*, *First Things*, and *The Jewish Review of Books*. Brown wrote a monthly column for the *New York Jewish Week*. She tweeted on one page of Talmud study a day @ DrEricaBrown. Her latest book is *Kohelet and the Search for Meaning* (Maggid).

Jeremy Bruce is Executive Director of The Rabbi Sacks Legacy Trust's operations across North America. Previously, he was Head of School of the Hebrew High School of New England and Principal of the Fuchs Mizrachi Stark High School in Cleveland, Ohio. Rabbi Bruce obtained his rabbinic ordination at Yeshivat Hamivtar, Israel, holds a BA in International History and Politics from the University of Leeds, a master's in Educational Management from King's College London, and is completing a doctorate in Educational Leadership. He has worked for over 20 years in the educational field in the United Kingdom and the United States and was also an adjunct lecturer at the London School of Jewish Studies, where he taught Bible and Jewish philosophy.

Shim Craimer is a musician and cantor. He studied at the Royal Academy of Music and is an accomplished pianist. Having served as Chazzan of the Riverdale Jewish Center for 15 years, Craimer travels the world leading synagogue prayers and performing in concerts and events with Jewish orchestras and ensembles. He has released a number of albums and videos of various musical styles and worked together with Rabbi Sacks on musical projects.

Joseph Dweck is Senior Rabbi of the S&P Sephardi Community of the United Kingdom, and the Rosh Beit Midrash of TheHabura.com. Rabbi Dweck studied in Jerusalem at Yeshiva Hazon Ovadia under the tutelage of former Sephardi Chief Rabbi Ovadia Yosef, has a Master of Arts degree in Jewish Education, and is working toward a master's in Psychotherapy. In his capacity as Senior Rabbi, he also oversees the Sephardi Beth Din and the Sephardi Kashrut Authority. He is Deputy President of the London School of Jewish Studies, President of The Council of Christians and Jews, and Ecclesiastical Authority to the Board of Deputies of British Jews. Rabbi Dweck also serves as a member of the standing committee of the Conference of European Rabbis.

Marc Eichenbaum is a doctoral candidate in Ferkauf Graduate School-Clinical PsyD Program and a Research Associate at the Sacks-Herenstein Center of Yeshiva University. He holds his BA in Psychology from Yeshiva

University and his rabbinic ordination from the Rabbi Isaac Elchanan Theological Seminary. He has worked as a Judaic Studies teacher at the Stella K. Abraham High School for Girls, as the rabbinic researcher for the Straus Center for Torah and Western Thought, and as the rabbinic intern for the Young Israel of Lawrence-Cedarhurst. He has authored several essays exploring the intersection of Torah and psychology.

Gila Fine is a teacher of Aggadah at the Pardes Institute of Jewish Studies, exploring the tales of the Talmud through philosophy, literary criticism, psychoanalysis, and pop-culture. She is also a faculty member of the London School of Jewish Studies, the Nachshon Project, and Amudim Seminary, and has taught thousands of students at conferences and communities across the Jewish world. As editor-in-chief of Maggid Books, Fine edited and published over a hundred titles of contemporary Jewish thought, including 16 books by Rabbi Sacks. *Haaretz* has called her "a young woman on her way to becoming one of the more outstanding Jewish thinkers of the next generation."

Steven Fine is the Dean Pinkhos Churgin Professor of Jewish History at Yeshiva University, Director of the YU Center for Israel Studies and the YU Israelite Samaritans Project. A cultural historian of ancient Judaism, Fine's books include *This Holy Place: On the Sanctity of the Synagogue During the Greco-Roman Period* (1997); *The Menorah: From the Bible to Modern Israel* (2016) and *Art and Judaism in the Greco-Roman World: Toward a New Jewish Archaeology* (2005, second edition 2010), which received the 2009 Jordan Schnitzer Book Award of the Association for Jewish Studies. His recent exhibition volumes are *The Arch of Titus: From Jerusalem to Rome and Back* (2021) and *The Samaritans: A Biblical People* (2022).

Eli Gottlieb is a cultural psychologist and advisor to government and nonprofit organizations on leadership and strategy. He is a visiting professor at the Interdisciplinary Institute of Innovation at Télécom Paris and a senior visiting scholar at the Graduate School of Education and Human Development at George Washington University. An expert in identity formation and leadership development, Gottlieb has led numerous initiatives in the fields of public leadership, Jewish education, and practice-focused research, including the Mandel Leadership Institute in Jerusalem, which he directed for over a decade. He holds degrees in philosophy and psychology from Cambridge and the Hebrew University of Jerusalem.

Michelle Greenberg-Kobrin is Clinical Professor of Law at Cardozo Law School and Founding Director of the Program on Leadership at the Heyman Center for Corporate Governance. She teaches in the areas of intellectual property, transactional law, corporations, negotiation, and leadership. Previously, Greenberg-Kobrin served as dean of students and taught at Columbia Law School. She is Lecturer in Law at Columbia Law School and Teachers College, Columbia. Prior to her appointment at Columbia, she was a corporate attorney at Arnold & Porter LLP. She holds both her BA and her JD from Columbia University. She was a Bruria Scholar at Midreshet Lindenbaum and a Torat Miriam Fellow. Greenberg-Kobrin has written and lectured extensively on a range of issues, including those related to intellectual property, negotiation, leadership, conflict resolution, sexual assault on campus, work-life balance, and women and Judaism.

Stuart W. Halpern is Senior Advisor to the Provost of Yeshiva University and Deputy Director of YU's Straus Center for Torah and Western Thought. He has edited 17 books, including most recently *Esther in America: The Scroll's Interpretation in and Impact on the United States*, *Proclaim Liberty Throughout the Land: The Hebrew Bible in the United States* and *Gleanings: Reflections on Ruth*. Rabbi Halpern's writing has appeared in *The Wall Street Journal*, *Newsweek*, *The Jerusalem Post*, *JTA*, *Tablet*, and *Jewish Review of Books*, and he has taught in Yeshiva University, synagogues, Hillels and adult educational settings across the United States, Europe and Israel.

Michael J. Harris is Senior Rabbi of Hampstead Synagogue and Senior Research Fellow at the London School of Jewish Studies (LSJS). He is a former affiliated lecturer in the Faculty of Divinity at the University of Cambridge and has been a visiting research fellow at the Jewish Studies Program of the Central European University. Rabbi Harris is the author of *Divine Command Ethics: Jewish and Christian Perspectives* and *Faith Without Fear: Unresolved Issues in Modern Orthodoxy*; he has co-edited *Radical Responsibility: Celebrating the Thought of Chief Rabbi Lord Jonathan Sacks* with Daniel Rynhold and Tamra Wright. His articles have been published in journals including the *Harvard Theological Review*, *The Torah U-Madda Journal*, *Tradition* and *Akdamot*. His most recent book, co-authored with Daniel Rynhold, is *Nietzsche, Soloveitchik and Contemporary Jewish Philosophy* (2018).

Michael A. Helfand is Brenden Mann Foundation Chair in Law and Religion and Co-director of the Nootbaar Institute for Law, Religion and Ethics at Pepperdine Caruso School of Law. A frequent author and lecturer, Helfand's work considers how US law treats religious law, custom and practice. In addition, he also serves as Visiting Professor and Oscar M. Ruebhausen Distinguished Fellow at Yale Law School, as well as Senior Fellow at the Shalom Hartman Institute of North America. He holds his BA from Yeshiva University, his JD from Yale Law School and his PhD in Political Science from Yale University.

Alex Israel teaches and directs educational programs at Yeshivat Eretz Hatzvi, Midreshet Lindenbaum and the Pardes Institute of Jewish Studies. He is the author of *I Kings – Torn in Two* and *II Kings – In a Whirlwind*. His writings may be found at www.alexisrael.org. Rabbi Israel holds degrees from London School of Economics; The Institute of Education, London; and Bar-Ilan University. He was awarded Semikhah from the Israeli Rabbinate after several years of study at Yeshivat Har Etzion.

Ari Lamm is the author of the "Why Read the Bible in Hebrew?" series on Twitter, and host of the weekly podcast on the Hebrew Bible and public affairs, Good Faith Effort. Rabbi Lamm is also President of SoulShop Studios, the premier media company for young, faith-driven audiences, and Chief Executive of the Bnai Zion Foundation. He holds ordination from RIETS and his PhD in Religion from Princeton University. His writings on religion and public policy have appeared in the *Wall Street Journal*, *Newsweek*, *Tablet* Magazine, *SAPIR Journal* and *The Jerusalem Post*.

Suzanne Last Stone is University Professor of Jewish Law and Contemporary Civilization at Yeshiva University, Professor of Law, and Director of the Center for Jewish Law and Contemporary Civilization and the Israel Supreme Court Translation Project at Cardozo Law School. She is also a visiting affiliated professor at Tel Aviv University Law School. Stone writes on the intersection of Jewish law and American legal theory. She has held the Gruss Visiting Chair in Talmudic Civil Law at both the Harvard and University of Pennsylvania Law Schools, and also has visited Princeton University, Columbia Law School, and Hebrew University Law. Stone is the co-editor-in-chief of *Diné Israel*, a Journal of Jewish Law co-edited with Tel Aviv Law School. Her work has been translated into German, French, Italian, Hebrew, and Arabic. In Fall 2010, she delivered the Franz Rosenzweig Lectures at Yale University.

Samuel Lebens is Associate Professor of Philosophy at the University of Haifa, as well as an Orthodox rabbi. His books and journal articles on a wide range of topics, including the philosophy of literature, the work of Bertrand Russell, and the philosophy of religion have been published. His most recent books include *The Principles of Judaism* and *A Guide for the Jewish Undecided*. Rabbi Lord Jonathan Sacks played an important role in his life, and Lebens has published articles in *Tradition* and *Religious Studies* that engage with Rabbi Sacks' work.

Liel Leibovitz is editor-at-large at *Tablet* magazine and the co-host of its popular podcast Unorthodox. He is the author of several books, including the forthcoming *How the Talmud Can Change Your Life: Surprisingly Modern Advice from a Very Old Book*.

Dov Lerner is a member of the faculty at Yeshiva University's Straus Center for Torah and Western Thought and teaches undergraduate courses exploring the intellectual legacies of Moses Maimonides, Dante Alighieri, John Milton, Meir Malbim, and Jonathan Sacks. He also serves as the Rabbi of the Young Israel of Jamaica Estates, where he preaches, teaches, and leads a passionately modern orthodox Jewish community. Rabbi Lerner holds his doctorate from the University of Chicago's Divinity School.

Benji Levy is a co-founder of the philanthropic advisory: Israel Impact Partners, and the interdisciplinary mental health center: Keshev and teaches extensively. He was the CEO of Mosaic United, a joint venture partnership between Israel and Jewish leaders to strengthen Jewish identity and, prior to that, Dean of Moriah College, one of the largest Jewish schools in the world. He authored *An Oasis in Time*, *Covenant and the Jewish Conversion Question: Extending the Thought of Rabbi Joseph B. Soloveitchik* (Palgrave Macmillan) and co-authored *Dreaming Bigger* with Erica Brown. Rabbi Levy was named a global change-maker working for global Jewry by Makor Rishon and awarded Educator of the Year by JNF Australia. He received rabbinic ordination following his years of study at Yeshivat Har Etzion and a doctorate in philosophy from the University of Sydney.

Noah Love is a psychological researcher at the University of Pennsylvania's Positive Psychology Center, where he assists Dr. Martin Seligman in his work studying agency and the history of human progress. He graduated from Biola University with a degree in psychology, having also graduated from the Torrey Honors College, in which he studied Classics, Christian theology, and the history of Western philosophy. His current research interests center around human agency, psychological rest and restoration, and the integration of the great wisdom traditions with modern science and technology.

Philip Maymin is Director of Asset Allocation Strategies at Janus Henderson and Associate Professor of Analytics and MSBA Program Director at Fairfield Dolan. He holds a Ph.D. in Finance from the University of Chicago, a Master's in Applied Mathematics from Harvard University, and a Bachelor's in Computer Science from Harvard University, as well as a J.D. and is an attorney-at-law admitted to practice in California. Maymin has been a portfolio manager at Long-Term Capital Management, Ellington Management Group, and his own hedge fund, Maymin Capital Management. A Rabbi ordained by the Jewish Spiritual Leaders Institute, he has published dozens of research papers, editorials, and books on behavioral and algorithmic finance, artificial intelligence, sports analytics, and law and economics, including one co-authored with his parents that solved several unsolved (teyku) problems from the Talmud that had remained unsolved for about 1500 years.

Rona Milch Novick is Dean of the Azrieli Graduate School of Jewish Education and Administration and holds the Raine and Stanley Silverstein Chair in Professional Ethics and Values. Novick also serves as Co-Educational Director of Hidden Sparks program which provides consultation and professional development to day schools and Yeshivas to support the success of diverse learners. She holds a PhD and has extensive clinical and research expertise in bullying and trauma, behavior management and child behavior therapy. Novick has delivered numerous presentations at national and international conferences and has authored numerous scholarly articles and book chapters. Along with her scholarly activities, she is the author of the children's books *Mommy Can You Stop the Rain?* (2020) and *Daddy, Can You Make Me Tall?* (2023) and a book for parents: *Helping Your Child Make Friends*, and edited the book series *Kids Don't Come with Instruction Manuals*.

Biti Roi teaches Kabbalah and Hasidut at the Hebrew University in Jerusalem, the Schechter Institute and the Zohar Chai Institute, and is a senior fellow at the Shalom Hartman Institute in Jerusalem. Her book, *Love of Shekhina: Mysticism and Poetics in Tiqqunei ha-Zohar*, was awarded the Matanel World Union of Jewish Studies Prize for the best book in Jewish Studies.

Daniel Rose is Director of Education at Koren Publishers, where he has developed several educational siddurim, and is working on an exciting new Tanach project. He also has an educational role at the Rabbi Sacks Legacy Trust, developing curriculum and educational resources to further the teachings and legacy of Rabbi Sacks. A British-born Jewish educator with over 30 years of experience working in informal and formal Jewish education, Rose has taught, developed curriculum, and consulted for Jewish day schools around the world, and lectured in Jewish education in various institutions and universities, including the Hebrew University, Tel Aviv University, the London School of Jewish Studies, and the Pardes Institute of Jewish Studies.

Daniel Rynhold is Dean and Professor of Jewish Philosophy at the Bernard Revel Graduate School of Jewish Studies, Yeshiva University. Born in London, England, and educated at the universities of Cambridge and London, Rynhold came to the United States in August 2007, after serving six years in the department of theology and religious studies at King's College, London. He also served as the Shoshana Shier Distinguished Visiting Professor at the University of Toronto in spring 2020. He has written extensively on Jewish philosophy, and is the author of *Two Models of Jewish Philosophy: Justifying One's Practices* (2005), *An Introduction to Medieval Jewish Philosophy* (2009), and co-author with Michael J. Harris of *Nietzsche, Soloveitchik, and Contemporary Jewish Philosophy* (2018), with whom he also, together with Tamra Wright, co-edited *Radical Responsibility: Essays in Ethics, Religion, and Leadership Presented to Chief Rabbi Lord Jonathan Sacks* (2012).

Dan Sacker worked alongside Rabbi Lord Jonathan Sacks for almost a decade, first as Director of Communications in The Office of the Chief Rabbi between 2011 and 2013, and then as Co-director of The Office of Rabbi Sacks between 2013 until Rabbi Sacks' passing in November 2020. He was subsequently Co-director of The Rabbi Sacks Legacy which exists today to perpetuate the memory and teachings of Rabbi Sacks. Though he remains involved with The Rabbi Sacks Legacy in an advisory capacity, he moved roles in March 2022 to join Milltown Partners, a global advisory and strategic communications firm.

Alan Sacks is the second of Rabbi Sacks' younger brothers. Like Rabbi Sacks, he studied at Cambridge University, and after qualifying as a lawyer in England (and a week after his wedding) he traveled to Israel, first to study in Yeshiva and then to pursue a legal career. He and his wife Judith are blessed with six children, whose outstanding service with the Israel Defense Forces (IDF) was a source of great pride for Rabbi Sacks, and with many grandchildren. Sacks is actively involved in continuing the legacy of Rabbi Sacks, both as Trustee of the UK Rabbi Sacks Legacy Trust, and as Director of the Legacy Trust's US and Israeli sister entities, assisting in developing educational and leadership programs in the spirit of the teachings of Rabbi Sacks.

Gila Sacks is the daughter of Rabbi Sacks and is a senior civil servant in the UK government. She serves at the Department for Health and Social Care, having held policy roles previously in the Departments for Business, Education, Digital, and the Prime Minister's Office. She has learnt and taught across the UK Jewish community, and lives in London.

Chaim Saiman is a scholar of Jewish law, insurance law and private law and Chair in Jewish Law at Villanova University's Charles Widger Law School. He has been the Gruss Visiting Professor of Talmudic Law at both Harvard Law School and the University of Pennsylvania Law School and a visiting fellow at Princeton University. Saiman serves as *dayyan* on the Beth Din of America, and as an expert witness in insurance law and Jewish law in federal court and has recently authored *Halakhah: The Rabbinic Idea of Law*. He learned for several years at Yeshivat Har Etzion (Gush) and Kerem B'Yavneh. Prior to joining the faculty at Villanova, he was a law clerk to Judge Michael McConnell on the Tenth Circuit Court of Appeals and an associate with the firm Cleary Gottlieb in New York.

Jeffrey Saks is the founding director of ATID—The Academy for Torah Initiatives and Directions in Jewish Education, in Jerusalem, and its WebYeshiva.org program. He is the editor of the journal *Tradition*, series editor of The S.Y. Agnon Library at The Toby Press, and Director of Research at the Agnon House. A three-time graduate of Yeshiva University (BA, MA, Semikhah), Saks has written widely on Jewish thought, education, and literature. He was formerly on the faculties of the YU High School for Girls in New York (NY), taught at various yeshivot in Israel, and teaches at Midreshet Amudim. Saks has edited the following books: *Wisdom from All My Teachers: Challenges and Initiatives in Contemporary*

Torah Education; *To Mourn a Child: Jewish Responses to Childhood Death*; *Agnon's Tales of the Land of Israel*. He has authored the book *Spiritualizing Halakhic Education*.

Jonathan D. Sarna is a university professor and the Joseph H. & Belle R. Braun Professor of American Jewish History at Brandeis University, where he directs its Schusterman Center for Israel Studies. He also is the past president of the Association for Jewish Studies and Chief Historian of the National Museum of American Jewish History in Philadelphia. Author or editor of more than 30 books on American Jewish history and life, his *American Judaism: A History* won six awards including the 2004 "Everett Jewish Book of the Year Award" from the Jewish Book Council. Sarna is a fellow of the American Academy of Arts and Sciences and of the American Academy of Jewish Research. His most recent books are *When General Grant Expelled the Jews*, *Lincoln and the Jews: A History* (with Benjamin Shapell), an edition of *Cosella Wayne*, by Cora Wilburn, the first (and hitherto unknown) American Jewish novel, and *Coming to Terms with America*, a volume of essays.

Jacob J. Schacter is University Professor of Jewish History and Jewish Thought at Yeshiva University. He is the author and editor of over a dozen books and over a hundred articles.

Mordechai Schiffman is an assistant professor at YU's Azrieli Graduate School, an instructor at Rabbi Isaac Elchanan Theological Seminary (RIETS), the Straus Center for Torah and Western Thought, and the Leadership Scholars undergraduate fellowship at Yeshiva University. He has been on the rabbinic staff of Kingsway Jewish Center in Brooklyn, NY, since 2010 and practices as a licensed psychologist in NY. His book *Psyched for Torah: Cultivating Character and Well-Being Through the Weekly Parsha*, his academic and popular articles, as well as many of his lectures, are accessible on his website, www.PsychedForTorah.com.

Martin Seligman is Director of the Penn Positive Psychology Center and Zellerbach Family Professor of Psychology in the Penn Department of Psychology. He is also Director of the Penn Master of Applied Positive Psychology program (MAPP). He was President of the American Psychological Association in 1998, during which one of his presidential initiatives was the promotion of positive psychology as a field of scientific study. Seligman is a leading authority in the fields of positive psychology, resilience, learned helplessness, depression, optimism and pessimism. He is also a recognized authority on interventions that prevent depression and build strengths and well-being. He has written more than 350 scholarly publications and 30 books, including *The Hope Circuit* (2018), *Flourish* (2011) *Authentic Happiness* (2002), *Learned Optimism* (1991), *What You Can Change and What You Can't* (1993) and *The Optimistic Child* (1995), and co-authored *Character Strengths and Virtues: A Handbook and Classification*, with Christopher Peterson (2004).

Malka Z. Simkovich is Crown-Ryan Chair of Jewish Studies and the director of the Catholic-Jewish Studies program at Catholic Theological Union in Chicago. She is the author of *The Making of Jewish Universalism: From Exile to Alexandria* (2016) and *Discovering Second Temple Literature: The Scriptures and Stories That Shaped Early Judaism* (2018), which received the 2019 AJL Judaica Reference Honor Award. Simkovich's articles have been published in journals including the *Harvard Theological Review* and the *Journal for the Study of Judaism*, and on online forums such as *The Times of Israel* and *The Ancient Near East Today*. She is involved in numerous interreligious dialogue projects which help to increase understanding and friendship between Christians and Jews.

Johnny Solomon is a teacher, writer, editor and "Virtual Rabbi" who provides online spiritual coaching, one-to-one learning, and halakhic consultations to those without a rabbi.

Meir Soloveichik is Senior Rabbi of Congregation Shearith Israel in Manhattan, and Director of the Zahava and Moshael Straus Center for Torah and Western Thought at Yeshiva University. Rabbi Soloveichik lectures internationally to Jewish and non-Jewish audiences on topics relating to faith in America, the Hebraic roots of the American Founding, Jewish theology, bioethics, wartime ethics, Jewish-Christian relations, and more. He writes a monthly column in *Commentary* magazine, and his writing has appeared in the *Wall Street Journal, New York Times, Mosaic, First Things, Azure, Tradition, Jewish Review of Books*, among other outlets. Rabbi Soloveichik graduated *summa cum laude* from Yeshiva University, received his rabbinic ordination from the Rabbi Isaac Elchanan Theological Seminary, and studied at its Beren Kollel Elyon. He has also studied at Yale Divinity School. He holds his doctorate in Religion (2010) from Princeton University.

Elana Stein Hain is Rosh Beit Midrash and a senior fellow at the Shalom Hartman Institute of North America, where she researches, teaches and writes, while consulting on educational programming for American Jewish leaders. In addition to authoring her forthcoming book, *Circumventing the Law: Rabbinic Perspectives on Loopholes and Legal Integrity* (University of Pennsylvania Press), she co-hosts a podcast, *For Heaven's Sake*, and teaches a periodic online series, *Talmud from the Balcony*, helping people see the big philosophical ideas embedded in legal *sugyot*. Stein Hain holds a PhD from Columbia University, where she studied with the late Professor David Weiss Halivni, is an alumna of both GPATS and the Cardozo Fellowship in Jewish Law and Civilization, and is a board member of Sefaria. She previously served as clergy at both Lincoln Square Synagogue and The Jewish Center.

Chaim Strauchler is Senior Rabbi at Congregation Rinat Yisrael in Teaneck, NJ. Rabbi Strauchler is an associate editor of *Tradition: A Journal of Orthodox Jewish Thought*. He had the privilege of meeting Rabbi Lord Jonathan Sacks while studying at Oxford University as a Rhodes Scholar—and continuing that relationship during his early rabbinic career in Connecticut and Toronto.

Sara Tillinger Wolkenfeld is Chief Learning Officer at Sefaria, an online database and interface for Jewish texts. She writes about Jewish texts and Jewish law and her current projects focus on applying Talmudic ideas to questions of advancements in digital technology. A Wexner Field Fellow, as well as a fellow of the David Hartman Center at the Shalom Hartman Institute of North America, her previous experience includes serving as Director of Education at the Center for Jewish Life—Hillel at Princeton University as part of the Orthodox Union's (OU's) Jewish Learning Initiative on Campus and serving as faculty at the Drisha Institute for Jewish Education. She studied Talmud and Jewish Law at many institutions of Jewish learning in Israel and America including Midreshet Lindenbaum, Drisha, Nishmat, and Beit Morasha and speaks on various Jewish topics in synagogues, schools, and university communities.

Hava Tirosh-Samuelson is Regents Professor of History, Irving and Miriam Lowe Professor of Modern Judaism, and Director of Jewish Studies at Arizona State University in Tempe, AZ. A Jewish intellectual historian (PhD Hebrew University, 1978), she focuses on the interplay of philosophy and mysticism, religion and science, and religion and ecology. In addition to over 60 essays and book chapters, she is the author of the award-winning *Between Worlds: The Life and Work of Rabbi David ben Judah Messer Leon* (1991), *Happiness in Premodern Judaism: Virtue,*

Knowledge, and Well-Being in Premodern Judaism (2003), and *Religion and Environment: The Case of Judaism* (2020). She is also the editor of several volumes, including *Women and Gender in Jewish Philosophy* (2004), *Jewish Philosophy for the Twenty-First Century: Personal Reflections* (2014), and *The Future of Jewish Philosophy* (2018). Tirosh-Samuelson is the editor-in-chief of the *Library of Contemporary Jewish Philosophers* (2013–2018).

Shaina Trapedo is Lecturer in English at Stern College and is a resident scholar at the Straus Center for Torah and Western Thought at Yeshiva University. She holds her PhD from the University of California, Irvine, where she specialized in early modern literature and religious studies. Her current book project *From Scripture to Script: The Hebrew Bible on the Early Modern Stage* considers Shakespeare and his contemporaries' indebtedness to Judaism and its exegetical traditions. In her teaching and scholarship, she explores the connections between literacy, cultural identity, and social engagement.

Shira Weiss is Assistant Director of the Rabbi Lord Jonathan Sacks-Herenstein Center for Values and Leadership, teaches Jewish Thought at Yeshiva University's Bernard Revel Graduate School and has previously taught at Stern College for Women. Weiss holds a PhD in Jewish Philosophy from Revel, an EdD from Azrieli, a BA from Stern College, and has been awarded fellowships from the National Endowment of Humanities, The Templeton Foundation, Oxford University and Ben Gurion University. She is the author of *Joseph Albo on Free Choice* (Oxford, 2017) and *Ethical Ambiguity in the Hebrew Bible* (Cambridge, 2018), co-author of *The Protests of Job: An Interfaith Dialogue* (Palgrave, 2022), as well as articles in academic journals and anthologies.

Tamra Wright specializes in twentieth-century Jewish thought. She is the author of *The Twilight of Jewish Philosophy: Emmanuel Levinas's Ethical Hermeneutics* (1999), and essays on Buber, Rosenzweig, Levinas and post-Holocaust Jewish thought. She co-edited *Face to Face with Animals: Levinas and the Animal Question* (2019) and *Radical Responsibility: Celebrating the Thought of Rabbi Lord Jonathan Sacks* (2012). Her research interests include exploring the connections between Judaism and positive psychology, with a view to creating a "new mussar" inspired by R. Sacks. Wright is Curriculum Development Adviser at Faith in Leadership, Scholar in Residence at the Council of Christians and Jews, and Senior Research

Fellow at the London School of Jewish Studies. She has held visiting lectureships and research fellowships at Oxford, Cambridge, and King's College London. During the pandemic, she founded 2020 Torah, an online Jewish learning platform.

Raphael Zarum is Dean of the London School of Jewish Studies (LSJS) and the Rabbi Sacks Chair of Modern Jewish Thought, established by the Zandan family. He lectures in Jewish Education and New Readings of Classical Texts, as well as training teachers, educators and rabbis for Anglo Jewry and beyond. Rabbi Zarum has rabbinic ordination from the Montefiore Kollel, a PhD in Theoretical Physics from King's College London, an MA in Adult Education from University College London, and is a graduate of the Mandel School in Jerusalem. He regularly writes journal essays and articles for the Jewish press, and has traveled the globe lecturing at many diverse Jewish institutions. His book, *Questioning Belief*, was recently published by Koren.

Yael Ziegler is Rosh Beit Midrash and Academic Director of Matan and Assistant Professor of Tanakh at Herzog College. She holds her BA from Stern College and an MA and PhD in Bible from Bar Ilan University. Ziegler has lectured widely on various Tanakh topics in Israel, the United States, Canada, South Africa, Australia, and Europe. Ziegler is the author of *Promises to Keep: The Oath in Biblical Narrative* and *Ruth: From Alienation to Monarchy*, which has been translated into Hebrew. Her book *Lamentations: Faith in a Turbulent World* was released in June 2021 and is being translated into Hebrew. She is working on a book on Exodus.

CHAPTER 1

Introduction

Erica Brown and Shira Weiss

The pursuit of happiness was a foundational theme in many of Rabbi Sacks' teachings and writings. It was central to his conception of Judaism, as he wrote in his *Essays on Ethics*: "I think of Judaism is an ode to joy."[1] As he develops this idea further, he acknowledges happiness not only as part of a healthy emotional range but as emblematic of a Jewish national soul all too often stamped by difficulty and oppression: "Jews have known suffering, isolation, hardship, and rejection, yet they never lacked the religious courage to rejoice. A people that can know insecurity and still feel joy is one that can never be defeated, for its spirit can never be broken nor its hope destroyed."[2] Ironically, persecution is so familiar to the Jewish people that happiness is sometimes harder to manufacture and sustain, as Rabbi Sacks observes in a *Covenant and Conversation* essay on the Torah reading for Deuteronomy, ("Collective Joy," *Re'eh* 5779): "It is easy to speak to God in tears. It is hard to serve God in joy."[3] Many of our contributors have highlighted these citations and discussed them on the pages ahead.

Jewish law, rituals, and the rich, multivalanced life of community are an important pathway to joy, but Rabbi Sacks did not believe that religion

---

E. Brown • S. Weiss (✉)
Yeshiva University, New York, NY, USA

© The Author(s), under exclusive license to Springer Nature Switzerland AG 2023
E. Brown, S. Weiss (eds.), *An Ode to Joy*,
https://doi.org/10.1007/978-3-031-28229-4_1

had a monopoly on happiness. He writes, "You do not have to be religious to be happy." Yet it is clear, as he continues, that intimacy with God and a life of faith are both propaedeutics for happiness and an outgrowth of them: "there is something profoundly spiritual about our capacity to live in a state of total insecurity and yet feel the joy of simply being, under the shelter of the Divine Presence."[4]

Happiness is also manifest, for Rabbi Sacks, in the love of friends, family and community, as he writes in *The Great Partnership*: "The most significant determinants of happiness are strong and rewarding personal relationships, a sense of belonging to a community, being valued by others and leading a meaningful life." Yet for Rabbi Sacks, these, too, were ultimately connected to faith: "These are precisely the things in which religion specialises: sanctifying marriage, etching family life with the charisma of holiness, creating and sustaining strong communities in which people are valued for what they are, not for what they earn or own, and providing a framework within which our lives take on meaning, purpose, even blessedness..." Religion provides the spiritual platform for joy's greatest expression: "The practices of religion - prayer as an expression of gratitude, ritual as enactment of meaning, sacred narratives as a way of understanding the world and our place within it, rites of passage that locate our journey as a shared experience connecting us to past and future generations, deeds of reciprocal kindness that bind us to a group in bonds of faith, loyalty and trust - create structures of meaning and relationships within which our individuality can flourish." Rabbi Sacks believed that, "This is where, for many of us, happiness is to be found."[5]

There are currently only a few book-length studies of joy or happiness in Judaism; works, for example, by Hava Tirosh-Samuelson, Gary Anderson, and Yochanan Muffs.[6] A limited number of scholarly essays on joy according to specific Jewish thinkers have also appeared in academic journals over the last several decades by authors including Moshe Sokol, Lawrence Kaplan, Alex Sztuden, and Elizabeth Hollender.[7] This volume aspires to provide the reader with a sense of the range of Jewish views on joy as they relate to the thought of Rabbi Sacks and beyond, through insightful essays spanning a broad array of genres. We hope it will expand on existing literature and stimulate additional research on this timely and important subject.

In this volume, we gather the voices of those who knew Rabbi Sacks personally, as well as academics, and educators to consider the significance of joy within the Jewish tradition. The section on personal reflections about Rabbi Sacks opens this volume. In other sections, the writings of Rabbi Sacks on joy are primarily used as a touchstone, as the authors bring their work into conversation with the views of Rabbi Sacks and other thinkers on the topic of joy through an analysis of traditional Jewish primary sources, including Biblical, Rabbinic, and Hebrew literature, Jewish philosophy, history, education, the arts, and positive psychology. While the volume is framed around Jewish thought, some of the contributions engage with non-Jewish thinkers and texts. Each chapter represents an original contribution to the respective field of its author and adds richness to the collection.

The reader will find overlapping themes in the chapters that follow. Just as Rabbi Sacks wrote about the same idea in different ways in his many books and articles, so too, do our authors, in some references, present similar concepts in different manners. For instance, though the distinction between 'happiness' being solitary and 'joy' being collective has been raised in numerous chapters, the unique contexts in which Rabbi Sacks' analysis is embedded offer new insight into his words from divergent perspectives. Several chapters mention the Aristotelian distinction between *eudaemonia* and *hedonia*, a juxtaposition that Rabbi Sacks highlights, but each author applies the contrast to support profoundly different arguments.

Words expounded upon by Rabbi Sacks, such as the *Ashrei* prayer, as well as exegetical interpretations of the same biblical books, including Psalms and Ecclesiastes, are discussed in various chapters because they were fundamental sources for Rabbi Sacks on the topic. A number of authors relate positive psychology to Rabbi Sacks' reflections on joy, yet each does so with creative and distinctive analyses. While not exhaustive, the chapters are complementary within a collection that we hope will make a meaningful contribution to the field of Jewish thought in a world sorely in need of more happiness, while promulgating the impact of Rabbi Sacks' teachings.

Rabbi Sacks' daughter, Gila, wrote in a foreword to this book that happiness may not come naturally. It requires hard work. Yet the work is one of the most important tasks of being human in an increasingly embattled climate. Piety depends on our capacity to transcend pettiness and harshness and reach for eternity. In *Studies in Spirituality*, Rabbi Sacks writes, "Joy helps heal some of the wounds of our injured, troubled world."[8] May this volume bring healing to the wounds caused by Rabbi Sacks' loss—to his family, to his students, and to his readers—and help us recognize and celebrate the joy he worked so hard to generate and to share.

NOTES

1. Jonathan Sacks, *Essays on Ethics* (Jerusalem: Maggid, 2016), 315.
2. Ibid.
3. *Covenant and Conversation: Deuteronomy*, 127.
4. Ibid., 147.
5. Jonathan Sacks, *The Great Partnership* (NY: Schocken Books, 2011), 280.
6. Hava Tirosh Samuelson, *Happiness in Premodern Judaism* (Cincinnati: Hebrew Union College Press, 2003); Gary Anderson, *A Time to Mourn, A Time to Dance* (PA: Penn State University Press, 1991); Yochanan Muffs, *Love & Joy* (NY: JTS, 1995).
7. Moshe Sokol, "Maimonides on Joy," in *Maimonides and his Heritage* (NY: SUNY Press, 2010), 37–50; Lawrence Kaplan, "Suffering and Joy in the Thought of Hermann Cohen," *Modern Judaism* 21, no. 1 (2001): 15–22; Alex Sztuden, "Grief and Joy in the Writings of Rabbi Soloveitchik," *Tradition* 44, no. 3 (2011): 9–32; Elizabeth Hollender, "Joy and Mourning in Medieval Ashkenaz: The Piyyutim of Abraham b. Joseph of Nuremberg," *Shirat Dvora* (2019): 103–27.
8. Jonathan Sacks, *Studies in Spirituality* (Jerusalem: Koren, 2021), 259.

PART I

Personal Reflections: Rabbi Sacks and Joy

CHAPTER 2

Rabbi Sacks and Joy: A Personal Reflection

Alan Sacks

This is my favorite photograph of my late brother, Rabbi Jonathan Sacks.

Rabbi Sacks has just addressed my son Dan and his bride Tehila under their Chuppah. Dan takes a step forward and gives his uncle a huge bear hug. For a split second, Rabbi Sacks is taken aback that someone should cross the divide of British formality and hug him, as if a long-lost "comrade-in-arms". But then, as the photograph shows, Rabbi Sacks leans forward into the deep emotion of joy.

As no doubt will be reflected in this volume, Rabbi Sacks thought a great deal about joy. For Rabbi Sacks, as he elaborates in a number of his *Covenant & Conversation* essays, happiness is the state of mind of an individual, but joy (*Simha* in the Torah) is never about individuals.

"*Simha* is joy shared. It is not something we experience in solitude … Happiness is something you pursue. But joy is not. It discovers you. It has to do with a sense of connection to other people or to God… It is the exhilaration we feel when we merge with others. It is the redemption of solitude."[1] So wrote Rabbi Sacks. Yet, I believe that under cross-examination, Rabbi Sacks would have been more nuanced on the point. Is it true that we cannot experience joy in isolation? To answer this question, we would have to understand a little more about how Rabbi Sacks himself experienced joy.

Rabbi Sacks had many reasons in life to be happy, and he often was. And for every one of those moments, he was grateful. For Rabbi Sacks, *hakarat ha-tov*, expressing gratitude, was a moral imperative. But happiness was not perhaps Rabbi Sacks' default mode. Rabbi Sacks was more often "concerned". He was constantly driven to do more, to influence more, to travel further along the road of his self-imposed mission in life. Had he done enough? What should he be doing next? And had he done well enough? That sense of questioning and self-doubt never left Rabbi Sacks.

Yet Rabbi Sacks was undoubtedly a man of joy. During the last decade or more of his life, Rabbi Sacks' greatest joy was his grandchildren. He found their individual personalities, their pursuits, their inquisitiveness, a source of energy and excitement. This was far more than the happiness and contentedness of seeing his own children settled and raising families. This interaction with his grandchildren brought Rabbi Sacks true joy, joy in knowing that in many respects his grandchildren would see further and go beyond what he had experienced, joy in knowing that his grandchildren would be the link connecting him to the collective future of the Jewish people. This was a joy that Rabbi Sacks experienced through his grandchildren. Happiness and joy combined. A private emotion, but at the same time, the "redemption of solitude".

Our late father was a man of few, but often-repeated, aphorisms. He would often say, citing Keats, that "A thing of beauty is a joy forever". In that sense, joy is like the comfort of a glowing hearth. It continues to give you warmth, whenever you go back to it. And in this sense, Rabbi Sacks found joy not only in people but also in music and art and prayer. My brother and I often discussed the spiritual joy of reading Shabbat morning prayers, comparing a slow read of the Psalms to a walk through an art gallery. For Rabbi Sacks, faith, like love, is the redemption of solitude. Alone, but not feeling alone. Alone, but not in isolation.

Rabbi Sacks certainly found joy in collaboration. With philosophers, with musicians, with schoolchildren, with whoever could bring out the best in him while Rabbi Sacks brought out the best in them. Rabbi Sacks found joy in the success of others. He found joy in encouraging others. Rabbi Sacks once told the teachers in a floundering school, "Celebrate something every day". Bring joy to the classroom, even (perhaps especially) over a minor improvement, and you will change the entire atmosphere of the school. And it worked. The joy was infectious and brought about a remarkable transformation in the attitude of the children and the teachers at the school.

Rabbi Sacks' enthusiasm was infectious. How many people have told us since his passing how he changed the course of their lives? "I would not be religious today, but for…" or "I am who I am because of Rabbi Sacks." Clearly, Rabbi Sacks touched many people, either through personal interaction or through his writing. But equally, Rabbi Sacks was touched by those same people. This is where he found his joy. In encouraging others, in teaching others, in learning from others. Time after time, Rabbi Sacks told me about meeting people who inspired him, who brought him a true sense of joy, in every walk of life. Schoolchildren, students, social workers, academics, and especially the Holocaust survivors and nonagenarians who overwhelmed him with their "sense of life", despite their age or experiences.

Rabbi Sacks understood that joy has different meanings in different situations. Noting the multiple references to the Hebrew term, *simha* in *Sefer Devarim (Deuteronomy)* Rabbi Sacks remarks on the emphasis that the *Torah* places on Jerusalem and the Temple as the focal point for communal joy (to the best of my knowledge, Rabbi Sacks first road-tested this idea in a sermon he gave at my son's *Aliyah LaTorah*, call to the Torah, before expanding on the idea in *Covenant & Conversation* and elsewhere). Time and again, the Jewish people are told to rejoice in the place that the Lord will choose.

> The nation was to be brought together not just by crisis, catastrophe or impending war, but by collective celebration in the presence of God. The celebration itself was to be deeply moral. Not only was this a religious act of thanksgiving; it was also to be a form of social inclusion. No one was to be left out: not the stranger, or the servant, or the lonely (the orphan and widow).[2]

Jerusalem and the Temple were the focal point of communal joy.

At the time, I pointed out to my brother Maimonides' definition of ultimate joy in "The Laws of Megillat Esther and Hanukkah:"

> One should rather spend more money on gifts to the poor than on his Purim banquet and presents to his friends. No joy is greater and more glorious than the joy of gladdening the hearts of the poor, the orphans, the widows, and the strangers. He who gladdens the heart of these unhappy people imitates God, as it is written: "I am ... to revive the spirit of the humble, and to put heart into the crushed" (Isaiah 57:15).[3]

"Hundred percent", my brother replied to me immediately and enthusiastically, congratulating me for my thought, but already two steps ahead of me. There are many manifestations of joy, but the highest manifestation, that Moses is articulating for the first time in *Deuteronomy*, is the idea of *simha* as communal, social, and national rejoicing. As Rabbi Sacks wrote:

> Our contemporary consumer is constructed in the first-person singular: I want, I need, I must have ... That, said Moses before the Israelites entered their land, would be their greatest challenge ... The only way to avoid it, is to share your happiness with others, and, in the midst of that collective, national celebration to serve God ... So blessings are not measured by how much we own, or earn, or spend or possess but by how much we share. *Simha* is the mark of a sacred society. It is a place of collective joy.[4]

Rabbi Sacks understood personal and communal crisis, and he perceived joy to be the antidote for both. For him, there were widening circles of joy, from the intimate personal joy of a spiritually uplifting encounter, to the wider joy of family and group encounters, to the widest idea of collective, communal joy. Rabbi Sacks understood this not only intellectually but also emotionally. Although not always the most expressive of individuals, I do not believe that Rabbi Sacks wrote anything that he did not believe and experience deeply within himself. And I believe that the sincerity with which he spoke with people, and wrote in his contemporary or religious writings, is the source of much of the influence that Rabbi Sacks leaves behind.

All of which brings me back to my favorite photograph of my brother, Rabbi Sacks. As I look at the photograph, as I do often, I am alone. But only on one level. Each time I stand in front of the photograph, I have with me the warm glow of all the time that my brother and I spent together, the uplifting feeling when I was in his company, the special feeling of proximity to greatness. And I realize that as I stand in front of that photograph, I am not alone. I carry with me the special joy of having been so close to such a fine human being, whose message, Lord willing, will continue to resonate for generations to come.

May his memory be a blessing.

Notes

1. Jonathan Sacks, "The Pursuit of Joy," *Covenant and Conversation: Ki Tavo*, 5782, https://www.rabbisacks.org/covenant-conversation/ki-tavo/the-pursuit-of-joy/.
2. Jonathan Sacks, "Collective Joy," *Covenant and Conversation: Re'eh*, 5779, https://www.rabbisacks.org/covenant-conversation/reeh/collective-joy/.
3. Maimonides, *Mishneh Torah*, Laws of Megillat Esther and Hanukkah 2:17.
4. Ibid.

CHAPTER 3

Joy as Challenge: Personal Reflections on Working with Rabbi Sacks

Dan Sacker

In September 2011, I began working as Director of Communications in the Office of the Chief Rabbi in London. By that point, Rabbi Sacks had already announced his intentions to step down from his position as Chief Rabbi in September 2013, yet the opportunity to support the work of someone I so deeply admired was too good to pass up. I figured that even if it was only for two years, it would be an experience like no other. Little did I know that my experience would last for nearly the next decade or that it would become such a defining chapter of my life in so many ways.

There was one experience that crystallized what Rabbi Sacks expected of me, and what, I would later appreciate, formed such a central and foundational element to his character and work. It happened about a week after I started the role.

When he was not undertaking various engagements in the United Kingdom or overseas, Rabbi Sacks enjoyed being at home, sitting at his large, wooden desk in his loft study, surrounded by shelves and piles of books. It was here where he engaged in his most creative, intellectual, and demanding work. And it was from here that he emailed me a draft of an

---

D. Sacker (✉)
London, UK

© The Author(s), under exclusive license to Springer Nature Switzerland AG 2023
E. Brown, S. Weiss (eds.), *An Ode to Joy*,
https://doi.org/10.1007/978-3-031-28229-4_3

article he was working on and asked for my thoughts. From memory, I think it was one of his monthly columns on faith for *The Times*, one of the most respected national newspapers in the United Kingdom.

Being new to the role and not wanting to put my dream job in instant jeopardy, I drafted a reply. "It's great," I wrote. Just two words. To be honest, there was not much more I felt I needed to say; the draft was articulately written, powerfully argued, and, in my opinion, seemed ready for publication. I ended my short email with a question: Was he happy for me to submit the article?

Less than thirty seconds later, my mobile rang. It was from a "Withheld" number, which meant it was Rabbi Sacks on the line. "Dan," he began, his voice gentle, yet firm. "There are a million people in the world that I could send this draft to and get that kind of feedback."

And then he paused, as if to leave me hanging, suspended mid-air, contemplating my own inadequacies and failings. "That's not your job," he said, leaving me feeling dejected. But before I could muster an apology, he rescued me with one of the most powerful and inspiring sentences he uttered in the time we worked together.

"You are empowered to say no."

You are empowered to say no. Just six words, but six words which instilled in me a deep sense of duty and responsibility. Rabbi Sacks was one of, if not *the*, smartest people I had ever met. Yet here he was, telling me, a thirty-something-year-old, that not only could I challenge his assumptions or opinions, but he was actively encouraging me to do so. He was letting me know that he trusted me, believing that I could, in whatever way possible, help him in his work. In that moment, my outlook changed. I began to understand, if not fully appreciate, what Rabbi Sacks expected and wanted from me.

"Don't worry," continued Rabbi Sacks refocusing my mind on the present assignment, "I know what changes I need to make to the draft."

And he hung up.

No more than ten minutes later, a second email arrived in my inbox. Attached was a significantly improved, tighter, and stronger article. The accompanying email contained one word: "Send."

I did exactly that and breathed a sigh of relief.

The following week, I was undertaking research for another article Rabbi Sacks had been asked to write. As before, it was for a national paper, though this time the focus of the piece was not on faith but on one of the current political and societal issues of the day. And as before, Rabbi Sacks sent me his draft to offer my thoughts. This time, however, I promised myself I would not repeat my previous mistake. I reviewed the article carefully, slowly, thinking about the meaning behind every word, judging the strength of every sentence, ensuring the paragraphs flowed and the argument developed and reached a crescendo in a logical form.

On practically every line, I left my mark. On some, I dared to change or delete words. On others, I offered comments that I hoped were insightful and demonstrated my willingness to challenge and confront any perceived weaknesses in his argument. By the time my review was over, hardly any aspect of the article remained untouched.

As I saved the document called "Version 2", attached it to the email, and drafted the short cover note about how I had made "a few suggested tweaks," my mouse hovered nervously over the 'Send' button. As I pressed it, I'm sure my heart skipped a beat. Possibly two.

Though it felt like hours, it cannot have been longer than a few minutes before my mobile rang, flashing the now familiar "Withheld" number. I hesitated, just for a moment. In my head, I was second-guessing how the conversation might go: "Dan," Rabbi Sacks would say, "I don't think this partnership is quite going to work out…"

Worried that my dream job was about to become my ex-job, I nervously answered the call. It was Rabbi Sacks, as expected, but it was his response that was entirely unexpected. He sounded neither angry nor resentful, disappointed nor discouraged with my reflections on his work. To my amazement, if anything, he sounded excited, happy, even joyful.

"Dan!" he exclaimed. "That's better. Much better!" Even at the end of a phone line, his delight at my changes and challenges was palpable.

Once again, I breathed a sigh of relief.

This is the story that first came to mind when I was asked to contribute to this wonderful anthology on joy. It was strange because, in the time I worked with Rabbi Sacks, I had certainly witnessed purer moments of joy and happiness in the more conventional sense of the words. Most of these moments revolved around his family. I saw the joy in Rabbi Sacks' heart whenever he spoke to me about his love and admiration for his wife Elaine, or for the important and influential presence she had been in his life. I heard the joy and pride in his voice whenever he told me about the professional or personal achievements of his three children. And I felt the joy in his laughter whenever he recalled a good joke or explained how his grandchildren were teaching him about astronomy or some other subject that he deemed outside his sphere of knowledge.

But the story I shared above was about a different kind of joy. It was about intellectual joy; the sense, as Rabbi Sacks believed, that beauty can be found in differing perspectives, in robust discussion and debate, in engaging others to help sharpen your argument. Indeed, whether on a small or large scale, and providing it was respectfully done, Rabbi Sacks saw being intellectually challenged as a Torah scholar, Jewish thinker, public intellectual, or moral philosopher, a deeply joyful experience for two reasons. Firstly, because it meant that people took his perspective seriously enough to intellectually engage with it, even if they disagreed with his position. And secondly, because through this engagement, Rabbi Sacks knew he would inevitably grow intellectually as a person, even if he didn't agree with what was said. For Rabbi Sacks, therefore, this kind of intellectual joy represented a non-zero-sum game, where whatever the outcome, he felt as though he had won.

Rabbi Sacks saw the roots of this idea in many places in Torah. For example, in one of his *Covenant & Conversation* essays, he offered a profound insight into the failed rebellion led by Korah against Moses and Aaron. He noted how Korah's attack was deeply personal, becoming, according to the Mishnah, a paradigm for the worst kind of disagreement: "Which is an argument for the Sake of Heaven? The argument between Hillel and Shammai. Which is an argument not for the Sake of Heaven? The argument of Korah and his company" (*Mishnah Avot* 5:17). Rabbi Sacks wrote: "The sages were drawing on a fundamental distinction between two kinds of conflict: argument for the sake of truth and argument for the sake of power."[1] It was this that defined what was an argument for the sake of heaven versus an argument that was for the sake of victory. Reflecting on this idea, Rabbi Sacks ended his essay with this compelling conclusion:

> In such a conflict, what is at stake is not truth but power, and the result is that both sides suffer. If you win, I lose. But if I win, I also lose, because in diminishing you, I diminish myself ... Argument for the sake of power is a lose-lose scenario. The opposite is the case when the argument is for the sake of truth. If I win, I win. But if I lose, I also win—because being defeated by the truth is the only form of defeat that is also a victory.[2]

It is for this reason, according to the Talmud, that Jewish law tends to follow the School of Hillel rather than the School of Shammai: because the School of Hillel were "kindly and modest" and studied the teachings of the School of Shammai not just as well as their own rulings but *before* their own rulings. As Rabbi Sacks wrote: "They [the School of Hillel] sought truth, not victory."[3]

Rabbi Sacks once famously said that Judaism was the only faith he knew of whose key texts—the Tanakh, Midrash, Mishnah, Talmud, the codes of Jewish law and the compendia of biblical interpretations—are "anthologies of arguments." This, he said, "was the glory of Judaism" noting that the Divine Presence is to be found "not in this voice as against that, but in the totality of the conversation."[4] There were no losers, just winners.

It was this sense that arguments or disagreements could be framed as the collective pursuit of truth that Rabbi Sacks always hoped to find in society at large. Indeed, he once defined the concept of society as "a conversation scored for many voices."[5] It was in the midst of this conversation, and in offering a meaningful contribution in the same kind and modest way as the School of Hillel once had, where professionally Rabbi Sacks was ultimately, I believe, at his most joyful.

Among the most intellectually joyful I saw him was at the 2017 TED Conference in Vancouver[6]—one of the world's premier platforms for the sharing of ideas—and when we recorded a series in 2018 for BBC Radio on "Morality in the 21st Century."[7] The joy at TED came not when he delivered his own TED Talk, but when we attended the other sessions to hear fellow presenters share their own ideas. The joy of the BBC series came not from the fact that he had been asked to make the series, but because it afforded him the opportunity to engage in extended conversations with some of the world's top thinkers and people whose ideas he found most fascinating, including Michael Sandel, Jonathan Haidt, Melinda Gates, Steven Pinker, Jordan Peterson, Jean Twenge, Robert Putnam, David Brooks, and others.

It was this that was so illustrative of his happiness because he loved reflecting on recent scientific discoveries or new theories on different elements of life. He read continuously and ferociously, seeking to be inspired or challenged by ideas in other people's work that might shed new light on dark areas of his knowledge. Most of all, he loved meeting people—especially fellow public intellectuals—and took great interest in their perspectives on the issues of the day, even if he didn't always agree with them.

Ultimately, Rabbi Sacks empowered those around him to challenge and question not just their views but his as well. He created a safe space for people in general, and especially his closest advisors like me, to do so because he wanted the next talk he gave or the next article he wrote to be better than the last. The result was that his entire life was a journey of continuous self-improvement, and it was within the journey itself that he found the deepest sense of joy.

Rabbi Sacks also knew that for everyone, this journey through life was not always one of joy. There were bound to be moments of real challenge as well. Several years before I started working for him, he wrote a book called *Celebrating Life: Finding Happiness in Unexpected Places*. He originally authored it, somewhat ironically given the title, as a means by which to pull himself out of the depression he fell into following the death of his father. Contained within the book is a beautiful piece called "The Art of Happiness" in which Rabbi Sacks reflects on the impact his late father had on his life. Towards its conclusion, Rabbi Sacks writes that:

> Something of him lived on in me. I could still see him, hear him, turn to him for advice, knowing what he would say… I knew that the people who change our lives do not die. They live on in us as we live on in our children. That is as much of immortality as we will ever know this side of the grave, and it is enough.[8]

During my time with Rabbi Sacks, the concept of legacy—of what lives on beyond our physical being—was something we spoke about a significant amount. Not for morbid reasons, but because it helped frame our decision-making process. For him, there was little doubt that despite all his achievement and the honors that had been bestowed on him in his lifetime, the most important title he ever earned was "Rabbi," teacher. It was his ideas, his books, and his teachings that gave him the deepest sense of professional satisfaction. They were his pride and joy, and what he hoped would live on long into the future, beyond his own life.

From that first week in September 2011 until the day that Rabbi Sacks passed away on 7 November 2020, I knew I was blessed. Truly blessed. Almost every day, I got to talk to him, marvel up close at his genius, and learn from his timely and timeless wisdom. It was—and will surely remain—one of the greatest educational and professional experiences of my career, and one that inspired me to engage in my faith and in the world around me with more depth and purpose.

Being in his presence changed my life forever and changed it for the better. That is why, even though I still mourn his physical passing daily, he very much remains with me, in the words I can read on the pages of his books, in the videos I can watch of him online,[9] and in the wise voice of his I can still hear in my head.

As a result, Rabbi Sacks was, and remains, my guiding light. He epitomized the kind of Judaism I believe in, one that is connected to its heritage and traditions and deeply engaged with the modern world. He also participated in the societal conversations that continue to interest me. Through his personal example, he showed me and so many others that joy can be found not just in people or things, but—when framed by a humble willingness to encourage challenge from others and a relentless drive for self-improvement—in the collective pursuit to discover not victory but truth.

Most importantly, Rabbi Sacks taught me that though we have a long way to travel yet, whatever challenges we face along the way, whether in a collective pursuit of truth or in this interesting road we call life, we should always recognize the journey for the blessing it is and ensure we move along it with joy. Such joy.

May his memory be an eternal blessing.

Notes

1. Jonathan Sacks, "Argument for the Sake of Heaven," in *Covenant & Conversation: Numbers—The Wilderness Years* (Jerusalem: Maggid, 2017), 204.
2. Ibid., p. 207.
3. Ibid., p. 209.
4. Ibid., p. 209.
5. Jonathan Sacks, *The Dignity of Difference: How to Avoid the Clash of Civilisations* (London: Continuum, 2004), 84.
6. You can watch Rabbi Sacks' TED Talk on the TED website here: https://www.ted.com/talks/rabbi_lord_jonathan_sacks_how_we_can_face_the_future_without_fear_together.
7. You can listen to all the extended interviews on the BBC website here: https://www.bbc.co.uk/programmes/p06jxvm9/episodes/downloads.
8. Jonathan Sacks, *Celebrating Life: Finding Happiness in Unexpected Places* (London: Bloomsbury, 2000), 64.
9. For an extensive digital archive of Rabbi Sacks' work including articles, videos, audio recordings, and much more, visit www.RabbiSacks.org.

CHAPTER 4

Beethoven's Last Sonata

Joanna Benarroch

I was privileged to work closely with Rabbi Sacks for over 23 years, both during his distinguished tenure as Chief Rabbi and those wonderful years after he stepped down. It was then that he moved into new territory, one he called LP—'Late Period,'—named after Beethoven's last sonatas. And this choice was not incidental. Rabbi Sacks' joy was profoundly connected to music.

Rabbi Sacks had a passion for music, music of every genre. He had eclectic taste—from Brahms to The Beatles, Mattisyahu to Mahler and everything in between. He was tickled pink to discover that I was a Queen fan—quite by accident—when my phone rang and Bohemian Rhapsody filled the room. Rabbi Sacks proceeded to give me a detailed shiur on how that song was produced. Watching him listen to a piece of music that he was playing at full volume on his computer—wanting to share the pleasure with me or our team—was wonderful—he loved nothing more than introducing us to music that we hadn't come across. He threw himself into the music and became immersed in it—it was true joy, the joy of sharing the moment. It reminds me of something he once wrote:

J. Benarroch (✉)
London, UK

© The Author(s), under exclusive license to Springer Nature Switzerland AG 2023
E. Brown, S. Weiss (eds.), *An Ode to Joy*,
https://doi.org/10.1007/978-3-031-28229-4_4

Happiness is something I can feel on my own. But joy in the Torah is essentially shared ... Unlike happiness, simcha only exists in virtue of being shared. It is a form of social emotion ... Joy is a Jewish wedding. It is dancing in the presence of the Divine ... It says: stop thinking of tomorrow. Celebrate, sing, join the dance however undignified it makes you look. Joy bathes life with light.[1]

When I remember times of joy and happiness experienced with Rabbi Sacks, in my mind's eye, I see his eyes light up, slightly crinkled with a distinct twinkle, or when he was savouring something really special his eyes closed, all the better to listen and inhale.

There were many occasions when Rabbi Sacks himself brought the music: in prayer, to schools, and to Israel.

The musicality of *tefilla* [prayer] inspired him. He was the heart and soul of community *tefillah*—joining in at the top of his voice, clapping along and encouraging the community to be part of this joyful celebration. His exuberance was infectious!

One Yom Kippur, my daughter and I decided to spend the *Yamim Noraim* [High Holidays] at Western Marble Arch, the community where Rabbi Sacks officiated. It was, without doubt, the most uplifting Yom Kippur we have ever experienced. Watching Rabbi Sacks leading *Neilah* [final prayer], surrounded by the choir and the children, was joy personified, the *ruach* [spirit] he created was electric. The whole community felt compelled to join in. Of particular note were the wonderful and inspiring Yom Ha'aztmaut celebrations at Finchley Synagogue (Kinloss) singing Hallel together. Rabbi Sacks would stand in front of the *Aron Kodesh* [ark], swaying and clapping and singing. The exultation he shared with the community was palpable.

Visiting schools and spending time with children singing brought such hope for the future to Rabbi Sacks. He believed that you could see Judaism being born again in their excited young faces, in hearing their *tefillot* [prayers] and knowing that Jewish continuity is strong. Looking back at old photos, I recently came across one where Rabbi Sacks was dancing with abandon and delight with Bnei Akiva youth. It was the true highlight of his year—connecting and sharing his love of Israel with the youth, many of whom looked forward, one day, to making Israel their home.

Being in Israel brought another layer of hope to Rabbi Sacks which was also reflected in music. Whether Rabbi Sacks spoke at a hospital, at a children's facility, to those wounded in a terrorist attack or those in an old age home, Rabbis Sacks always had the perfect words—crafting them carefully so that they would resonate with and touch each person—so many people told us they felt he was speaking directly to them. He loved nothing more than singing with others to bring them comfort. The Shabbaton Choir 'Solidarity through Song' missions, which you can read about in Shimon Craimer's reflections, were a highlight in Rabbi Sacks' calendar.

Rabbi Sacks came up with a novel idea to celebrate Israel's 60th birthday. He produced a double CD of over 24 pieces of music interspersed with his commentary. One of those pieces, written especially for the album by Steven Levey, *Oseh Shalom*, became an iconic piece of music synonymous with Rabbi Sacks. We gathered at Trevor Horn's recording studio in West London to record this piece with the three *chazzanim* [cantors] of the Shabbaton Choir: Jonny Turgel, Lionel Rosenfeld, and Shimon Cramer. We were joined by the children of the Moriah Jewish Day School choir. The delight on everyone's faces was something to behold, but it was mesmerising watching Rabbi Sacks' unbridled joy at bringing everyone together in song to celebrate Israel. For me, it was a truly emotional experience.

Just before Rabbi Sacks stepped down as Chief Rabbi, we visited Netiv Tefahot in the Galil because a *beit midrash* was being dedicated in his name. Spontaneous dancing broke out in the courtyard. Rabbi Sacks threw himself into the dancing with great exuberance.

On a more personal note, watching the beaming smile on Rabbi Sacks' face as he addressed my daughter and son-in-law under the *chuppah* [marriage canopy] was very moving for me. He watched my children grow up and took great personal pleasure and interest in their development. Despite my protestations that he and Elaine could quietly slip out if they were tired (he was having such a wonderful time enjoying the festivities), he didn't want to leave.

Rabbi Sacks and I shared the joy of children and grandchildren, a bond that was deep and memorable. I was blessed to receive calls from Rabbi Sacks on the birth of my three youngest children. Each time I sat up straight at the end of the phone and received his blessings and tales of the joys that children bring. We were blessed to have him name our boys at their *bris milahs* [circumcisions]. Just a few months before he passed away, we were expecting our first grandchild. Rabbi Sacks called me daily, in the run-up to the impending arrival, to check in and ask if there was any news. He told me that I was joining the best club in the whole world and that grandchildren were the greatest source of joy one could imagine. I saw that joy on his face when he was with his grandchildren or talking about them. They gave him much *nachat* [gratification]; he loved the fact that one of his granddaughters was the spitting image of his mum, a child who brought him such pleasure. When one of his grandsons taught him about astronomy, he quipped, "Don't worry Saba [Grandpa] I'll make it easy for you." This brought him pure delight. Rabbi Sacks believed "to bless grandchildren and be blessed by them, to teach them and be taught by them, these are the highest Jewish privileges."

Carrying the torch of Rabbi Sacks' light and his joy is an incredible honour and privilege and I hope that I, together with our wonderful team, can do Rabbi Sacks' legacy proud. Joy wasn't necessarily Rabbi Sacks' natural habitat. He was a natural worrier, who was always striving to do better and climb the next mountain. But everywhere he went, Rabbi Sacks sought joy, brought joy, and taught joy to others because, in his own words, "Joy bathes life with light."[2]

Notes

1. Jonathan Sacks, *Ceremony and Celebration: Introduction to the Holidays* (Jerusalem: Maggid, 2017), 127.
2. Ibid., 129.

CHAPTER 5

The Language of the Soul

Shim Craimer

Rabbi Lord Sacks loved music.

His joy in music transcended our conventional thought and, like so much in his life, he understood why God had gifted us this medium.

Before his untimely passing, I was very fortunate to have spent twenty-one years of my life helping Rabbi Sacks spread his message to the world through the power of music.

My good friend and mentor, Rabbi Chazzan Lionel Rosenfeld, invited me in 1999 to join him for the midnight choral *Selichot* service when I was 21. We were accompanied by the Shabbaton Choir led by Stephen Levey, in London, where I grew up.

With this invitation, I was given my first chance to listen to a modern *Gadol Hador*—a great scholar—of our generation prepare us for the prayers we were about to recite. His very presence allowed me to harness his aura into my own soul. Seeing how the combination of music and prayer affected him so deeply helped me reach a higher spiritual plane.

He could channel the notes and, in turn, feel that power enhances the understanding of the words.

S. Craimer (✉)
Modiin, Israel

Even more than that, Rabbi Sacks felt there was a whole new language contained in music. A language with no words. To him, music gave meaning to written texts, but it also had the ability to create a spiritual text of its own without the need for grammatical content. Our minds need words to generate thought, but our souls need something more. Rabbi Sacks expressed this idea beautifully in one of his most famous phrases, "Words are the language of the mind, music is the language of the soul."[1]

Throughout Jewish history, music has played a very important part in helping our souls connect to our faith. There is not one area of prayer or Torah reading which doesn't have a musical theme running through it. Specific melodies were written for particular texts, linked to the time of the year at which they are recited. For example, there is one for reading the Torah, a different one for the Haftorah, and a totally separate one for the Megillot, the scrolls read on certain holidays. As Rabbi Sacks writes, "When we engage with sacred texts, we don't recite. We chant!"[2]

Music helps create different moods for specific holidays, one for Shabbat, a separate one for the *Shalosh Regalim*, the three pilgrimage festivals, and a completely different set of melodies for the *Yamim Noraim*, the Days of Awe.

Each prayer, *tefilah*, has its own unique sound and is instantly recognizable when sung, allowing everyone to feel the particular emotions connected to that period of the year. "There is a map of holy words and it is written in melodies and songs."[3]

There are even moments in davening when the music overtakes the emotion of the words. A prime example of this is the Kol Nidrei prayer on the holiest night of the year.

"It is a dry legal formula for the annulment of vows,"[4] less a prayer, more a statement.

And yet, it is one of the most magical moments of Yom Kippur. The melody sets the tone for the whole day of repentance. The atmosphere in the synagogue becomes one of contemplation and trepidation for the upcoming twenty-five hours. It is an instant transformation for the one leading prayers and for the congregation, who are transfixed with every utterance.

The sheer power of something not of this earth, created purely by the human voice, is a gift to release emotion in so many ways.

Our faith takes on a new meaning with the emotion attached to it. Sometimes words, however powerful, are not enough to break through to that area of our soul where we internalize what we are saying and feeling.

How have we used music in ways other than prayer and connection to ancient Holy texts to reach our inner soul?

What is it about this medium that affects us in such a spellbinding way?

I have often marveled at the number of different cultural styles of music that exist. Just as there are a multitude of languages in the world, similarly there are an abundance of musical strands. Every corner of the globe defines the "mindful" and "soulful" language in their own way. It's almost as if "spoken" and "musical" languages are connected to beat as one heart within each nation.

What is also very interesting to note is how it is more the country than the religion that defines styles of music. When I take a deeper look at our Jewish heritage, I always find a prime example of this in the wide geographical spectrum, and integration into each society has seeped into our religious musical language. Focusing on our Ashkenazic and Sefardic traditions, since their center of development stems from different areas of the world, we see how the musical style of a region has influenced melodies in Jewish prayer. Ashkenazic melodies produce a different range of emotions to Sefardic melodies to the same words and vice-versa.

We have so far focused on the effect of music within a religious text-based setting, as well as linking the geographical nuances of a place to the way a prayer is recited. If we start to focus a bit more on the melodies themselves, however, we can trace the effect it has on our inner soul beyond the structure of prayer, and how in some incredible, sacred, and transcendent way, it draws us to want to pray more.

We have all experienced it. Those unforgettable moments, sitting or standing with thousands of other people. Our eyes focused on the stage, our ears taking in every sound, listening intently to the performers, feeling the emotion as they sing, or deliver their personal interpretation of a well-known song or piece.

It's a unique experience, each individual listener feels the power of the collective.

The atmosphere connecting their shared love of music of all kinds flows through the air.

Here is where the power of this gift takes on a different spiritual role. Yes, we want to be entertained and feel good at the end of a show, but the songs that move us to emote and uplift us create memories we never forget.

On many occasions, I have been blessed to have had the opportunity to become the interpreter of these experiences to others through my music. To share my musical soul. There are similarities to leading a congregation in prayer, but there are also major differences. We don't have the comfort of a holy place, the structure of the services, or the feeling that the congregation is there to talk to God with you.

Music has the ability to become the ultimate mode of communication with others and with God. Words of a song form the context of what we are trying to say. They are not words of written prayer; they are the personal expression of an individual. But it is the music, the melodies, the rhythms, the instrumentation, accompanying those lines that give it the emotional soul needed to break through to a higher level of feeling.

It is this inner soulful blanket wrapped in words and the melody that carries the lyrics from the mind that helps channel these emotions into the soul.

Now we have an answer to our first question. Music is multifaceted. It is capable of reaching our innermost feelings in so many ways and can create a variety of emotions depending on setting and style.

That is why many people leave a musical performance feeling spiritually uplifted. They have not been praying as such, although the connection between body and sound can feel almost prayer-like. Even more fascinating to me is the way non-verbal instrumental pieces, from early classical to modern day, affect our thoughts and moods. The melodies and harmonies produced by pieces of wood and plastic and string possess the ability to make us cry one minute and dance the next.

Rabbi Sacks understood that power, and he used music in his teachings to great effect in various ways. I had the honor of helping to produce and record, with many artists from around the world, a number of musical projects and videos with him. Using words and music, for example, we created unique musical pieces for the High Holidays and did the same for the celebration of Israel's 60th anniversary Israel. We journeyed for thousands of years together through the music.

The culmination of that project was the filming of the first viral Jewish music Youtube video, called *Oseh Shalom*.

Rabbi Sacks joined us front and center, singing a new anthem for peace composed by Stephen Levey and lead by Chazzan Jonny Turgel, Chazzan Lionel, and myself. The video also featured the Shabbaton Choir and schoolchildren from the Moriah Jewish Day school in London. The video has over three million hits.

Rabbi Sacks also attributed to music the power to heal.

In his essay on music as part of his "Covenant and Conversation" series, Rabbi Sacks writes about the famous musicologist Clive Wearing, who struggled to remember anything for more than a few seconds after being struck by a devastating brain infection. Rabbi Sacks describes how Wearing's life was "caught in an endless present that had no connection with anything that had gone on before."[5] One time Wearing held a chocolate bar in one hand and repeatedly covered and uncovered it with his other, unaware that it was the same piece of chocolate. And yet, Clive could still sing and play and conduct whole pieces of music with the same mastery before he got sick.

One of the most famous crooners of our generation, Tony Bennet, suffererd from Alzheimer's. He struggled to put sentences together or even converse with others. Every single day, however, the accompanist who had been working with him for decades, came around to the house. As soon as the accompanist started to play the first notes of one of Bennet's songs, the transformation was instantaneous. He bounded into the room with a spring in his step and sang the entire song from memory.

There are numerous accounts of patients with amnesia or Alzheimer's who cannot remember from one moment to the next but can recite whole songs or play long pieces from beginning to end. It is quite extraordinary.

But there's another kind of healing through music that Rabbi Sacks sensitized me to in 2002 that became one of the most uplifting and spiritual moments of my musical life. During the Second Intifada of 2002, I came to Israel as a featured soloist together with Rabbi Lionel and Chazzan Jonny on a trip organized with the Office of Chief Rabbi Lord Sacks to bring strength to the country through music. Citizens all over Israel were suffering from daily, debilitating terror attacks. Our itinerary included visits to hospitals, special needs schools, and army bases as well as giving concerts in various areas around the country.

Rabbi Sacks joined us for most of the tour, giving words of inspiration to us and to everyone present at each event. To have him and his special wife Lady Elaine with us as we traveled the length and breadth of the country was truly special and inspiring. We all shared in the emotion of what we were witnessing and achieving. Rabbi Sacks guided us through the tough times with his natural ability to make everything meaningful.

That first trip was so successful, we had 17 more.

Many of the missions were specifically targeted to coincide with painful moments, such as the missile attacks in the south and the 2008 conflict on the northern border. Our music and energy stirred, moved, and healed everyone we met. There were many magical moments, pain mixed with joy, tears mixed with smiles.

I will never forget one particular visit that demonstrates the true, healing power of music.

We went to visit Hadassah Hospital during a very trying time, traveling the wards singing and dancing with anyone we met. On that trip, we brought a talented child soloist with us, adding even more color and depth to some of our performances. Just before we left the hospital, we were asked by a nurse to come into the room of a young boy who had been tragically involved in a suicide bombing. We were told to prepare ourselves for what we were about to see. He had lost both his arms and legs and was now blind. The doctors told us that the boy hadn't said one word since that fateful day and was just lying there in silence with his parents by his bedside.

Ten of us, including the child soloist, walked in, surrounded the bed, and stood there, unsure what to song to perform. We finally settled on an *Ein Kelokainu*, a soft, beautiful piece of music, written by the famous *hazzan*, composer and conductor, Zvi Talmon featuring the young soloist. We all closed our eyes and began to sing.

A few moments later, we suddenly heard another voice joining us. I opened my eyes to see the mouth of the young boy in that hospital bed moving, the sweet melody permeating from what remained of his shattered body. We were overwhelmed. We cried together with his parents, and for hours after. That is the healing, spellbinding beauty of music, its connection to the soul, a part that transcends the physical body.

Rabbi Lord Sacks was an integral part of my entire life, but especially my musical life. He was my mentor and gave me inspiration and strength to lead with the gifts that God gave me. I miss him deeply. He left behind a legacy like no other. His aura is still with me and it will live long in my heart and soul. I know he is up in Heaven, looking down, singing joyously together with the angels.

Notes

1. Jonathan Sacks, "Music, Language of the Soul," *Covenant and Conversation: Beshallach*, 5772, https://www.rabbisacks.org/covenant-conversation/beshallach/music-language-of-the-soul/.
2. Ibid.
3. Ibid.

4. Jonathan Sacks, "The Spirituality of Song," *Covenant and Conversation: Ha'Azinu*, 5776, https://www.rabbisacks.org/covenant-conversation/haazinu/the-spirituality-of-song/
5. Sacks, "Music, Language of the Soul".

PART II

Joy in the Bible

CHAPTER 6

"What Good Is That?" Happiness and the Emotional Range of Ecclesiastes

Erica Brown

"To desire only happiness in a world undoubtedly tragic is to become inauthentic," writes Eric G. Wilson in his book, *Against Happiness: In Praise of Melancholy*.[1] For Wilson, the shelves of recent books on happiness promote a life that is not only unrealistic but one that is also emotionally flat and robbed of the range that makes life both interesting and worthwhile.[2] Elsewhere, Wilson makes the case for what we might call negative emotional reactions and responses:

> [Y]ou are most you, at your best, when you create the roles that make you feel most alive: witty, lyrical, speculative, loving, but also, and here's the rub, cynical, sarcastic, angry, muddled, sad—for negative states can be just as vital as positive ones. Fullness is the goal, myriad-mindedness (a happy phrase Coleridge conjured to describe Shakespeare): to be as varied and capacious as the cosmos…The best actor, Hamlet asserts, uses all gently.[3]

E. Brown (✉)
Yeshiva University, New York, NY, USA

It is in this spirit that the book of Ecclesiastes[4] is best read, as wisdom literature that acknowledges and validates a healthy range of emotions, one that does not bypass the grim and maudlin aspects of human life to advance an ever-sunny disposition. The hopeless, the despairing, the indignant, the cynic, and the contented can all find themselves on its pages and, more importantly, as the stirrings of the same author. Those who mistake this vitality for contradictions[5] fail to see that the scope, array, and transient nature of emotions represented in Ecclesiastes provide the book's perennial appeal and save readers from a life that is static and tedious: "The porcelain rose is not as pretty as the one that decays."[6]

Happiness has its place but can only be truly experienced with intensity alongside other dramatic feelings. R. Joseph Soloveitchik, for example, mentions in the name of the 'Kabbalist Sages,' that the soul has two sets of forces: constructive and destructive.

> Love is a constructive force; it is opposed by the destructive forces of jealousy and hatred. The positive-constructive forces are by and large static and passive, while the negative forces are dynamic and aggressive. Hatred is more emotional and fiercer than love; the destructive forces more powerful than the constructive forces.[7]

Because the destructive forces, to use R. Soloveitchik's language, in Kohelet are so strong, the repeated mentions of joy and the importance of its pursuit are often lost in the study of the book. But happiness punctuates Ecclesiastes, and the sudden and often unexpected endorsement of joy throughout the book, especially in the context of a heartbreaking sentiment or a meditation on injustice, makes the book's emotional scope more penetrating and realistic.

The first group of 'joy verses' in Ecclesiastes 2 test the durability of material joy just as Kohelet interrogated and found it wanting at the end of chapter 1: "For as wisdom grows, vexation grows; to increase learning is to increase heartache" (1:18). Right after this statement Kohelet examines the fleeting value of happiness.

> I said to myself, "Come, I will treat you to merriment. Taste mirth!" That too, I found, was futile. Of revelry I said, "It's mad!" Of merriment, "What good is that?" I ventured to tempt my flesh with wine, and to grasp folly, while letting my mind direct with wisdom, to the end that I might learn

which of the two was better for men to practice in their few days of life under heaven.[8]

Kohelet indulges in merriment—"*anaskha b'simkha*" (loosely translated as "I will try my hand at happiness") as if joy were subject to the controls and variables of a scientific experiment. Yet he quickly arrives at pleasure's limitations, summarized with a question: "What good is that?" This question that Kohelet ponders—*ma ze oseh?*—is refashioned by Rashi on 2:10 to a more existential register: "What good is that if it [life] ends in grief?"[9] Joy can only ever be temporal because life ends in death. Contemporary Bible scholar Michael V. Fox, in contrast, contends that Kohelet is pitting pleasure against meaning: "His purpose is to discover what is good to do. The answer is pleasure, though this too is senseless. The feeling of pleasure is not enough to imbue pleasurable actions with meaning. Therefore, the toil that produced the means of pleasure proved to be absurd."[10] To work hard to afford pleasure is itself an act of futility. Elsewhere, in the *Jewish Publication Society Ecclesiastes* commentary, Fox translates the question and adds another aspect to his reading, that of genuine productivity and value: "Literally, 'What does this do?' Even if it feels good, it *does* nothing, accomplishes nothing, and Kohelet longs to do something *effective*, to achieve something substantive. He finds, however, that wine, women, song and even achievements in building and land development (vv. 4–8) fail to provide a sense of achievement and efficacy."[11] Kohelet demonstrates experientially that, for him, the accumulation of wealth was enjoyable but not inherently valuable: "I got enjoyment out of all my wealth. And that was all I got out of my wealth" (Eccl. 2:10). To this Robert Alter adds, "The purely hedonistic probe of Qohelet's experiment with experience fails." For Kohelet, it "proves to be no more than a transient excitation, leading to nothing and providing no lasting satisfaction."[12]

These interpretations confirm Kohelet's early rejection of pure hedonism as a reason for living. Yet, near the chapter's end, after a lengthy description of Kohelet's many excesses that include the planting of orchards and groves, the building of houses and pools, the amassing of servants, gold, and silver, Kohelet arrives at an unexpected conclusion: "There is nothing worthwhile for a man but to eat and drink and afford himself enjoyment with his means. And even that, I noted, comes from God" (Eccl. 2:24). The rhetorical flourish of our earlier question, "What good is that?" finds its answer in the simplicity of food and drink. Lest a reader think that this unexpected praise of the joy that emerges from material enjoyment is itself just another random thought in Kohelet's arsenal of adages, we have it as a repeated leitmotif throughout the book:

> Thus I realized that the only worthwhile thing there is for them is to enjoy themselves and do what is good in their lifetime; also, that whenever a man does eat and drink and get enjoyment out of all his wealth, it is a gift of God. (Eccl. 3:12–13)

> I saw that there is nothing better for man than to enjoy his possessions, since that is his portion. For who can enable him to see what will happen afterward? (Eccl. 3:22)

> Only this, I have found, is a real good: that one should eat and drink and get pleasure with all the gains he makes under the sun, during the numbered days of life that God has given him; for that is his portion. Also, whenever a man is given riches and property by God, and is also permitted by Him to enjoy them and to take his portion and get pleasure for his gains—that is a gift of God. For [such a man] will not brood much over the days of his life, because God keeps him busy enjoying himself. (Eccl. 5:17–19)

> Here is a frustration that occurs in the world: sometimes an upright man is requited according to the conduct of the scoundrel; and sometimes the scoundrel is requited according to the conduct of the upright. I say all that is frustration. I therefore praised enjoyment. For the only good a man can have under the sun is to eat and drink and enjoy himself. That much can accompany him, in exchange for his wealth, through the days of life that God has granted him under the sun. (Eccl. 8:14–15)

> Go, eat your bread in gladness, and drink your wine in joy; for your action was long ago approved by God. (Eccl. 9:7–9)

With so many verses praising enjoyment, it is difficult to know whether or not to trust Kohelet's condemnation of pleasure elsewhere. It also means that Kohelet did not praise joy incidentally. He returns to it and repeats his claim, much the way that he returns to other, more despondent thoughts. Alter claims that this supposed contradiction is "another expression of Qohelet's dialectic thinking. Immersion in sensual pleasure, especially in its extreme forms, may bring no lasting good, but in the futility of our ephemeral lives, the simple pleasures of the senses here and now are all we have, and we might as well take advantage of them."[13] A passage in the

Talmud also notes the contradictory appreciation of pleasure and its condemnation and then resolves it by distinguishing the laughter and pleasure of the righteous from]| that of the wicked.[14]

One need not, however, go to these theological lengths to reconcile the challenge because the verses themselves reveal the solution. Joy is not a "fleeting amusement," in the words of one scholar.[15] Material joy is a gift from God, as is evident from a review of the above verses.[16] Professor of Bible, Mark R. Sneed, argues that such pleasure is not vanity precisely because it comes from God and "does not involve the strife and toil that accompany human agnostic aspirations."[17]

Temporal, sensual joy is one of the few diversions God provides to distract human beings from life's bruising injustices, as explicitly stated in chapter eight, where Kohelet shares a constant irritation: "Sometimes an upright person is requited according to the conduct of the scoundrel; and sometimes the scoundrel is requited according to the conduct of the upright. I say all that is frustration. I therefore praised enjoyment" (Eccles. 8:14–15). Indulgence in the life of the senses cannot replace the true elation of justice and fairness, but it, nevertheless, can have a palliative effect. Confront despair with good wine and good food and perhaps the personal anguish will lessen for the moment; since injustice itself cannot always be repaired, the perception of it can be temporally diminished and blurred with feasting and alcohol. Kohelet, on some level, offers us a theology of distraction. God gave us material delights to smooth out the deeper wrinkles of pain, if only for a time.

Kohelet also implies that the experience of excessive pleasure without God leads to emptiness, as Hebrew Bible scholars Adele Berlin and Marc Zvi Brettler discuss: "The one who displeases God … suffers the fate depicted in the experiments above, namely, that God makes him focus simply on accumulating wealth, only then to see it handed over to another who pleases God."[18] Failure to enjoy life's limited pleasures may be itself construed as a rejection of God's beneficence.[19] Philip Browning Helsel, a professor specializing in pastoral care, writes:

> Ecclesiastes suggests that the "basic pleasures that sustain life" have theological significance, suggesting that the ability to experience pleasure and satisfaction are intimately connected with our experience of God. For Ecclesiastes, experiencing enjoyment and pleasure is part of what it means to live in faithful response to God's call in our lives, and the inability to enjoy "one's portion" in life is a serious ethical and interpersonal problem, one

that leads to violation of the self, the other, and the world ... an important aspect of the spiritual journey is the "stewardship" of joy.[20]

The spiritual stewardship of joy may be the ultimate answer to the question Kohelet posed in chapter two, "What good is that?" Kohelet's question may not be rhetorical after all. He tells you what joy is and asserts its religious worth, as Rabbi Jonathan Sacks sums up in a description of the biblical book that points to his own deepest held values:

> What redeems life and etches it with the charisma of grace is joy: joy in your work ("The sleep of a worker is sweet"—5:11), joy in your marriage ("See life with the woman you love"—9:9), and joy in the simple pleasures of life. Take joy in each day. Above all, rejoice when you are young. Kohelet is an old man. No one has written a more moving description of the dying of the light in old age than does Kohelet in the last chapter of the book. Yet his conclusion yields to neither cynicism nor despair. You do not need to be blind to the imperfections of the human world or the slow ravages of age in order to rejoice. You can know life with all its flaws and still have joy.[21]

Rabbi Sacks found great joy in work, joy in family, joy in reading, and joy in community. He did not yield to cynicism or despair. During the two years I lived in London and had the great good fortune of studying with Rabbi Sacks, running programs at Jews' College, the institution he ran before becoming the Chief Rabbi, and working closely with him as my thesis advisor, I saw not only a man of tremendous intellect and elegance. I also saw a scholar unlike many academics I knew and would come to know, who was lifted and energized by his teaching, learning, and thinking. As a rabbi, he did not wear religion like a heavy cloak of theological angst or loneliness that separated him from those he led. Teaching, like the happy moments that punctuate Kohelet, was his feast that was a gift from God. Observing him over the years taught me by example that there is great piety in pleasure when it expands one's religious horizons.

Instead of abnegation to achieve spiritual closeness to God or denial of pleasure to achieve piety, Kohelet advises us to deepen our relationship with God and others through the simple variety of smells, tastes, and textures of a this-worldly existence. If his conclusion is that happiness has only transient value, it is no more or no less than any other human emotion. All are fleeting. Kohelet helps his readers embrace the emotional range of living because just as joy suddenly turns into misery, disappointment can abruptly morph into delight. "*What good is that?*," Kohelet ponders. For a life void of stasis and filled with wonder, there is much good in that.

Notes

1. Eric G. Wilson, *Against Happiness: In Praise of Melancholy* (New York: Sarah Crichton Books, 2009), 6.
2. A quick search on Amazon with the word "happiness" in the search engine produced 60,000 books.
3. Eric G. Wilson, *Keep It Fake: Inventing an Authentic Life* (New York: Sarah Crichton Books, 2015), 99.
4. One of the oddities of Kohelet is its spelling in English, as will be evident in the scholarly citations throughout this essay. I have opted for the easiest phonetic spelling and will refer to Kohelet both as the book and as the author of the book.
5. For an introduction to the many contradictions in Ecclesiastes, see Michael V. Fox, "On Reading Contradictions," in *A Time to Tear Down and a Time to Build Up: A Rereading of Ecclesiastes* (Eugene, Oregon: Wipf and Stock, 2010), 1–26.
6. Wilson, *Against Happiness*, 110.
7. Joseph D. Soloveitchik, *On Repentance* (Paramus, New Jersey: Jason Aaronson, 2000), 39. I am grateful to Dr. Shira Weiss for bringing this citation to my attention.
8. Eccl. 2:1–2.
9. This explains Rashi's use of *Kohelet Rabba* 2:24 on 3:13 to support a non-literal reading of eating and drinking throughout Ecclesiastes as a reference to Torah study and *mitzvot*, good deeds.
10. Michael V. Fox, *A Time to Tear Down and a Time to Build Up* (Grand Rapids, Michigan: William B. Eerdmans, 1999), 175.
11. Michael V. Fox, *The JPS Bible Commentary: Ecclesiastes* (Philadelphia: Jewish Publication Society, 2004), 12. Italics are the author's.
12. Robert Alter, *The Wisdom Books: Job, Proverbs, and Ecclesiastes* (New York: W.W. Norton, 2010), 349.
13. Ibid.: 352.
14. BT *Shabbat* 30b.
15. See Aerre Lauha, *Kohelet*, Biblischer Kommentar, Altes Testament 19 (Neukirchen-Vluyn: Neukirchner Verlag, 1978): 52, as translated by Mark R. Sneed, *The Politics of Pessimism in Ecclesiastes: A Social-Science Perspective* (Society of Biblical Literature, 2012), 167.

16. Robert Gordis in *Koheleth: The Man and His World: A Study of Ecclesiastes* writes that, "For Koheleth, as for Biblical writers generally, the physical pleasures of life were divine in origin, as this verse eloquently attests" (New York: Schocken Books, 1978), 226.
17. Sneed: 168.
18. Adele Berlin and Marc Zvi Brettler, eds., *The Jewish Study Bible* (Oxford: Oxford University Press, 2004), 1609.
19. This view appears as early as Deuteronomy 28: 47–48.
20. Philip Browning Helsel, "Enjoyment and Its Discontents: Ecclesiastes in Dialogue with Freud on the Stewardship of Joy," *Journal of Religion and Health* 49, no. 1 (March 2010): 106.
21. Jonathan Sacks, *Ceremony and Celebration: Introduction to the Holidays* (Jerusalem: Maggid, 2017), 126.

CHAPTER 7

Joy to Shushan: The Book of Esther's Radical Cocktail of Happiness

Stuart W. Halpern

I'm a grape-juice-at-the-Seder kind of guy. It's because alcohol—the taste, the temptation of shedding inhibitions and the loosening of logic—is just not my thing. Relying on modern-day rabbinic opinions that the four cups of redemption can be brought to you by Kedem, I've been able to picture myself as if I left Egypt without being enslaved by the choice of red or white.

So I've always had a particularly hard time imbibing on Purim.

"One must drink on Purim until that person cannot distinguish between cursing Haman and blessing Mordecai," the Talmud instructs in Tractate Megilla.[1] Alas, the years of experience I've accrued downing the same drinks as my three young children have led me to believe the road to joyfully confused inebriation on the fourteenth of Adar is ruefully closed to me, even if I topped things off with a glass of *sparkling* grape juice. Some years I've tried to sneak in a nap—some commentators suggest this liedown-for-a-few-minutes loophole since while you're dozing, you can't differentiate between the Purim story's hero and villain. Other years, I've

S. W. Halpern (✉)
Yeshiva University, New York, NY, USA

© The Author(s), under exclusive license to Springer Nature Switzerland AG 2023
E. Brown, S. Weiss (eds.), *An Ode to Joy*,
https://doi.org/10.1007/978-3-031-28229-4_7

comforted myself with the thought (hope?) that the intention behind the rabbinic edict can be found by finding unabashed bliss amidst the holiday's carnivalesque climate, bouncing between homes after the *Megilla* reading with little Luke, Leia, and Boba Fett in tow, handing out *mishloach manot* [gifts of food and drink], giving charity to the poor, and chowing down on the festive meal with family and friends.

The concoction of intoxication and elation, spirits and scrolls, delirium and danger, and ultimately delight is, after all, the maze through which the ancient Jews of Shushan navigated. "When Adar enters, joy increases,"[2] the rabbis stated in another part of the Talmud, an adage about which one could not distinguish whether they were being prescriptive or descriptive. That is because the story of Esther offers, amidst its poured glasses, politics of power, beauty contests, and military clashes, a perspective on joy that predates today's pundits by millennia.

The actual word for joy, *simha*, appears eight times amidst the Megilla's ten chapters. Its first occurrence is hardly an auspicious one and is rather unexpected. Although a new queen has been found, an assassination attempt foiled, and a plot hatched by Haman to dispose of his enemy Mordecai and all his fellow Jews, no one is yet described as being happy. It is only in the book's fifth chapter, after Esther works up the courage to enter Ahasuerus's throne room and invites him and Haman to a feast, and then to a second feast, that the reader even catches the possibility of joy, but even then, only as an aspiration. Zeresh, Haman's wife, offers a suggestion to her depressed husband. Haman's hyper-exclusive series of invitations to the king and queen's private dining room is not enough of an ego boost as long as that pesky Mordecai refuses to bow down to him. "Build gallows fifty cubits high," she suggests. "And tomorrow morning, recommend to the king that Mordecai be hung on them." This way, "you will go to the next feast with the king *joyfully*."[3]

Offering the possibility of peace of mind, victory, and even joy through the murder of his personal foil, Haman and his family undoubtedly spent the evening celebrating like any good Shushanite, offering toasts as they hammered the gallows up high.

One royally disturbed night of sleep later, Mordecai ends up ceremoniously paraded through the streets instead of pulverized by Haman. And when Esther reveals both her hidden Jewish identity and Haman's plot to destroy her people to an enraged King Ahasuerus, Haman and his lot end up being the ones hanging from the gallows.

And it is then that joy in the book is made manifest. And multiplies—appearing seven times in the book's closing three chapters and concludes with this use: "And Mordecai went from the presence of the king in royal apparel of blue and white, and with a great crown of gold, and with a robe of fine linen and purple; and the city of Shushan shouted and was *joyful*."[4] Letting loose not because of libations but because their very lives had been liberated, the Jews of Shushan, and in fact all the city's inhabitants, are unabashedly happy. Unlike Haman's attempt at joy-through-murder, the Jews' joy is that of relief, gratitude, and national pride.

Celebrating their salvation, the Jews enjoyed "light and joy, happiness and honor." Through a series of proclamations ensuring the commemoration of the salvation that had been achieved, the fourteenth of Adar is declared a "day of feasting and joy." So is the fifteenth of the month for the Jews of Shushan.

The joy enshrined in Purim's practices, the call to cultivate that original outpouring of happiness, couldn't be more different than that which Zeresh attempted to offer her pouting husband. It is a joy emerging not out of the need to destroy difference but rather of the possibility of delighting in inclusivity: "Observe the fourteenth day of the month of Adar," the Scroll instructs, "and make it a day of joy and feasting, and as a holiday and an occasion for sending gifts to one another."[5] The same month during which the Jews had faced destruction at Haman's hands "turned from one of grief and mourning to one of festive joy."[6] Sending gifts to one another, and charity to the poor, were the ways to observe these "days of feasting and merrymaking." Sure, drinking will make an appearance at the feasts, but the ethos is less bartending than brotherhood.

In 2020, a team of international scholars set out to uncover the formula for joy. Distilling the findings of these "distinguished and prolific academic experts on the science of happiness" in a 2022 article for the *Atlantic*,[7] former think-tank president turned Harvard social scientist Arthur Brooks listed ways to get happier that "work and are workable." And they will come as little surprise to those who have ever felt even a little bit sloshed in celebration of Shushan's salvation.

"Invest in friends and family was the first recommendation"—say, by hosting them for a *seudah*, for example.

"Join a club" because it fosters a sense of belonging and protects against loneliness. You can't do much better than delivering *mishloach manot* to welcome new neighbors, reconnect with old friends, and foster a sense of communal solidarity.

"Be physically active"—anyone who's ever climbed in and out of a minivan with young kids in tow for half a day while balancing cardboard boxes stacked with *mishloach manot* can most definitely most definitely can skip "leg day" at the gym.

"Practice your religion"—as spiritual experiences go, it's kind of hard to top a wall-rattling, grogger-spinning *megilla* reading.

"Act nicely" and "be generous"—say, by giving funds and food to those less fortunate.

"Don't leave your happiness up to chance," Brooks concludes. Make sure you proactively cultivate it and "share it with others."

Mordecai and Esther and our wise ancient rabbis understood what today's credentialed elite only now discovered. "The Jewish response to trauma is counterintuitive and extraordinary," wrote Rabbi Lord Jonathan Sacks in an essay titled "The Therapeutic Joy of Purim." "You defeat fear by joy. You conquer terror by collective celebration. You prepare a festive meal, invite guests, give gifts to friends."[8]

What was true in ancient Shushan remains timeless. True joy can be found not in elite invitations to exclusive soirees but in the "my roommate's best friend is visiting for the day—can she pop by ... and also bring a friend and can that friend bring a friend?" *balagan* that is de rigueur at Purim seudahs. Deeply felt smiles emerge not from accumulating power but from spotting Spider Man praying at the Western Wall and clown cars blasting "Mi She, Mi She, Mi She, Mi She" down Broadway. Serenity is achieved not through dunking on (let alone hanging) our enemies but through delivering smiles, sustenance, and sure, some spirits, to both those less fortunate and those more familiar—all while carrying your five-year-old's plastic lightsaber. Adar's month-long merrymaking, and Purim's mix of generosity, spirituality, community, and connection offer a cocktail of joy ... even to Purim prudes like me.

Notes

1. BT Megilla 7b.
2. BT Ta'anit 29a.
3. Esther 5:14.
4. Esther 8:15.
5. Esther 9:19.
6. Esther 9:22.

7. Arthur Brooks, "Ten Practical Ways to Improve Happiness," *The Atlantic*, April 21, 2022, https://www.theatlantic.com/family/archive/2022/04/happiness-research-how-to-be-happy-advice/629559/.
8. Jonathan Sacks, "The Therapeutic Joy of Purim," 2015, https://www.rabbisacks.org/archive/therapeutic-joy-purim/.

CHAPTER 8

Odes to Joy in Sonnets and Psalms

Shaina Trapedo

For centuries, the Psalms have served as a touchstone for exploring the texture, edges, and impediments of pleasure, happiness, and joy as meaning-seeking and connection-craving beings. While the Hebrew Bible conveys God's desire for a relationship with us, it also "contains words of human search and concern" for Him, most notably in the *mizmorim, shirim, pesukei d'zimra,* and collected compositions of the authors of *Tehillim,* in which "the spontaneity of the Biblical man found its expression."[1]

"Let all those who take refuge in You rejoice," King David intones, "let them ever sing for joy as You shelter them" (Ps. 5:12).[2] And yet, such lyrics of delight both follow and precede various verses of pain, angst, self-doubt, and suffering all the way through the collection. For the casual reader of *Tehillim,* David's majestic range and rapid tone shifts are enough to induce a type of emotional whiplash.

Although the pain of feeling distanced from the Divine resounds throughout *Tehillim,* heartache is not its main melody. As Rabbi Sacks writes, "King David in the Psalms spoke of danger, fear, dejection,

S. Trapedo (✉)
Yeshiva University, New York, NY, USA

© The Author(s), under exclusive license to Springer Nature Switzerland AG 2023
E. Brown, S. Weiss (eds.), *An Ode to Joy,*
https://doi.org/10.1007/978-3-031-28229-4_8

sometimes even despair, but his songs usually end in the major key."[3] Gratitude, praise, contentment, joy, and hope find full-throated expression in this "lexicon of the Jewish soul."[4] And if *Tehillim* offers a soundtrack for life, then its leitmotif is *Ashrei*.

Variously translated as happy, blessed, or fortunate, the word *Ashrei* appears thirty-one times throughout the Psalms (nearly as many as all its other uses in *Tanach* combined) and bookends the score.

> Happy (*Ashrei*) is the one who does not walk in the counsel of the wicked, who does not stand on the path of sinners, who does not sit among the jeering cynics—instead, the Lord's teachings is all his desire, and he contemplates that teaching day and night. (Ps. 1:1–2)

Like the opening note of an opus, the first word of *Tehillim* invites curiosity. Happiness—how it is achieved, maintained, and protected—has universal appeal. As Rabbi Sacks reminds us in his reading of this verse, for Aristotle, happiness (in Greek *eudaemonia*) "is the ultimate purpose of human existence."[5] Yet *Tehillim* resists a teleological conception of the good life and hints at its countercultural vision by defining happiness through negation. Despite popular practice, *Ashrei* is not achieved by pursuing our heart's desires. This approach often begets self-centered, self-sabotaging, and transgressive behaviors, which (as the Psalmist shows through nature metaphors) yield volatility and detachment. Rather, desiring what God desires from and for us leads to tranquility and stability, though this path is not without its challenges.

The emotional modulation of *Tehillim* reveals we rarely experience one feeling at a time and resists the harmful notion that we can incrementally work toward a happiness that is realized when all other sensations and obstacles are removed. Instead, the "Sweet Singer of Israel" (2 Sam. 23:1) and his collaborators embrace a more nuanced, complicated joy that emerges within a network of darker emotions yet is ever-available throughout life's ups and downs. And it is the poets who have turned to *Tehillim*'s teaching against the decontextualization of joy who have found the most success and resonance in their own explorations and articulations of the human condition.

In the fourteenth century, Francesco Petrarch fostered Renaissance humanism with meditations on the nature of love and religion, the virtuosity of verse, and the impulse to glean sacred insight from secular wisdom. Yet the devout Catholic struggled to justify the joy he found in the aureate language of antiquity and prove that the arts serve a spiritual purpose. Taking evidence from the "Old Testament fathers," Petrarch argued, "one may almost say that theology actually is poetry, poetry concerning God" arising from humankind's innate drive to seek truth and "win the favour of the deity by lofty words."[6] Although Petrarch placed Greco-Roman writers at the apex of artistic achievement, throughout his career he studied the Psalms in Hebrew. Their stylistic influence is palpable in the language of longing and other poetic features that have come to constitute Petrarchism and the sonnet form he popularized. In memorializing his unrequited love for Laura (which incites his greatest joy and deepest anguish), Petrarch repeatedly pulls from Psalms. To offer just one of many examples, in the poet's sigh, "Sorrow and tears, I feed my weary heart,"[7] we hear murmurs of David's despondence, "My tears have been my fare day and night" (Ps. 42:4). Though Petrarch and David's objectives cannot be compared, the former repeatedly looked to the lyrics of the Israelite king as a guide for gauging joy in relation to pain on both a visceral and spiritual scale. Though Petrarch often confessed to loving Plato, Homer, Cicero, and Virgil, in his later years he resolved, "my philosopher shall be Paul, my poet David ... I want to have his Psalter always at hand [and] beneath my pillow when I sleep and when I come to die."[8]

During the Renaissance and Reformation, David captured the imagination of early modern English monarchs, ecclesiastics, and artists as a biblical figure who skillfully navigated the fields of diplomacy, religion, and literary invention.[9] The most prominent Renaissance poets—including but not limited to Wyatt, Spenser, Sidney, Shakespeare, Jonson, Donne, and Milton—"translated, paraphrased, or alluded to the Psalms in their major works"[10] which infused Renaissance England with the lyricism and wisdom of ancient Israel that has profoundly shaped Western literature and culture to this day.

Although Shakespeare's sonnets are more secular than spiritual, the bard engaged with the Bible throughout his career and acknowledged the "force of heaven-bred poesy" in his plays and poetry.[11] Echoes of Psalm 23 ("though I walk through the valley of the shadow of death") are heard in Sonnet 18 when the speaker claims his verse will immortalize his beloved such that death shall not "brag that thou wander'st in his shade." In Sonnet 91, after cataloging sources of "delight" that still speak to our modern moment—"birth," "skill," "wealth," "bodies' force," even fashion and animal companions—the poet certifies the subjectivity of satisfaction, granting that "every humor hath his adjunct pleasure / Wherein it finds a joy above the rest." But "Thy love," the speaker tells his beloved, surpasses all these "measures" and is "better" than every "best," a superlative sentiment that strikes a chord similar to Asaf's estimation of a relationship with the divine. After pondering the "revelers" pursuing "fancies" and amassing wealth, the composer concludes "With You, I desire nothing else on earth" for the "nearness of God is my good" (Ps. 73:25—28).

The metaphysical poets of the seventeenth century vigorously explored God's presence and proximity in a style blending rational meditation, religious fervor, and witty wordplay. George Herbert, who played the lute and studied the Psalms, enjoyed a successful academic career at Cambridge and spent the last few years of his short life as an Anglican priest. In "Man's Medley," Herbert contemplates how the nature of human beings—"With th' one hand touching heav'n, with th' other earth"—affects their experience of happiness. Like John Donne in his Anniversary poems, Herbert advises those suffering the "griefs" of mortality—whether emotional or physical—to find solace in the knowledge that "in flesh he dies" but in "soul he mounts and flies," and achieve a degree of "relief" by alchemizing pain into purpose with poetry: "Happy is he, whose heart / Hath found the art / To turn his double pains to double praise." In these lines, I hear the steady beat of *Tehillim*, in which praising God becomes a universal imperative and panacea: "Happy are the people who know the joyful shout, Lord, they walk in the light of your presence. They rejoice in Your name all day long, raised up through Your righteousness" (Ps. 89:16–17). Underpinned by a Protestant perspective on Cartesian mind–body dualism, Herbert offers his Christian audience the familiar faith tenet that only after death can one convene with godliness and fully experience bliss. We might "taste of the cheer" here, the poet asserts, "Yet if we rightly measure, Man's joy and pleasure, Rather hereafter, than in present, is."

In Jewish tradition, happiness is not a dream deferred to the World to Come. By divine design, it is achieved by engaging with the material aspects of living.

> A song of ascents. Happy are all who fear the Lord, who *walk* in His ways. You shall eat the fruit of your *labor;* You shall be happy and thriving. (Ps. 128:1–2)

As Rabbi Sacks observes in the first verb of Psalms and repeatedly throughout *Tanach*, Jewish identity calls for forward momentum in the here and now.[12] "This principle of 'walk on ahead,' the idea that the Creator wants us, His greatest creation, to be creative, is what makes Judaism unique in the high value it places on the human person and the human condition."[13] The Mishnaic concept of *Tikkun Olam* (repairing the world) and the Midrashic notion of *Dirah Bitachtonim* (building a dwelling for God in the lower realms) endorse the centrality of virtuous behavior in Jewish life and practice. But it is the Psalms that suggest generative work is essential for *Ashrei*—a happy and good life. As Rabbi Sacks has shown, Judaism has much to offer positive psychology:

> The ancient Hebrew word for hard work is *avoda*. It is also the word that means 'serving God.' What applies in the arts, sciences, business, and industry, applies equally to the life of the spirit … Halakha (Jewish law) involves a set of routines that—like those of the great creative minds—reconfigures the brain, giving discipline to our lives and changing the way we feel, think, and act … Judaism is about changing us so that we become creative artists whose greatest creation is our own life.[14]

Imagine the impact of recontextualizing happiness as the product of effort and ingenuity, as spoken about in the Psalms. *Tehillim* hits its highest and most evocative notes when David channels his energy, expertise, and spiritual insight into composing a *shir chadash*, a *new* song.[15]

Simcha (joy), another term in *Tanach* aligned with *avoda*, further expands our understanding of human flourishing and offers artists another avenue for exploration.

> *Serve* the Lord with *joy*, come before Him in glad song. (Ps. 100:2)

For Rabbeynu Bahya, exhibiting *Simcha* "is considered as fulfillment of a commandment by itself, meriting additional reward."[16] The Lubavitcher Rebbe spoke about *Simcha* as necessary to break "through barriers, including the barriers of exile."[17] Though *Ashrei* and *Simcha* are obtained through observance of God's commandments, the difference, Rabbi Sacks explains, is that while individuals can achieve *Ashrei* independently, *Simcha* "is better defined as 'the happiness we share, or better still, the happiness we make by sharing.'"[18] If *Ashrei* is an aria, *Simcha* is a symphony. King David declares, "*Happy* are those who give thought to the weak" and "make the Lord their trust" (Ps. 40:2–5); though worthy endeavors, these are solo performances. Joy, however, requires a collective: "Let Israel rejoice in his Maker; let the children of Zion be joyful in their King" (Ps.

149:2). And as Rabbi Sacks notes, *Simcha* appears almost ten times as often as *Ashrei* in *Tanach*, underscoring its centrality in Jewish life as the "supreme religious emotion" that creates connection, community, and partnership.[19] While joy "lies at the heart of the Mosaic vision of life in the land of Israel," it is also a universal social emotion that enacts the "redemption of solitude."[20]

In opposition to the widespread alienation and political strife that emerged from the Enlightenment, the redemption of the individual is precisely what the Romantic poets of the late eighteenth century hoped to achieve. English poet laureate William Wordsworth, orphaned by the age of thirteen and predeceased by three of his children, spent much of his career contending with loneliness and reflecting on the emotional complexities and "deep power of joy."[21] One of his most poignant sonnets, written as an elegy for his three-year-old daughter Catherine, begins with a startling sensation:

> Surprised by joy—impatient as the Wind
> I turned to share the transport—Oh! with whom
> But Thee, long buried in the silent Tomb

The poet's elevation of joy is infused with the impulse to connect, but sadly, it dissipates quickly. The speaker is left "forlorn," reliving the "worst pang that sorrow ever bore" when he recalls the loss of his daughter that "time, nor years unborn" can restore. Although the poem springs from "faithful love" befitting a sonnet, its metrical breaks and disruptions to the Petrarchan structure remind us that bereavement does not obey boundaries. While there is much wisdom to be mined from Wordsworth, this sonnet ends with the mournful assertation that although joy and grief emanate from a shared urge to unite souls, they are mutually exclusive emotions. However, just a generation later and an ocean away, Transcendentalist poet Walt Whitman draws inspiration from the wonders of the natural world wrought by "God's beautiful eternal right hand"[22] and the subtlety of the Psalms to proclaim, "I contain multitudes."[23]

In his spiritual autobiography, which takes its title from Wordsworth's sonnet, C.S. Lewis reflects on the writers who shaped his early life and his discovery that joy is not the satisfaction of a desire, but a *longing* for what is most desirable: "we yearn, rightly, for that unity which we can never reach except by ceasing to be the separate phenomenal beings called 'we.'"[24] For Lewis, who reflected on the Psalms throughout his lifetime, joy is the "[ache] for that impossible reunion" which pulls us closer to God. For Rabbi Sacks, the Hebrew term for the Divine Presence, *Shekhina* (etymologically linked to *shakhen* meaning neighbor) bespeaks this belief.[25] And for David, this yearning leads to his discovery that pleasing the Lord *is* pleasing, and he shares his hard-won wisdom through song.

In his decades of writing, Rabbi Sacks attuned us to the range of human emotions. He drew inspiration and wisdom from the eloquence and elevated thoughts of Shakespeare, Wordsworth, Lewis, and countless others. But David was his poet and philosopher, whose "soul thirst[ed] for God" (Ps. 42:3, 62:2). With the words of *Tehillim* on hand and in heart, he taught us that we can hold grief in one hand and joy in the other. We can feel good will toward someone who becomes pregnant while struggling with fertility. We can celebrate the marriage of a sibling while longing for companionship. We can embrace a complicated joy. Happiness "is not the absence of suffering but the ability to take its fractured discords and turn them into music that rescues from the darkest regions of the soul a haunting yet humanizing beauty—surely the supreme achievement down here on earth. Some of the greatest Psalms come from this realm of pain, as do the finest works of art."[26]

If poetry "begins in delight and ends in wisdom," as Robert Frost wrote, then we are blessed indeed by the poetic Torah of Rabbi Sacks, who saw Judaism itself is "an ode to joy."[27] If we want to feel close to those who have walked ahead, we can study their teachings—in word or deed—and they accompany us. And if we want to experience the highest levels of joy, we must utilize our unique strengths and gifts to collaboratively transform the world around us as illustrated in the crescendo of *Tehillim*, in which "every living soul" (Ps. 150:6) is called upon to express gratitude to God and partner in the ongoing process of creation and redemption.

Notes

1. Abraham Joshua Heschel, *God in Search of Man* (Farrar, Straus and Giroux, 1976), 26.
2. All Psalms quotations from *The Koren Illustrated Tehillim*, trans. Rabbi Jonathan Sacks and Sara Daniel (Koren, 2021).
3. Rabbi Jonathan Sacks, *Studies in Spirituality* (Koren, 2021), 256.
4. *Studies in Spirituality*, xx.
5. *Studies in Spirituality*, 257.

6. Petrarch, *Petrarch: The First Modern Scholar and Man of Letters*, trans. James H. Robinson (Knickerbocker Press, 1914), 261.
7. Petrarch, *Canzoniere*, trans. Mark Musa (Indiana University Press, 1996), 342.
8. Petrarch, *Letters From Petrarch*, trans. Morris Bishop (Indiana University Press, 1966), 191–92.
9. See Debora Shuger, *The Renaissance Bible* (University of California Press, 1998); Hannibal Hamlin, *Psalm Culture and Early Modern English Literature* (Cambridge University Press, 2004); Heather Dubrow, *The Challenges of Orpheus: Lyric Poetry and Early Modern England* (Johns Hopkins, 2011).
10. Hamlin, *Psalm Culture*, 1.
11. William Shakespeare, *Two Gentlemen of Verona* (Folger), 3.2.71.
12. *Studies in Spirituality*, 115–18. In his commentary on the *Tehillim*, Rabbi Shimshon Rafael Hirsch explains that root of the word *Ashrei* is *ashur* ("strive forward").
13. *Studies in Spirituality*, 12.
14. *Studies in Spirituality*, 101–02.
15. See Ps. 33:3, 40:4, 96:1, 98:1, 103:5, 144:9, 149:1. The term poetry is derived from the ancient Greek *poiesis* meaning to create or make something that did not exist before.
16. In his commentary on Deu. 28:47, Rabbeynu Bahya also notes that "The Torah also makes a point of underlining the joy in Aaron's heart when he saw his brother Moses again after so many years. Had he known that his feelings would be commented upon favorably (Exodus 4:14), he would have gone out to meet his brother accompanied by an orchestra of many different musical instruments." Other commentaries on this verse, including Yalkut Shimoni and Torah Temimah, also identify joyful service as *shira* (song) modeled by the Leviim.
17. Rabbi Menachem Mendel Schneerson, Sichas Shabbos Parshas Ki Seitzei 5748.
18. Rabbi Jonathan Sacks, *To Heal a Fractured World* (Schocken, 2007), 5.
19. *Studies in Spirituality*, 258.
20. Rabbi Jonathan Sacks, *Essays on Ethics* (Koren, 2016), 314.
21. "Lines Composed a Few Miles above Tintern Abby, On Revisiting the Bands of the Wye during a Tour. July 13, 1798." Rabbi Sacks draws on Wordsworth's thinking and uses this phrase as the title for his essay on Parsha Re'eh in (5776) and the relationship between *Simcha* and covenant.
22. Walt Whitman, "Death's Valley," *Harper's Monthly Magazine*, April 1892.
23. Whitman, *Leaves of Grass, Song of Myself*, 51. On the influence of the Hebrew Bible on Whitman see Gay Wilson Allen's "Biblical Echoes in Whitman's Works," *American Literature VI* (1934): 302–15.

24. C.S. Lewis, *Surprised by Joy: The Shape of My Early Life* (Houghton Mifflin Harcourt, 1995), 271.
25. Rabbi Jonathan Sacks. October 18, 2010. "Happiness in the Jewish Perspective." Center for the Study of Law and Religion at Emory video, https://www.youtube.com/watch?v=2S_rqcJnvpE (5:40 and following).
26. *To Heal a Fractured World*, 232.
27. *Essays on Ethics*, 315.

CHAPTER 9

Flowing with Joy

Raphael Zarum

The hope for a happy life filled with joy is certainly a universal human aspiration, but most of us are uncertain as to how to achieve it. Together with life and liberty, the American Declaration of Independence proclaims that the pursuit of happiness is one of the unalienable rights endowed on all humanity by the Creator. But how is this happiness meant to be pursued? How do we find joy?

Rabbi Sacks discusses these questions when analyzing the Torah's use of the Hebrew term, *simha*. He writes: "*Simha* is usually translated as joy, rejoicing, gladness, happiness, pleasure, or delight. In fact, *simha* has a subtle meaning that is untranslatable into English. Joy, happiness, pleasure, and the like are all states of mind, emotions. They belong to the individual. We can feel them alone. *Simha*, by contrast, is not a private emotion. It means happiness shared. It is a social state, experienced as a "we," not as an "I." There is no such thing as feeling *simha* alone."[1]

He points out that all seven instances in which *simha* appears in the Torah portion, *Re'eh*, refer to occasions of collective religious celebration. We are instructed to rejoice before God at the Temple in Jerusalem by

R. Zarum (✉)
London, UK

© The Author(s), under exclusive license to Springer Nature Switzerland AG 2023
E. Brown, S. Weiss (eds.), *An Ode to Joy*,
https://doi.org/10.1007/978-3-031-28229-4_9

coming together to eat sacred food or to share festive meals on *Shavuot* and *Sukkot* (Deut. 12:7,12,18; 14:26; 16:11,14,15). By noting that these are all essentially *group* experiences, Rabbi Sacks deduces that collective joy is the essential nature of *simha*.

In this chapter, I would like to explore the biblical use of the term *simha*, focusing on four specific narrative episodes. This will unearth some of its psychological contours, which may aid us in our hope for a life of happiness and joy today.

The Torah's first two references to *simha* appear in complementary circumstances: one a farewell, the other a greeting. After two decades working for Laban, marrying his daughters Leah and Rachel, producing eleven children with them and their handmaidens, and gaining substantial wealth, Jacob is ready to move on. Noticing a downturn in relations with his father-in-law and ranch staff, he opts for a quiet exit with his family. Laban is offended, and on catching up with Jacob exclaims: "Why did you flee secretly, and steal away from me; and not tell me? For I would have sent you away *with joy (b'simha)*, and with songs, with tambourine, and with harp! And why did you not let me kiss my sons and my daughters?"[2] The rituals of leave-taking are as old as civilization, and Laban was upset at missing them. Recalling the devious ways in which Laban had already treated Jacob, we may suspect that Laban was overstating feelings for his offspring, and that the financial loss resulting from Jacob's departure was much more his concern. Either way, we observe *simha* occurring in the primal desire to give a joyous and heartfelt send-off to loved ones.

The next reference to *simha* appears in the book of Exodus, during Moses' first encounter with God at the burning bush. Reticent for being appointed to redeem the Israelite slaves from their Egyptian oppressors, Moses highlights his weak oratory skills, but God replies: "Is not Aaron the Levite your brother? I know that he can speak well, and also, behold, he comes forward to meet you; and when he sees you, he will *be joyous in his heart (vesamach belibo)*."[3] One midrash states that had Aaron known God would mention him at that very instant, "he would have gone out to greet Moses with drums and dancing."[4] Similar to the previous story, music and movement are expressions of *simha*.

What else do these two episodes have in common? Both refer to the joy experienced at moments of significant social change when people separate or reconnect. These, it would seem, are best expressed energetically: by Laban organizing a live band for Jacob's departure and Aaron moving to the beat as Moses arrives. I would like to suggest that these narratives are the paradigm for the religious moments of *simha* Rabbi Sacks discussed in Deuteronomy. Each moment is a rendezvous with God, made up of an arrival and a departure, in between which there is a memorable period of *simha* expressed through food, service, and celebration. Thus, the innate *simha* of family members, when they part or greet, is extended to the Israelites getting together to share rituals on sacred occasions.

Another intriguing aspect of both Laban's farewell to Jacob and Aaron's meeting with Moses is that though they were meant to be expressed with joyous dancing and singing, it turned out that these were absent on both occasions. We learn of what Laban and Aaron *would have done* if they had been more fully conscious of their respective situations. Thus, the collective joy intended in both these episodes is not realized. The social norm is not expressed by those present. This too is instructive. Family get-togethers are generally happy occasions, but there can be particular pressures—such as external stresses, intense micropolitics, unsatisfied expectations and so on—which mar the moment and cause the inherent joy to be dampened or aborted altogether. This might be why, the Torah instructs us to celebrate some collective religious events with joy, ensuring that there, at least, we will come together *b'simha*.

Two further narratives in which *simha* occurs add another important dimension to its biblical understanding. When Jonah retired from Nineveh to see if the city would heed his prophetic warning, God miraculously grew a plant over his head to shade him from sunstroke. "And Jonah was joyous ... a great joy *(simha)*."[5] Additionally, when Esther invites Haman to a second exclusive banquet with the king, he was "joyous *(sameach)* and happy-hearted."[6] A common element of these two episodes is that the joy experienced is transitory and is rapidly replaced with frustration. When the plant withers and the sun beat down the following day, Jonah is so upset he tells God, "I am good and angry, to the point of death" (Jonah 4:9). Meanwhile, Haman's joy ends as abruptly as it began. For when, in the very same very verse, Mordechai does not rise or stir in his presence: "Haman was filled with rage at him" (Esther 5:9).

What is the cause of Jonah's and Haman's rapid switch from elation to misery? Neither individual did anything to make himself joyous. Both were unexpected gifts from others. As a result, there was no personal investment in the emotion so it could easily be dispelled. Rather than making themselves happy, they were *made happy*, and that is a piecrust feeling—easily made, easily broken.

This is reiterated in a second moment of joy that Haman experiences. Again, it does not originate from him. This time it comes but from his wife Zeresh (Esther 5:14). The emotion is experienced briefly and, as is clear from the following chapter, does not even last the evening. Haman's fleeting feelings of joy starkly contrast with the end of the Megilla. There we read of the establishment of Purim as "a day of feasting and joy *(simha)*... for holidaymaking and for sending gifts to one another."[7] This is an annual expression of deep joy because it requires investment and participation. *Simha* is mentioned eight times in this context. Surviving the threat to survival, Jews gather to share and celebrate the continuity of Jewish life with *simha*.

Identifying the need for enduring joy to have personal involvement rather than coming from an external source enables us to uncover another insight into how it plays a role in religious ritual. *Simha* is the *method* of religious celebration, never the *aim*. There is no command to be happy per se, rather it is the way of performing a *mitzvah*: "Serve the Lord *with joy (b'simha)*; come before him in glad song."[8] This, in turn, implies that lasting joy is not something to be directly pursued. Rather, it is an outgrowth of a powerful and significant experience. Joy is an emergent phenomenon that arrives when you are not looking for it. You are so immersed in what you are doing, it happens organically.

The American psychologist, Mihaly Csikszentmihalyi, published a book on the psychology of happiness, called *Flow*. Flow is his term for an optimal experience. He describes it as "a sense that one's skills are adequate to cope with the challenges at hand, in a goal-directed, rule-bound action system ... Concentration is so intense that there is no attention left over to think about anything irrelevant... Self-consciousness disappears, and the sense of time becomes distorted... [it] is so gratifying that people are willing to do it for its own sake."[9] The experience of flow is clearly related to Torah concepts concerning the mitzvot, such as *kavannah* (intention) and *lishma* (for its own sake). Rabbi Sacks referred to Csikszentmihalyi's work on a number of occasions and how it can help us with *avodat Hashem* (service of God). To my mind, *simha* is an outcome of flow.

Csikszentmihalyi writes about the conditions needed for flow to occur. Included in these is a lessening of both self-consciousness and self-centeredness. "Both lack the attentional fluidity needed to relate activities for their own sake; too much psychic energy is wrapped up in the self... Under these conditions it is difficult to become interested in intrinsic goals, to lose oneself in an activity."[10] Similarly, we saw earlier that Jonah was too self-centered and Haman was too self-conscious to experience more than passing joy. Their lack of investment and focus was fatal. Maimonides relates to these issues in his discussion of religious practice, "The *simha* which a person derives from doing good deeds and from loving God, who has commanded us to practice them, is a supreme form of divine worship ... Anyone who is arrogant and insists on self-glory on such occasions is both a sinner and a fool."[11]

We find seemingly contradictory comments about *simha* in the book of Ecclesiastes. Early on we read, "I said, let me quench myself with joy; let me sate myself with good living. I found that, too, but fleeting breath *(havel)*. Of delirium I said it was a joke, and of joy I asked: What's the point?"[12] Yet later we find, "And so I praise joy—for there is nothing as good for man beneath the sun to eat and drink and be happy; this is what he has to accompany him in his labors throughout the life that God has given him beneath the sun."[13]

So, does the book condemn or advocate joy? A close reading reveals important differences in the language that reflect the distinctions I have been making. Joy's worth is questioned in chapter two because it is being directly pursued, "let me quench myself" and so it does not last, it is "but fleeting breath." Conversely, in chapter eight, joy complements a purposeful life, "this is what he has to accompany him in his labors," and thus is meaningful and praiseworthy.

The Talmud distinguishes between these two comments in Ecclesiastes in a similar way. The first is "joy unrelated to a *mitzvah* (commandment)" while the second is "joy related to a *mitzvah*."[14] In other words, joy for self-gratification is denounced, but joy that comes through doing something worthwhile—and what is more worthwhile than the performance of a divine command?—is lauded. *Simha* is not valuable in and of itself and thus should not be pursued, but *simha* does *come along* when you are fully invested in a meaningful experience. It emerges when you are doing a *mitzva*, when you are in flow.

Writes Csikszentmihalyi, "Flow and religion have been intimately connected from earliest times. Many of the optimal experiences of mankind have taken place in the context of religious rituals. Not only art but drama, music, and dance had their origins in what we now would call "religious" settings; that is, activities aimed at connecting people with supernatural powers and entities ... This connection is not surprising, because what we call religion is actually the oldest and most ambitious attempt to create order in consciousness. It therefore makes sense that religious rituals would be a profound source of enjoyment."[15]

Had Jacob and Laban been in a good relationship, their parting would have been an intense and meaningful experience, one which would have exuded joy. But this was not the case, and so all we are left with is a mildly cynical comment by Laban of what might have been. Meanwhile, Aaron was unaware that he was greeting his brother after his first ever encounter with God. He was happy when they met because they were close, but had he known of Moses's divine mission, and the role he too was to play in releasing the Israelites from slavery, he would have had a much more intense and joyous experience. Together they were about to embark on the fulfilment of God's grand command.

These are some of the ideas behind Rabbi Sacks' discussion of joy in *Re'eh*. He himself was a man full of *simha* because he never chased it. Instead, he found it because he was passionate about everything he did. He would always commit fully. He was flowing with joy.

Notes

1. *Covenant & Conversation: Deuteronomy* (Jerusalem: Maggid, 2019), 127.
2. Gen. 31:27–28.
3. Ex. 4:14.
4. Ruth Rabbah 5:6.
5. Jonah 4:6.
6. Esther 5:9.
7. Esther 9:18–19.
8. Ps. 101:2.
9. Mihaly Csikszentmihalyi, *Flow: The Psychology of Happiness* (NY: Penguin 2022), 86.
10. Ibid., 102–103.
11. Maimonides, *Mishneh Torah*, Laws of Shofar, Lulav and Sukkah 8:15.
12. Eccl. 2:1–2.
13. *Ibid*. 8:15.
14. BT Shabbat 30b.
15. Csikszentmihalyi, *Flow*, 2022, 92.

CHAPTER 10

Joy and Trembling

Alex Israel

Nothing would seem more uncomplicated than Judaism's embrace of joy. "Serve the Lord with joy,"[1] urges Psalms, and, as Rabbi Sacks reminded us, the biblical word for happiness, *Ashrei*, is Psalms' opening word, and a key to our daily prayers."[2] The ultimate manifestation of a functioning Jerusalem is *"kol sasson, kol simha*: the sound of jubilation, the sound of rejoicing."[3] Deuteronomy bemoans those who "did not serve God in joy and gladness amidst every abundance."[4] We commence our Jewish week by chanting the verse from Esther: "The Jews enjoyed light and gladness, happiness and honor."[5] And we respond, "So may it be for us!"[6]

And yet, many sources express a pronounced discomfort with joy, an uneasiness and apprehension. It is not merely Ecclesiastes' curmudgeonly comment: "Rejoicing! What good is that?"[7] There is a sense that excessive joy is problematic: "Better to go to a house of mourning than to a house of feasting."[8] In this mindset, the Talmud quotes an alternative verse from Psalms: "Serve the Lord in fear and rejoice with trembling."[9]

> What is meant by "rejoice with trembling"? R. Adda bar Mattana said that Rabba said: Where there is rejoicing, there should be trembling. Abaye sat

A. Israel (✉)
Midreshet Lindenbaum, Yeshivat Eretz Hatzvi, The Tanakh Podcast, Jerusalem, Israel

© The Author(s), under exclusive license to Springer Nature Switzerland AG 2023
E. Brown, S. Weiss (eds.), *An Ode to Joy*,
https://doi.org/10.1007/978-3-031-28229-4_10

before Rabba. Rabba saw that he was excessively joyful. He said: It is written: Rejoice with trembling. Abaye responded: I am wearing phylacteries … R. Ashi made a wedding for his son. He saw the Sages were excessively joyous. He brought a valuable cup of white glass and broke it before them and they became sad … At the wedding of Mar, son of Ravina: The Sages asked R. Hamnuna Zuti to sing. He sang: Woe to us, for we shall die! Woe to us, for we shall die. They said to him: What shall we respond after you? He replied: "Where is Torah and where is mitzva that protect us?"[10]

Something is agitating these scholars when it comes to excessive levity. Why do they feel a need to puncture the bubble of joy? Possibly it relates to a fear of sin; after all, Rabbi Akiva warns that, "Merriment and frivolity accustom one to sexual license."[11] In environment of levity, inhibitions fall, and caution is often thrown to the wind. In this Talmudic passage, we see two solutions. The first involves a constant God-awareness, a serious frame of mind—*koved rosh* (in contrast to *kalut rosh*, lightheadedness), which is achieved by donning phylacteries. There is joy, but it is tempered by an action that makes the divine presence more palpable. This sort of demeanor is presented as exemplary: "The Divine Presence rests neither through gloom nor through lethargy, not through laughter nor levity, not through talk nor through idle chatter; rather, from the joy of a mitzva."[12]

Here we have a Golden Mean of sorts—neither ecstatic mirth on the one hand, nor melancholy on the other, but rather a sense of purpose, a joy in the Divine relationship, in commandment.

In contrast, in the other anecdotes of the Talmudic passage we quoted, R. Ashi smashes an expensive glass and R. Hamnuna Zuti recalls the day of death. This is more radical. This is not a steady, happy medium but an antidote, a counterbalance. It is a more literal reading of "rejoice with trembling" whereby each emotion struggles in a dialectical tension.[13]

Sukkot

In order to further navigate the tensions inherent, the pull and tug of "rejoicing with trembling," let us turn our attention to the festival of Sukkot. It will prove a useful arena in which to explore this theme. Our liturgy applies the moniker *Zman Simhateinu*—the Time of Our Rejoicing—to Sukkot, due to the repeated biblical instruction of joy on this celebration, so we might anticipate unbridled rejoicing.[14] And yet, as we shall demonstrate, Sukkot—in its observance and literature—expresses an ambivalence of joy, a paradoxical blend of jubilation and unease.[15]

The Fragile Sukka

Why is Sukkot—of all festivals—marked specifically by expressions of particular happiness? It is an ingathering festival. At this season, the farmer happily revels in a barn filled with an annual yield of grain, nuts, fruits, wine and oil—the labor of an entire year. The farmer's family knows that they will survive the winter in comfort; maybe their crops will even make them a little wealthy. That financial stability, the understanding that one is safe and secure and not subject to vulnerability will most certainly engender a deep sense of contentment!

But, as the Rashbam notes, it is precisely this feeling of abundance that might lead to a sense of arrogance and pride, and forgetfulness of God:

> We leave our houses that are filled with every good at the time of the ingathering and we dwell in booths as a reminder that they did not have an inheritance in the wilderness, nor houses to dwell in, so that their hearts not swell on account of their houses that are filled with every good, lest they say, "Our hands have gotten us this wealth."[16]

We are invited to recall the era of the wilderness, when God provided Israel's every need, as an antidote to a feeling of invulnerability, self-sufficiency, and conceit. A number of Sukkot's laws, rituals, and practices reflect this dialectic tension that embodies the human condition.

The Sukka reflects a sense of fragility and temporality. By its definition, it must be a temporary structure. But the vulnerability of the Sukka is reflected more deeply in the laws of its construction. The Sukka must have two walls and a handbreadth. As such, it offers more than fifty percent protection; likewise, its canopy should offer more shade than sun.[17] It is, by definition, a structure that protects. And yet, it is permeable to the heat and the rain.[18] It is a halfway house between exposure and protection. But it is liminal in a further sense. The material of the canopy must be fashioned from natural materials, but not too natural—if it is still growing, it is disqualified. And yet, if it has been crafted into a household object, it is again disqualified. The Sukka exists in the space between the raw and natural on the one side and the processed, the industrialized, the technological, on the other.

The Sukka of the harvest and the Sukka of the Exodus are oriented to the same point. They seek to remind us that though we craft our physical and social environment, it will never be complete, never hermetically sealed. Even the most sophisticated society is but a temporary dwelling. Prof. Eliezer Schweid writes of the rules guiding Sukkot observance:

> What do these laws express? The consciousness that humans do not have full and total ownership and control of our land and its produce, and we may not make claim to that ownership ... Precisely at the moment in which one fills one's hands with the bounty of one's land, the gesture of leaving the home, into a fragile, temporary hut testifies that the farm produce is a divine kindness. The joy [of Sukkot] is awakened precisely by overcoming the penchant for absolute acquisition and the delusions of mastery. [19]

At the ingathering, as the farmer is celebrating, filled with the feeling that the keys to prosperity lie in his control, in his ingenuity and skill, we are called to remember God's protection and our human fragility; we are invited to check our hubris in a liminal space that reminds us that our "permanent" abode is, in fact, a temporary abode. In this way, the wild levity that might characterize the ingathering in many agricultural societies is given balance and direction, one might even say a weightiness, a *koved rosh*.

THE BOUND LULAV

The Four Species are also designated as expressions of joy. We are instructed: "Rejoice before the Lord your God for seven days."[20] In our Hallel prayers, we shake or wave the Four Species in celebration and thanks—*Hodu LaShem ki Tov* [Praise God for He is good; His kindness everlasting]. But in contrast, the same gestures are marshalled in a cry for help: *Ana Hashem Hoshiya Na!* [Please God! Save! Please!] Likewise, the Talmud gives the Four Species a heavier and more somber dimension: "We wave them back and forth to counter harmful winds (from the four directions) and up and down to counter harmful dews."[21]

The ritual of the Four Species is framed here as a prayer of fraught anticipation of the rain.[22] When we shake the Lulav or as we circuit the synagogue pleading *Hosha Na!* [Save us!]—we are expressing our nervousness and apprehension regarding future prosperity; the national economy is governed by rainfall.

The dialectic inherent in Sukkot's particular notion of joy is further reflected in the choice of the palm branch for use on Sukkot. For an ingathering festival, we might expect to wave an open, lush, palm branch, expressive of the plenty of the harvest. However, the Talmud mandates a "bound lulav"[23]—a young, immature branch that has yet to open. This is indicative of a clenched anxiety, it expresses prayers of anticipation of future rains and crops, not those that have already ripened and been gathered.[24] In short, intertwined with the joy of the past season is the trepidation regarding the next season—and the prayers, only hinted at, for the rain of the coming year.[25]

THE REJOICING OF THE WATER-DRAWING

"One who has not witnessed the rejoicings at the *Simhat Beit Hashoeva* [Temple Water-Drawing] has never witnessed real rejoicing."[26] The Mishnah describes the music, the procession, the dancing with glorious superlatives—"the righteous ... **would dance with flaming torches singing praises to God**"; even the street lighting: "There was not a court in Jerusalem that was not illuminated. A Baraita taught: A woman could pick wheat by this light."[27]

What could go wrong with such a celebration? A short phrase in the Mishnah becomes the prevailing theme of an entire Talmudic chapter. The Mishnah reads: At the close of the first holiday of the festival they came down to the women's court, where a great transformation was made.[28] What is this "great transformation"? It is the construction of a balcony or a *Mehitza* [partition]!

> The rabbis taught: Formerly the women sat in inward chambers and the men in outer ones; but thereby was produced some levity, and therefore it was ordained the men should sit inwardly and the women outwardly; but still levity arose, and therefore it was ordained that the women sit above and the men below ... they were occupied in rejoicing, and the passions can overwhelm them.[29]

Celebration is often expressed in an overwhelming surge of emotion and passion that sweeps both the individual and the collective into elation, to ecstasy. The carnivalesque celebration of the Water-Drawing sees the enactment of a gender separation. Following from this detail, the Talmudic discussion turns to the topic of the "evil inclination" and the issue of sexual temptation. At the Temple, joy and revelry cannot be simple or carefree. Joy engenders levity, and the evil inclination awaits: "The greater the person, the greater the temptation of the evil inclination."[30]

The Reading of Kohelet

Lastly, we should note the book of Kohelet—Ecclesiastes—designated to be read on Sukkot. It is the most melancholic of all the Megillot and one which returns, over and over, to the ultimate test case—death—as it examines and explores the value and meaning of life, with its achievements and abundant pleasures. What is this bleak book doing on a festival of joy? Yet again, our tradition feels a need to push back upon the lightness of *zman simhateinu* and ask the question: What is it all for? To what end? Are the pleasures to which people aspire genuinely valuable?

Let us close our discussion of "the Festival of Joy." We have identified at every turn, a sense of rejoicing that is tempered "with trembling"— whether it seeks to assail the human tendency to self-assurance and vanity, whether it is concerned with sexual license, abandonment, and excess amid the revelry, or whether in the carefree merriment of the ingathering, it raises a healthy anxiety for the upcoming season. Sukkot, as a test-case, offers us a nuanced, regulated and qualified jubilation.

The Confrontation with Western Culture

We have presented this antithetical mix of joy and fear as a normative Jewish gesture, as a fundamental awareness, a deep sensibility. But before we close, I would like to apply this sensibility to one final sphere, far wider than a particular event or holiday; it is the encounter between Judaism and other cultures, sometimes called *Torah im derekh Eretz*, or as Rabbi Sacks preferred, Torah and *Chokhmah*—wisdom, "the Universal heritage of humankind." "To be sure," Rabbi Sacks wrote, "the world of wisdom is a danger-zone." The "culture saturated combination of fact and value … may be incompatible with, or subversive of, or antagonistic towards the values to which Jews have been called." And yet, Rabbi Sacks contends: "We cannot apply Torah to the world unless we understand the world," and "a Judaism divorced from society will be a Judaism unable to influence society."[31]

This confrontation then, is not an uncomplicated one. And here I return to our peculiar confederation of joy and fear, and one particularly auspicious moment in history—the opening of the Hebrew University in Jerusalem in 1923. Rabbi Abraham Isaac Hakohen Kook, the Chief Rabbi of Palestine, was invited to address the celebratory event. He chose to speak about the encounter between the Jewish and the academic, the particular and the universal. Rav Kook deeply appreciated the value of both dimensions and sought a fusion between them. His speech drew from Isaiah chapter 60, and the phrase: "Your heart will fear and rejoice."[32] He directed Isaiah's amalgam of "fear and rejoicing," apprehensiveness and jubilation, to the interchange between Jewish and general culture, which he saw as beneficial—hence the joy—and yet hazardous—hence the fear. He said:

> But why "fear"? Why did the prophet preface the phrase "Your heart will rejoice" with the notion of fear? When we look back on the previous generations ... we realize that neither the fear nor the rejoicing was in vain. ... This much is clear: Regarding those circles that welcomed absorption and propagation joyously, with unmitigated optimism and with no trepidation, very few of their descendants remain with us today ... the vast majority of them have assimilated among the nations.[33]

In other words, Jewish history has many instances of groups who welcomed wider culture—from the Hellenists of the Second Temple to the Enlightenment. This has always been a feature of Jewish life. Rav Kook was suggesting that a lack of caution and an easy attitude of unmitigated joy in the engagement with general culture opened a fast route to assimilation and would engender a swift disappearance from the future of Jewish peoplehood. In contrast:

> Only from those who resided securely in our innermost fortresses, in the tents of Torah, enmeshed in the sanctity of the law, did emerge the truly creative Jews ... They exported and imported ideas and values on the spiritual highway that mediates between Israel and the nations. Their attitude, however, toward this undertaking was never one of rejoicing only. **Fear accompanied their joy** as they confronted the vision of the "wealth of the sea" belonging to the "riches of the nations."[34]

For Rav Kook, the encounter between the particular and the universal, between Torah and world knowledge, harbors great potential. There is much to be gained, but also existential dangers. To be successful, it must be approached in two ways: First, from an immersion in "the tents of

Torah", when one is filled with Jewish devotion, practice, and learning. But second, Rav Kook advocates a certain reticence, a sensibility of caution, an underlay of fear. This caution and apprehensiveness will in itself, serve as a preservative measure. In short, the engagement with world ideas and culture is—for a Jew—both a goldmine and a minefield. Here yet again, we discover an arena in which the dialectical tension, the balancing of joy and fear finds its place.

* * *

In this chapter, we have engaged in an examination of the Jewish ethic of joy and celebration. We have discovered a "music of ambivalence,"[35] a highly nuanced disposition, which the Talmud terms "rejoice with trembling." It is a dialectical mindset that allows one to dance at a wedding and at the ingathering, to engage with the exciting ideas of the world, to experience happiness and contentment. And yet, it reflects a sobriety, a resistance to the carefree demeanor, a rejection of exhilarated delirium; it is imbued with an awareness of human failing and an attentiveness to the call of God.

Notes

1. Ps. 100.
2. https://www.rabbisacks.org/covenant-conversation/reeh/deep-power-of-joy/; for a comprehensive treatment by Rabbi Sacks on the topic of happiness in Judaism see: "Happiness: A Jewish Perspective," *Journal of Law and Religion* 29, no. 1 (2014): 30–47.
3. Jer. 33:11.
4. Deut. 28:47. Rabbeinu Bahya interpreted this verse as reflecting an instruction to serve God with joy "for the notion of serving God in joy is in itself a command [mitzva]." Bechor Shor reads the verse in a more circumstantial manner: Since you neglected service of God amidst luxury, you will now have to suffer, and still serve Him. For Bechor Shor, the verse is not instructive.
5. Esther 8:16.
6. The Havdalla service
7. Eccl. 2:2, and the discussion in BT Shabbat 30b.
8. Ibid. 7:2.
9. Ps. 2:11.
10. BT Berakhot 30b–31a.
11. Avot 3:13.

12. BT Shabbat 30b and in a variation at the end of the passage in 30a.
13. See Yehuda Brandes, *Applied Aggada: Studies on Family, Society and Worship* [Hebrew] (Jewish Agency for Israel—Eliner Library / Beit Morasha of Jerusalem, 2005), 29.
14. Deuteronomy 16:14–15.
15. Please see Rabbi Sacks' article "Sukkot: Season of Joy," in *Ceremony and Celebration. Introduction to the Holydays* (Jerusalem: Maggid, 2017), 99–166, in which he establishes many conflicts and dialectics associated with Sukkot: Universalism and particularism, Temple and Tabernacle, Joy and Happiness, stability and uncertainty, security and insecurity.
16. Commentary to Lev. 23:47, drawing heavily on Deut. 8.
17. Mishna Sukka 1:1.
18. Rain—Mishna Sukka 2:9; Sun—BT Avodah Zara 2b.
19. This section draws on the wonderful work of Prof. Eliezer Schweid, *The Cycle of Appointed Times—The Meaning of Jewish Holidays* [Hebrew] (Am Oved Publishers, Tel Aviv, 1986), 86–105.
20. Lev. 23:40.
21. BT Sukka 37a.
22. Mishna Taanit 1:1 raises the ambivalence regarding rain on Sukkot. On the one hand rain is seen as a curse, after all, rain will eject us from the Sukka. On the other hand, we need to pray for it. How do we request rain, without wanting it right this moment? The Mishna's discussion reflects this tension.
23. BT Sukka 32a: ""Branches [*kappot*] of a date palm," i.e., bound [*kafut*]; if the leaves were spread, one should bind it."
24. I heard this idea from Rav Yoel bin-Nun.
25. Similarly, the Water-Drawing ceremony would appear to be part of a ritual of prayer for rain, See Rabbi Dr. Yaakov Nagen, *Water, Creation and Divinity: Sukkot in the Philosophy of Halacha* [Hebrew], Yeshivat Otniel (2008) in particular, chapter 4.
26. Mishna Sukka 5:1.
27. BT Sukka 53a.
28. Mishna Sukka 5:2.
29. BT Sukka 51b.
30. Ibid. 52a.
31. All quotes are from Jonathan Sacks, *Future Tense* (Hodder and Stoughton, 2009), 219–28.
32. Is. 60:5.
33. Translation S.Z. Leiman, *Tradition: A Journal of Orthodox Jewish Thought* 29, no. 1 (1994): 87–92.
34. Ibid.
35. https://www.rabbisacks.org/covenant-conversation/vayera/the-music-of-ambivalence/

PART III

Joy in Rabbinic Literature

CHAPTER 11

Reflections on the Human Experience of Joy

Jacob J. Schacter

Life is not lived in extremes. In the course of our lifetimes we rarely, if ever, experience emotions in their extreme forms. We are neither fully calm, peaceful, relaxed, delighted on the one hand, nor are we fully agitated, angry, irritated, or hostile on the other.

The same is true with joy. We rarely, if ever, experience joy in its extreme, total joy or no joy at all. We live our lives in the in-between, experiencing some joy, while at the same time facing challenges—be they personal, familial, economic, or even national—that elicit feelings of anxiety and trepidation. Our joy is never absolute, full and complete. At times, we feel joy, at others we do not, and often we feel them both at the same time.

The Talmud (*Pesaḥim* 109a) states that a person is obligated to gladden (*le-sameaḥ*, to bring joy to) his children and the members of his household on a festival. Rabbi Judah states that everyone does not fulfill this requirement in the same manner, but each person needs to engage in an activity that will be pleasing to him or her. He determined that for men this means drinking wine while for women this means wearing new clothes. The Talmud continues quoting Rabbi Judah ben Beteira who taught that when the Temple was standing, men would rejoice only through the eating of

J. J. Schacter (✉)
Yeshiva University, New York, NY, USA

© The Author(s), under exclusive license to Springer Nature Switzerland AG 2023
E. Brown, S. Weiss (eds.), *An Ode to Joy*,
https://doi.org/10.1007/978-3-031-28229-4_11

the sacrificial meat, but in the absence of the Temple, they fulfill their obligation only by drinking wine. This position is uncontested and appears to be the final word on this matter.

In codifying this law in his *Mishneh Torah*, however, Maimonides seems to chart his own course. He writes that for men to fulfill their obligation of joy on the festival they are required to eat meat *and* drink wine, "for joy is generated only by meat and joy is generated only by wine."[1] And this ruling of Maimonides is cited in the fourteenth-century code written by Rabbi Jacob b. Asher.[2]

Rabbi Joseph Karo drew attention to the fact that Maimonides was not following the position of Rabbi Judah ben Beteira. "One is astounded at Maimonides," he writes. Why does Maimonides mandate that men should eat meat *and* drink wine when the Talmud states that "these days" when there is no Temple, *only* drinking wine is required? On what basis does Maimonides mandate the eating of meat? He leaves this question open.[3]

A number of answers have been suggested to resolve this dilemma,[4] but there are two in particular that, I believe, speak to the general human experience of joy. R. Joel Sirkis (16th-17th century) suggests that eating the meat of the sacrifice that was brought in the Temple generated two types of joy: one was the "main joy (*ikkar simḥah*)" of partaking in a sacrifice bought for God and the other was simply the enjoyment of eating the meat. But once the Temple was destroyed, only "the secondary joy (*eino ikkar simḥah*)" of eating meat itself remained.[5] R. Joshua Falk (16th-17th century) presents a similar explanation and suggests that even after the destruction of the Temple, eating meat generates "some joy (*simḥah kezat*)," albeit not the full joy that would have been experienced from eating the meat of the sacrifice in the time of the Temple.[6] Both of these interpretations explain Rabbi Judah ben Beteira's statement to mean that in the absence of the Temple, full joy can only be experienced through the drinking of wine, but less than full joy can also be experienced through eating meat.

Technology executive, Sheryl Sandberg, and Wharton School of Business professor, Adam Grant, co-authored a book in 2019 entitled *Option B*. Option A, the best and most desirable alternative in any scenario, is not always available. We wish that life would always be wonderful, but it isn't. All of us have faced—and will face—adversity at one point or another. We all deal with loss. The challenge we have is how to respond to it. The subtitle of their book is, "Facing Adversity, Building Resilience, and Finding Joy." After the sudden death of Sandberg's husband, she found herself adrift. Slowly, she found a way out of the darkness of her situation and formulated an approach to helping others. Sandberg realized that she had been holding herself back from joy. But joy is also possible in Option B.

This very important lesson lies at the core of this halakhic discussion. Joy need not be full, unadulterated, and complete. Indeed, it cannot be. Option A, namely the Temple in its full glory, is no longer possible. We now live in the world of Option B. There is no Temple. But joy is possible there as well. *Ikkar simḥah* is not necessary. *Kezat simḥah* is not optimal or preferred, but it, too, is *simḥah*.

This notion is also expressed in other Jewish ritual contexts as well. Rabbi Joseph B. Soloveitchik often drew attention to the dual nature of *mitzvah* [commandment] observance, what he referred to as the "formal compliance with the law" and the law as "a living experience." He wrote that "the religious gesture" in Judaism consists of both "strict objective discipline and exalted subjective romance."[7] It is not only the *act* of the *miẓvah* which is important, as it surely is; also important is the *emotion* or *experience* of the *miẓvah*.[8]

Sometimes the experience of the *miẓvah* is clear and self-evident. When it comes to prayer, for example, the *maʿaseh ha-miẓvah*, act of the *miẓvah*, consists of reciting words; the *kiyyum ha-miẓvah*, inner fulfillment of the *miẓvah*, consists of "experiencing the complete helplessness of man, his absolute dependence upon God."[9] But sometimes, the precise contour or parameter of the experience of a *miẓvah* is complicated, and even the subject of no small amount of dialectical tension. Take Rosh Hashanah, for example. The act of the only positive *miẓvah* associated with those days is clear, blowing or listening to the shofar. But what should one be *feeling* on those days? What emotion should characterize one's personal experience on those days?

This is not an easy question to answer. The days of Rosh Hashanah and Yom Kippur are Days of Judgment and, if taken seriously, can only elicit within us feelings of trepidation, anxiety, and even fear. The Talmud explains that God Himself told the angels that Hallel is not recited on these days because "is it possible that when the king is seated on the Throne of Judgement, and the Books of the Living and the Books of the Dead are open before Him, that Israel should recite song!"[10] The books of judgment are open! Who can possibly be in an emotional state to be able to sing! In Maimonides's *Commentary to the Mishnah*, he writes that Hallel is not recited on those days "because they are days of service, submission, fright and fear of God and awe of Him…and repentance, supplication, entreaty, atonement and forgiveness."[11]

The most well-known expression of this visceral sense of fear we experience on these days is found in the *UNetaneh Tokef* prayer that is a centerpiece of the *Musaf* Service on both Rosh Hashanah and Yom Kippur. There we refer to them as "awesome and terrible," and we assert that even the angels are "trembling and shaking." On these days, all of humankind will pass under God's penetrating gaze and He will determine the fate of every human being for the coming year. What is at stake is as straightforward as "who will live and who will die."

But yet there is another, directly opposite, perspective. The Jerusalem Talmud contrasts the Jewish people with other nations. In the normal course of events, if someone is facing a serious court case with potentially very dangerous far-reaching implications, "he will dress himself in black, wrap himself in black, and will let his beard grow because he does not know the outcome of his case. But Israel is different. Rather, they dress in white, wrap themselves in white, shave their beards, and eat, drink and are joyous (*ve-okhlin ve-shotin u-semehin*) for they know that God will perform a miracle for them."[12] In this telling, these days are not days of awe. On the contrary, they are holidays, on which a Jew feels optimism and even joy.

This perspective is echoed widely in Jewish law. For example, Rabbenu Asher cites the opinion of those who maintain that characterizations of these days as times of "happiness and joy" belong in the prayer services recited on those occasions.[13] *Sefer Mordecai* cites this passage from the Jerusalem Talmud and asserts that fasting on Rosh Hashanah is prohibited because those two days are holidays.[14] Further examples abound.[15]

So, which is it? Are these Days of Judgment or are they holidays or days of joy? Here a phrase in Maimonides' *Mishneh Torah* is very instrumental in helping resolve this dilemma and also further underscores the intermediate role that joy plays in our lives. He refers there to Rosh Hashanah and Yom Kippur as "days of repentance, fear and fright, not days of excessive joy (*simḥah yeterah*)."[16] The clear implication is that in spite of the "fear and fright," there is, indeed, *some* level of joy.[17] In fact, these two perspectives are not contradictory or mutually exclusive. These days are both days of awe *and* days of joy. Yes, we recognize that we are being judged and that the stakes of that judgment are very high, but at the same time we are joyously optimistic that God will judge us favorably.

Once again, joy need not be full, unadulterated, and complete. Joy can be joy even if it is imperfect or incomplete. *Keẓat simḥah* is also *simḥah*.

Knowledge that incomplete happiness is also happiness is itself cause for happiness. This is a fundamental reality of the human condition.

Notes

1. Maimonides, *Mishneh Torah, Hil. Shevitat Yom Tov* 6:18.
2. *Arba'ah Turim, Oraḥ Ḥayyim* 529.
3. *Bet Yosef* on *Oraḥ Ḥayyim* 529, s.v. *katav ha-rambam*, end.
4. See, for example, R. Moses ibn Habib, *Kapot Temarim, Sukkah* 42b; R. Shlomoh Luria, *Yam Shel Shlomoh, Bezah* 2:5. For these references, and others, see Meir Gloiberman, "Be-Inyan Simḥat Yom Tov ve-Hamista'ef (2)," *Kovez Bet Aharon ve-Yisrael* 24, no. 2 (Kislev-Tevet 5769): 123–31; Moshe Sasson, "Be-Inyan Ḥiyyuv Simḥah be-Yom Tov," *Kol ha-Torah* 53 (Tishrei 5763): 68–73.
5. *Baḥ, Oraḥ Ḥayyim* 529, s.v. *mizvat yom tov*.
6. *Derishah, Oraḥ Ḥayyim* 529, s.v. *ve-ha-anashim okhlim basar*.
7. See Joseph B. Soloveitchik, "A Tribute to the Rebbitzen of Talne," *Tradition* 17, no. 2 (1978): 77; idem., *Family Redeemed: Essays on Family Relationships*, ed. David Shatz and Joel Wolowelsky (Jersey City: Ktav, 2000), 40.
8. I discuss this aspect of Rabbi Soloveitchik's thought, and cite many more examples of where this notion appears prominently in his writings, in my "Tazri'a: Rabbi Joseph B. Soloveitchik on Marriage, Mitzvot and a Jew's Relationship to God," in *Wisdom by the Week: The Weekly Torah Portion as an Inspiration for Thought and Creativity*, ed. Naftali Rothenberg (Ktav, 2011), 324–31; "Halakhic Authority in the World of Personal Autonomy," in *Radical Responsibility: Celebrating the Thought of Chief Rabbi Lord Jonathan Sacks*, ed. Michael J. Harris, Daniel Rynhold, and Tamara Wright (New Milford and Jerusalem, 2012), 155–76, esp. pp. 171–72, and n. 45; "The Discipline of Law and the Subjectivity of Spirituality," *Tradition* 53, no. 3 (2021): 232–39, esp. pp. 232, 236–37, and n. 11.
9. *Family Redeemed*, 40.
10. BT *Rosh Hashanah* 32b; *Arakhin* 10b.
11. Maimonides, *Commentary on the Mishnah, Rosh Hashanah* 4:7.
12. YT *Rosh Hashanah* 1:3.
13. *Rosh, Rosh Hashanah* 4:14.
14. *Sefer Mordekhai, Rosh Hashanah* 708.
15. See, for example, *Shulḥan Arukh, Yoreh De'ah* 399:6; *Magen Avraham, Oraḥ Ḥayyim* 581:4.
16. Maimonides, *Mishneh Torah, Hil. Ḥannukah* 3:6.
17. See Uriel Bener, "Shitat ha-Rambam be-Mizvot Simḥah be-Rosh Hashanah ve-Yom Kippur," *Mevakshei Torah* 3, nos. 16–17 (Elul 5755): 382–83.

CHAPTER 12

All for the Best: Rabbi Akiva's Theodicy of Joy

Gila Fine

Few themes were as central to Rabbi Sacks' thought as the theme of joy. In his writings, in his talks, even in personal conversation, it was a subject Rabbi Sacks returned to again and again ("What are you doing to keep yourself happy?," he once asked me; his own answer was whiskey and Schubert). From its prevalence in the Book of Ecclesiastes to its alarming decline in the liberal West, joy was, for Rabbi Sacks, one of the greatest challenges of human existence.

Yet in his lifelong exploration of joy—in the Bible and Aristotle, Locke and Beethoven, positive psychology and cognitive science—one work is all but absent: the Talmud. And with good reason; the rabbis of the Talmud, wise and noble and heroic though they were, were not particularly cheerful. At least not explicitly so (of the few hundred appearances of the root s-m-h, joy, in the Talmud, only a handful are used to describe rabbis). But scratch the surface of the Talmudic page, look beyond text to subtext, and you will find moments of profound, if unstated, happiness. The following story is, I believe, one such moment.

G. Fine (✉)
Pardes Institute of Jewish Studies, Jerusalem, Israel

© The Author(s), under exclusive license to Springer Nature Switzerland AG 2023
E. Brown, S. Weiss (eds.), *An Ode to Joy*,
https://doi.org/10.1007/978-3-031-28229-4_12

Rabbi Akiva was walking along the road.
He came to a certain town and sought lodging, but they did not grant it.
He said, "All God does, He does for the best."
He went and slept in a field.
He had with him a rooster, a donkey, and a candle.
A gust of wind came and extinguished the candle; a cat came and ate the rooster; and a lion came and ate the donkey.
He said, "All God does, He does for the best."
That night, bandits came and took the town into captivity.
The next day he entered the town and did not find anything in it.
He said, "It is as I have told you: 'All God does, He does for the best.'"[1]

A favorite in Jewish children's books (and works of similar hagiographical nature), the story is widely cited as an exemplum of the power of faith. The eternal optimism of Rabbi Akiva, his repeated insistence that "All God does, He does for the best," is rewarded, as he is saved from the fate of the ransacked town. Faith, according to this reading, is a self-fulfilling prophecy.

* * *

Yet there are a number of questions such an interpretation leaves open. Why does Rabbi Akiva return to the town that had turned him away? Who, in the final line, is he talking to (the townsfolk have all been taken captive)? And, if a narrative is predicated on the change of its hero,[2] where is the change in Rabbi Akiva, who begins and ends the story saying the precise same words?

The children's books and their simple message of faith notwithstanding, the truth of our story, it seems, lies further afield.

* * *

To fully understand the text, we must begin by examining its context. Preceding our story is a Talmudic discussion, toward the end of Tractate Berakhot, on the Mishna's edict, "One must bless the bad just as he blesses the good."[3] A tall order indeed, for how is one meant to bless fortune and misfortune, tragedy and triumph, equally? The Talmud offers the following answer: "Said Rava: This was only said to teach us to receive bad tidings with joy.... And so it was taught in the name of Rabbi Akiva: One must always accustom oneself to say, 'All God does, He does for the best.'"[4]

Blessing the bad, says Rava, means receiving it with joy. A comment which does little to solve the problem, for how exactly are we meant to do that? Enter Rabbi Akiva with his trusted mantra, which serves as the story's epigraph and refrain: "All God does, He does for the best." If we accustom ourselves to believe that all bad ultimately leads to good, we will be able to accept everything—the good and the bad—with equal joy. Happiness, for Rabbi Akiva, is a derivative of faith.

This is not the only instance in rabbinic literature when Rabbi Akiva is portrayed as unfailingly optimistic. Living through one of the darkest periods in Jewish history, Rabbi Akiva experienced the aftermath of the failed Bar Kokhba Revolt firsthand: exile and enslavement, national oppression and religious persecution, mass killing and martyrdom (which was the lot of Rabbi Akiva himself). Bad things were happening, brutally and constantly, to good people. The biblical doctrine of reward and punishment had broken down, as the most righteous suffered the worst of fortunes, and the rabbis, in this and in subsequent generations, had to propose alternative theodicies to take its place.[5] One popular response was that reward and punishment still exist, but are deferred to the afterlife;[6] another was that the righteous suffer because they are held to a higher standard,[7] or for the sake of the greater good;[8] a third was that affliction is a sign of Divine love.[9]

Within this matrix of rabbinic responses, Rabbi Akiva emerges as rabbinic culture's greatest Pollyanna. He becomes the spokesman for a radical theodicy, one that disputes the existence of evil altogether. Bad things don't happen to good people; in fact, bad things don't happen at all. "All God does, He does for the best." If something bad happens, it must be God's doing. But if it is God's doing, it must be for the best. Ergo, it cannot be bad. It only appears as such, but will be revealed to be good (or at least, a necessary step toward the good) in the end.

Accordingly, Rabbi Akiva declares that "suffering is precious," because it brings people closer to God.[10] He argues that "a man must rejoice in suffering more than in good, since ... [it] atones for his sins."[11] When he witnesses his beloved Rabbi Eliezer ailing, he exclaims, "I am happy," confident that the latter will receive a handsome reward in Heaven.[12] Where his rabbinic friends mourn the sight of the Destruction, he sees the beginnings of redemption.[13] And when he is being tortured to death, he laughs, savoring his chance to express his love of God, until "a Divine

Voice emerged and said, 'Happy are you, Rabbi Akiva, as you are destined for life in the World to Come.'"[14] In the face of suffering and pain, personal tragedy and national disaster, Rabbi Akiva's faith is steadfast, his joy unwavering. "All God does, He does for the best."

* * *

In light of the story's context, let us now attempt a close reading of the text:

> Act 1
> Rabbi Akiva was walking along the road.
> He came to a certain town and sought lodging, but they did not grant it.
> He said, "All God does, He does for the best."
> Act 2
> He went and slept in a field.
> He had with him a rooster, a donkey, and a candle.
> A gust of wind came and extinguished the candle; a cat came and ate the rooster; and a lion came and ate the donkey.
> He said, "All God does, He does for the best."
> Act 3
> That night, bandits came and took the town into captivity.
> The next day he entered the town and did not find anything in it.
> He said, "It is as I have told you: 'All God does, He does for the best.'"

At first glance, our story is a classic rabbinic three-act drama, with each of the acts ending in the refrain, "All God does, He does for the best." The three acts form a chiastic A-B-A structure, drawing on the larger Talmudic discussion of good and bad: Acts 1 and 3 take place in a civilized town and during the light of day (good), while Act 2 is set in a desolate field and during the dead of night (bad).

The story begins with Rabbi Akiva "walking along the road." We don't know where he has come from or where he is going, simply that he is in transit. The Talmudic motif of "walking along the road" commonly refers to the vulnerable state of being away from one's home and exposed to the elements;[15] it is, in this sense, a clear metaphor for exile. Rabbi Akiva is presented as an exilic everyman, a typical Jew in the post-Destruction world.

He arrives at a town where he hopes to spend the night but is refused lodging. Receiving these bad tidings with joy, Rabbi Akiva says, "All God does, He does for the best" (refrain #1).

And so he is forced, in Act 2, to leave the protection of the town for the perils of the field, just as the safety of daylight gives way to the dangers of the dark. He has with him, we are told, the essential luggage of a second-century traveler: a donkey, to travel upon; a rooster, to rouse him; and a candle, to light his way (today we might speak of a car, an alarm clock, and a flashlight). There, in the middle of nowhere and in the heart of darkness, disaster strikes. A gust of wind blows out the candle and, with no light to ward off predators, a cat comes and eats the rooster, and a lion devours the donkey. The drama reaches its nadir, as Rabbi Akiva has lost everything—his hoped-for lodging, his vehicle, all of his possessions. Alone and vulnerable, a lion still prowling nearby, he nevertheless affirms, "All God does, He does for the best" (refrain #2).

Act 3 opens with a flashback to the events of the night in the nearby town. Unbeknownst to Rabbi Akiva, at the very same time that predators were attacking his animals, a gang of bandits had attacked the town, looting its homes and taking its inhabitants captive. There is a hint of measure for measure in the structural parallel between Acts 1 and 3, as the townsfolk, who would not grant Rabbi Akiva shelter, have now lost it themselves.[16]

The following day, Rabbi Akiva returns to the town, presumably to buy another donkey, rooster, and candle so that he may continue on his way. He is met with the damage and devastation of a plundered city. The houses are empty. The shops are bare. The people are all gone. He certainly will not be able to replace his luggage. And yet, Rabbi Akiva doesn't lament his fate, doesn't complain about having to resume his journey on foot. Instead, standing at the site of the wreckage, he once again proclaims, "It is as I have told you: 'All God does, He does for the best'" (refrain #3).

Who is he speaking to? There's no one else there.

Rabbi Akiva, I submit, is speaking to Rabbi Akiva. Rabbi Akiva has only ever spoken to Rabbi Akiva (indeed, rabbinic storytelling often uses "he said" to mean "he said to himself"[17]). Herein is the dramatic change in our hero: In the first two refrains, and throughout his life, Rabbi Akiva's mantra was a profession of faith. Staunch faith perhaps, unwavering faith, but faith nonetheless. He had no proof that "All God does, He does for the best"; he simply believed. This is the first time in his long and difficult life that Rabbi Akiva doesn't believe. He knows. He is certain. He has seen it with his own eyes. The disasters had come to protect him. Had the candle continued to shine, the rooster crowed, or the donkey brayed, it would have revealed his whereabouts to the bandits. Everything God did was, in fact, for the best.

So now, when Rabbi Akiva speaks, it is not with faith but with full-throated certainty: "All God does, He does for the best." He will still have to go on traveling. His journey, his exile, has not yet come to an end. He'll still be forced to wander the wilderness, without a donkey to ride or a candle to show him the way. But now, he'll have his optimism—his once faith, now knowledge—to comfort him. And with him, us, the readers of his story, the Jews still in exile.

★ ★ ★

Thus is Rabbi Akiva's lifetime of faith confirmed. This, I believe, is the ultimate lesson of our story. Faith, it seems, is indeed a self-fulfilling prophecy, but not in the way the children's books meant. It doesn't make everything turn out for the best; according to Rabbi Akiva's theodicy of joy, everything turns out for the best anyway. *But it is only through faith that we are able to see it.* Only by steadfastly believing in the good, seeking it, will we ever come to find it. "If you keep resting your mind on good events and conditions," contemporary neuroscience tells us, "over time your brain will take a different shape, one with strength and resilience hardwired into it, as well as a realistically optimistic outlook.... Bit by bit, synapse by synapse, you really can build happiness into your brain."[18] It is Rabbi Akiva's cockeyed optimism, honed over years of saying, "All God does, He does for the best," that allows him to find joy in the midst of suffering, to look past the desolation and loss and see his own deliverance.

In this sense, Rabbi Akiva's legacy of joy is beautifully reiterated in the words of his theodical successor, Rabbi Sacks:

> Happiness is not far away. It is here, but first we have to know how to look.... It is not somewhere else; it is where we are. It is not something we do not yet have; we already possess it. It is not fantasy; it is reality experienced in a certain way. Happiness is a close relative of faith ... an astonishing affirmation [that] life is beautiful.[19]

Like Rabbi Akiva, Rabbi Sacks faced difficulty in his life; happiness, for him, wasn't just a theoretical question but a deeply personal matter. Like Rabbi Akiva, he held fast to his faith in times of darkness. And, like Rabbi

Akiva, he searched tirelessly, insistently, for happiness, believing it was always there to be found.

Notes

1. BT Berakhot 60b–61a. The text is from the Oxford manuscript; the printed version, which appears to be far less accurate, omits the penultimate line of Rabbi Akiva's return to the town (without which it's unclear how he would have known of its fate), and features an unaccounted-for shift from Aramaic to Hebrew in the final line (in the Oxford manuscript, the story is entirely in Aramaic).
2. This is particularly true of travel narratives (and Rabbi Akiva, at the very outset, is portrayed as "walking along the road"—an archetypal traveler): "Journey [is] an idea that can contain any narrative of change, change that requires leaving one's original space (whether physical or mental) to be able to view that space in a new light, or to see things that could not be seen within that space ... The physical journey becomes a narrative device, a cover for the second, internal journey." Hannah Naveh, *Men and Women Travelers: Travel Narratives in Modern Hebrew Literature* (Tel Aviv: Ministry of Defense, 2002), 7–9 [Hebrew].
3. Mishna Berakhot 9:5.
4. BT Berakhot 60b.
5. "Jews who lived in the centuries following the Bible carried with them the legacy of this all-powerful, all-knowing, just, and caring God. As their history brought pain and bitterness ... the answers provided in their sacred scripture often did not suffice. So the religious imagination of these centuries repeatedly returned to the related problems of suffering, evil, and injustice, and a variety of explanations, both eclectic and original, found ample expression." David C. Kraemer, *Responses to Suffering in Classical Rabbinic Literature* (New York: Oxford University Press, 1995), 6.
6. Sifrei Numbers 103, Sifrei Deuteronomy 117, Y Peah 1:1, Y Sanhedrin 1:11, BT Kiddushin 39b–40b, BT Avoda Zara 4a.
7. Mekhilta DeRabbi Yishmael 22:22, BT Taanit 11a, Numbers Rabba 20:24.
8. BT Moed Katan 28a, BT Bava Metzia 85a, BT Sanhedrin 39a, Genesis Rabba 96, Exodus Rabba 35.
9. Sifrei Deuteronomy 311, BT Berakhot 5a, Genesis Rabba 92.
10. Sifrei Deuteronomy 32.
11. Mekhilta DeRabbi Yishmael 20:20.
12. BT Sanhedrin 101a, Genesis Rabba 33:1.
13. BT Makkot 24b.
14. Y Berakhot 9:5, BT Berakhot 61b.

15. Rabbis who are found "walking along the road" regularly run into hazards such as earthquakes (BT Berakhot 59a), storms (BT Taanit 24b), rapid rivers (BT Bava Metzia 81b), and wild animals (BT Sanhedrin 59b).
16. The parallel is emphasized by the similarity between the Aramaic phrases "they did not grant" in Act 1 and "[he] did not find" in Act 3.
17. "[Talmudic] stories reveal a marked preference for representing thought as speech and representing consciousness through interior monologue." Jeffrey L. Rubenstein, *Talmudic Stories: Narrative Art, Composition, and Culture* (Baltimore: Johns Hopkins University Press, 1999), 248.
18. Rick Hanson, *Hardwiring Happiness: The New Brain Science of Contentment, Calm, and Confidence* (New York: Harmony, 2013), 10–15.
19. Jonathan Sacks, *Celebrating Life: Finding Happiness in Unexpected Places* (London: Continuum, 2000), 3–4.

CHAPTER 13

Inclusive Joy: On Maimonides' Definition of Meaningful Happiness

Ari Berman

Early Greek philosophers, most notably Aristotle, made an important distinction between joy and happiness. There is hedonic happiness, from the Greek word *hēdonē*, which is achieved through experiences of pleasure, and there is eudemonic happiness, from the Greek terms *eû* (goodness) and *daímōn* (deity), which is achieved through experiences of meaning. At first glance, one might think that these two respective paths are mutually exclusive, but as we will see with two examples in the thought of Maimonides, they can intersect and be mutually enhancing.

While there is no specific religious obligation in the Jewish tradition to be joyful every single day, there are two repeated occasions during the year in which there is a particular focus on happiness: the holidays and the Sabbath.

A. Berman (✉)
Yeshiva University, New York, NY, USA

The Inclusive Joy of Holidays

When Jews made pilgrimages to Jerusalem during the Three Festivals, the Torah specifically notes that happiness was to be an integral part of the experience:

> [You shall rejoice in your festival, with your son and daughter, your male and female slave, the [family of the] Levite, the stranger, the fatherless, and the widow in your communities.][1]
>
> One of the sacrifices that each pilgrim offered during the Three Festivals was known as a *shalmei simha*, literally a joyous sacrifice. Maimonides elaborates on this obligation:
>
> When a person sacrifices festive and celebratory peace-offerings, he should not eat while secluded, together with his children and his wife and think he is performing a perfect mitzvah. Instead, he is obligated to bring joy to the poor and unfortunate. Thus, it states: "the Levite, the stranger, the orphan, and the widow" (Deut. 16:14). One should grant them food and drink according to his wealth. If one partook of his sacrifices and did not bring joy to these together with him, to him are applied the words of censure, "Their sacrifices will be like the bread of mourners, of which all who partake of it become impure. But their food will be only for themselves and should not come into the House of the Lord" (Hos. 9:4)[2]

The ultimate sacrificial embodiment of joy includes within it a commandment to bring others joy. A joyous sacrifice that does not better other people's lives is considered an affront.

Maimonides' position on the *shalmei simha* is similarly in line with how he describes the general obligation of joy on the holidays.

> While eating and drinking, one must feed the stranger, the orphan, the widow, and other poor unfortunates. Anyone, however, who locks the doors of his courtyard and eats and drinks along with his wife and children, without giving anything to eat and drink to the poor and the desperate, does not engage in the joy of a mitzvah but indulges in the celebration of his stomach.[3]

Maimonides distinguishes between a selfish pursuit of pleasure, the joy of the stomach, with the noble experience of joy of a commandment. Later in this chapter, Maimonides (6:20) explains that this directive for joy on a holiday discourages levity and drunkenness since its focus is only on joy that serves the Creator. In fact, Maimonides amplifies this point in his discussion of the laws of Purim (Laws of Megilla 2:17), a festival that mandates feasting and drinking wine. He contends that the most religious expression of joy is achieved through giving gifts to the downtrodden and needy; those who engage in such pursuits are imitating God who similarly cares for those who are weak and humbled.

This description of the commandment of joy on the holidays fundamentally alters the nature of the obligation. Rabbi Joseph B. Soloveitchik, for example, explains that based on Maimonides' writings, the *simha* on a holiday is not considered simply an obligation on the individual but an "*aseh de-rabim*," a public positive command.[4] The fact that it is a commandment that encompasses many people around the individual gives it an elevated status and priority when other "individual obligations," like the private case of mourning, come into conflict with it.[5]

This notion of joy for Maimonides reflects a profound connection between the two Greek concepts of joy: *hedonia* and *eudamonia*. For it is through the concern for the *hedonia* of others that one reaches *eudamonia*, a joy that is virtuous and meaningful. Moreover, opening one's table to others is a redemptive act in which one's own eating becomes sanctified. The commandment of joy on the holiday is not just fulfilled by distributing sustenance to the poor. It is fulfilled by eating as well. But only consumption that also considers the physical wants and needs of others is deemed meaningful.

THE RESTIVE JOY OF THE SABBATH

Another manifestation of this extended notion of inclusive happiness appears in the Maimonides' understanding of the commandment to rest on the Sabbath. In Talmudic literature, there is a tannaitic teaching that the verse "your maidservant's son [*ben 'amatekha*] and the *ger* may be refreshed,"[6] which commands rest on Shabbat, refers specifically to an uncircumcised slave and a *ger toshav*,[7] a resident alien. Maimonides, in codifying this teaching, writes that this verse specifically obligates an employer:

> Since a *ger toshav* may do *melakhah* [work] for himself on the Sabbath, and a *ger zedek* is like a Jew for all matters, concerning whom does it state: "And that your maidservant's son [*ben 'amatekha*] and the *ger* may be refreshed"? It refers to a *ger toshav* who is the harvester or hired laborer of the Jew, similar to his maidservant's son. He is not to do *melakhah* for his Jewish master

on the Sabbath, but he may do so on his own behalf. And even if this *ger* was his slave, he may do *melakhah* for himself.[8]

A *ger toshav* worker should rest from work for his employer even though he is permitted to do work for himself. Similarly, if the *ger toshav* was a slave, he is to rest from work for his master but is allowed to do work for himself. Maimonides, in this ruling, appears to adopt a distinction between *shevitah* and *nefishah*, cessation of work and rest. While there is no obligation to refrain from doing *melakha*h (*shevitah*) for the non-Jewish *ger toshav* employee, there is an obligation for the employer to ensure that the restorative rest that underlies all of the Sabbath applies to this worker.

Maimonides' concern for the treatment of one's workers is reflected by his well-known directive at the end of *Mishneh Torah*, Laws of Slaves 9:8 in which he writes that a Jewish owner should model *midat ḥasidut* [pious measures], strive to be merciful and not treat his slaves unkindly by speaking to them harshly and imposing onerous labor on them. But in this ruling, Maimonides goes one step further. He states that the restorative rest of the Sabbath needs to be extended beyond oneself to include one's employees. Maimonides limits this ruling to those non-Jewish employees who accept to observe the Noahide rules. While this is not the place to discuss extensively Maimonides' positive views of *ger toshav*, suffice it to say that this ruling highlights Maimonides' thinking: the workplace environment must include space for a true and comprehensive restorative break. One cannot rest if his laborer is not also resting.

In Maimonides' thinking *hedonia* and *eudomonia* are intertwined.

By extending the parameters of happiness found on the holy days of the Jewish calendar, Maimonides highlights that the experience of meaningful *simha* and rest is only complete when ensuring that others similarly are feeling joy and experiencing rest. Through service to others, this more inclusive notion of joy elevates personal happiness to communal celebration and transforms activities of consumption into moments of meaning.

Notes

1. Deut. 16:14.
2. Maimonides, *Mishneh Torah*, Laws of Hagigah 2:14.
3. Maimonides, *Mishneh Torah*, Laws of Holiday Rest 6:18.
4. Joseph Soloveitchik, *Shiurim le-Zecher Avi Mori*, vol. 2 (Jerusalem: Mossad Rav Kook, 1984), 210.
5. BT Moed Katan 14b.

6. Ex. 23:12.
7. BT Yebamot 48b; *Mekhilta de-Rabbi Yishmaʿel, Massekhta de-be-Ḥodesh* 7, p. 230 and *Mishpaṭim Massekhta de-Kaspa*, par. 20, p. 331. See also *Mekhilta de-RaSHBY, pereq* 20, p. 151, for a related but different *derashah* that deals with the issue of the Sabbath rest for slaves and *ger toshav*. See M. Kasher, *Torah Shelemah*, vol. 16 (Jerusalem, 1992), *Miluʿim* 17, 252–256, who analyzes the differences between the two *midrashim*.
8. In the older printed versions of the *Mishneh Torah*, this whole passage which is divided into three sections is mistakenly placed into one Halakhah, Laws of Sabbath 20:14. J. Qafih in his edition of *Mishneh Torah* (Jerusalem, 1986), 434, claims that this error caused later commentaries to misinterpret Maimonides' ruling.

CHAPTER 14

Show Me Those Pearly Whites: Divine and Human Smiling

Elana Stein Hain

It is truly a testament to the work and life of Rabbi Jonathan Sacks that we are addressing the topic of joy in this book. He was someone who presented an optimistic Judaism to the world. Moreover, as I recall specifically from hosting him at Lincoln Square Synagogue for a memorable Shabbat during my tenure there, Rabbi Sacks radiated joy, laughing often and extending a heartfelt smile to the many people he encountered.

In his honor, this chapter will address a rare if not unique phenomenon within rabbinic literature: a passage that focuses on the importance of a smile, and even its religious significance. While people may be familiar with the idiom *sever panim yafot*, a "friendly countenance," from *Ethics of the Fathers (Pirke Avot)*, there is an example in rabbinic literature which speaks more specifically about the significance of the facial gesture of smiling. It is a creative reading of Jacob's blessing to his son Judah at the end

E. Stein Hain (✉)
Shalom Hartman Institute of North America, New York, NY, USA

© The Author(s), under exclusive license to Springer Nature Switzerland AG 2023
E. Brown, S. Weiss (eds.), *An Ode to Joy*,
https://doi.org/10.1007/978-3-031-28229-4_14

of Genesis. In Genesis 49:12, Jacob includes mention of wine and milk in this blessing:

חַכְלִילִי עֵינַיִם מִיָּיִן וּלְבֶן־שִׁנַּיִם מֵחָלָב

His eyes are darker than wine. His teeth are whiter than milk.
While we have translated the verse, it has several possible meanings. One possibility is that wine and milk are metaphorical. They reflect the opposition of dark and light, based on their respective red and white hues: *His eyes are darker than wine and his teeth are whiter than milk*, as in the translation above. This may allude to the topography of Judah's land— perhaps referring to mountains that offer distant views (hence, *"his eyes"*). Alternatively, the verse might promise abundance, for example, vineyards of red wine and sheep whiter than milk.[1]

A second translation suggests that Judahites literally will drink wine and milk: *His eyes are darkened/reddened from wine, and his teeth are whitened from milk.*

This squarely emphasizes the tribe's material wealth: vineyards from which to make wine and cattle, sheep and goats from which to extract milk. Its members will live on wine and milk, which will be reflected in their facial features: their eyes will be reddened/dark, and their teeth will be whitened from these drinks.

In both translations, the word יללכח (*ḥakhlili*), found nowhere else in the Bible, means either "reddened" or "darkened," a cognate to the Akkadian word *ekelu*, "to be dark."

The Sages, however, offer a homily which relates *ḥakhlili* to the Aramaic word אכוח (*ḥukha*)—meaning laughter or playfulness. And rather than being a descriptor of the tribe of Judah, this homily reads the verse as a request by the Jewish people of God to "be playful with me"—the end of יללכח meaning "to me (יל)." The homily cited in Ketubot 111b reads as follows:

> When Rav Dimi arrived, he said, "The congregation of Israel said before the Holy Blessed One: 'Sovereign of the universe, hint to me with Your eyes, for that is sweeter than wine, and show me Your teeth, for that is sweeter than milk.'"

The speaker of this *midrash* is R. Dimi, one of the most prominent *neḥutei*. The *neḥutei* were a class of people who traveled back and forth between the Land of Israel and Babylonia as transmitters of rabbinic knowledge between the two rabbinic centers. As a Babylonian, R. Dimi traveled to the Land of Israel and returned with information gleaned from the rabbinic community there.

Often, it was specifically the explanation of a Hebrew term or phrase that benefited from the linguistic knowledge of Palestinian rabbis. While Babylonian rabbis might explain such terms or phrases associatively, Palestinian rabbis may be informed by a deeper appreciation of Hebrew language and the historical realities of the region often described by the Bible.[2] In this passage, however, R. Dimi makes use of Aramaic, spoken in both Babylonia and the Land of Israel, albeit using different dialects.

R. Dimi reinterprets the verse as follows: *hakhlili* is a request for God to be "playful with me"—the "me (*li*)" referring to the Jewish people as a whole. Rather than as a blessing that the tribe of Judah will have abundant wine and milk, R. Dimi reads the verse as a request made by the Jewish people of God: show us love. To arrive at this reading, the word "*hakhlili*" (now understood as *hukha li*, "be playful with me") is expanded into hint to me (*remoz li*) and show me (*ahvi li*).

First, "hint to me:" the Jewish people ask God to wink at them, indicating a coded sense of intimacy. Such tenderness is better (more valuable? more intoxicating? more pleasurable?) than wine. This echoes Song of Songs 1:2, where God's love is pronounced "better than wine." Next—"show me"—show me Your white teeth, that is, smile at me. God smiling at the Jewish people is better (more nourishing? more valuable? more delicious?) than milk.

This text stands out within rabbinic literature: while multiple texts describe God as laughing and experiencing joy, a discussion of Divine smiling is rare, if not unique to this passage.[3] Like the winking of an eye, a smile acknowledges connection, a positive and even close relationship between two beings. R. Dimi's explanation renders the verse a plea for God to express approval, tenderness, and joy towards the Jewish people: wine and milk reflect material plenty, good socioeconomic standing. But a wink or a smile from God is even sweeter.

While requesting a smile is innocent enough, it may reveal a deep need felt by those living after the fall of the Temple. Whether or not they achieved material success, the Jewish people still lived under a foreign regime, lacking their Temple. This created a theology, if not the actual experience, of distance between the Jewish people and God. Read in this context, this homily may represent a plea for a return to the Divine intimacy that had been compromised with the fall of the Temple. Whether a Divine sign of enduring relationships or a full reprieve from the post-destruction remoteness, they sought a demonstration of God's love, a gesture that indicated that the Jewish people still mattered to God.

Alternatively, this may not be about aspiration for repair but a call for recognition of proper priorities. This is, after all, a rather subversive rereading of Gen. 49:12. The rabbis reread a verse in which Divine blessing refers to material success as suggesting that material success is in fact not the ultimate blessing. This reading shifts the focus away from physical wealth toward a relationship with God, asserting that the latter is the greatest source of blessing.[4] God's wink or smile indicates that the Jewish people's relationship with God is solid and steady. An intimate bond with God offers greater value than the gratification of satiation, material abundance, or intoxication.

As R. Dimi often cites his teacher, R. Yohanan, when bringing teachings back to Babylonia, it is fitting that the next part of the passage describes how this interpretation supports R. Yohanan's similar but distinct reading of the same verse:

> This supports Rabbi Yohanan. As Rabbi Yohanan said: One who whitens their teeth to their friend is better than one who gives them milk, as it is said: "And his teeth, white [*leven shinayim*] from[5] milk" (Genesis 49:12). Do not read this expression as *leven shinayim*; rather, read it as *libbun shinayim*, the whitening of teeth.

R. Yohanan also reads smiling into the verse. The terminology for smiling used is *libbun shinayim*, literally the whitening of the teeth. In other words, flashing one's pearly whites. And again, one's teeth are not white *from* drinking milk; rather, whitening one's teeth—smiling—is better *than* milk. For Rabbi Yohanan, this means that one who smiles at someone does more than one who gives that person milk to drink. Once again, stability, intimacy, and communication of an affective bond are considered more valuable than the material sustenance of a drink. But rather than referring to the relational bond between God and the Jewish people, R. Yohanan refers to the emotional bond between two human beings.

R. Yohanan favors emotional generosity over material generosity, though the two are not mutually exclusive and can reinforce one another.[6] Nonetheless, offering someone approval, intimacy, connection, and the confidence to know that they bring you happiness is loftier than giving a person something to drink. This brings to mind a parallel yet inverse statement attributed to R. Yohanan about favoring emotional concerns over other significant concerns. This second statement also incorporates white imagery:

> Rabbah bar bar Hanna said in the name of R. Yohanan: it is better for a person to sleep with a woman who may be married rather than to whiten their fellow's face (*yalbin penei ḥavero*) in public.[7] (Bava Metzia 59a)

Rather than a smile, whitening here indicates a ghostly pallor caused by intense embarrassment.

Both of the above teachings stated in R. Yohanan's name refer to emotions reflected by the color white: the whitening of teeth is a smile while the whitening of the face indicates embarrassment. Both declare a surprising prioritization between two options: smiling is better than offering milk, and causing embarrassment is worse than possibly committing adultery. Kind emotional treatment of others is preferred to other weighty considerations.[8] Thus, Rabbi Yohanan's comments about smiling fit perhaps within a broader picture of the importance of emotional awareness and generosity.

There is much to learn from this brief Talmudic midrash and the complementarity of the explanations in R. Dimi and R. Yohanan's respective readings:

First, this *midrash* emphasizes the power of a simple wordless gesture, of body language, in forging, maintaining, and possibly repairing relationships.

Second, asserting the superiority of smiling over more concrete forms of support speaks to the importance of relational rather than transactional connections on both the giving and the receiving ends.

Third, reinterpreting a verse that is literally about material abundance to be about kindness and intimacy challenges a paradigm of wealth as the dominant marker of Divine love and acceptance.

And lastly, bringing together R. Dimi and R. Yohanan's statements has the effect of offering a new form of *imitatio dei*: human beings should smile at others just as God does. This linkage is simple but profound. May we merit the Divine closeness aspired to by R. Dimi and fulfill the interpersonal adage of R. Yohanan. And critically, may we always experience the two as intertwined.

Notes

1. See Rashi's comments on this verse.
2. See Yehoram Bitton, "Ki ata Rav Dimi—bein historia la-'arikha," *Millin Havivin (Beloved Words)* 3 (2007/5767): 42–53.
3. Perhaps the most famous is the image of God laughing and saying "My children have triumphed over Me" in Bava Metzia 59b.
4. This is made more subversive by the seemingly editorial introduction to R. Dimi's appearance, asking, "About what is the plain meaning of the verse written?" Clearly, R. Dimi's gloss does not actually provide the plain meaning of the verse. If anything, it undermines that very meaning.
5. Based on the homily, *me-halav*, means "more than" milk.
6. The Torah Temimah points out that both giving a smile and giving milk can be considered acts of love.
7. R. Yohanan is not the first to use this terminology to mean embarrassing someone. *Pirke Avot (Ethics of the Fathers)* 3:11 cite R. Elazar ha-Moda'i that one who "whitens the face of their fellow in public" has not share in the World-to-Come.

    There is another attribution of a similar statement to R. Yohanan regarding embarrassing one's fellow in public, namely that one should throw oneself into a fiery furnace rather than shame someone. This is based on the Tamar and Judah story in Genesis 38. However, that attribution is debated within the Talmud itself. (Berakhot 43b)
8. As my son Azzan pointed out to me, committing (possible) adultery might embarrass someone as well. This is why the context of this passage is important. The statement refers to a story in which King David complains of embarrassment when is taunted by the rabbis about sleeping with Bathsheba (II Samuel 11), who was technically still married at the time. He claims that his own sin of adultery is less egregious than their sin of embarrassing him in public. See Bava Metzia 59a and Sanhedrin 107a.

CHAPTER 15

Bright Yellow Judaism

Chaim Strauchler

Rabbi Lord Jonathan Sacks wore bright yellow neckties, bringing a touch of sunshine to his outward appearance. In a 2020 interview with Tim Ferriss, Rabbi Sacks explained his preferred sartorial choices:

> *I always used to wear silver ties. This kind of dignified thing that ministers of religion do. And I had a huge, but HUGE collection of silver ties. Then at a certain point in time, I'm not sure whether it was 2016 or a little earlier than that, the world began to fall apart. And that was when I realized that part of my job was not just to speak or to write, but to cheer people up. And I think Little Miss or Mr. Cheerful has to be colored yellow. So I thought, "Wearing a yellow tie cheers people up." And by and large, consciously or subconsciously, it does.*[1]

In contrast, twenty years ago, I witnessed a fellow rabbinic student introduce a model sermon by asking his audience to imagine that behind him hung the famous black-and-white photograph of Rabbi Elchonon Wasserman. For those unfamiliar, the photo contains a solitary figure against a gray background. He wears a black cap and black cloak over a

---

C. Strauchler (✉)
Congregation Rinat Yisrael, Teaneck, NJ, USA

white shirt that barely peaks out beneath his wispy broad white beard. His mouth is drawn into a frown that doesn't convey sadness so much as a concern bordering on apprehension. Yet, all these details pale in comparison to the penetrating gaze of his jet-black eyes. Framed with arched eyebrows, those eyes look out across time into the person who would have the temerity to gaze at his image, as if to borrow God's words to Adam, "Where are YOU?"[2] In conjuring this stern haunting image, my classmate adopted the classic stereotypes of religious authority—the anger and foreboding doom of ultimate judgment.[3]

I mention Rabbi Sacks' ties and Rabbi Wasserman's eyes to underscore a sea change not just in rabbinic dress and demeanor but also in the emotional hues in which Torah is communicated and understood. Rabbi Sacks' ties reflect something about his approach to Judaism and Jewish education that are both unique to him but also typify larger trends in society and Jewish life, more particularly. The colors of effervescent joy have not just entered Jewish life, they have become iridescently dominant. "Little Rabbi Cheerful" was a dramatic alteration from classic rabbinic understandings of emotion and religion. Jews now expect happiness from their religion. They, we, shun sadness and apprehension.

To underscore the trend that Rabbi Sacks' exemplified, it is worthwhile to look beyond the images of early twentieth-century rabbinic figures like Rabbi Wasserman. In "Rupture and Reconstruction," Rabbi Dr. Haym Soloveitchik describes how modernity has changed the way traditional Jewish communities understand both body and mind. He notes the disappearance of a Jewish moral tradition that conceived of Judaism in opposition to the physical world:

> Little of all this [ceaseless warfare between will and instinct and the pessimistic feeling that the "crooked timber of humanity" will never quite be made straight] is to be found in the moral literature of the past half century. There is, to be sure, much criticism of hedonism; restraint in all desires is advocated, as is a de-emphasis of material wellbeing. However, what is preached is "plain living and high thinking," rather than any war on basic instinct. The thousand-year struggle of the soul with the flesh has finally come to a close.[4]

Now, Judaism—like all great religions—appreciates the breadth of human emotion. The Torah describes the obligation to rejoice on the holidays (Deut. 16:11, 14). Ecclesiastes teaches the value of joy by personal example, "I therefore praised enjoyment. For the only good a man can have under the sun is to eat and drink and enjoy himself" (8:15). Yet, Soloveitchik understands that historically these emotions were but one hue in a complex religious life that had contained many other shades. Soloveitchik sees in Judaism's transition into modernity a loss of range in its ascetic notes that might have balanced modernity's preoccupation with happiness.

While certainly valid, a narrative that focuses on the loss of an ascetic tradition is insufficient to a moment when rabbis spread cheer and congregations expect such inspiration from them. It is not simply that people no longer think in terms of soul versus flesh, rather the entire emotional vocabulary of religious life has changed. Yes—most people don't cry in terror at *neila* anymore—but they do sing at *kumzitzes* on Tisha b'Av with expectations of religious inspiration. The popularity of *daf yomi* and other daily learning programs signals a renewed understanding of the life-giving force that is Torah and the desire to belong to a global learning community. Schools and shuls are expected to not only teach skills for Jewish conduct and ongoing learning but also to deliver uplifting religious experiences that will sustain life-long engagement in communal life. Judaism is increasingly seen not just as a source of mitzvot, rituals, and ethics but also as a source of exhilarating emotional positivity.[5]

In the past twenty years, a new discipline within the study of history has contextualized emotions, exploring how they have changed through time. The history of emotions is based on the assumption that not only the expression of feelings but also the feelings themselves are learned. Culture and social mores are always changing and so are feelings, including the means of their expression. That the social relevance and potency of emotions are historically and culturally variable has great importance for our self-understanding as religious people. The emotions encoded in our Jewish lives shifted during Rabbi Sacks' lifetime, and he was an important part of that movement.[6]

Rabbi Sacks' writings on joy tracked and encouraged this emotional change. Rabbi Sacks turned the meaning of the depressing phrase "It's hard to be a Jew" into a point of pride and blessing:

> There is grandeur in this refusal to abandon the struggle, this sustained reluctance to accept the world as it is, conforming to the conventional wisdom, following the herd. Jews have always been pioneers of the spirit, disturbers of the peace. The path chosen by Jacob/Israel is not for the

fainthearted. Zis schver zu sein a Yid, they used to say: "It's hard to be a Jew." In some ways, it still is. It is not easy to face our fears and wrestle with them, refusing to let go until we have turned them into renewed strength and blessing. But speaking personally, I would have it no other way. Judaism is not faith as illusion, seeing the world through rose-tinted lenses as we would wish it to be. It is faith as relentless honesty, seeing evil as evil and fighting it in the name of life, and good, and God. That is our vocation. It remains a privilege to carry Jacob's destiny, Israel's name.[7]

For Rabbi Sacks, "It's hard to be a Jew" becomes a transformative calling. In place of a fatalistic judgment on Jewish existence, Rabbi Sacks interprets the phrase to contain opportunities to face a broken world and to derive inspiration, purpose, and happiness from its repair.

In a 2014 lecture at Yeshiva University, Rabbi Sacks borrowed from Stephen Covey in formulating his title, "The Seven Principles to Inner Happiness." Weaving together rabbinic sources, popular social science, and masterful storytelling, he adopted the self-help movement's "happiness" narrative while correcting for many of its excesses. As he says about principle seven, gratitude: "Happiness isn't out there, in what you don't yet have. You already have all the ingredients for happiness. It's just that you need to open your eyes and see what you are surrounded by."[8]

Yet, Rabbi Sacks' approach to happiness was not contained in his speeches and essays, alone. The public persona that Rabbi Sacks embodied was a force for joy within Jewish and general society. It is instructive to note the penultimate sentences of former Archbishop of Canterbury Rowan Williams' obituary for Rabbi Sacks:

> We shared meals, conversations, journeys, frustrations with the internal divisions within our own communities, and ultimately a pervasive sense of joy in the God who keeps promises. Jonathan may not have entirely transformed the face of Anglicanism with his Lambeth address; but he did give us a taste of that joy, so confident and forceful in Jonathan's personality.[9]

That a rabbinic leader should be associated primarily with joy is a dramatic counterpoint to the frightening stare of rabbinic images from decades past. Rabbi Sacks was not alone in effectuating this change. Many of his contemporaries also wore colorful ties. Yet, no one climbed the pinnacles that Rabbi Sacks did in not just spreading Torah, but also bringing a warm smile to the face of Judaism and the rabbinate.

Notes

1. Tim Ferris, host, "Rabbi Lord Jonathan Sacks on Powerful Books, Mystics, Richard Dawkins, and the Dangers of Safe Spaces" The Tim Ferriss Show (podcast #455), August 26, 2020, accessed November 24, 2022, https://tim.blog/2020/08/26/rabbi-lord-jonathan-sacks-2/.
2. When considering photographs of rabbinic leaders of the past, we would do well to contextualize such portraits to prevailing conventions. Wide smiles were associated with madness, lewdness, loudness, and drunkenness. See Angus Trumble, *A Brief History of the Smile*. (United Kingdom: Basic Books, 2004).
3. Why did my friend do this? He set the stage for a jocular riff on those stereotypes, with which to demonstrate his homiletic and comedic chops.
4. Haym Soloveitchik, "Rupture and Reconstruction," *Tradition* 28, no. 4 (Summer 1994): 80.
5. Peter N. Stearns tracks a parallel but distinct change in general American culture between the Victorian Age emotional culture with a preoccupation with a dispassionate "cool" disposition. He analyzes a major change between World War I and midcentury when a dramatic break took place in "feeling rules"—socially shared norms that influence how people want to try to feel emotions in given social relations. Stearns Peter N. *American Cool: Constructing a Twentieth Century Emotional Style* (New York: NYU Press, 1994), 193–228.
6. Such changes in rabbinic demeanor parallel changes in general society. Christina Kotchemidova describes how the primary strategy of American advertising shifted during the 1920s, when the "warning" type of ad gave way to the "product-satisfaction" ad. Advertisers emphasized the positive experience of using a product. Stressing a healthy and happy life, "portraying consumer happiness became the paramount directive of advertising." Kotchemidova, Christina, "Why We Say 'Cheese': Producing the Smile in Snapshot Photography," *Critical Studies in Media Communication* 22, no. 1 (2005): 2–25.
7. Jonathan Sacks, *Covenant & Conversation: A Weekly Reading of the Jewish Bible* (Jerusalem: Maggid Books & The Orthodox Union, 2009), 140–141.
8. Jonathan Sacks, "The Seven Principles to Inner Happiness," recorded January 28, 2014 at Yeshiva University, New York, NY, audio, https://www.rabbisacks.org/archive/the-seven-principles-to-inner-happiness/.
9. Rowan Williams, "The Joy of Jonathan Sacks" *First Things* 11/30/20. https://www.firstthings.com/web-exclusives/2020/11/the-joy-of-jonathan-sacks.

CHAPTER 16

Simha Shel Mitzvah: The Commandment of Joy, or the Joy of a Commandment?

Sara Tillinger Wolkenfeld

We live in a culture that celebrates joy. The self-help section of the bookstore overflows with works designed to coach people suffering from twenty-first century malaise to adopt a posture of happiness. This focus on happiness can be, in turn, either inspiring and uplifting, or burdensome and guilt-inducing. Happiness enthusiasts believe that a more joyful existence is inherent in the purpose of life, and allows us to be better, more productive human beings.[1] Authors arguing from the opposite perspective contend that happiness is not a cure-all,[2] and that joy is not always the most generative state for creativity and healthy human functioning.[3] Perhaps the most famous Jewish expression of the idea that joy is a necessity in our religious lives is the saying of Rabbi Nahman of Bratslav, whether quoted sincerely or sung without much forethought: "It is a great *mitzvah* [commandment] to be joyous constantly."[4]

Yet, Rabbi Nahman notwithstanding, there is no biblical or rabbinic commandment to be joyous at all times. The Jewish calendar has occasions that call for joy, while others call for sadness, seriousness, self-examination, and a variety of other internal states. In cases where specific

S. T. Wolkenfeld (✉)
New York, NY, USA

© The Author(s), under exclusive license to Springer Nature Switzerland AG 2023
E. Brown, S. Weiss (eds.), *An Ode to Joy*,
https://doi.org/10.1007/978-3-031-28229-4_16

emotions are mandated, the *halakhic* [Jewish legal] tradition tends to prescribe actions that will prompt the relevant emotion. This concretizes the requirement to feel a certain way by providing instructions for evoking that emotion and shifts the focus from a purely internal state to recognizable and measurable actions.[5]

Whenever Jewish tradition endorses happiness, one can ask, "Joy to what end?" Not all forms of happiness, in Judaism, are created equal. Rabbinic literature contains multiple sources that endorse a more nuanced form of joy called "*simha shel mitzvah*" [joy of the commandment] and it is this more subtle and refined emotion that I wish to explore and suggest as an antidote to the extremes of today's happiness culture.

The Talmud, in BT Shabbat[6] introduces the concept of *simha shel mitzvah*:

> "So I commended mirth (Ecclesiastes 8:15)," that is **the joy of a commandment**. "And of mirth: What does it accomplish?" that is joy that **is not** the **joy of a commandment**. The praise of joy mentioned here is **to teach you that the Divine Presence rests** upon an individual **neither from** an atmosphere of **sadness, nor from** an atmosphere of **laziness, nor from** an atmosphere of **laughter, nor from** an atmosphere of **frivolity, nor from** an atmosphere of **idle conversation, nor from** an atmosphere of **idle chatter, but rather from** an atmosphere imbued with **the joy of** a commandment (*simha shel mitzvah*).[7]

Using a verse from Ecclesiastes as a springboard, the Talmud contrasts two different types of joy. Ordinary happiness is unproductive and unimportant, but there is a kind of happiness that is praiseworthy: *simha shel mitzvah*, or the joy of a commandment. This form of joy is what allows a person to feel the presence of the Divine, while other emotions prevent us from being able to commune with the Divine presence.

Similarly, the Talmud in Berakhot endorses *simha shel mitzvah* as the appropriate emotional state when engaging in prayer.[8] In the context of a series of recommendations as to how to foster a compelling prayer experience, the Talmud in Berakhot mentions *simha shel mitzvah*:

> [T]he **Sages taught: One may neither stand to pray from** an atmosphere of **sorrow nor from** an atmosphere of **laziness, nor from** an atmosphere of **laughter, nor from** an atmosphere of **conversation, nor from** an atmosphere of **frivolity, nor from** an atmosphere of **purposeless matters.**

Rather, one should approach prayer from an atmosphere imbued with the joy of a commandment.[9]

This statement seems like a logical extension of the passage in Tractate Sabbath: If joy is the appropriate state of mind for encouraging the presence of the Divine, it follows that this emotional state is the ideal one for preparing to pray. In both texts, the rabbinic sources emphasize that they are describing a particular type of joy, one that accompanies or stems from commandment performance, and not mere laughter or frivolity.

At no point is *simha shel mitzvah* defined by the Talmud; it is merely contrasted with lesser forms of happiness. The medieval commentaries and philosophical writings do elaborate on *simha shel mitzvah*, and the ways in which this category can be used to understand more deeply the ways that joy might enrich our spiritual lives. What follows are three rabbinic approaches to conceptualizing the idea of *simha shel mitzvah*:

SIMHA SHEL MITZVAH: THE JOY OF DOING THE RIGHT THING

Joy is an expression of virtue. In order to explain the category of "*simha shel mitzvah*," Rashi provides an example: "such as accompanying a bride."[10] Not all commandments bring about the same level of happiness as being involved in a wedding. Other sources assert that joy is inextricably bound up in all areas of Jewish law: it is both a required component of performing commandments as well as a natural outcome of a life structured around Divine command. Maimonides writes in his codification of the laws of Sukkot about the importance of performing commandments with a sense of joy:

> The joy which a person derives from performing commandments and from loving God, who has commanded us to practice them, is a supreme form of divine worship. Anyone who refrains from experiencing this joy deserves punishment, as it is written: "Because you have not served the Lord your God with joy and with a glad heart" (Deuteronomy 28:47).[11]

In this formulation, "performing commandments" and "loving God" are almost synonymous and are overlapping components of the same actions. To carry out the commandments is to do the will of the Divine, whom we are obligated to love. Rabbi Vidal of Tolosa, author of the Maggid Mishnah, explains this comment:[12]

> The words of our teacher are explained in several places in the Talmud, and in Sabbath 30b ... the essence of the idea is that it is not appropriate for a person to do commandments because they are obligatory, and they are forced and coerced into doing them. Rather, one is obligated to do them and rejoices in doing them and will do what is good because it is good, and will choose the truth because it is the truth, and so performing them will not seem burdensome. People will understand that this is why they were created: to serve the Creator, and when one does what one was born to do, one rejoices and celebrates.

As the Maggid Mishnah understands Maimonides, it is a joy to have a Creator who is also a Commander, and to be obligated to do things which are definitionally good and true. We choose truth, precisely because it is the truth; the joy of doing the right thing—of living virtuously—relieves the perception that fulfilling 613 commandments is burdensome. One who does not feel joy as a result of performing commandments—and then, in turn, does not perform commandments with a sense of joy—is doing it wrong, as evidenced by the quote from Deuteronomy.

A more modern iteration of this idea appears in the writings of Rabbi Abraham Isaac Kook. His twentieth-century commentary on Tractate Sabbath includes an extensive explanation of the idea of *simha shel mitzvah*. Happiness, argues Rabbi Kook, is the natural state of a person who is physically and mentally healthy. The function of commandments is not to curb natural human inclinations but rather to direct and elevate those tendencies. Ordinary happiness, which might stem from physical pleasures, is transformed by Torah and commandments. Rabbi Kook defines *simha shel mitzvah* as:

> the joy in understanding the truth, knowledge of God and God's Torah, and in the joy of the soul that is engaged with justice and righteousness, to fulfill all the obligations of Torah and intellect that are incumbent upon a person in action and thought, with joy and good-heartedness.[13]

This elevated form of happiness is born of the connection between a person's natural desire to be happy, and the Divine commandments, which provide a path to righteousness and justice. It is a kind of redeemed happiness that presents itself to one who observes mitzvot.

Simha Shel Mitzvah: Love for the One Who Commands

This is joy as a relational concept. The performance of commandments is often envisioned as a conduit for the love between humans and the Divine, between Commander and Commanded. Numerous sources point to the Torah as a gift that provides expression for the loving bond between God and the Jewish people,[14] and the idea is expressed daily in the blessing preceding the Shema:

> With unbounded love You have loved us ... Our Father, merciful Father, Who acts with compassion have compassion on us and put into our hearts to comprehend, and to be intellectually creative, to listen, to learn, and to teach, to preserve, to practice, and to fulfill all the words of instruction in Your Torah with love.[15]

This loving relationship is both the reason for the commandments and the context in which commandments are performed. Serving another from a place of love evokes feelings of happiness because the deeds being performed are done as part of building an ongoing, intimate, relationship. The midrash provides the following formulation:

> For example, when a son serves his father, he does so in gladness, saying to himself: If I should commit an error in my father's presence, he will not be angry with me, for he loves me. Hence, he serves him with gladness. However, when a stranger serves a master, he does so with trepidation, saying to himself: If I should commit an error in his presence, he will become angry with me.[16]

Like a child doing things for a parent's approval, the happiness we feel in performing commandments is a sign of a healthy, loving relationship. This provides a lens for understanding the idea of *simha shel mitzvah*: The particular joy that emerges from performing commandments, which serve as signs of God's care for us and as part of our own expression of love for the Divine.

An even stronger formulation of this position is expressed by Rabbi Moshe Chaim Luzzato, in his ethical treatise, *Mesilat Yesharim* [*The Path of the Just*]. He refers to joy as "an important essence of service of God," and elaborates as follows:

For this is the true joy, namely, that a person's heart delights that they merit to serve before the blessed Master ... and to toil in Torah and commandments which are the true perfection and the eternal worth. And Solomon said in a parable on wisdom: "Draw me, we will run after You. The King has brought me into His chambers; we will be glad and rejoice in You." (Song of Songs 1:4)[17]

The connection to Song of Songs is indicative of the joy that emerges from another model of the relationship with God: that of lover and beloved. In the rabbinic understanding of Song of Songs, the Jewish people and the Divine are partners in an intense and loving relationship. This source portrays *simha shel mitzvah* as the inevitable consequence of acting in service of one to whom we always want to grow closer.

The evocation of love between partners draws renewed attention to the contrast between "ordinary" happiness, and the nuanced, elevated joy of *simha shel mitzvah*. The other forms of happiness that are mentioned in both Talmudic sources, "laughter" (*shok*), and "frivolity" (*kalut rosh*), as well as "conversation" (*siha*) are all modes of interaction that are typically referenced as trivial ways that men and women might interact.[18] At best, these types of enjoyment are seen as a waste of time, and at worst, they are portrayed as leading to a kind of casual sexuality. *Simha shel mitzvah*, on the other hand, is the result of a serious investment in our relationship with God; the emotional state of one doing commandments is the joy of drawing closer to one's soul mate.

SIMHA SHEL MITZVAH: EXPANDING THE CIRCLE OF JOY

This is the joy of unbounded happiness. One of the frequently cited modern maxims about happiness is that being happy will make those around you happy as well.[19] This is not always true; there are certain forms of rejoicing that can seem selfish or even callous to those who are outside. Seeing happy people can sometimes make those who are depressed feel even more isolated. But the nuanced joy of *simha shel mitzvah* is that it is an inclusive form of joy. The extension of one's relationship with God is bringing others into the circle of love and joy described above.

Maimonides describes this phenomenon in writing about the commandment to rejoice on holidays:[20]

While eating and drinking, one must feed the stranger, the orphan, the widow, and other poor unfortunates. Anyone, however, who locks the doors of his courtyard and eats and drinks along with his wife and children, without giving anything to eat and drink to the poor and the desperate, does not experience commandment-related joy, but rather indulges in the celebration of his stomach.

This final phrase evokes the self-satisfied, miserly joy of someone who keeps what they have all to themselves. In fact, the Torah's commands to rejoice in the festivals are frequently accompanied by reminders of the need to include those who lack the physical means to celebrate. In Deuteronomy, the culmination of the bringing of the first fruits is described as follows: "And you shall enjoy, together with the Levite and the stranger in your midst, all the bounty that the Lord your God has bestowed upon you and your household."[21]

Commandments are sometimes accompanied by, or fulfilled through, forms of physical enjoyment. Only when those who have more than enough include those who lack means is the joy complete. Rabbi Naftali Tzvi Yehuda Berlin explains the happiness in this verse as the joy of "soul and body," as one eats and drinks and also expands the impact of that happiness by spreading it to others. The happiness we feel in these commandments is meant to create a ripple effect that ultimately impacts the entire community, from the teacher to the stranger, and everyone in between.

Conclusion

There are spiritual dangers in not cultivating an intentional sense of joy in commandment performance. Viewed through the lens of an opportunity to rejoice in doing what is right, the absence of *simha shel mitzvah* can make the many demands of a religious life feel burdensome. Without a sense of connection to the One Who Commands, the one performing commandments is in spiritual danger of feeling distant from the Divine. Joy without an emphasis on commandedness can create a feeling that happiness is entirely about one's own experience of the world, without realizing that happiness also confers its own obligations to others. This, too, presents a danger: the peril of narcissism.

Simha shel mitzvah is rabbinic literature's reminder that not all forms of happiness help refine a person's character or improve the world. Joy is intricately bound up in a healthy relationship with commandments, and by extension, a healthy relationship with the Divine and with the people around us. To inculcate this particular form of happiness into our lives is to invite the Divine presence to dwell within ourselves and our communities.

Notes

1. One example of this approach is presented by Gretchen Rubin, creator of a book, app, and podcast called "The Happiness Project." The book was first published in 2009.
2. See for example Barbara Ehrenreich, *Bright-Sided: How Positive Thinking is Undermining America* (London: Picador, 2010).
3. See for example Susan Cain, *Bittersweet: How Longing and Sorrow Make us Whole* (New York: Crown, 2022), and Eric G. Wilson, *Against Happiness: In Praise of Melancholy* (New York: Sarah Crichton Books, 2009).
4. Rabbi Nachman of Breslov, *Likutei Moharan* Tinyana, 2:24:1, rabenu-book.com/ליקוטי-מוהר"ן-תנינא-תוכן-עניינים/
5. Rabbi Y.D. Soloveitchik writes about the distinction between the act of a commandment and its fulfillment in a number of places, including *Shi'urim le-Zekher Abba Mori* (Jerusalem: Mossad Harav Kook, 2002), Volume II, 188–190.
6. BT Shabbat 30b. Text from The William Davidson digital edition of the Koren Noé Talmud, with commentary by Rabbi Adin Even-Israel Steinsaltz, License: CC-BY-NC. A parallel passage appears in BT Pesahim 117a.
7. The following line in the Talmud contains a prooftext that references joy, but which does not obviously connect with *simha shel mitzvah* specifically. Textual witnesses make it clear that earlier versions of this text read simply "*simha.*" The Maharsha, in his *Hidushei Aggadot* (*ad loc*) explains that joy is sometimes the prerequisite for doing a commandment, which may, in turn, bring about greater happiness.
8. BT Berakhot 31a. Text from The William Davidson digital edition of the Koren Noé Talmud, with commentary by Rabbi Adin Even-Israel Steinsaltz.
9. There are a variety of textual variants in earlier editions of this text. The parallel statement in the Tosefta (BT Berakhot 3:21) says *devarim shel hokhma*, and other editions have *simha shel Torah* (Oxford 366), *simha shel halakha* (Paris 671), among other related variations. A full exploration of the evolution of the phrase is beyond the scope of this article, but it seems that there may be movement over time to broaden the category of happiness beyond the intellectual, study-focused form that would presumably be

available to a smaller number of people, in favor of the more general *simha shel mitzvah*.

10. BT Shabbat 30b, s.v. *simha shel mitzvah*. Translation is my own.
11. Mishneh Torah, Laws of Shofar, Sukkah and Lulav, 8:15. Adapted from the Sefaria Edition, Translated by R. Francis Nataf, 2019, Maimonides' Mishneh Torah, edited by Philip Birnbaum, New York, 1967.
12. Maggid Mishnah ad loc. Translation is my own.
13. Rabbi Abraham Isaac Kook, *Ein Ayah on Tractate Sabbath* (Jerusalem: Merkaz HaRav, 1995), 118.
14. There are multiple relevant references in Biblical literature, including Deuteronomy 26:17–18, and associated commentaries, particularly HaKtav VeHakabalah ad loc. For a relevant Talmudic discussion, see BT Sabbath 88a-b.
15. Weekday Morning Services. Adapted from the translation of Avrohom Davis, Metsudah Linear Siddur (New York: Metsudah, 1981), License CC-BY
16. Midrash Tanhuma, Noach 19:2. Translation from the digital edition of Samuel A. Berman, *Midrash Tanhuma-Yelammedenu* (New York: Ktav, 1996), License CC-BY
17. Mesilat Yesharim 19:100. Adapted from the translation of Yosef Sebag, *Mesilat Yesharim: With Commentaries* (Published by author, 2018).
18. See, for example, Pirkei Avot 1:5, Pirkei Avot 3:13, Berakhot 62a, Maimonides, Laws of Forbidden Sexual Relations, 21:1–2, and Sukkah 51b, among others.
19. "The Eight Splendid Truths of Happiness," *The Happiness Project*, accessed June 28, 2022, https://the-happiness-project.com/blogs/tools/the-eight-splendid-truths-of-happiness
20. Shevitat Yom Tov 6:18. Adapted from the Sefaria Edition, Translated by R. Francis Nataf, 2019, Maimonides' Mishneh Torah, edited by Philip Birnbaum, New York, 1967.
21. Deut. 26:11.

CHAPTER 17

Finding Happiness in the Transience of Sukkot

Joseph Dweck

The Torah commands us to be happy,[1] to make others happy,[2] and to serve God in happiness.[3] So central is happiness in Torah that severe repercussions are promised should we fail to engage with God and His commandments out of happiness.

> *And all these ill tidings will come upon you…for you did not serve God your Lord in joy and with good heart… (Deut. 28:45,47)*

Happiness is a cornerstone of Judaism.

Sukkot, the festival of happiness, is a good place to start an exploration of Judaism and happiness. It would make sense then, to study the core principles of Sukkot and to see if we can learn more from them about what it means to be happy and fulfill the Torah's charge.

On the surface, however, it is difficult to find anything overtly happy about Sukkot. To the contrary, it seems like it is a festival that revolves around elements that tend to make us quite sad. As a harvest holiday,[4] it is celebrated at a time when the northern hemisphere is moving into the

---

J. Dweck (✉)
Spanish and Portuguese Sephardi Community of the UK, London, UK

© The Author(s), under exclusive license to Springer Nature Switzerland AG 2023
E. Brown, S. Weiss (eds.), *An Ode to Joy*,
https://doi.org/10.1007/978-3-031-28229-4_17

dormancy of winter. There are fewer daylight hours and the fields stop producing. In society, these melancholy months are marked by holidays that focus on morbidity and death. In the West, it is the time of Halloween. Catholics commemorate All Soul's Day, and in Mexico, *Día de los Muertos* (Day of the Dead). The reaping season has long been associated with mortality. Consider the Angel of Death's moniker "The Grim Reaper." Sukkot is not as far removed from these undertones as we might initially believe.

The central concept of Sukkot is that everything is temporary, and all things pass. In recognition of this, we build a hut that by Jewish law must be impermanent by nature.[5] And for seven days we must treat this hut, this sukkah, as though it is our home. We must "sit in it as if we are dwelling in it"[6] only to take it all down seven days later. Somehow it is meant to be a source of happiness for us; we must not hold back from putting within the sukkah all that is important and precious[7] even though we know it won't last beyond a week. If, at any time, we find ourselves in what in Hebrew is called *tsa'ar*, which is essentially some form of discomfort, we are exempt from sitting in it for it is no longer a place in which we can be happy.[8]

Yet, perhaps it is this very stark contrast between the intended joy of the festival and the darker aspects it seems to include that invites us to uncover something counter-intuitive about the deeper nature of happiness.

Happiness and sadness are two sides of the same coin, and if we are to understand them at all, we must understand them in light of each other. In this world, happiness does not last for us.[9] Its very manifestation is fleeting, and as we rejoice, we also keenly sense its transience. The fullness, meaning, joy, contentment, and satisfaction that we experience in happiness fades even as it appears. Rabbi Sacks recognized this very point as the base upon which the entire book of Ecclesiastes (traditionally read by many on Sukkot) is set.

[The author] is obsessed by the fragility and brevity of life, as contrasted with the seeming eternity of the universe ... Kohelet is a sustained meditation on mortality ... he is traumatized by the "unbearable lightness of being", the fact that life is lived toward death, that our days are numbered.[10]

Still, there is a depth of meaning in this happy–sad state that often brings us to tears. That depth itself comes from its very transience. Transience gives us something as it takes away. Consider the following story recounted in the Talmud about R. Elazar ben Pedat and R Yohanan:

R. Elazar ben Pedat was ill and R. Yohanan, who was known to be especially beautiful,[11] went to visit him. Upon entering, R Yohanan rolled up his sleeve and the Talmud says that the house "filled with light," as a result of this minor exposure of R. Yohanan's forearm. And upon seeing this, R. Elazar started crying. R. Yohanan asked him why he was crying, and he said, "I am crying because of the beauty that stands before me that will one day whither in the earth." To which R. Yohanan himself said, "Yes, that is indeed a reason to cry." R. Elazar's tears emerged from knowing that R. Yohanan's was not going to live for an eternity. When R. Elazar recognized the fleeting nature of beauty, he wept.[12]

Nahmanides called attention to this tragic truth at the opening of his book on the laws of mourning. Why is it, he asked, that after time immemorial, we all encounter death yet, we still have not come to terms with it? Why is it that something so ubiquitous still elicits such deep sadness and resentment? It is because, he says, we know deep down that we are meant to be eternal; that something as precious as a human soul should never be extinguished. And when we see it happen, we are broken all over again. We cry over the meaning that we see in it all. And that meaning and, therefore, both the happiness and sadness, manifest themselves in the transience.[13]

This is so central a condition to the human experience that Sigmund Freud thought it important enough to write an essay elaborating upon the idea. He did this after an interlude he had with the poet, Rainer Maria Rilke, which bears a similar theme to the story of R. Elazar and R. Yohanan. Freud and Rilke were once walking in a beautiful meadow together. He noticed that the poet was deeply distraught. Freud asked why, and Rilke said, "all of this beauty is going to die." Freud, did not see this simply as an extenuating incident of overwhelming emotions. He understood that Rilke's distress came from a serious existential problem—the same problem that moved R. Elazar to tears, the same problem that prompted Nahmanides to highlight our inability to come to terms with death. This episode with Rilke prompted Freud to write an essay he called "On Transience."[14] In it, I believe he highlights the core of Sukkot's meaning. He noted that it is the very transience we lament that gives us all our sense of preciousness, and in that preciousness, beauty and happiness.

This juxtaposition of eternity and death, this happy–sad state with the profundity of its value and meaning, is the bedrock of Sukkot and the foundation of what the Torah calls *simha*—happiness. It is an experience that moves the human heart; our usual response to it is to cry, not because it is purely sad, but because it is overwhelmingly meaningful. This meaning is the true source of human happiness, and when we know it, we are happy. It is why the Sages see one who is "happy with his portion" as the sign of true wealth.[15] Being happy with one's portion has nothing to do with what one has, but who one is. Each and every one of us is a beauty that is irreplicable. And each and every one of us in our lives in the universe that we build and nurture, has a beginning and an end. That beginning and end illuminate every moment in splendor and exquisite preciousness. When we discover these special moments, we come to know true happiness.

With this, we might better understand why the prophet Zekharia[16] establishes Sukkot as the ultimate challenge for the world.

> And it shall be that all who remain among the nations coming up to Jerusalem shall go up year after year to bow to the King, the Lord of Armies, and to celebrate the festival of Sukkot.

Here the prophet places Sukkot as a festival for all humanity in which a human being comes to accept the world on its own terms by learning Sukkot's lessons and understanding the path to happiness.

Reading these texts, we begin to discover that happiness is not a feeling of elation or contentment alone but one where we must honor the full meaning of life, including our own. Yes, our precious moments pass us by, but it is in their very passing that their value and meaning is found. Endings firmly define the irrevocable stored reality of the past.[17] These moments behind us have happened. We have seen them and are richer for it. When we can come to this understanding about the world, we can truly embrace and welcome life on its own terms. In that acceptance lies true happiness.

NOTES

1. Deut, 16:14; MT Hilkhot Shofar, Sukkah ve'Lulav 8:15.
2. MT Hilkhot Avel 14:1; ibid., Hilkhot Megilla veHanuka 2:17.
3. Deut. 28:47.
4. Exodus 23:16; 34:22.
5. BT Sukkah, 2a; MT Hilkhot Sukkah 6:5.
6. BT Sukkah 28b; MT, ibid.
7. BT Sukkah 28b; MT Hilkhot Sukkah, 6:5.
8. MT, 6:2

9. Cf. Tanhuma, Shemini 2:1.
10. Jonathan Sacks, "Season of Joy," *Koren Sukkot Mahzor* (Jerusalem: Koren Publishers, 2015), xli–xlii.
11. BT Baba Mezia 84a.
12. BT Berakhot 5b.
13. Nahmanides, *Torat Ha'Adam* (Jerusalem: Mossad HaRav Kook, 1994), 12.
14. Sigmund Freud, "On Transience", in *The Standard Edition of the Complete Psychological Works of Sigmund Freud*, https://www.sas.upenn.edu/~cavitch/pdf-library/Freud_Transience.pdf.
15. *Ethics of the Fathers* 4:1.
16. Ibid., 14:16–19.
17. Viktor Frankl, *Man's Search for Meaning* (Boston: Beacon Press, 2006), 120.

PART IV

Joy in Legal Thought

CHAPTER 18

Law's Joy: Celebrating the Study and Practice of Law

Michael A. Helfand and Chaim Saiman

Jewish law stands at the center of the Jewish experience and worldview. Yet, the compound concept of Jewish law is literally complex—as in "a whole made up of complicated or interrelated parts."[1] Law, as a term and concept, has long been the subject of intense debate,[2] and Judaism has received analogous conceptual treatment; is Judaism a religion, family, race, ethnicity, nationality, culture, political community—or all of the above?[3] It is hardly surprising that an amalgam of these terms—Jewish Law—captures a range of meanings under even its most narrow interpretations.[4]

Within the Jewish tradition, Jewish law straddles the fence between two of the most religiously essential activities: study and practice. Broadly construed, Jewish law is the subject of study as captured in the obligation of

---

M. A. Helfand (✉)
Pepperdine Caruso School of Law, Malibu, CA, USA

C. Saiman
Villanova University Charles Widger School of Law, Villanova, PA, USA

© The Author(s), under exclusive license to Springer Nature Switzerland AG 2023
E. Brown, S. Weiss (eds.), *An Ode to Joy*,
https://doi.org/10.1007/978-3-031-28229-4_18

the *Talmud Torah*. At the same time, the content of Jewish law serves as the body of religious obligations to be followed by Judaism's adherents.[5] This division typically serves as a conceptual fault line when it comes to religious experience. The Talmud most famously captures this dichotomy between study and action in the reporting of a rabbinic convocation where the matter was put up for debate. Rabbi Tarfon argued mitzva observance is superior, while Rabbi Akiva countered that study takes precedence.[6] The assembled rabbis, possibly seeking a compromise, responded that the study of Torah is greater because it leads to mitzva observance.[7] Yet, this apparent unanimity did little to settle the matter. The Talmud continues to record additional statements explaining that Torah study is more important as demonstrated by the fact that its command preceded the giving of some mitzvot.[8] Moreover, following a person's time on earth, the Talmud records that they are judged first with respect to their Torah study while evaluation of their performance of mitzvot comes second.[9]

In addition to its apparent primacy over observance, the rabbinic tradition understands the study of Torah, *Talmud Torah*, as providing happiness or joy. While mourners are required to perform most mitzvot, they are prohibited from studying Torah, because, in the words of the psalmist, "The precepts of the Lord are right, rejoicing the heart" (Psalms 19:9). The same prohibition against study applies to all Jews on the Ninth of Av since rejoicing is antithetical to the mourning that a Jew must observe when commemorating the destruction of the Temple or the death of a close loved one.[10]

The association of study with joy tracks the way in which the study of Jewish law is understood as a devotional activity—one that is not merely an intellectual endeavor but is intended to generate religious fervor and spiritual fulfillment. As one of us has explained, the "Talmud brims with encomiums to the study of Torah … Torah is described as the elixir of life, the tree of life, and the life-giving force of water … As the Talmud sees it, through the study of Torah man comes to understand his God, himself, and his world."[11] For the religious adherent, few activities can inspire more joy.

The contrast between the joyous approach to law as Torah that is studied and the far more somber understanding of law as a tool of social control, and ultimately power, obtains its most haunting exploration in the work of Robert Cover. Cover's celebrated article, *Nomos and Narrative*, draws on Torah study as a paradigm to explain that "[l]aw as Torah is pedagogic." Its discourse "is initiatory, celebratory, expressive, and performative."[12] By contrast, his essay *Violence and the Word*, which focuses on state law, opens with the following provocative insight: "Legal interpretation takes place in a field of pain and death."[13] On Cover's account, the goal of authoritative legal interpretation—that is, removed from the *beit midrash* and pursued through the regulatory apparatus of the state—inevitably uses coercion, pain, and sometimes even death to destroy competing understandings of the normative universe. In this way, it is not simply that the practical imposition of authoritative legal interpretations "kill the diverse legal traditions that compete with the State," but that official judicial decision-making feeds off of actual violence in order to achieve domination.[14]

In making this argument, Cover brings the dual aspects of law and Jewish law, in particular, into stark relief. Freed from the coercive power of enforcement, the study of law can be a joyful communion under the Divine canopy. Moreover, even the internal drive towards halakhic obedience can be joyful—since, to use Cover's turn of phrase, obedience is "correlative to understanding."[15] So long as law avoids the coercive power of the state, law can be the locus of personal fulfillment and joyous celebration. On the other hand, once law—including Jewish law—is imposed and enforced by human agents, there is no escaping the ever-present coercion, in the form of the interpretive and actual violence that stands behind it. When the law moves from study to human enforcement, the inevitable need for coercion drains law of its joy and happiness, and instead injects law with pain, horror, and agony.

Cover's scholarship looms large in the academic field of Jewish law. Indeed, with his powerful arguments and imagery, it is hard to think of a legal scholar who has more influence, both inside and outside the academy, on perception of Jewish law. Indeed, Rabbi Sacks himself periodically cites Cover's work—far from surprising, given the frequency with which Jewish scholars have tangled with Cover's ideas.[16] That being said, Cover's sharp distinction between the joy of study and the pain of regulatory enforcement stands in stark opposition to Rabbi Sacks' own vision of law—an approach that focuses far more on its emancipatory power than its coercive dark side.

Writing about the holiday of Shavuot, Rabbi Sacks links Jewish continuity with the joy Jews have found in the study of the Torah. In explaining this link, Rabbi Sacks made use of the oft-invoked metaphor of a marriage between God and the Jewish people where the Torah served as the "never-to-be-rescinded marriage contract with God." Thus, even without land

and sovereignty, Jews were able to breathe life into their collective experience by studying the Torah and writing commentaries on the Torah; it was rejoicing in the discovery and challenge of old and new interpretations that Jews could "rejoic[e]," especially on the holiday celebrating God's revelation of the Torah.[17]

Rabbi Sack's characterization of *Talmud Torah* as a joyous activity largely tracks this conventional view of the Talmudic sages. His more novel intervention, and what set him apart from writers like Cover, lies in his treatment of the regulatory state and his unbridled optimism in the redemptive power of legal enforcement. In an essay originally published in *The Times*, Rabbi Sacks celebrated the practice of law with all its demands of obedience by illustrating the novelty of Judaism's other Torah-themed holiday, Simchat Torah. Rabbi Sacks asked his primarily non-Jewish readers to "[i]magine the following scene. The Lord Chief Justice, together with his senior judges, decide that law is a wonderful thing. They resolve to set aside a day each year to celebrate it. They write poems and compose songs in its honour. When the day comes, they each take a weighty tome—Halsbury's Statutes would do nicely—and dance round the House of Lords, singing the songs and reciting the poems."[18] It was against the "whack[iness]" and "impossib[ility]" of such a scene that Rabbi Sacks demonstrated why the holiday where Jews rejoice with the Torah stands out as undeniably unique.[19]

Rabbi Sacks begins by reiterating the joyousness found in Torah study: "In a sense the entire history of Judaism is the story of a love affair between a people and a book." But Rabbi Sack's association of joy with law is not limited to Torah and the Jewish people. In fact, he goes so far as to encourage the entire world to celebrate the existence of sovereignty and the mechanism of legal enforcement, notwithstanding all the conflicts inherent to the process of legal coercion. Writing in 2004, he argued:

> One of the most important things religion does is to get us to celebrate things we would otherwise take for granted. That includes law. Usually, it is just there in the background. But as we have seen in Iraq, Sudan, and so many of today's failed, failing or rogue states, it is not easy to create the rule of law. Yet without it, there is no freedom, justice or human rights. Law is humanity's single greatest non-violent form of conflict resolution. That is why Jews saw law as the most precious gift of God, and why we still try to spend as much time as possible studying it.[20]

Note the weaving together of practiced law and studied law. Jews study law because it is precious. But that preciousness is most palpable because enforced observance provides freedom, justice, and human rights. And this is a reason not simply to abide by the law but to celebrate the law and rejoice in its implementation. Because Sacks emphasizes that law is an alternative to violence, he celebrates the conventional view of law as grounded in the state's ability to establish order.

Cover also appreciates the redemptive possibilities of law but conceptualizes it in an entirely different manner. Cover emphasizes the rule of law is not simply "established" but can only come about through coercion and violence that inevitably suppresses alternative legal meanings and worldviews. Per Cover, this process is always working in the background even when no shots are fired.

Thus, while Cover also celebrates the law, it is specifically the law of the *beit midrash* that peers into the realm of the ideal. Set at a remove from enforcement, "law reflects a tension between what is and what might be,"[21] where the Jewish people adopt the legal idiom to formulate their understanding of God's covenant. As with so many facets of the human condition, Rabbi Sacks adopted a more joyous view, seeing both devotional study and tangible enforcement as part of a divine gift that ought to be celebrated.

Notes

1. https://www.merriam-webster.com/dictionary/complex.
2. https://plato.stanford.edu/entries/lawphil-nature/.
3. The best example of this fault line is Leora Batnitzky's seminal work, Leora Batnitzky, *How Judaism Became a Religion: An Introduction to Modern Jewish Thought* (Princeton: Princeton University Press, 2011).
4. One of us has explored elsewhere the way in which these conceptual debates play out in U.S. courts. See Michael A. Helfand, *What Is Jewish Law? A Conceptual View from U.S. Courts*, Oxford Handbook on Jewish Law, eds. Zev Eleff, Roberta Kwall, and Chaim Saiman (forthcoming 2024).
5. Indeed, it is precisely because Jewish law, as a term, can be deployed in these different ways that one of us has differentiated between the terms *Torah*, *Halakhah*, and Jewish Law in an effort to bring conceptual—as well as substantive—clarity to the field. See generally Chaim N. Saiman, *Halakhah: The Rabbinic Idea of Law* (2018).
6. BT Kiddushin 40b.

7. Ibid. "Is study greater or is action greater? Rabbi Tarfon answered and said: Action is greater. Rabbi Akiva answered and said: Study is greater. Everyone answered and said: Study is greater, but not as an independent value; rather, it is greater as study leads to action."
8. Ibid. "It is taught in a baraita that Rabbi Yosei says: Torah study is greater, as it preceded the mitzva of separating ḥalla by forty years."
9. Ibid. "Just as study takes precedence over mitzva performance, Divine judgment regarding Torah study takes precedence over judgment of mitzva performance."
10. BT Ta'anit 30a.
11. Saiman, *Halakhah* at 65.
12. Robert M. Cover, "The Supreme Court, 1982 Term-Foreword: Nomos and Narrative," *Harvard Law Review* 97 (1983): 7, 13.
13. Robert M. Cover, "Violence and the Word," *Yale Law Journal* 95 (1986): 1601.
14. Id. at 1610. "I have written elsewhere that judges of the state are jurispathic—that they kill the diverse legal traditions that compete with the State. Here, however, I am not writing of the jurispathic quality of the office, but of its homicidal potential," Robert M. Cover, "Nomos and Narrative," *Harvard Law Review* 97 at 40–44.
15. "Nomos and Narrative," *Harvard Law Review* 97 at 13.
16. E.g., Jonathan Sacks, *Covenant and Conversation*, Leviticus, 376 (Koren, 2015).
17. Jonathan Sacks, "Shavuot/Pentecost Israel's Wedding," in *Faith in the Future* (1984), 145, 149.
18. Jonathan Sacks, "The Children of Israel Dance for their Portable Homeland," *The Times*, October 9, 2004, https://www.rabbisacks.org/archive/the-children-of-israel-dance-for-their-portable-homeland/.
19. One of us has examined the unique practices of Simhat Torah from a different perspective. See Chaim Saiman, The Inverted Halakhah of Simhat Torah, https://thelehrhaus.com/holidays/the-inverted-halakhah-of-simhat-torah/.
20. Ibid.
21. "Nomos and Narrative," *Harvard Law Review* 97 at 39.

CHAPTER 19

Joy as a Legal Metaphor

Suzanne Last Stone

In biblical literature, the three pilgrimage festivals are most commonly associated with the emotion of joy while in rabbinic literature, joy is most commonly associated with Torah study and the performance of the commandments. Does the joy invoked in these contexts refer to a subjective, personal feeling experienced by the individual who celebrates the festival, performs a *mitzvah* [commandment], or engages in Torah study? Or is joy an objective experience, the same for everyone within a particular culture because the culture transmits clear expectations about what emotions are appropriate in different circumstances?[1] For that matter, is joy an experience of the individual or an emotion that can only be experienced collectively? And do the meaning of emotions—even within a distinct culture—shift over time? In other words, can we assume that joy, as used in the Hebrew Bible and early rabbinic sources, has the emotional sense we expect today?

In his study of rabbinic thought, Ephraim Urbach surveyed the sources and concluded that the sages created the concept of "joy in the precept"— *simha shel mitzva*—in order to cultivate a "feeling of gratification and joy"

S. Last Stone (✉)
Cardozo Law School, Yeshiva University, New York, NY, USA

© The Author(s), under exclusive license to Springer Nature Switzerland AG 2023
E. Brown, S. Weiss (eds.), *An Ode to Joy*,
https://doi.org/10.1007/978-3-031-28229-4_19

in the person who obeys the Torah.[2] Urbach's focus is on the feeling state of the individual person who fulfills the commandment. Joy, in this view, is a subjective, personal experience with which we moderns can easily identify. But recent studies of joy in the Bible and even in rabbinic literature cast considerable doubt on this way of understanding the term joy.

In an all too short yet intriguing sermon on the Torah portion, *Ki Tavo*, in the Book of Deuteronomy,[3] Rabbi Sacks noted that the root for the Hebrew word joy (*simha*) appears often in Deuteronomy, in contrast to its scant appearance in the other five books of Moses. Joy, Rabbi Sacks wrote, "lies at the heart of the Mosaic vision of life in the land of Israel ... where we serve God with joy." He calls particular attention to the appearance of the word in connection with the curses outlined in Deuteronomy. While in Leviticus, the curses are invoked as a result of "the total abandonment of Judaism by the people," in Deuteronomy, the curses are invoked "because you did not serve your God with joy and gladness of heart out of the abundance of all things" (Deut. 28:47). Rabbi Sacks asks why national disaster is attributed to a lack of joy and, more generally, why joy matters more than happiness? Happiness is the state of mind of an individual, he concludes, whereas joy, in the Torah, is never about individuals but rather points to a shared or collective experience. Joy is the emotion that describes the experience of a couple, such as husband and wife or God and the people. The festivals are days of joy because they are a collective celebration. That is, joy is a social emotion that involves capturing and celebrating the moment.

The insight that joy in the Bible is a social, and not an individual, emotion is elaborated on in Anderson's study of the ritual expression of grief and joy in the Hebrew Bible and in early rabbinic literature.[4] Anderson argued that both joy and mourning are emotional states Israel is expected to embody and perform that are keyed to the presence or absence of God in the community. For example, the Torah commands that three times a year Israel must rejoice before God (Deut. 16:11). This is not spontaneous joy. Joy, rather, is part of the obligation of observing the holiday. Moreover, the obligation is a collective one, not a personal one. And the obligation falls at fixed or prescribed times. Joy in this context, seems to function as a general expectation that emerges from concrete acts or behaviors—eating, drinking wine, singing, and so on. These behaviors, especially when done collectively and taken together, create an affective state of affairs. The theological significance is primarily collective; the main axis revolves around God's presence or absence in the community. The proper disposition before God "is a joyful one."⁵ Conversely, the mourner or one who is unclean is cut off temporarily from the community and from the presence of God. Communal mourning necessarily follows the destruction of the Temple. Eventually, Anderson argues, the rabbis had to face the question of whether the destruction of the Temple meant an end to joy or whether joyful celebration could be extended to contexts outside the Temple. Joy first was extended to festal joy outside the Temple and finally to the act of Torah study, culminating in the post-Talmudic festival, Simhat Torah.⁶

But the ritual aspects of joy do not exhaust joy's meaning in biblical and in rabbinic sources. I want to focus on a different definition of joy: joy as willingness and wholeheartedness. In many biblical and rabbinic sources, joy is a legal metaphor for a state of mind made possible by human freedom. Thus, joy can refer to a gift given freely and unconditionally, without any mental reservation, and, conversely, sadness is associated with a contract or sale made under duress. Understanding joy as a legal metaphor does not reduce joy solely to a technical, cognitive state of mind, of interest only within the halakhic framework. Rather, the use of the term joy to connote willingness and lack of inner mental reservation highlights a human capacity for wholeheartedness that has been largely obscured by the contemporary tendency to view the self as inevitably conflicted and ambivalent.

Over a century ago, the legal philosopher, Wesley Newcomb Hohfeld, pointed to the pervasive use of metaphors in law. "Much of the difficulty, as regards legal terminology, arises from the fact that many of our words were originally applicable only to physical things; so that their use in connection with legal relations is, strictly speaking, figurative or fictional."⁷ And so we find words that seem out of place in law and legal analysis, and yet these words convey, in poetic language, important legal concepts. The term joy is no exception. In a fascinating study of love and joy in biblical religion, Yochanan Muffs drew a comparison between the biblical and early rabbinic use of the terms joy and love as legal idioms with Akkadian and Aramaic sources.⁸ Muffs pointed to the expression "in the joy of his heart he gave," appearing in Neo-Babylonian legal documents, which scholars had already translated as "he gave it in altogether willing fashion."⁹ In other words, the word joy in these documents had a legal function, marking that the act was done willingly and with volition. More importantly, for our purposes, Muffs showed that the word *simha* functioned as a legal idiom in biblical and Mishnaic Hebrew and even non-legal rabbinic texts retained its original meaning of joyful willingness or wholeheartedness.[10] Conversely, sadness can express mental reservation. Such juridical sadness is already hinted at in Deuteronomy, Muffs points out. Deuteronomy 15:10 commands the bestowing of gifts on manumitted slaves and instructs: "Do not give it to him with a sad heart, with mental reservation or reluctance."[11]

Many of Muffs' examples center on gift-giving. Thus, Rabbi Yishmael, commenting on the divine grant of the *terumot* to Aaron, translates the biblical term *va-ani hinei nattati* [Behold, I have given] as *beratzon ve simha*[with willingness and joy], terms that are commonly paired together.[12] *Simha*, thus, is an analogue to *razon*, both connoting willingness. Commenting on the giving of the Torah, the Talmudic text (BT Berakhot 5a) states: "It is the way of human beings that when one sells a desired item to another, the seller grieves while the buyer rejoices. The Holy One, Blessed Be He, however, is different. He gave the Torah to Israel and rejoiced." Muffs interprets the passage as follows: "Whereas humans part with their goods half-heartedly—even for a price—God parts with his precious possession—the Torah, with complete willingness."[13]

Muffs' philological excursion through the biblical and later rabbinic sources, from the legal and non-legal midrash to the clearly liturgical, is in the service of exposing the religious phenomenology that animates the Bible and the early rabbis. Joy, he writes, is the word used to express the free and gracious will that underpins a divine gift; the willing and joyful alacrity with which a human reciprocates the divine gifts and blessings with sacrifices, tithes, and offerings and, finally, the spontaneity with which individuals accept divine grace or the free resignation with which one accepts divine punishment.[14]

Thus, the rabbinic *simha shel mitzvah*, "the joy of the commandment," means the spontaneous willingness with which one performs the commandment rather than the emotion generated by performing the commandment. And we can now also revisit the verse in Deuteronomy, to which Rabbi Sacks drew attention, which linked the curses to an absence of joy. The curses are invoked "because you did not serve your God with joy and gladness of heart out of the abundance of all things" (Deut. 28:47). Israel, in turn, did not reciprocate God's gracious bounty with a wholehearted performance of God's commands.

We live in a very different culture today. Even a cursory look at the self-help section of a bookstore reveals numerous guides to coping with a fragmented, divided, and ambivalent self. Thus, we are accustomed to beginning sentences by referring to multiple identities (such as our professional identity, our religious identity, or our gender identity) all competing for expression and priority. We make decisions against the background of this ambivalence and mental reservation but, as the philosopher, Harry Frankfurt reminded us about human freedom: only wholehearted decisions are true decisions.[15] Joy, understood as a legal metaphor that condenses both a cognitive state of mind and a religious phenomenology reconnects us to that human capacity for wholeheartedness.

NOTES

1. See Ari Mermelstein, *Power and Emotion in Ancient Judaism* (New York: Cambridge University Press, 2021), 11–12.
2. Ephraim E. Urbach, *The Sages* (Jerusalem: Magnes Press, 1975), 390–99.
3. Rabbi Lord Jonathan Sacks, *The Pursuit of Joy*, https://aish.com/323359281.
4. Gary Anderson, *A Time to Mourn, a Time to Dance: The Expression of Grief and Joy in Israelite Religion* (Pennsylvania: Pennsylvania State Univ. Press, 1991).
5. Ibid.,108–9.
6. Ibid., 130.
7. Wesley Newcomb Hohfeld, "Some Fundamental Legal Conceptions as Applied in judicial Reasoning," *Yale Law Journal* 23 (1913): 16.
8. Yochanan Muffs, *Love and Joy: Law, Language, and Religion in Ancient Israel* (Boston: Harvard University Press, 1995).
9. Ibid., 124.
10. Ibid., 121–93.
11. Ibid., 185.
12. Ibid., 127.
13. Ibid., 130.
14. Ibid., 165–66.
15. Harry Frankfurt, *The Importance of What We Care About* (Cambridge: Cambridge University Press, 1988).

CHAPTER 20

Emotion, Connection, and Motion: Deploying Positive and Negative Emotions in Conflict Resolution

Michelle Greenberg-Kobrin

> *Peace cannot be kept by force. It can only be achieved by understanding.*
> —Albert Einstein (See Ronald W. Clark, *Einstein, The Life and Times* (New York: Avon Books, 1972), 158.)
>
> *Happiness is a byproduct of function, purpose, and conflict; those who seek happiness for itself seek victory without war.*
> —William S. Burroughs (See "An Interview with William S. Burroughs," McCaffery, Larry. and McMenamin, Jim. in Hibbard, Alan, ed. *Conversations with William S. Burroughs* (Jackson: University of Mississippi, 1999), 185ff.)

Rabbi Lord Sacks understood that positive emotions fall into three categories: prophetic happiness, which relates to the recognition of suffering and gratitude for survival; wisdom happiness, which relates to peace; and covenantal happiness, which relates to the joy of communal shared

M. Greenberg-Kobrin (✉)
Cardozo Law School, New York, NY, USA

experience. Rabbi Sacks often reflected on the role of joy. His understanding of joy is tied to community, to the acceptance of one's fate, and to the gratitude that emerges for resilience in the face of suffering. Joy, in the words of Rabbi Sacks, is "a combination of thanksgiving, humility, gratitude and memories of suffering."[1] In Rabbi Sacks' conception, joy is linked to feelings of empathy—both a connection to a past that is marked by suffering and gratitude at being alive in the moment.

Rabbi Sacks returned, again and again, to the idea of joy as a relational emotion. We are grateful that although life is fleeting, there is time to savor what has been accomplished: a job well done, a moment of spiritual reflection, and even a moment of compassion for the suffering of others. This conception of joy is inextricably linked to other people. Happiness may be the pursuit of individual fulfillment, but joy is a deeper emotion, one that is found in connective love.

These emotions—of empathy derived from having suffered, of a desire to live without conflict, and of our need for connection—can each be harnessed in the service of building peace. They can lead to a more thoughtful understanding of creative and robust approaches to conflict resolution. Such approaches go beyond assigning blame and move us forward to improving relationships and community.

There is conflict all around us: we experience it in business, politics, family, religious, and communal life. Our trending modes of communication and media thrive on drama, on pitting parties against each other and creating seemingly irreparable dichotomies. In the midst of so much conflict, it is critically important to think about negotiation and difficult conversations—moments when we try to repair arguments and smooth out differences to move forward. Historically, both popular wisdom and academic theorists have rejected the role of emotion in these challenging spaces: our shared cultural understanding is that the best negotiator is dispassionate and focused on facts and results rather than on feelings and relationships. Emotions should be repressed, remain on the side—or, better yet, at home.

Even as more modern frames around the work of peacebuilding move away from understanding the negotiator as the impersonal, emotionless automaton who leaves her feelings at the door, there are still echoes in the literature that the most successful negotiators keep their emotions firmly in check.[2] This is particularly true when we are talking about the role of positive emotion: displaying pleasure, joy, happiness, or gratitude is seen as leaving oneself open for exploitation.

We often focus primarily on substance: the nature of the disagreement, the question of who was wronged, and the matter of who is to blame. Of necessity, this is a retrospective, backward-looking interrogation, one which seeks to determine who is to blame for various elements of the dispute, whom to punish, and then whom to allocate benefits going forward to the less-blameworthy parties.

In this approach to conflict resolution, we appoint (often in actuality, sometimes only figuratively) a factfinder to determine the truth of what happened. Who did what? To whom? Who said what? Who started it? Who continued it? Who intended what? The inquiry focuses on past actions and how to best understand what happened in the past, mapping contributions to the various issues and then figuring out a future direction.

These factfinders are at best, neutral actors whose goal is to remain as passionless as possible: expressing emotion would skew (and prolong) the work of conflict resolution. The best negotiators do not display any emotion. The slightest whiff of a positive or negative emotion, the thinking goes, and the outcome would tilt in an opponent's favor.

Until recently most negotiation texts have regarded emotion—whether hot or cold—as an impediment to reaching constructive agreements. The classic book in the field, *Getting to Yes*, by Roger Fisher, William Ury, and Bruce Patton, earnestly advises readers to "separate the people from the problem," as if negotiators should be like the coolly analytic Spock in *Star Trek*, rather than flesh-and-blood human beings.[3]

In fact, this theory doesn't hold up. There are many examples where the exact opposite is true: displaying emotion can often lead to *better* outcomes. Fear can be an important driver in determining how conflict resolves, and anger, legitimately expressed, can communicate sincerity and commitment. Positive emotions can help build empathy and understanding and can facilitate communication.[4] Demonstrating and being open about positive emotions—conveying joy, satisfaction, and gratitude—can help build trust with the other parties, lead to the open communication necessary to reach mutually beneficial outcomes, and move towards problem-solving for the future rather than the retrospective blame game.[5] Expressing empathy and understanding of the other side's suffering often opens path to mutually beneficial solutions.

Rabbi Sacks' idea of joy derived from grappling with suffering and emerging more resilient can lead to peace and a focus on shared communal goals that perfectly capture a recipe for a more thoughtful, successful approach to conflict resolution, one that allows and facilitates peacebuilding. A study where outcomes are optimized demonstrates that we are better able to reach successful outcomes when we ourselves are happy. We are more generous towards others when we are in a magnanimous mood ourselves.[6] We display more goodwill towards others when someone takes the time to apologize. For example, patients are less litigious when doctors apologize for medical mistakes. These Communication-and-Resolution programs reduce malpractice suits by up to thirty percent.[7]

An oft-cited study of Israeli parole review boards demonstrated that while our understanding of the judicial review of parole decision is governed by set law, regulations, and legal formalism, these complex decisions are also informed by emotion and psychology. In the case of parole hearings, outcomes can even depend on time of day, blood sugar, and the feelings of the judges involved.[8] As human beings, rational consideration and intellectual discussions only take us so far. We are not dispassionate creatures—and emotion draws us closer or distances us, establishes connection and disconnection, and creates community or disunity. Forthright acknowledgment of our emotions around both the conflict and our interests creates a holistic experience that builds space for the repair and reconstruction of the self and of the relationship.

A secondary reason why we do not notice how costly it is to remove emotion from our deal-making is because our notions of how to resolve conflict focus on resolving the substance of the issue. We forget that in order to resolve conflicts meaningfully, we must focus not only on substance but also on the process we use to resolve the conflict, as well as the relationship between the parties themselves. For parties to progress, both need to feel that a fair process was utilized: one that felt right and good to the parties. The perception of fairness is often grounded more deeply in the process than in the outcome. We are often able to accept outcomes less favorable to us if we feel that the process utilized was a fair one.

Almost by definition, significant conflict implies that there is a challenge between parties that needs to be resolved in a way that creates the possibility and structure for reconciliation and a future relationship. The critical emotional element to this work is trust. Trust-building helps parties assume equal footing and a parity of emotions on issues of disagreement. Understanding that there has been suffering, pain, and loss on both sides, and that both sides are capable of emerging from suffering rather than each elevating victimhood, is a significant step towards rebuilding the relationship that can lead to meaningful reconciliation.

Rabbi Sacks understood the role emotions play in outcomes. He writes both about the importance of reason and logic as well as the limits of wisdom. He writes of the need for emotion and an emotional connection to religion and to others. His emphasis on joy, as a rational and intellectual philosopher speaking primarily to a rational and intellectually minded audience, underscores this. We exist in various states of conflict—of our secular selves in conflict with our religious identities, within our individual goals, work, and family, and times when we feel in conflict with larger communal, political, and spiritual goals. There's a way across the aisle, a way in and a way to reconcile. That way includes our emotions. Expressions of emotion can unlock a sealed door. Joy, gratitude, and remembrance of past suffering build connections, open us up to community, and bring us closer to the forces around us. Admitting our vulnerabilities and proclivities allows us to move beyond a papering over of past conflict towards a more restorative state of peacebuilding.

Notes

1. Rabbi Lord Jonathan Sacks, *Introduction to the Koren Sukkot Machzor* (Jerusalem: Koren Publishers, 2015), xxii–xxiii.
2. ADR Times, "Mastering your Emotions in Conflict Resolution," *Alternative Dispute Resolution Times* (June 16, 2021). See https://www.adrtimes.com/master-your-emotions/, last viewed on 1/22/23.
3. Kimberlyn Leary, Juliana Pillemer, and Michael Wheeler. "Negotiation with Emotion," *Harvard Business Review* (January–February 2013), https://hbr.org/2013/01/negotiating-with-emotion.
4. Studies have shown that positive emotions can actually help facilitate a more favorable outcome, and feelings like anxiety or nervousness can be channeled to achieve success. When people reframe their anxiety as excitement, they perform better. A. W. Brooks, "'Get Excited: Reappraising Pre-Performance Anxiety as Excitement,'" *Journal of Experimental Psychology: General* 143, no. 3 (June 2014): 1144–58.
5. Robert S. Adler, Benson Rosen, and Elliot M. Silverstein, "Emotions in Negotiation: How to Manage Fear and Anger," *Negotiation Journal* 14, no. 2 (April 1998): 168.
6. See, for example, S. Lyubomirsky, L. King, and E. Diener. (2005) "The Benefits of Frequent Positive Affect: Does Happiness Lead to Success?" *Psychological Bulletin* 131, no. 6 (2005): 803–55.

7. F. R. LeCraw, S. C. Stearns, and M. J. McCoy, "How U.S. Teams Advanced Communication and Resolution Program Adoption at Local, State and National Levels," *Journal of Patient Safety and Risk Management*, 26, no. 1 (March 2021): 34–40.
8. Shai Danziger, Jonathan Levav, and Liora Avnaim-Pesso, "Extraneous Factors in Judicial Decisions," *Proceedings of the National Academy of Science of the United States* (PNAS), 108 (2011): 17.

PART V

Joy in Jewish Philosophy and Kabbalah

CHAPTER 21

Happiness and Joy: Rabbi Sacks' Dialogue of Athens and Jerusalem

Hava Tirosh-Samuelson

The dialogue of "Athens" and "Jerusalem" was the life's project and legacy of Rabbi Lord Jonathan Sacks. Rabbi Sacks engaged Western culture critically from a Judaic perspective, and, conversely, he interpreted Jewish tradition in the light of Western culture, especially its philosophy, history, and literature. In so doing, Rabbi Sacks left for posterity not only a coherent vision for how Jews could and should live in the contemporary secular world but also a compelling model for how the dialogue among civilizations, cultures, and ideologies could and should be conducted. His dialogical model is based on mutual respect, genuine curiosity, intellectual openness, civility, and compassion.[1] Perpetuating and expanding Rabbi Samson Raphael Hirsch's vision of *Torah im derekh eretz* [Torah and the way of the land], Rabbi Sacks responded to the challenges of contemporary life which Hirsch could not have anticipated: modern secularism, globalized capitalism, deconstructive postmodernism, hedonistic atheism, evolutionary Darwinism, and technoscientific transhumanism. In his critical but respectful conversation with contemporary Western culture, Rabbi

H. Tirosh-Samuelson (✉)
Arizona State University, Tempe, AZ, USA

© The Author(s), under exclusive license to Springer Nature Switzerland AG 2023
E. Brown, S. Weiss (eds.), *An Ode to Joy*,
https://doi.org/10.1007/978-3-031-28229-4_21

Sacks universalized Jewish particularity.[2] Namely, he presented the beliefs, practices, and values of Judaism as a universal vision for humanity, offering a radical notion of freedom and responsibility that addresses contemporary social ills.[3] The Judaic worldview and way of life, he maintained, assures the attainment of what all humans seek—that is, happiness—while teaching humanity the true meaning of happiness—that is, joy.

Rabbi Sacks' upbringing illustrated the integration of Judaic and secular knowledge characteristic of modern Orthodoxy. Although he was born into a traditional Jewish family, Rabbi Sacks was educated at Saint Mary's Primary School and Christ's College High School in London, and thereafter at Cambridge University, where he read philosophy under the tutorship of Bernard Williams (d. 2003). The atheist Williams compelled him, in his words, "to examine my own faith in depth,"[4] and to wrestle not only with the Tertullian's old question, "What does Athens have to do with Jerusalem?" but also with the internal contradictions within his own religious faith. As a philosophy student, Sacks was fully aware of the changes in British academe: logical positivism, which had dominated academic philosophy since the 1920s, "has reached a dead end,"[5] and the dominant theories of moral philosophy—deontology and consequentialism—were challenged as inherently flawed. The charge was articulated by G.E.M Anscombe, a Catholic philosopher, in her essay "Modern Moral Philosophy," in which she charged that the secular approaches to moral philosophy are unjustified because they use concepts such as "morally ought," "morally right," or "morally obligated," which are legal concepts that presuppose a legislator as the source of moral authority.[6] In the past, God occupied that role, but since modern secular moral philosophies dispensed with God, they lacked the proper foundation for meaningful employment of those concepts. Anscombe called for developing an alternative theory to the dominant moral theories, a theory that would be based on moral psychology, moral virtue, the facts of human nature, and an account of the good for humans. Moral philosophy should center on the concept of virtue and human flourishing, or happiness (*eudaimonia*), as Aristotle taught in the *Nicomachean Ethics* and all ancient moral philosophers accepted in their theorizing about happiness.[7]

Thus began the revival of virtue ethics in contemporary philosophy that would shape the intellectual identity of Rabbi Sacks.[8] Interpreting Judaism through the prism of virtue ethics, the young Sacks emerged as a "religiously committed moral philosopher who must live by the precepts of his or her religion but, as a philosopher must remain open to further dialogue."[9] Throughout his adult life, Rabbi Sacks reflected on happiness by taking Aristotle as his point of departure because "Aristotle gave the West its most influential analysis of happiness … We undertake all activities for the sake of some good, but there is only one good that we seek as an end in itself and for no other reason: namely *eudaimonia*, his term for happiness."[10] But as a traditional Jew, an ordained rabbi, and a scholar of Judaism, Rabbi Sacks had to ask: Does Aristotle's analysis of happiness accord with the values of Judaism, or does Judaism offer an alternative understanding of happiness? Is it true that happiness is "an activity of the soul in accordance with virtue," as Aristotle said, or does happiness mean "living in accord with the world and will of God, which is how the Bible construes moral life?"[11] For Rabbi Sacks, as for many Jewish philosophers who preceded him, happiness was the lens through which to explore the relationship between "Athens" and "Jerusalem," that is, between religion and philosophy, between Torah and Wisdom.[12]

In his essay, "Happiness: A Jewish Perspective," Rabbi Sacks succinctly summarizes his view on Judaism and happiness: "Happiness is not central to the Judaic value system. It is not the telos of human activity. Judaism is the pursuit of holiness, not the pursuit of happiness. Happiness may be the result, but it is not the aim."[13] This statement juxtaposes "Athens" and "Jerusalem;" whereas the former is interested in the pursuit of happiness, the latter is interested in holiness. Rabbi Sacks, of course, was fully aware that the Hebrew Bible does not ignore "happiness" (*osher*). After all, the Book of Psalms opens with the following statement:

> Happy is the man who has not walked in the counsel of the wicked, nor stood in the way of sinners or sat where scoffers sit. But his desire is in the Torah of the Lord; on his Torah he meditates day and night. He shall be like a tree planted by streams of water, bearing its fruit in its season, and its leaf does not wither, and in all that he does he prospers.[14]

The powerful imagery of Psalm 1 expresses the Judaic understanding of happiness: the best-lived life is one devoted to the Torah of God; through it one can become righteous, just as God is righteous. The study of God's Torah itself constitutes the life in which humans can flourish, or more to the point: Jews can flourish if and only if they live the life of Torah. In a Torah-centered life, Rabbi Sacks explains, "*Ashrei* is a state of one who has lived in accordance with the will of God, a person who is good and does good, who honors God and his or her fellow creatures, who has been blessed in life and who, living among the righteous is held in high regard. The is the happiness of balance and virtue, of justice and compassion, of living well and faring well."[15] For Jews, "living well and faring well," which is how Aristotle defined *eudaimonia*, is inseparable from a range of religious values, such as blessedness, righteousness, justice, lovingkindness, loyalty, love, and, above all, holiness.

Although traditional Jews recite the *Ashrei* prayer three times a day,[16] Rabbi Sacks insists that "*ashrei* is not the central value of the Hebrew Bible."[17] If so, what is the central value of the Judaic life of holiness? Sacks answers that joy (*simha*) is the key value of Judaism, and he explains: "the noun *simha* and the verb *s-m-ch* ... [mean] joy, rejoicing, elation, celebration. It is a mood, but it is also a mode of being, of living in a state of thankfulness."[18] Put differently, the life of religious Jews is not governed by the pursuit of happiness, as Aristotle and Western philosophers have maintained and as popular culture takes for granted, but is rather a life in "the pursuit of joy," the title of Rabbi Sacks' exposition of *Parashat Ki Tavo*.[19] Rabbi Sacks, then, differentiates between "happiness" and "joy." He explains their difference as follows: "unlike *osher/ashrei*, which is predicated on the individual as individual, *simha* is essentially collective. It only exists in virtue of being shared. It is a form of social happiness."[20] The Book of Deuteronomy, where the root *s-m-ch* appears 12 times, captures what is distinctive about the Judaic conception of joy. Joy, Rabbi Sacks teaches, is communal rather than individual; it is relational rather than self-centered; it is rooted in memory and history, and it is "the way a culture is geared to sense of gratitude."[21] Deuteronomy, in short, articulates what Rabbi Sacks names "covenantal happiness" or "social happiness," a vision of a good society in which all members experience happiness and not just the philosophical elite.

The biblical vision of "covenantal happiness" is distinguished by several features.[22] First, covenantal happiness is experienced in the here and now rather than in the afterlife; second, covenantal happiness eschews asceticism, involving embodied activities and physical pleasures derived from food, drink, and sexual relations; third, covenantal happiness is linked to justice, addressing the needs of the poor and the socially marginal; third, covenantal happiness privileges the social order over the civic or political order. The covenantal virtues of righteousness (*tzedek*), justice (*mishpat*), loving-kindness (*hessed*), and compassion (*rahamim*) are practiced in the extended family and the local community rather than in the civic arena of the state as it was for the Greeks; fourth, covenantal happiness is egalitarian and non-hierarchical since everyone shares a "sense of human dignity and inclusion, especially when it comes to the festivals, the moments of collective celebration;"[23] fifth, memory of God's intervention in history and gratitude for God's benevolence are central elements of joy because they focus "our attention on what we have not on what we lack; on what we possess, not what others possess."[24] This societal understanding of happiness is celebrated every week in the Sabbath, a ritual that enables Jews to have "a foretaste of the ideal society which is the opposite of Egypt in which there is a hierarchy of power and in which strangers are enslaved."[25] The Sabbath and its openness toward the undetermined future establishes a "culture of hope," a culture that is based on "strong emotional bonds of love and loyalty" because it does not regard the universe as "fundamentally hostile or indifferent."[26] In short, according to Rabbi Sacks, Judaism's vision of covenantal or social happiness was an alternative to the Aristotelian conception of happiness (as he interprets it). Whereas the Aristotelian vision is individual, passive, cerebral, and contemplative, the Judaic vision is communal, relational, affective, and action-oriented.

Rabbi Sacks' rendering of Judaism as the happy life of Torah is powerful and compelling, and it offers a very viable response to the social ills of contemporary society. But did Rabbi Sacks do justice to the dialogue between Judaism and the Aristotelian tradition? I humbly submit that he did not. Medieval Jewish philosophy was much more indebted to Aristotle's analysis of happiness than Rabbi Sacks acknowledges. A case in point is Maimonides who, as Diana Lobel nicely put it, "interprets Biblical texts and oral rabbinic traditions in light of Aristotelian thought in a way that is highly original and creative."[27] Maimonides was familiar with Aristotle's *Nicomachean Ethics* through the Arabic translation of Alfarabi, and Maimonides was the first Jew to interpret the rabbinic notion of religious perfection (*shlemut*) in the context of Aristotelian virtue ethics. For Maimonides, there was no conflict between Judaism and Greek philosophy, provided both were properly understood. Moreover, it is only the mastery of Aristotelian physics, metaphysics, psychology, and ethics along with Plato's political theory that enables the Jewish believer to interpret the Torah of Moses correctly. Indeed, in the *Guide of the Perplexed*, Maimonides presented Moses as the "masters of all philosophers" as well as the "master of all prophets" and suggested that the inner, esoteric meaning of the Torah is identical to what is true in philosophy since truth cannot be self-contradictory. Focusing on Maimonides, modern historians of medieval Jewish philosophy have wrestled with the relationship between "Athens" and "Jerusalem," and this scholarship made it clear that Maimonides was deeply indebted to Aristotle and his Muslim interpreters, Alfarabi, Avicenna, ibn Bajja, and ibn Tufail. The literature on Maimonides's conception of happiness is too extensive to be cited here in full,[28] but remarkably Rabbi Sacks made no mention of it in his reflections on happiness and joy.

When contemporary scholarship on Maimonides is consulted, it is difficult to accept the radical differentiation between Aristotelian "happiness" and Judaic "joy" posited by Rabbi Sacks. To begin, Aristotle's analysis of happiness left for posterity an ambiguous legacy that requires close reading: in Books 8–9 of the *Nicomachean Ethics*, the ideal life is experienced in the socio-political sphere, especially with friends with whom one can cultivate the virtues, but in Book 10, Aristotle presented contemplation of necessary truths (*theoria*) as the ideal life for humans. Modern scholars of Aristotle have long debated this tension and sought to resolve it differently, but without reaching consensus.[29] Maimonides inherited that ambiguity and made it even more complicated because he accessed Aristotle through the Muslim philosophers who were divided on the issue. Furthermore, Maimonides intentionally obfuscated his views by conveying them through parables, following Plato, who believed that philosophy could only be taught through parables. Thus, Maimonides left for posterity an insoluble puzzle that invites all future readers to unpack it without a simple resolution.[30] How one interprets Maimonides tells us more about the interpreter than about Maimonides' original intent, and each interpretation is necessarily partial and incomplete.

It is well known that in the *Guide of the Perplexed* III: 27; III:51, and III: 54, Maimonides differentiated between "perfection of the body" (*tikkun ha-guf*) and "perfection of the soul" (*tikkun ha-nefesh*), explaining how the acquisition of virtues facilitates the attainment of happiness.[31] Crucially, Maimonides classified the moral virtues as part of the former category, and he made it quite clear that moral perfection in the sociopolitical sphere is not the ultimate end of human life. Maimonides stated that true human perfection

> consists in the acquisition of the rational virtues—I refer to the conception of the intelligibles which teach true opinions concern the divine things. This is in true reality the ultimate end; this is what gives the individual true

perfection, a perfection belongs to him alone; and it gives him permanent perdurance; through it man is man.[32]

The ultimate end of human, the *sommum bonum*, consists of the perfection of the intellect and requires the acquisition of intellectual virtues. Attaining intellectual perfection requires contemplation of necessary truths, an activity that requires some degree of social isolation. Moreover, only contemplation leads to the immortality of the intellect when the human soul is separated from the corporeal body at death. Precisely because Maimonides read Aristotle through the mediation of Muslim philosophers, Maimonides' view of the ultimate end of human life was intellectualist, elitist, individualistic, and quite ascetic.[33]

If so, can Maimonides' conception of intellectual perfection be reconciled with the halakhic obligation to rejoice? What is the place of joy in the teachings of Maimonides? In 1980, two years before Rabbi Sacks received his Ph.D. from King's College London, Gerald Blidstein addressed these questions in an essay on joy in the writings of Maimonides.[34] Consulting Maimonides's halakhic and philosophic works, Blidstein explained how Maimonides linked joy to physical and mental health, how joy functions in moral and spiritual growth, how joy is translated into social action and care for the marginal, and how joy is connected to the knowledge and love God, all the aspects of joy that Rabbi Sacks would later explicate. Blidstein further showed that for Maimonides, joy also has an ecstatic dimension because it is a precondition to prophecy, but prophecy, he was careful to note, is an intellectual phenomenon: an overflow from the Active Intellect onto the human intellect. The more liberated one's intellect is from corporeal embodiment, the more one is prepared to receive the prophetic overflow. Joy, then, was not simply an affective emotion that one experiences in the worship of God and through interaction with people. For Maimonides, joy was predicated on knowledge of God.

The connection between joy, intellectual perfection, and knowledge of God was further explicated by Moshe Sokol, who showed how Aristotle's *Nicomachean Ethics* shaped Maimonides' interpretation of the commandment to rejoice in the festival of Sukkot, since "leisure provides the possibility of the contemplative life."[35] Sokol compellingly argued that the three pilgrimage festivals pertain only to "*tikkun ha-guf* morality," unlike the commandment to rejoice in Purim, since "Purim more than any other holiday provides insights into the astonishing work of providence."[36] Purim is different because "it reveals the meaning behind the suffering its story relates, and the ways in which Jewish tragedy providentially gives way to salvation. So too the messianic era will reveal that same providence hidden behind exile."[37] Sokol's analysis of joy in Maimonides' teachings exposes a much deeper reliance on Aristotle than Rabbi Sacks allows, but on reading Sokol (and Blidstein) one could see that Sacks' analysis of joy as "social happiness" took its cue from Maimonides's halakhic works.

The tension between the social and intellectual dimensions of happiness is explored in another insightful essay by Moshe Sokol, where he pondered the paradox of Maimonides' life; his busy professional life as a court physician and his responsibilities as a communal leader prevented him from "achieving human excellence as he Maimonides himself understood it."[38] Sokol shows how "the highly intellectualist conception of the good, explained in the context of Maimonides' account of mitzvot and ultimately drawn from Aristotle, explicitly excludes actions or moral qualities."[39] Carefully considering Maimonides's view on the relationship between philosophy and prophecy, between the sage (*hakham*) and the saint (*hasid*), Sokol highlights the "tragic conflict in which Maimonides is trapped between two incommensurable goods, two competing obligations much like the heroes of ancient Greek tragedies were themselves caught in such irreconcilable conflicts."[40] Sokol concludes that "it is altogether likely that at some point in his life he [i.e., Maimonides] was beset by serious conflict as he sought to reconcile his Jewish and philosophical commitments."[41] If Sokol is correct, this tragic view of life did not characterize ancient Greek philosophers alone, as Rabbi Sacks suggested[42]; it afflicted Maimonides as well, even though as an observant Jew he experienced the joy of worshipping God.

I do not know why Rabbi Sacks, whose knowledge was so extensive and inclusive, chose to ignore the scholarship on medieval Jewish philosophy, especially on Maimonides. I can only conjecture that when he embraced the rabbinate as his chosen path in life, he renounced academic scholarship produced by historians of Jewish philosophy. Instead, he preferred to become a teacher for all people, philosophers and non-philosophers, academics and non-academics, Jews, and non-Jews. Viewing teaching as a mode of leadership, it was leadership (rather than the academic study of Judaism) that the Jewish people needed most in his judgement, because "in Judaism leadership is not a luxury but a necessity."[43] Emulating *Moshe Rabeinu* ("Moses, our teacher"),[44] Rabbi Sacks was committed to making Judaism as accessible as possible to all, using a literary style that interwove personal narratives, anecdotes, and encounters to illustrate Judaism as an ethics of freedom and responsibility. Rabbi Sacks preferred to teach through the heuristic device of the "drama of ideas," which made his writings accessible, interesting, and personally meaningful to everyone. He could not have become the leader he was had he adopted the lugubrious, pedantic, and cautious style of academic scholarship. Using ideal types to illustrate the drama of ideas, Rabbi Sacks practiced the dialogue between Athens and Jerusalem effectively, while defending "the dignity of difference."[45] The conversation between Athens and Jerusalem was not to erase the particularity of Judaism; it was to universalize that particularity.

Rabbi Sacks' exposition of happiness and joy was not intended to be a lesson in the history of philosophy but an invitation for Jews and non-Jews to reflect on the meaning of the well-lived life. To non-Jews, who know little about Judaism or who hold misleading views (e.g., that Judaism is only about law but not about love), and to secular Jews, who greatly contributed to contemporary culture but who forsook their own religious identity, Rabbi Sacks explicated the radical insights of Judaism about freedom and responsibility, which he believed are most meaningful to addressing our contemporary social ills. Today, happiness is misunderstood because it is identified with hedonistic consumerism, self-absorbed individualism, and irrational emotionalism. In his last publication, *Morality: Restoring the Common Good in Divided Times*, Rabbi Sacks critiqued the culture of "I" that has corroded the common good, led to the breakdown of society, and to the inability to reason together civilly. To this divided, fragmented, and broken social world, Rabbi Sacks presented his interpretation of Judaism in which love, loyalty, commitment, compassion, and joy constitute "covenantal happiness."

In the Judaic vision of the ideal society, people care for each other, support the poor and the socially marginal, and resist consumerism, hedonism, and the commodification of life by technology. Because he was immersed in contemporary culture, Rabbi Sacks was aware of the "science of happiness" developed by economists, sociologists, and psychologists.[46] Although he used their empirical findings, he did not think that the science of happiness could lead us to live well and fare well because it lacks the relational dimension that only religion can offer, and it ignored the fact that happiness and joy resist quantification because they are predicated on human freedom. Privileging the "We" over the "I," Rabbi Sacks promoted pluralism that defended "the dignity of difference" against multiculturalism, and that called all people to rebuild our social home together freely and responsibly.[47] In his socially and politically engaged life, Rabbi

Sacks served as a spiritual guide to the contemporary perplexed, showing how a philosopher-teacher could lead, and how Judaism could "heal a fractured world."

Notes

1. This dialogue model is explicated in Jonathan Sacks, *The Dignity of Difference: How to Avoid the Clash of Civilizations*, rev. edition (London: Bloomsbury, 2003).
2. See *Jonathan Sacks: Universalizing Particularity*, eds. Hava Tirosh-Samuelson and Aaron W. Hughes (Leiden: Brill, 2013).
3. Jonathan Sacks, *Radical Then, Radical Now: On Being Jewish* (London: Bloomsbury Academic, 2004). For analysis of Sacks' message see Michael J. Harris, Daniel Rynhold, and Tamra Right, eds., *Radical Responsibility: Celebrating the Thought of Chief Rabbi Lord Jonathan Sacks* (Jerusalem: Maggid Books, 2012).
4. Jonathan Sacks, "Finding God," in *Jonathan Sacks: Universalizing Particularity*, 25.
5. Sacks, "Finding God," ibid.
6. G.E.M. Anscombe, "Modern Moral Philosophy," *Philosophy* 33, no. 4 (1958): 1–19.
7. The literature on Aristotle's *Nicomachean Ethics* is too extensive to be cited here. Most useful is Sarah Broadie, *Ethics with Aristotle* (Oxford: Oxford University Press, 1993).
8. For an overview of virtue ethics and the major contributors to the discourse see, Daniel C. Russell, *The Cambridge Companion of Virtue Ethics* (Cambridge: Cambridge University Press, 2013). On Rabbi Sacks' integration of virtue ethics and Judaism, see Alasdair MacIntyre, "Torah and Moral Philosophy," in *Radical Responsibility*, 3–16.
9. Michael J. Harris and Daniel Rynhold, "Torah and Wisdom in a Secular Age," in *Radical Responsibility*, xix.
10. Jonathan Sacks, *Morality: Restoring the Common Good in Divided Times* (New York: Basic Books, 2020), 100.
11. Ibid., 101.
12. On the history of Jewish discourse on happiness, see Hava Tirosh-Samuelson, *Happiness in Premodern Judaism: Virtue, Knowledge and Well-Being* (Cincinnati: Hebrew Union College, 2003).
13. Rabbi Lord Jonathan Sacks, "Happiness: A Jewish Perspective," *Journal of Law and Religion* 29, no. 1 (2014): 30–47, quote on 32.
14. Ps. 1:1–3.
15. Sacks, "Happiness: A Jewish Perspective," 34.

16. The prayer known as *Ashrei* consists of Ps. 145 in its entirety to which were added Ps. 84:5 and Ps. 144:15 in the beginning and Psalm 115:18 in the end and the prayer links happiness to the sacred myth of Judaism.
17. Sacks, "The Pursuit of Joy," in *Covenant and Conversation*", Parashat Ki Tavo, 5775, available at https://www.rabbisacks.org; Cf., Sacks, "The Deep Power of Joy," *Covenant and Conversation*, Parashat Re'eh, 5776, available at https://www.rabbisacks.org.
18. Sacks, "Happiness: A Jewish Perspective," 38.
19. Sacks, "The Pursuit of Joy," *Covenant and Conversation*, 5775.
20. Sacks, "Happiness: A Jewish Perspective," 38.
21. Ibid., 39.
22. This paragraph summarizes Sacks, "Happiness: A Jewish Perspective," 40–44.
23. Ibid., 42.
24. Ibid., 43.
25. Ibid., 43.
26. Ibid., 44.
27. Diana Lobel, *Philosophies of Happiness: A Comparative Introduction to the Flourishing Life* (New York: Columbia University Press, 2017), 163.
28. Among the numerous studies are Norman Roth, "Attaining 'Happiness (*Eudaimonia*) in Medieval Muslim and Jewish Philosophy," *Centerpoint* 4 (1981): 21–32; Daniel H. Frank, "The End of the *Guide*: Maimonides on the Best Life of Man," *Judaism* 34 (1985): 485–95; Lawrence V. Berman, "The Ethical Views of Maimonides within the Context of Islamicate Civilization," in *Perspective on Maimonides: Philosophical and Historical Studies*, ed. Joel L. Kraemer (Oxford: Oxford University Press for the Littman Library, 1991), 13–32; Howard Kreisel, "Individual Perfection vs. Communal Welfare and the Problem of Contradictions in Maimonides Approach to Ethics, *Proceedings of the American Academy for Jewish Research* 58 (1992), reprinted in his *Maimonides' Political Thought: Studies in Ethics, Law, and the Human Ideal* (Albany, NY: 1999), 159–88; Raymond L. Weiss, *Maimonides' Ethics: The Encounter of Philosophic and Religious Morality* (Chicago: University of Chicago Press, 1991); Steven Harvey, "Maimonides in the Sultan's Palace," in *Perspectives on Maimonides*, ed. Joel I. Kraemer (Oxford University Press, 1991), 47–75; Lenn E. Goodman, *Maimonides and His Time* (Albany, NY: SUNY Press, 2009).
29. See Tirosh-Samuelson, *Happiness in Premodern Judaism*, 40–45.
30. See, ibid., 192–245, and the secondary literature cited there.
31. For analysis see Menachem Marc Kellner, *Maimonides on Human Perfection*, Brown Judaica Series (Atlanta: Scholars Press, 1990).
32. Maimonides, *The Guide of the Perplexed* III:54, trans. and ed. Shlomo Pines (Chicago: University of Chicago Press, 1963), 635.

33. This interpretation was promoted especially in David R. Blumenthal, *Philosophic Mysticism: Essays on Rational Religion* (Bar Ilan University Press, 2006).
34. Gerald Blidstein "*Ha-Simha be-Mishnato Ha-Musarit shel Ha-Rambmam,*" *Eshel Beer Sheva* 2 (1980): 145–63.
35. Moshe Sokol, "Maimonides on Joy," in *Judaism Examined: Essays in Jewish Philosophy and Ethics* (New York: Touro College Press and Boston: Academic Studies Press, 2013), 12–29; citation on p. 20. The essay originally appeared in *Maimonides and His Time*, ed. Lenn E. Goodman (Albany, NY SUNY Press, 2009).
36. Sokol, "Maimonides on Joy," 26.
37. Ibid., 29.
38. Moshe Sokol, "The Tragedy of Excellence: Maimonides on the Philosophical Life," in his *Judaism Examined: Essays in Jewish Philosophy an Ethics*, 31–66, citation on p. 33.
39. Sokol, "The Tragedy of Excellence," ibid.
40. Ibid., 54.
41. Ibid., 64.
42. On the contrast between the tragic view of life characteristic of Greek philosophy and the Judaic commitment to joy see Jonathan Sacks, *To Heal a Fractured World: The Ethics of Responsibility* (New York: Schocken Books, 2005), 175–81.
43. Rabbi Jonathan Sacks, *Lessons in Leadership: A Weekly Reading of the Jewish Bible* (Jerusalem: Maggid Books, 2015), 234.
44. Sacks, *Lessons in Leadership*, 242.
45. Jonathan Sacks, *The Dignity of Difference: How to Avoid the Clash of Civilization* (London: Bloomsbury, 2003).
46. The *Journal of Happiness Studies: An Interdisciplinary Forum on Subjective Well-Being* was founded in 2000 by Ruut Veenhioven, Ed Diener, and Alex C. Michalos. Since then, the literature on the science of happiness has proliferated. Major contributions include Robert Layard, *Happiness: Lessons from a New Science* (2005, 2011); Martin Seligman, *Authentic Happiness: Using the New Positive Psychology to Realize Your Potential for Lasting Fulfillment* (2002); Jonathan Haidt, *The Happiness Hypothesis: Finding Moral Truth in Ancient Wisdom* (2006), and Sonja Lybomirsky, *The How of Happiness: A Scientific Approach to Getting the Life You Want* (2007).
47. Jonathan Sacks, *The Home We Build Together: Recreating Society* (London: Bloomsbury, 2007).

CHAPTER 22

Crescas and Rabbi Sacks on Happiness and Joy

Samuel Lebens

To the extent that happiness and joy were a preoccupation for Rabbi Sacks, it might be fruitful to curate a conversation between him and the great medieval philosopher of joy, Ḥasdai Crescas. In what follows, I seek to lay the foundation for just such an encounter between these two thinkers.

From Maimonides to Crescas

Medieval philosophers tended to view our emotional life as a function of our animality. Positive emotions would be associated with the satisfaction of our appetite and imagination, and negative emotions with their frustration. This conception of our emotional life is ultimately credited to Aristotle.[1] Perhaps unsurprisingly, Maimonides adopted this Aristotelian view without question, even though it entails that God, being pure intellect, and possessing no animal soul, and having no need for anything, and, therefore, having no appetite, could have no emotional life. But doesn't the Bible describe God as having all sorts of emotions?

S. Lebens (✉)
University of Haifa, Haifa, Israel

© The Author(s), under exclusive license to Springer Nature Switzerland AG 2023
E. Brown, S. Weiss (eds.), *An Ode to Joy*,
https://doi.org/10.1007/978-3-031-28229-4_22

Here's how Maimonides resolves the problem. Whenever the Bible says that "God has emotion X", it *really* means that God's causal imprint on the world around us corresponds to the causal imprint that *our* actions tend to have when *we* are motivated by X.[2] In other words, given the causal imprint that God leaves on the world, we experience Him *as if* He experiences changing emotional states. Sometimes we experience Him as if He's angry, and sometimes as if He's happy or sad. Nevertheless, and despite these appearances, there are no emotions in the mental life of God Himself.

In a sense, Maimonides was being more Aristotelian than Aristotle. In his book, the *Metaphysics*, Aristotle describes God as the object of the *eros* of the world (in other words, as the Being that all creatures desire to approach),[3] but he also claims that God experiences pleasure (in Greek: *hedone*).[4] In other words, according to Aristotle, God somehow enjoys being God! But Maimonides would have none of it. Pure intellect, with no appetite, can experience no emotion.

Many other influential Aristotelians in the Middle Ages were somewhat less austere than Maimonides when it came to Divine emotions. Following Aristotle's lead, they were happy to say that there is one exception to the emotional vacuum in the Divine mind. The one emotion that God constantly experiences, they claim, is joy. In the Christian tradition, this position is advanced by Aquinas (among others).[5] In the Jewish Aristotelian tradition, it is advanced, most famously, by Gersonides.

Gersonides accepts that God is pure intellect and that he has neither appetite nor passion. But there is one form of joy that Gersonides (like Aquinas) would insist we should relate to, not as animalistic but as an *intellectual emotion*, and that emotion is "intellectual pleasure." In actual fact, even Maimonides was committed to the existence of this phenomenon (if only in the case of human intellects). Afterall, Maimonides endorsed a conception of the afterlife as a blissful *disembodied* experience in which only the intellect survives and *enjoys* an uninterrupted beatific vision (i.e., a Divine revelation).[6] In other words, the intellect in heaven, without any bodily form, and without any appetite, can still enjoy itself. But what does it enjoy? Well, it enjoys thinking. The better the thing it's thinking about, the more it enjoys itself. It was with this sort of intellectual joy in mind that Aquinas and Gersonides attribute joy to God. Gersonides writes:

> It may be demonstrated that His pleasure and joy in His apprehension is the most perfect possible, as the philosopher [i.e., Aristotle] has made clear. For

apprehension is pleasurable to those who apprehend, and the more numerous and noble the objects of apprehension, the greater the pleasure and joy. Accordingly, His joy and pleasure in what He apprehends is the ultimate of what is possible, for He apprehends all things, and apprehends them in the most noble way possible.[7]

Crescas was unimpressed by this attempt to introduce joy into the mental life of God. In fact, he thinks it would be wholly inappropriate to predicate intellectual joy of God. That sort of joy would be an appropriate response either to the *surprise* of discovering a new fact or to overcoming an intellectual obstacle. But God never transitions from ignorance to knowledge. Accordingly, He's never surprised. Moreover, there are no intellectual obstacles in His way. For these reasons, God would never have the sort of experience that gives rise to intellectual joy.[8]

In order to make sense of the claim that God experiences joy, Crescas would have us distinguish between two *types* of joy. The first is a *passion* that we human beings experience as we "transition from potentiality to actuality in the attainment of a desired goal."[9] The greater the transition, or the greater the challenge, the greater the joy. But, as we've seen, God doesn't face any challenges. God is also unchanging since He never has any *need* to change. After all, He's totally independent and self-sufficient. Accordingly, He never undergoes transition, from ignorance to knowledge, or from hunger to satiation, or from any one state to another. Without transition and without challenge, God can't experience the passion of joy.

Once we rule out joy as a passion, we can move over to the notion of joy as an *action*. According to Crescas, God's joy is nothing more than the action of creation. He enjoys giving being to others.[10] As Warren Zev Harvey memorably puts the point:

> When [Crescas] attributes joy and love to God, he attributes them to Him not as *passions*, but as *actions*. In Crescas' Hebrew terminology, God, in His joy, is *po'el* (Agent, Maker, Efficient Cause), not *mitpa'el* (suffering passion or emotion). *Our* joy and love are effects and are affective, but *God's* joy and love are causes and not affective. *Our* joy and love are in our being actualized, *God's* is in His actualizing.[11]

God's joy is not a passion because it isn't *passive*. That doesn't mean joy as an action feels like nothing. If God were feeling nothing on the inside, after all, we'd be back to the Maimonidean God of pure intellect. We've come a long way from there. For Maimonides, it is God's intellectual activity that is the cause of the universe. For Crescas, by contrast, the ultimate cause of the universe is nothing other than God's infinite joy and love.[12] Moreover, as far as Crescas is concerned, the very same joy that we experience as passive recipients is what God experiences, so to speak, from the other side, as its cause. It is joy that we share.[13]

Crescas and Rabbi Sacks

On one crucial issue, there is a great lacuna between the thought of Crescas and the thought of Rabbi Sacks. As far as Rabbi Sacks is concerned, the belief in the radically free will of human beings is a fundamental principle of Judaism as a religion. Indeed, he went so far as to call it the "fourteenth principle of faith."[14] Crescas, by contrast, is famous for being the main rabbinic philosopher to have believed in a rigid determinism and to have thought that, at best, we have a so-called compatibilist freedom (that is to say: a species of freedom that's compatible with the fact that all of our thoughts and actions are determined by prior causes), and at worst, to have thought that our free will is nothing more than an illusion.

But, when it comes to the study of joy, it seems that Crescas and Rabbi Sacks would have made especially good *chevrutot* (study partners). I say this because each of them held views about the nature of joy that shed light upon, or offered interesting support to, the views of the other.

Rabbi Sacks was keen on the distinction between zero-sum goods and social goods. Zero-sum goods are those goods that get distributed by the market and the State, such as money and power. They are zero-sum because the more that you share them, the less you end up with:

> That is why governments and markets are arenas of conflict, mediated on the one hand by democratic elections and on the other by monetary exchange. We need such institutions. Without them, as Hobbes said, life would be nasty, brutish and short.[15]

Social goods, by contrast, are an almost magical commodity in that the more you share them, the more you have:

[I]magine that you have a certain quantum of love, or friendship, or influence, or loyalty, and then you share it with nine others. Do you have less than when you started? In fact, you have more.

Rabbi Sacks—who wasn't yet making any distinction between joy and happiness (a distinction that would become important to him later)—was clear that true happiness is a social good.[16] True happiness, when shared, is multiplied, and not diminished.

In addition to situating happiness (or true happiness) among social goods, Rabbi Sacks also argued that the key to true happiness is to seek the happiness of others. This, he dubbed, "the paradox of volunteering" since:

> the more we give, the more we are given. I lose count of the number of times I have thanked people for their voluntary work, only to be told: 'It is I who want to give thanks for the chance to serve.' Lifting others, we ourselves are lifted. Happiness—the sense of a life well lived—is born in the blessing we bestow on others. Bringing hope to someone else's life brings meaning to our own.[17]

There are a number of ways in which Rabbi Sacks' observations about happiness are elevated in light of Crescas' philosophy. The idea that happiness is a social good finds a number of resonances in the world of Crescas: first of all, joy is, for Crescas, an experience that even God couldn't have on His own, since true joy, as we human beings passively receive it, is—at root—the creative activity of a God of love, loving His creations into being. It is something that emerges only in the context of more than one being—a *po'el* and a *mitpa'el*.

Secondly, the notion that happiness is ampliative—that the more you give the more you have—is given a new force when joy is thought to be the very thing that brings the creation into being; the very power that emanates from a single God, only to give rise to the dazzling multiplicity that is this universe, with all of its gigantic stars, and minute atoms, is ampliative indeed.

Finally, the notion that lifting others is the key to a life well lived, and, therefore, to human happiness, when transposed into a Crescian key, becomes the claim that making others happy is the ultimate form of *imatatio Dei* (walking in the path of God). To experience joy, not merely as a passive recipient but as the creator of the joy of others, is to attain Divinity.

In his later work, Rabbi Sacks came to draw a key distinction between joy and happiness. Joy, he associates with the Hebrew word, *simḥa*; happiness, with *ashrei*.[18] Rabbi Sacks recognizes that happiness is a virtue in Judaism. A person can only be described as *ashrei* if he is "doing well and faring well."[19] Such a person is:

> blessed with a good marriage, children, a reputation for integrity ("the crown of a good name"—(*Avot* 4:17), an honoured place within the community, and the feeling of a life well lived. He or she sleeps well at night, knowing they have done nothing of which to be ashamed.[20]

Ideally, happiness should be the automatic "outcome of a moral life," but in actual fact, it is too dependent upon external circumstances beyond our control, however moral we may be.

> What of the poor, the exploited, the unemployed? What, asks the Torah repeatedly, of the orphan, the widow, and the stranger within the gates? What, asks Kohelet [in Ecclesiastes], of the tears of the oppressed who have no comforter? What of the wise man who saved the city only to be unthanked, ignored, forgotten? What, we might ask nowadays, of the victims of terror, or those who live under tyranny? To speak of happiness under such circumstances is almost to mock the afflicted.[21]

Joy, by contrast, as Rabbi Sacks came to understand it, depends upon nothing more than the experience, in the present, of being alive, of having being.

> The Talmud says that each Sunday, Shammai, the great sage of the late Second Temple period, was already preparing for Shabbat. Hillel, however, lived by a different principle: "Blessed be God day by day" (*Beitza* 16a). Joy blesses God day by day. It celebrates the mere fact of being here, now, existing when we might not have done, inhaling to the full this day, this hour, this eternity-in-a-moment that was not before and will not be again … It is a state of radical thankfulness for the gift of being. Even in an age too fraught for happiness, there can still be joy.[22]

Indeed, as Rabbi Sacks pointed out, the notion that joy, unlike happiness, isn't contingent upon things going well, is expressed by Habakkuk in a beautiful passage of the Bible:

> Though the fig tree does not blossom,
>   and no fruit is on the vines;
> though the produce of the olive fails
>   and the fields yield no food;
> though the flock is cut off from the fold
>   and there is no herd in the stalls,
> yet I will rejoice in the Lord;
>   I will exult in the God of my salvation.[23]

Rabbi Sacks makes clear—in his later work and armed with his new distinction—that it is joy, rather than happiness, which is truly reliant upon being shared. Perhaps you can be happy alone. But "*simḥa* only exists in virtue of being shared."[24]

This distinction between happiness and joy, is once again, lifted by Crescas. In Crescas' view, the joy in which God is active, and of which we are His passive recipients, is manifest in nothing more (and nothing less) than our continued existence from moment to moment. Giving us our being, from second to second, is the joy of God. And thus, of course, there *must* be a crucial notion of joy in which the substance of our joy is nothing more (and nothing less) than our mere existence in the moment. To experience that moment as joy, is, in a sense, to experience an aspect of God's own joy in that moment. Happiness can have all sorts of objects—a full belly, a nice car, a comfortable home, and so on. Joy, by contrast, is simply to be, and to recognize that our very being is a joyful expression of God's infinite love.

Rabbi Sacks' distinction between *simḥa* and *ashrei* helps, in turn, to strengthen Crescas' point. The Hebrew Bible never describes God as *ashrei*, but it does describe Him in terms of *simḥa* (Psalms 104:31). This is just as we should expect. The notion of *ashrei* only makes sense for someone who has desires that can be fulfilled or an appetite to satiate. *Simḥa*, by contrast, requires no such limitation. Likewise in the classical Rabbinic texts, it's almost unheard of for God to be described as *ashrei*.[25] By comparison, God is regularly described as being in a state of *simḥa*.[26] Moreover, the Talmud teaches that a prophet who isn't in a state of *simḥa* isn't able to receive the Divine word.[27] Paying attention to the distinction between *simḥa* and *ashrei* and the association between God and the former, rather than the latter, helps to bolster Crescas' distinction between happiness as a human passion (i.e., *ashrei*) and joy as a Divine activity of which we can be the recipients (i.e., *simḥa*).

In these ways and more, Rabbi Sacks' and Crescas' meditations on the nature of joy shed light upon one another and upon the Jewish tradition from which they both emerged, and to which they both contribute so much.

Notes

1. Aristotle, *De Anima*, III, 10, 433a.
2. Maimonides, *Guide to the Perplexed* 1:54, trans. S. Pines (Chicago: University of Chicago Press, 1963).
3. Aristotle, *Metaphysics*, XII, 7, 1072b 3.
4. Ibid., 1072b 16.
5. E.g., Aquinas, *Summa Theologica*, II–II Q. 28, article 3.
6. See Maimonides' introduction to Chapter 10 of Tractate Sanhedrin, in his commentary to the Mishna.
7. Gersonides, *Wars of the Lord*, 5:3:12, as translated by (Harvey, 1998, 102–3).
8. Hasdai Crescas, *Light of the Lord*, 1:3:5.
9. Warren Zev Harvey, *Physics and Metaphysics in Ḥasdai Crescas* (Amsertdam: J. C. Gieben, 1998), 106.
10. Crescas, *Light of the Lord*, 1:3:5.
11. Harvey, 1998, 106–7.
12. Crescas, *Light of the Lord*, 2:5:5, and Harvey, 1998, 118.
13. Crescas, *Light of the Lord*, 2:5:5, and Harvey, 1998, 107.
14. Jonathan Sacks, *Covenant & Conversation: A Weekly Reading of the Jewish Bible; Deuteronomy: Renewal of the Sinai Covenant* (Jersualem: Maggid Books, 2019), 283–87.
15. Jonathan Sacks, *The Politics of Hope* (London: Vintage, 2000), xv.
16. Ibid., 202–9.
17. From an article first published in 2005, reprinted in Sacks, *The Power of Ideas: Words of Faith and Wisdom* (London: Hodder and Stoughton Ltd., 2021), 78.
18. Jonathan Sacks, *The Koren Sukkot Maḥzor* (Jersualem: Koren Publishers, 2016), xlvii.
19. Ibid.
20. Ibid.
21. Ibid.
22. Ibid., p. xlviii.
23. Hab. 3:17–18.
24. Sacks, 2016, p. xlix.

25. All I could find in the classical Rabbinic texts was (1) a case in which God likens himself to a king who is *ashrei*, which is hardly a direct predication of the term (Tractate Brachot 3a, repeated in *Otzar Mizrashim, Pirkei Rabeinu Hakadosh* 1:18); (2) a case in which a Roman Caesar, who can hardly be described as an authority on matters of theology, describes God as *ashrei* (*Tanna debei Eliyahu Zuta, Pirkei DeRabbi Eliezer* 5); and (3) a very obscure Midrash in which the wicked in hell, who also cannot be described as great authorities on matters of theology, describe God as *ashrei* (*Otzar Midrashim, Gan Eden, Gehinom, Seudat Levyatan*).
26. A non-exhaustive list of examples: *Tosefta Sanhedrin* 14:2; *Tractate Derech Eretz Zuta, Perek Shalom* 3; *Mekhilta d'Rabbi Yishmael* 23:15; *Mekhilta DeRabbi Shimon Bar Yochai* 17, s.v., *Vayiven Moshe*; *Sifra, Shimini, Mekhilta d'Miluim* 15; *Sifrei Bamidbar, Korach,* 117; *Sifrei Devarim* 326; *Bereshit Rabba* 3:3; *Shemot Rabba* 20:14; and *Bamidbar Rabba* 2:19. Less explicit, but more influential, is the blessing formulated in *Tractate Ketubot* 8a, which refers to God, "in whose habitation there is joy."
27. *Tractate Pesachim* 117a, and *Tractate Shabbat* 30b. The *simha* in question has to be the *simha* associated with observing the commandments, although the proof-text used in *Tractate Pesachim* would seem to indicate that the simple *simha* of listening to music could suffice.

CHAPTER 23

Standing Before God in Joy and Fear

Shira Weiss

"At Sinai, God reveals Himself equally to everyone," writes Rabbi Jonathan Sacks. "At Israel's founding moment, every individual is a party to the covenant and none stands higher than any other. Revelation creates a republic of free and equal citizens under the sovereignty of God."[1] Rabbi Sacks notes how each member of Israel had the opportunity to approach God and enter into a covenantal relationship. It is this sensation of standing before God, achievable by every individual, that Rabbi Joseph Soloveitchik describes as the very essence of joy. He elaborates upon the dialectic of terror and ecstasy that humans experience when encountering the divine presence through *de'ot* (beliefs) and *mitzvot* (performance of commandments), as it states in Chronicles,[2] "Might and joy are in His place."[3] In his classic medieval philosophical work, Joseph Albo reconciles the tension between fear and joy and focuses on both beliefs and observance as a means towards the achievement of true happiness by all of humanity.

Albo, a fifteenth-century Jewish philosopher who also played a rabbinic and political role in the Jewish community in Spain during the Inquisition,

S. Weiss (✉)
Yeshiva University, New York, NY, USA

uniquely presents the dogma of Judaism within the universal context of divine law in his popular *Sefer ha-'Iqqarim* [*Book of Principles*]. He aimed to teach his coreligionists the doctrine of Judaism in order to provide them with a uniform defense against their Christian persecutors, as well as to bolster their commitment to the divine covenant. Before he delineates his *'iqqarim* [foundational principles] in an effort to demonstrate that Judaism is the authentic divine law, he asserts the necessity of divine law altogether as a guide for humanity to achieve true happiness, that of the soul. Divine law, he argues,

> shows them the way they must follow to obtain it, teaches them the true good that they may take pains to secure it, shows them also real evil that they may guard against it, and trains them to abandon imaginary happiness so that they may not desire it and not feel its loss.[4]

Albo explains the need for divine law to guide humanity towards the true God and the immortality of the soul. Only divine law can regulate actions, as well as beliefs (*de'ot*), leading humanity to spiritual perfection. Albo writes that human happiness depends upon theoretical knowledge and practical conduct, but human intellect cannot attain perfect knowledge and understand how to achieve ethical conduct; therefore, there must be a divine law above human intellect through which knowledge and conduct can be comprehended without doubt.

Albo further explicates what belief and observance of God's Torah entail and introduces in this context the seemingly opposing values of fear and joy. He identifies the essence of the performance of a commandment as fear of God. He also affirms that divine service must be inspired with joy if it is to be complete but acknowledges the difficulty of reconciling fear with joy.[5]

As the virtue of the soul and the intellect increases, one comes to a greater appreciation of the sublimity and exalted character of God, standing in awe and fearing the transgression of any divine commandments. Albo writes, when one "finds in himself this degree of fear, he should rejoice in this fear, for it shows health of soul and perfection of intellect."[6] He explains that not fearing that which should be feared reflects a defect. For instance, if one is not afraid to put his hand into the fire, one demonstrates either an aberration of mind or insensibility of the hand. Accordingly, Albo innovatively interprets David's words, "Serve the Lord with gladness," as referring not to a light and frivolous fulfillment of commandments but rather an observance inspired with fear, "Serve the Lord with fear, and rejoice with trembling."[7] He explains how the soul considers the sublimity of God in contrast to one's personal lowliness, and thus, one simultaneously rejoices and trembles, apprehending that God is deserving of fear—an indication of intellectual perfection and health. Albo affirms, "This joy, therefore, makes the service perfect and complete."[8]

Albo reconciles such fear and joy by conceiving of the trembling which one suffers when inspired with fear of God as the toil which one exerts in pursuit of a valuable goal. Despite the arduous effort, one rejoices when reflecting upon the purpose of the fear, namely, submission to God. As an illustration, Albo references Abraham following his trial at the Binding of Isaac. God proclaims, "Now I know that you are a God-fearing man, seeing you have not withheld your son, your only son, from Me."[9] Albo comments, "Then, when Abraham stood his test joyfully and with good humor, the Bible called him friend. All this shows that the cheerful endurance of toil and trouble in the service of God gives perfection to the service and the fear of God."[10]

Albo's conception of happiness not only reflects his engagement with Maimonides' thought which focuses on the development of the intellect, or one's *de'ot* about the divine, to achieve human perfection, but also stresses the practical performance of the commandments. For Albo, "Belief in God and in His Torah brings man to eternal happiness and causes his soul to cleave to the spiritual substance."[11] Whereas Maimonides presents a naturalistic explanation of an impersonal God and humanity's striving for intellectual communion with the Active Intellect, Albo supports his notion of a personal God and his belief in the supernatural. "This is proved by experience, as we know from continuous tradition. We know of no instance of a philosopher or other investigator attaining to the degree of the prophet, which means the union of the divine spirit with the human intellect. We do find that the devotees of the Torah came into such close intellectual union with God that they were able to change the laws of nature, cause the latter to do their bidding and perform miracles against the laws of nature."[12] It is this notion of a personal God that underlies Albo's third principle (*'iqqar*) of divine law, namely reward and punishment. He asserts that the noble and worthy deed should be rewarded by God and that punishment should be given for its violation. Albo goes on to specify the reward and punishment associated with joyful worship.

There is no deed that is more noble, and more worthy, and more deserving of reward, according to the truth and the consensus of mankind, than the service of God. And we find that the Bible announces severe punishment for not serving God joyfully: "Because you did not serve the Lord your God with joyfulness, and with gladness of heart, by reason of the abundance of all things; therefore, shall you serve your enemy..."[13]

Albo's emphasis on faith, performance of commandments, proper intention,[14] and fear of God,[15]—achievable by anyone—as central to religious life and meriting the reward of miracles, divine union,[16] immortality,[17] and prophecy,[18] was more accessible than Maimonides' focus on the intellectual development, achievable only by the elite. Albo, like other fifteenth-century Spanish Jewish philosophers, deviated from the Maimonidean notion that rational speculation constitutes the purpose of Torah and can lead an individual to human felicity and perfection, the ultimate human end. Instead, Albo stresses that humanity, due to limited knowledge, must rely on divine law for guidance both to proper truth and conduct. Albo rejects Aristotle's and Maimonides' conception of human perfection in intellectual terms since such perfection is unattainable by most people whose lives would then be in vain. God, he assures, would not have made the desired purpose of humankind capable of being fulfilled only by a small minority.[19]

Rather, for Albo, individuals of every intellectual capacity have the ability to reach happiness and spiritual perfection, as the entire nation of Israel achieved prophecy at Mount Sinai, during which they trembled and rejoiced.[20] At the establishment of His nation, all members were invited to appear before God and commit themselves to His covenant through *de'ot* (beliefs) and *mitzvot* (performance of commandments). Rabbi Sacks writes, "For Judaism, this was the supreme moment of revelation, and it remains unique in the religious literature of mankind... The difference between revelation to a holy individual and to a nation as a whole is fundamental and defines the unique character of the Jewish project." He stresses not only the public character of Sinai, but the significance of the experience shared by men and women, young and old, righteous and ordinary alike. "At Israel's founding moment, every individual is a party to the covenant and none stands higher than any other. Revelation creates a republic of free and equal citizens under the sovereignty of God." Rabbi Sacks cites Exodus 19:8, that it is only when "*all* the people responded together, 'We will do everything the Lord has said' that the revelation could proceed." This, he highlights, "is the first time in history that individuals—ordinary individuals, not an elite—were asked to give their consent to a political order ... a revolution in the concept of human dignity."[21] Recognition of the awe and joy that accompany such responsibility continues to be integral to the experience of every human who stands before God and achieves true felicity.

Notes

1. Jonathan Sacks, *A Letter in the Scroll* (New York, NY: Free Press, 2000), 119.
2. I Chronicles 16:27.
3. *Sefer Shiurei Harav on Aveilut and Tisha B'Av* (New York, NY: OU Press), 82.
4. Joseph Albo, *Sefer ha-'Iqqarim* [*Book of Principles*], trans. Isaac Husik (Philadelphia: The Jewish Publication Society of America, 1930), I:7.
5. Ibid., III:34.
6. Ibid., III:33.
7. Ps. 2, 11.
8. *Book of Principles*, III:33.
9. Gen. 22:14.
10. *Book of Principles*, III:34.
11. Ibid., 1:21.
12. Ibid.
13. Deut. 23: 47–48.
14. *Book of Principles*, III:28.
15. Ibid., III:27.
16. "Belief in God and in His Torah gives perfection of the soul ... Through faith the soul rises high above the things of nature, and can therefore control them... This is why we find that miracles are performed for men of faith, and not for men of speculative knowledge, so as to show that faith stands higher than speculation and the things of nature. Therefore, one may through it attain true union with God during life after death" (*Book of Principles*, I:21).
17. "Divine righteousness decrees that those who believe should obtain that degree of eternal life which is promised in the Torah, because they trust and believe in His Torah, though they are not able to acquire an intellectual comprehension" (*Book of Principles*, II:15).
18. "We never find the gift of prophecy in any of the philosophers, though they were wise men in theoretical speculation; whereas we do find prophecy among the Jewish people. This shows that it is not a natural phenom-

enon associated with theoretical speculation. For if it were so, why should this gift have been kept from the other nations, so that their wise men despite their perfection of intellect and imagination are devoid of the prophetic inspiration?" (*Book of Principles*, III:8).
19. Ibid., III:3.
20. Ibid., III:11.
21. Jonathan Sacks, *A Letter in the Scroll*, 117–119.

CHAPTER 24

Joys, Oys, and the Pursuit of Happiness

Daniel Rynhold

As I sit and type the word "joy," one of the words that appear in the list of synonyms proffered by an online thesaurus is "happiness." Such an equivalence will make any philosopher pause for thought, for philosophers have long approached "happiness" from two very different perspectives. On the one hand, there are those who, following Aristotle, ask what it is that constitutes a life of happiness or *eudaimonia*. The question Aristotle is asking—to which "happiness" is the answer—concerns what constitutes a flourishing life, one that we would consider a life worth living. Aristotle, and Jewish Aristotelians such as Maimonides, give very particular answers to that question, to which we will return. But the point is that a life of happiness is one that is well-lived according to some set of criteria that the thinker in question considers the best possible life. There will, of course, be disputes regarding what the best way to live is. Accounts of happiness are hotly disputed. Hedonists will look to pleasure; others will appeal to some set of objective values they deem the right or virtuous way to live, regardless (at least up to a point) of the pleasure it may yield. Either way, some forms of happiness will not necessarily yield a life that we would call

D. Rynhold (✉)
Bernard Revel Graduate School of Jewish Studies, Yeshiva University, New York, NY, USA

© The Author(s), under exclusive license to Springer Nature Switzerland AG 2023
E. Brown, S. Weiss (eds.), *An Ode to Joy*,
https://doi.org/10.1007/978-3-031-28229-4_24

joyous (and, of course, some theories will be non-starters from a Jewish perspective).

To consider several examples from modern Jewish thought, Yeshayahu Leibowitz often opposes what he calls an "endowing" religion—"a means of satisfying man's spiritual needs and of assuaging his mental conflicts"[1]— to a "demanding" religion—one that "imposes obligations and tasks and makes of man an instrument for the realization of an end which transcends man."[2] Leibowitz uncompromisingly, as was his wont, identified Judaism as a demanding religion, since for Judaism, "faith is nothing but a system of Mitzvoth [commandments]."[3] There is some "satisfaction" that "[derives] from the performance of one's duty,"[4] but it need not yield anything that we would call joy. Indeed, for Leibowitz, "[m]ost characteristic of the Halakhah is its lack of pathos. The Halakhah does not depend upon the incidence of religious experience[.]"[5] Judaism according to Leibowitz, does not care about our feelings, only "the permanent habit of performing one's duty."[6] For Leibowitz, the joy one takes in the performance of a mitzvah is entirely irrelevant to its religious value. Arguably, it could even potentially distract an agent from taking up the appropriate religious attitude.

While some in the Jewish world would hesitate to cite Yeshayahu Leibowitz as a source of support for their claims, the idea that Judaism prioritizes commandments that demand our allegiance regardless of their "feel-good" factor is certainly not out of kilter with mainstream views. To take a less controversial figure, Rabbi Joseph Soloveitchik is renowned for his views on the faith experience—and of Judaism in particular—as "[oscillating] between ecstasy in God's companionship and despair when he feels torn asunder by the heightened contrast between self-appreciation and abnegation." The faith experience, for Soloveitchik, has "been a difficult one since the time of Abraham and Moses … the Biblical knights of faith lived heroically with this very tragic and paradoxical experience."[7] While both Leibowitz and Soloveitchik would certainly see their lives as flourishing and worthy, dedicated as they each were to the highest possible value, one would be hard-pressed to describe them as lives of joy. Indeed, when one considers such lives, one might conclude that they were filled with challenges—more lives of "oys" than of joys.

This brings us to the second way in which one can approach the idea of happiness, for often when we speak of someone being happy, we mean that they are in a certain psychological state. Happiness, therefore, can be defined as a psychological state that need not relate directly to theories of well-being. All manner of things might yield a psychological state of happiness, and not all of them need to contribute to "happiness" in the more evaluative sense with which we began. For convenience in what follows, we will use happiness$_1$ to refer to the idea that happiness is a "flourishing life" in an evaluative sense, and happiness$_2$ to refer to the accounts of happiness that focus on it as a psychological state.

Just as with happiness$_1$, we can discriminate between different versions of happiness$_2$. To mention just two, some take a view whereby what counts is pleasure, such that pleasurable experiences outweigh unpleasurable experiences; others define happiness as an emotional state. The non-equivalence of these two accounts emerges when one considers a person who may suffer emotionally, while nonetheless having quantitatively more pleasurable experiences than unpleasant ones, by, for example, constantly occupying themselves with diversions to bring on such pleasurable experiences.

If anything, the word "joy" seems more suited to this latter psychological approach—to happiness$_2$ more than to happiness$_1$. Yet it often seems as if Jews are more focused on the latter. Some might say that we Jews don't really "do" joy. As the old joke goes: An Englishman, a Frenchman, and a Jew are sitting on a park bench. The Englishman says, "I'm so tired and thirsty. I must have a beer." The Frenchman says, "I'm so tired and thirsty, I must have a glass of wine." The Jew says, "I'm so tired and thirsty, I must have diabetes."

By this point, you may be thinking that this is all very well, but what does it have to do with Jonathan Sacks? Well, quite a lot, it turns out. To start with, and in opposition to Rabbi Soloveitchik, Rabbi Sacks often noted that "Jews never coined a word that meant 'tragedy' in the Greek sense," since "Judaism is the principled rejection of tragedy in the name of hope."[8] Countering Leibowitz, one can argue that joy features among Judaism's demands, in relation to such commandments as the Sabbath and holidays, for example. More importantly, Rabbi Sacks when writing about "joy" as understood in Judaism, recognizes the non-equivalence of happiness$_1$ and happiness$_2$. In so doing, he managed, as so often, to tread a conciliatory path that brought them together in his characteristic way—one that was particular to Judaism, while nonetheless containing a universal message.

In his final monograph, Rabbi Sacks has a chapter titled "Consuming Happiness," where he tells the story of a societal shift from happiness$_1$ to happiness$_2$, from "*eudaimonia*, happiness as a state of being-and-doing, to *hedonia*, a state of feeling, the pursuit of pleasure."[9] We are today sold the need for things that will bring us "happiness" in the form of pleasurable experiences, and end up, with or without intent, competing to accumulate more and more things that will yield those experiences. And while we have more access than ever to the things that will bring us such experiences, we nonetheless find ourselves in an increasingly dysfunctional society in which depression and stress-related illnesses are skyrocketing. For Rabbi Sacks, our dissatisfaction is in part a casualty of the shift in our understandings of happiness, from one rooted in values to one that reflects "the mindset of the market"[10] and "encourages us to spend money we don't have, on products we don't need, for a happiness that won't last."[11]

This modern form of happiness seems more focused on the psychological state of joy—on happiness$_2$ rather than happiness$_1$—and it's not clear it can be successfully pursued, at least as a stable lasting state. While one can accumulate all manner of experiences to give us experiential highs, those highs often lead to an endless pursuit of ever greater "pleasures" in pursuit of ever greater highs, ultimately in pursuit of a "happiness" that seems doomed to make us far from happy. More than that, some people take pleasure in some truly dreadful things.

For Rabbi Sacks then, the first thing that we need to recover is the ancient link between virtue and happiness; a return to the Aristotelian model that we also find in Jewish Aristotelians such as Maimonides. Maimonides' own view was that the life of *eudaimonia* is the life devoted to intellectual contemplation. As Maimonides tells us in his *Guide of the Perplexed*, III. 54: "The true perfection which gives human beings 'permanent perdurance' is one that consists in the acquisition of the rational virtues."[12]

For Maimonides, intellectual contemplation—to which, incidentally, "there do not belong either actions or moral qualities … it consists only of ideas towards which speculation has led and that investigation has rendered compulsory"[13]—is what constitutes the life of happiness$_1$. While many dispute the elitism of his approach,[14] it is important to note that for Maimonides, it *is* a life of pleasure. More than that, the pleasure of intellectual contemplation yields a form of joy the likes of which we can barely imagine. For Aristotle "life in accordance with intellect is best and pleasantest."[15] That we are unable to recognize this is no surprise to Maimonides, who tells us in his well-known Introduction to *Helek*: "Just like the blind man does not grasp appearance of colors and the deaf man does not grasp the sound of voices … so too bodies do not grasp spiritual pleasures …

[for] in this physical world, pleasures of the spiritual world are not known."[16]

Thus, an important element of the Aristotelian picture is that while the life of *eudaimonia* is a life worth living *lishmah* [for its own sake] (I'm paraphrasing...)., and pleasure is most certainly not *the* good, Aristotle thought it essential that pleasure "weaves"[17] into *eudaimonia*—happiness "must have pleasure mixed in with it."[18] Though pleasure is not the telos of life, it nonetheless "completes the activity not as the inherent state does, but as a sort of supervenient end, like the bloom on the faces of young men."[19]

For both Maimonides and Aristotle, therefore, the intellectual life of the individual is the highest form of happiness$_1$; a form of happiness$_2$ is a benefit of living such a life. For these thinkers, moral virtue, while an essential component of such a life, only serves as a necessary foundation for intellectual perfection, and as happiness "in a secondary way."[20] Part of the reason for this hierarchy is the idea of self-sufficiency—that the best life must be one that is entirely within one's own control and not reliant on someone or something else. A life of practical virtue minimally requires other people among whom the virtues can be practiced. The life of intellectual contemplation may also require a virtuous society as a condition, but it can then be maintained in solitude.

Rabbi Sacks follows these thinkers in linking happiness$_1$ to happiness$_2$, but as with tragedy, he rejects the Greek idea of self-sufficiency. Joy, for Rabbi Sacks, also supervenes on what really matters, but it cannot be achieved in isolation. The idea that runs through Rabbi Sacks' writings is the fundamental religious insight that, "Joy in the Hebrew Bible is essentially shared."[21]

Though he is not always consistent in his use of terminology, we can reconstruct the following picture from Rabbi Sacks' writings. Virtues, according to Rabbi Sacks "are born and sustained in particular institutions, the family, the congregation, the neighborhood, the voluntary organization, which give shape to our individuality and moral substance to our sociability."[22] Moreover, these forms of community are nurtured by the central Jewish idea of the covenant. Covenants—unlike contracts, which yield "the instrumentalities of the state—governments, nations, parties"— give rise to "families, communities, peoples, traditions, and voluntary associations."[23] These are the settings in which we achieve happiness$_1$.

The fundamental biblical insight for Rabbi Sacks, though, is that "Joy is *happiness* shared" (emphasis added).[24] Contra Maimonides, Rabbi Sacks finds in texts such as Ecclesiastes that the frustrations of the author are attached to all the things he achieves as an "I." We find biblical happiness$_2$ or joy in such things as the collective celebration of the festivals, or in "the woman you love." (Eccl. 9:9). That is, we experience joy not through our own individual perfection but in our commitment to the very communities formed through the covenant, for Judaism, through a life of fulfilling commandments.

According to Rabbi Sacks, we can seek ways to an essentially communal life well lived—for happiness$_1$—and then joy, happiness$_2$, supervenes on happiness$_1$. And that is because in Judaism happiness$_1$ emerges in the context of relationships, not in isolation. Joy, or *simha*, then follows since it is "not a private emotion. It means happiness shared. It is a social state, a predicate of 'we,' not 'I.' There is no such thing as feeling *simha* alone."[25]

Interestingly, this also means—with apologies to my American readers—that the pursuit of happiness$_2$, or joy, is a bad idea for Rabbi Sacks: "[h]appiness can never be obtained by being pursued … It comes from a life well lived, in pursuit of the good for its own sake."[26] It seems to me that Rabbi Sacks here is actually speaking of joy, not happiness; or rather happiness$_2$ rather than happiness$_1$. As we have seen, the "good" is a life of commandments, which one *can* pursue. I even have some friends who do so. But it is precisely because we are pursuing a life of commandments and *not* a state of joy that we are able to achieve a state of joy. And not just joy as fleeting states of pleasure that the consumerist version of happiness can provide but joy as a more lasting and general psychological state of emotional well-being.

Rabbi Sacks puts it more precisely elsewhere, "Happiness is something you pursue. But joy is not. It discovers you."[27] It is through performing commandments that we find the joy that eludes us if pursued, and one of the key reasons that this form of life brings joy is because of the relationships that it generates. These relationships help us navigate the "oys." Relationships are worth more than any transaction and cannot be bought. They are the foundation of love. Indeed, if we treat our families and friends in a transactional manner, they won't be our families and friends for long. Rabbi Sacks teaches us that covenant begets the seat of love, relationships, and they, in their reciprocity beget joy.

I recall long ago, while still living in London, reading a profile of the then Chief Rabbi Jonathan Sacks in the *Daily Telegraph* newspaper.[28] The journalist began by setting the scene, having walked into Rabbi Sacks' office to find a Bee Gees track playing in the background. Unsurprisingly, it wasn't "Tragedy." It was "Staying Alive." But if I were creating a soundtrack to accompany these brief ruminations on Rabbi Sacks' approach to joy, it would be Nat King Cole's "Nature Boy:"

> The greatest thing you'll ever learn
> Is just to love and be loved in return.

Notes

1. Yeshayahu Leibowitz, "Religious Praxis," in *Judaism, Human Values, and the Jewish State*, ed. Eliezer Goldman (Cambridge, MA: Harvard University Press, 1995), 14.
2. Ibid.
3. Ibid., 38.
4. Ibid., 14.
5. Ibid., 13.
6. Ibid.
7. Joseph B. Soloveitchik, *The Lonely Man of Faith* (New York: Doubleday, 1992), 2. That is not to say that there is no pleasure in Judaism for Soloveitchik for whom "Halakhah enjoins man to take no less pleasure than the hedonist in the glory and splendor of the creation." (Soloveitchik, *Uvikkashtem miSham*, trans. Naomi Goldblum as *And From There You Shall Seek Seek* (Jersey City, NJ: Toras Horav Foundation/Ktav, 2008), 111). But it is a pleasure that is specific to discrete halakhic acts that is still couched within the tragic faith context.
8. Jonathan Sacks, *To Heal a Fractured World: The Ethics of Responsibility* (London: Continuum, 2005), 177.
9. Jonathan Sacks, *Morality: Restoring the Common Good in Divided Times* (New York: Basic Books, 2020), 101.
10. Ibid., 102.
11. Ibid.
12. Moses Maimonides, *The Guide of the Perplexed*, 2 vols., trans. Shlomo Pines (Chicago: University of Chicago Press, 1963), 635.
13. Ibid., 511.
14. I should note that as with all interpretations of Maimonides, this intellectual interpretation (though correct in my opinion) is disputed. For extensive discussion, see Menachem Kellner, *Maimonides on Human Perfection* (Atlanta, GA: Scholars Press, 1990).
15. Aristotle, *Nichomachean Ethics*, trans. Roger Crisp (Cambridge: Cambridge University Press, 2000), 196.

16. Moses Maimonides, *Commentary to the Mishnah*, accessed June 23, 2022, https://www.sefaria.org/Rambam_on_Mishnah_Sanhedrin.10.1.15?lang =bi&with=all&lang2=en.
17. Aristotle, *Ethics*, 139. While the life of practice always has a role to play, I would contend that it is similarly a "side-effect" for Maimonides. See Daniel Rynhold, *An Introduction to Medieval Jewish Philosophy* (London: I.B. Tauris, 2009), Chapter 7, section 4.
18. Aristotle, *Ethics*, 195.
19. Ibid., 189.
20. See ibid., 196.
21. Sacks, *Morality*, 113.
22. Jonathan Sacks, *The Politics of Hope*, 2nd edn. (Vintage: London, 2000), 169.
23. Ibid., 64.
24. Sacks, *Morality*, 113.
25. Jonathan Sacks, "Collective Joy," accessed June 17, 2022, https://www.rabbisacks.org/covenant-conversation/reeh/collective-joy/.
26. Sacks, *To Heal a Fractured World*, 209.
27. Jonathan Sacks, "The Pursuit of Joy," accessed June 17, 2022, https://www.rabbisacks.org/covenant-conversation/ki-tavo/the-pursuit-of-joy/.
28. Before, it seems, newspapers had an online presence—I searched and was unable to find the article.

CHAPTER 25

Affirming Life in Joy Across the Divinity Divide: Rabbi Jonathan Sacks and Friedrich Nietzsche

Michael J. Harris

The German philosopher Fredrich Nietzsche (1844–1900) does not have any single consistent conception of joy or happiness across his writings but articulates "multiple attitudes toward happiness."[1] There is no attempt in this chapter to address all of these attitudes but only to focus on those which can be fruitfully juxtaposed to R. Sacks' teachings.

Nietzsche is something of a *bête noir* for Rabbi Sacks:

> I, for one, find Nietzsche the very antithesis of Jewish values. I take no pleasure in the fact that, from time to time, he found nice things to say about Jews ancient and modern. The man who expressed contempt for "pity, the kind and helping hand, the warm heart, patience, industriousness, humility, friendliness" defined for all time what Judaism is not. I read him to know what Judaism is the battle against, then, now, and for the future.[2]

M. J. Harris (✉)
London School of Jewish Studies, London, UK

Paradoxically, however, R. Sacks' reflections on joy display something of a Nietzschean sensibility. There is no claim here of direct influence of Nietzsche's writings on R. Sacks or that R. Sacks is consciously responding to Nietzsche. I do, however, want to argue that R. Sacks' reflections on joy often intersect in interesting and unexpected ways with some of Nietzsche's meditations on this concept.

Of particular importance for our purposes, Nietzsche sometimes uses "joy" (*Lust*) as a synonym for a radical affirmation of life that embraces all of life's difficulties, suffering, and agony. According to the dominant scholarly interpretation of Nietzsche's famous doctrine of eternal recurrence, Nietzsche even advocates being prepared to welcome the never-ending repetition of all the misery one has undergone were one's life to recur in perpetuity in all its details.[3] This thoroughgoing affirmation of life, from within Nietzsche's uncompromisingly atheistic framework, is a, indeed arguably *the*, core component of Nietzsche's thought.[4]

Joy is a central feature of R. Sacks' conception of Jewish tradition. He acknowledges that happiness (*osher, ashrei*) is a salient value in Judaism but reminds us that "[t]he Torah's key word for positive emotion is not happiness but *simha*, joy".[5] The term *simha*, R. Sacks points out, occurs in the Bible almost ten times as often as *ashrei*.[6] Strikingly, R. Sacks reminds us that whereas the curses of Leviticus 26 are described against a backdrop of total desertion of the Torah by the Jewish people, they nevertheless conclude on a note of hope. The curses set out in Deuteronomy 28, however, conclude without any solace whatsoever. Yet the sin that invites the curses is nothing like the wholesale abandonment of Judaism. The sin is simply that "you did not serve the Lord your God with joy [*simha*] and gladness of heart, out of the abundance of all things" (Deut. 28:47).[7] Joy, one might almost say (though R. Sacks himself does not put it this way), is equivalent to the sum of all the other commandments.

R. Sacks again underscores the centrality of joy in the following passage:
> Joy is at the heart of Judaism ... The one defence against national entropy—the loss of collective energy over time—would be joy itself, a combination of thanksgiving, humility, gratitude, and memories of the suffering that had to be endured in the course of arriving at this place and this estate. Judaism is not a religion of austerity, self-denial and stoic endurance... Time and again it arose, phoenix-like, from catastrophe, demoralization, and defeat, and each time renewed itself, gathering ever greater strength in the process. True faith, in Judaism, is marked by the capacity for joy.[8]

The multiple Nietzschean resonances here are striking: the emphasis on joy, the admiration of the steadfastness of the Jewish people throughout a history blighted by suffering,[9] the rejection of austerity and self-denial,[10] the deployment of catastrophe and suffering to advantage,[11] and the reference to the key Nietzschean value of "strength".

We have noted that Nietzsche advocates a radical affirmation of life despite its brevity. R. Sacks writes that for Kohelet, who is obsessed with mortality and considers it the central fact of human (and animal) existence, what redeems us from the shadow of death is joy, "joy in the simple pleasures of life".[12] R. Sacks points out that "[a]fter every one of his meditations on the pointlessness of life, Ecclesiastes ends with an exhortation to joy".[13] Ecclesiastes finds the meaning of life in joy, "the grateful acceptance and celebration of today" and the blessings it brings from God.[14] R. Sacks stresses the religious nature of joy, which he calls "a form of thanksgiving ... dancing in the presence of the Divine".[15] Joy is "gratitude for the gift of life that we feel in the presence of the Giver of life."[16] Nietzsche and R. Sacks are operating from within diametrically opposed metaphysical systems, one atheistic and the other theistic, but the emphasis on joyous affirmation of transitory earthly life is shared.

One might have thought a traditional theistic system incapable of seriously affirming earthly life, intent on escaping it and ascending to the heavenly realms where God resides. This is certainly how Nietzsche perceives Christianity. Nietzsche consistently rails against what he sees as the radical devaluation of this world and this life (the only ones that exist, in his view) by the Christian and some Western philosophical traditions which claim the existence of truer, more real or more significant worlds beyond this one.[17] Yet R. Sacks champions the affirmation of this life and the attainability and centrality of joy within it—life's ineluctably fleeting and fragile nature notwithstanding—from within the matrix of traditional Jewish belief. He thus shows how a theistic faith which believes in the existence of a better world beyond this one can nevertheless, as Nietzsche would have put it, say 'Yes' to this world—and a resounding 'Yes' at that.[18] It need not be the case, as Nietzsche complains concerning what he calls ["t]he Christian idea of God", that God is the "*contradiction of life* ... the formula for every slander against 'the here and now'".[19] R. Sacks insists that a joyful affirmation of mortal life is, from a traditional Jewish perspective, not only possible but necessary.

R. Sacks repeatedly underlines the essentially interpersonal nature of joy, *simha:* "[J]oy in the Torah is essentially shared".[20] R. Sacks points, for example, to the Torah's exhortation to rejoice on holidays not only with one's family but also with the stranger, the orphan, and the widow.[21] Joy "liberates the soul from the prison of the self"; it "defeats the fear of death, because it lifts us beyond the self, the insistent, interminable 'I'".[22] Interestingly, while not conceiving of joy as necessarily a social phenomenon, Nietzsche comes a long way towards recognizing the profound significance of its social dimensions. He points out that an indirect social benefit arises from individual joy: the deeper one's own capacity to feel joy, the less vindictive one will be towards others. "[L]earning better to feel joy", he observes, "we learn best not to hurt others or to plan hurts for them."[23] Moreover, the ability to rejoice in the joy of others is something of great value: "[T]o imagine the joy of others and to rejoice at it is the highest privilege of the highest animals, and among them it is accessible only to the choicest exemplars—thus a rare *humanum* [human quality]."[24] It is the capacity to feel and share the joy of the other that gives birth to friendship: "Fellow rejoicing [*Mitfreude*], not fellow suffering [*Mitleiden*], makes the friend".[25] Nietzsche exhorts us "to share not pain, but *joy*".[26]

There is a distinct commonality between Nietzsche and R. Sacks in terms of dissatisfaction with a smug, comfortable, "bourgeois" kind of happiness. In a celebrated aphorism, Nietzsche remarks: "If you have your '*why?*' in life, you can get along with almost any '*how?*'. People *don't* strive for happiness, only the English do".[27] The famous first sentence is cited approvingly and elaborated upon in one of R. Sacks' essays.[28] The English target of the second sentence appears to be the utilitarian philosopher John Stuart Mill, who maintains that the morally correct course of action in any instance is that which results in "the greatest happiness of the greatest number" and who Nietzsche views as risk- and danger-averse. There is something shallow about this kind of happiness, which Nietzsche terms "English happiness", "striving … for comfort and fashion".[29] Nietzsche is contemptuous of the over-cautious, anemic happiness of the "Last Man," the paradigm of mediocrity whom Nietzsche contrasts with his Superman.[30] For Nietzsche, a significant measure of *discomfort* is essential to growth, achievement, and ultimate joy:

> [S]hould you refuse to let your suffering lie on you even for an hour and instead constantly prevent all possible misfortune ahead of time; should you experience suffering and displeasure as evil, hateful, deserving of annihilation, as a defect of existence, then you have … *the religion of snug cosiness*. Oh, how little do you know of the *happiness* of man, you comfortable and

good-natured ones! For happiness and misfortune are two siblings and twins who either grow up together or—as with you—*remain small together!*[31] [emphases in original]

To resolutely pursue comfort and recoil from danger and from any risk of suffering, for Nietzsche, restricts one to a "small" kind of happiness.[32] Only a more courageous attitude to the possibility of suffering, a willingness, in one of Nietzsche's most famous exhortations, to "live dangerously", holds out the promise of a full-blooded happiness worthy of the name.

R. Sacks, for his part, notes that historically, Jews have not "tended to seek the risk-free life".[33] The one festival that Jewish tradition terms *zeman simhateinu*, "the season of our joy", namely Sukkot, is precisely that on which "we leave the security and comfort of our houses and live in a shack exposed to the wind, the cold, and the rain".[34] Developing a contrast between joy (*simha*) and happiness and privileging the former, R. Sacks approvingly cites Rilke: "How superficially must happiness engage us, after all, if it can leave us time to think and worry about how long it will last".[35] Making the joy/happiness contrast once again, R. Sacks writes:

> The pursuit of happiness … can lead to risk-averse behaviour and a failure to "dare greatly". Not so joy. Joy connects us to others and to God. Joy is the ability to celebrate life as such, knowing that whatever tomorrow may bring, we are here today, under God's heaven, in the universe He made, to which He has invited us as His guests".[36]

God is explicitly focal here. But the emphasis on daring and on responding with joy to our ephemeral existence echoes Nietzsche.[37]

Rabbi Sacks, exhorting us to feel joy in the knowledge that "it is a privilege simply to be alive"[38] has shown how a deep, life-affirming joy need not be rooted in Nietzsche's trenchant atheism. It is achievable within the life of traditional Jewish faith.

Notes

1. Richard Bett, "Nietzsche, the Greeks and Happiness (with Special Reference to Aristotle and Epicurus)," *Philosophical Topics* 33, no. 2 (Fall 2005): 45–70, at 66.

2. Jonathan Sacks, review of *Nietzsche and Jewish Culture* (ed. Jacob Golomb), *Le'ela* 47 (April 1999), 62.
3. See *Thus Spoke Zarathustra* Part IV, 10–11; *Ecce Homo* Part III, "The Birth of Tragedy", 2; *Beyond Good and Evil*, 56; *The Gay Science*, 341. All references are to section numbers unless otherwise stated. Except where otherwise indicated, all translations from Nietzsche's works are from the Cambridge Texts in the History of Philosophy editions. Translations from *Thus Spoke Zarathustra*, except where indicated, are from Graham Parkes's edition (Oxford: Oxford University Press, 2005).
4. See, for example, Lawrence J. Hatab, *Nietzsche's On the Genealogy of Morality: An Introduction* (Cambridge: Cambridge University Press, 2008), 17: "[L]ife-affirmation—in response to the *question* of meaning in life and the danger of nihilism after the death of God—is the core issue in Nietzsche's thought" (emphasis in original).
5. *Covenant and Conversation: Deuteronomy*, 146.
6. *Essays on Ethics: A Weekly Reading of the Jewish Bible*, 311.
7. Ibid., 312.
8. Koren Sukkot Mahzor, xxviii–xxix.
9. See Nietzsche, *Daybreak*, section 204: "Every Jew possesses in the history of his fathers and grandfathers a great fund of examples of the coldest self-possession and endurance in fearful situations, of the subtlest outwitting and exploitation of chance and misfortune; their courage beneath the cloak of miserable submission, their heroism in *spernere se sperni* [being contemptuous of the fact that they are an object of contempt], surpasses the virtues of all the saints".
10. Nietzsche, while certainly not advocating that our passions be allowed free rein, strongly condemns their "castration", which he views as an attack on life itself. See *Twilight of the Idols*, V, 1.
11. Note the reference in *Daybreak* 204 (see n.9 above) to "the subtlest outwitting and exploitation of chance and misfortune". In a letter of 1867, Nietzsche writes: "It does ... lie in our power, to use every event, every small and large accident, for our improvement and proficiency, to derive benefit from them" (cited and translated in Julian Young, *Friedrich Nietzsche: A Philosophical Biography* (Cambridge: Cambridge University Press, 2010), 67).
12. Koren Sukkot Mahzor, l–li.
13. *Essays on Ethics*, 313.
14. Ibid., 314.
15. Koren Sukkot Mahzor, liii.
16. Ibid., lxiii.
17. The attitude to this world which Nietzsche ascribes to Christianity is very close to that of Rav Soloveitchik's *homo religiosus* in *Halakhic Man*.

R. Soloveitchik's Halakhic Man, in contrast, vigorously affirms earthly existence. The interface here between R. Soloveitchik's thought and that of Nietzsche is discussed in detail in Daniel Rynhold and Michael J. Harris, *Nietzsche, Soloveitchik and Contemporary Jewish Philosophy* (Cambridge: Cambridge University Press, 2018), ch. 3.
18. There is a strong parallel here with the thought of Rav Soloveitchik. See Rynhold and Harris, esp. ch. 3.
19. *The Antichrist*, section 18; emphasis in original. See also *Ecce Homo* IV:8.
20. Koren Sukkot Mahzor, liii. See also, e.g., *Covenant and Conversation: Deuteronomy*, 125–29, 143–48; *Essays on Ethics*, 311–15.
21. See also *Covenant and Conversation: Deuteronomy*, 127–29; *Essays on Ethics*, 312–13.
22. Koren Sukkot Mahzor, liv.
23. *Thus Spoke Zarathustra* Part II, 3. Translation from *The Portable Nietzsche*, ed. and trans. by Walter Kaufmann (New York: Viking Penguin 1954), 200.
24. *Human, All Too Human*, vol. II, Part I, 62.
25. Ibid., vol. I, 9.
26. *The Gay Science*, 338; emphasis in original.
27. *Twilight of the Idols*, "Arrows and Epigrams," 12.
28. "In Search of the Why" in *Judaism's Life-Changing Ideas: A Weekly Reading of the Jewish Bible*, 181–84.
29. *Beyond Good and Evil*, 228.
30. *Zarathustra*, Part 1, 5.
31. *The Gay Science*, 338.
32. See also *Zarathustra*, Part Three, 5:2.
33. *Essays on Ethics*, 315.
34. Ibid., 315.
35. Koren Sukkot Mahzor, lii.
36. *Essays on Ethics*, 315.
37. See also Koren Sukkot Mahzor, xc: "To know that life is full of risk and yet to affirm it, to sense the full insecurity of the human situation and yet to rejoice: this, for me, is the essence of faith".
38. Koren Sukkot Mahzor, lxxxviii.

CHAPTER 26

Sacks on Sisyphus and Soloveitchik: From Myth to Meaning

Dov Lerner

Though Rabbi Jonathan Sacks and Rabbi Joseph Soloveitchik occupy distinct places in the constellation of modern Jewish giants, popular appreciation of their individual talents tends to see them in relative continuity. Both paired erudition with eloquence and modesty with confidence; both shared a commitment to Jewish tradition and a vision for a Jewish mission that responds to shifts in history. Both defended a blended education and attended eminent universities while pressing their listeners to invest this world with the spirit of the next. And yet, on a matter of inordinate consequence, these two titans were divided by an abyss—and that matter regards the pursuit of happiness.

Defining happiness is indeed a complex project as the word can connote several divergent, even adverse meanings.[1] For our purposes, we take the word 'happiness' to indicate a state of being characterized by a combination of calm, serenity, and harmony, one that stands in opposition to turmoil or pain. And it is this opposition, between forms of peace and

---

D. Lerner (✉)
Straus Center for Torah and Western Thought, Yeshiva University,
New York, NY, USA

© The Author(s), under exclusive license to Springer Nature Switzerland AG 2023
E. Brown, S. Weiss (eds.), *An Ode to Joy*,
https://doi.org/10.1007/978-3-031-28229-4_26

grief, that lies at the core of a rift between R. Sacks and R. Soloveitchik. The division can be evidenced simply by contrasting two virtually irreconcilable citations. R. Sacks writes, "In Judaism joy is the supreme religious emotion."[2] R. Soloveitchik, on the other hand, contends that "The religious act is fundamentally an experience of suffering."[3] For the sake of making the case a little clearer, however, we will go deeper.

* * *

At the turn of the twentieth century, in the wake of widespread secularization, a growing sect of philosophers known as existentialists drew attention to what they saw as a pervasive sense of loss and futility in Western society. Among others, it was Albert Camus who captured the mood in his 1942 essay entitled *The Myth of Sisyphus*. According to Greek myth, Sisyphus was the founder of Ephyra who, cheating death twice, infuriated Zeus and consequently was sentenced to spend eternity pushing a boulder, repeatedly, to the top of the same hill.

In his essay, Camus gives voice to a vision of the modern world defined by what he calls 'the absurd'—where Earth is a place ultimately bereft of hope. Through his lens, human beings are left tormented by the absence of purpose or essence and must climb, like Sisyphus, up the incline of life without any expectation of reaching a redemptive, or even a conclusive, destination. But Camus offered a path forward toward what he calls happiness, ending his essay with the words: "The struggle itself toward the heights is enough to fill a man's heart. One must imagine Sisyphus happy."[4]

R. Sacks, commenting on Camus' final sentence, simply writes: "Must one? Really? If that is happiness, what is misery? What is despair?"[5] He goes on to characterize Camus' vision as "coherent, consistent, lucid, perfectly rational within its own terms of reference," but fundamentally tragic and unredeemed. For R. Sacks, the mere refusal of purposelessness does not amount to true happiness, if there is no accompanying reason to believe that life has meaning. It is here that he makes his case for God.

In the final chapter of his *The Great Partnership*, he offers three arguments for belief in divinity—from biology, history, and entropy—though he notes that none of them truly settles the issue. In what might amount to a stunningly candid admission for a religious scholar, he writes: "None of this is intended as proof of the existence of God … Contemplation of the natural universe is an intimation, no more and no less, of the presence of a vast intelligence at work in the universe."[6] Where others have seen conclusive proof of the divine presence or providence, R. Sacks sees only possibility; in other words, it is not irrational, he writes, to be in awe of the cosmos yet remain skeptical about a creator.

Belief in God, for R. Sacks, is ultimately a matter of choice between two mutually exclusive, equally rational options. However, there is far more than mere intimations to assist in making this critical decision, which is why R. Sacks presents a fourth and final argument for faith, what he calls "The Argument from Happiness." In his words: "There either is or is not the Presence who brought it, and life, and you, into being. You have to make a choice and it will affect the whole of your life."[7]

Reacting to an advertisement placed on the sides of London buses by the British Humanist Association that read "There's probably no God. Now stop worrying and enjoy your life," R. Sacks suggests that quite on the contrary, happiness is more likely in the presence of God than in God's absence. He labels the ad as "One of the less profound propositions to have been produced by the collective intelligence of people who pride themselves on their intelligence," and adds that "If I wanted to stop worrying, I would not choose a world blind to my existence, indifferent to my fate, with no solace in this life or any other."[8] Citing the research and work of Tal Ben-Shahar, he writes: "The practices of religion—prayer ... ritual ... sacred narrative ... rites of passage ... deeds of reciprocal kindness...—create structures of meaning and relationship within which our individuality can flourish. This is where, for many of us, happiness is to be found."[9]

The case for religious faith is, for R. Sacks, made most compelling by contrasting it to Camus' modern myth and the new atheists' astonishingly shallow version of bliss, in which human beings are bidden to find joy in a meaningless existence. In summation, R. Sacks says: "I see people grow taller under the sunlight of divine love than they might have done under a godless sky."[10] Where Camus suggests that purposelessness can be overcome by a stubborn refusal to submit, R. Sacks suggests that life is far richer when "transfigured by a sense of dimly discerned significance," for, ultimately, "Religion is a sustained process of using the deep power of joy to see into the life of things."[11] Happiness is not a guaranteed consequence of a commitment to religious faith, but it is, for R. Sacks, an unambiguous aspiration.

* * *

R. Sacks' vision of Jewish tradition's embrace of an aspiration for human happiness begins at the dawn of his public record, in a 1973 essay entitled "Alienation and Faith"—which also marks the start of his dissent from R. Soloveitchik's defense of inner torment (or 'alienation') as an ideal, or at least, a necessity. As R. Sacks himself put it later in life: "The first article I ever published was a critique of Rabbi Joseph Soloveitchik's essay, 'The Lonely Man of Faith.' In Judaism, I argued, faith is not lonely. It is the redemption of solitude, not its celebration."[12]

And while R. Sacks does note a fundamental chasm between R. Soloveitchik's depiction of the self and that of the secular existentialists—rooted in the divergent sources of their respective perspectives—he sees them as emotionally or tonally analogous. For both Camus and R. Soloveitchik, there is an irreconcilable tension at the core of the human condition—for the former, as a product of a world without faith, and for the latter, as a result of faith itself; for both, life is—at its best—defined by a sense of intentional psychic suffering, what R. Soloveitchik calls, a "feeling of loneliness and being unwanted."[13] In his *Halakhic Man*, R. Soloveitchik goes even further: "Religion is not, at the outset, a refuge of grace and mercy for the despondent and desperate, an enchanted stream for crushed spirits, but a raging clamorous torrent of man's consciousness with all its crises, pangs, and torments."[14]

For R. Sacks, the tone of R. Soloveitchik's outlook is in consonance with the sense of loss that permeates existential sensibilities and thus affords a measure of empathy for those who participate in contemporary life. But, for him, Judaism offers something far better than empathy: redemption. In his words:

> I want ... to describe an alternative phenomenology of the Jewish self ... in which ... alienation and loneliness are defective states, the consequence of sin, and that the religious man of any age transcends divisions, [and] subsumes contrasts into harmonious emotion ... In short, I want to argue that Judaism stands to contemporary alienation in a redemptive ... relation.[15]

Though this early passage is rhetorically distinct from R. Sacks' later signature polish, his sense is clear: Jewish tradition sees faith as a means to breed joy in its adherents and seeks to present a pathway from alienation to harmony. First, he critiques R. Soloveitchik's reading of the first two chapters of Genesis, which serves as the latter's prism for promoting a vision of inexorable and essential spiritual tension—showing divergent, but equally attentive, readings produced by other Jewish exegetes. Then he argues that R. Soloveitchik's notion that a sense of alienation is, philosophically, a necessary consequence of faith is, rather, "the untestable record of his private impressions" and is ultimately subjective. And that is why he feels at liberty to disagree—and disagree deeply. In his words: "At a time when loneliness is the condition of the estranged Jew, one reading offers empathy, the other, healing."[16]

* * *

As part of R. Sacks' defense of religious faith, he paints the picture of a "life-changing" encounter that he had as a student with R. Soloveitchik.[17] He credits the latter with challenging him to think; but more important than the content of their conversation, for R. Sacks, was the impact of his presence. Along with Rabbi Schneerson, who R. Sacks also met at that time, he describes R. Soloveitchik as conveying "the gravitas and depth of the Jewish soul" and writes of feeling the divine presence in his company.[18] So, while R. Sacks thoroughly rejected dimensions of R. Soloveitchik's phenomenology, he saw his thought as seminal and felt him to be a sort of mentor. In fact, even in the essay in which he contests R. Soloveitchik's perspective, he notes that: "To state this contrast is not to formulate an opposition; simply to open another gate."[19]

However way we may characterize his critique though, it is clear that R. Sacks sought to forge a new way that deviated from the aspirations of both Camus' secular *Myth of Sisyphus* and R. Soloveitchik's religious *Lonely Man of Faith*. Where R. Soloveitchik's ethos seems to advocate a profound admiration for those who feel a deep and unassailable religious alienation, R. Sacks begs to differ. For him, Jewish faith does not demand that we embrace, even crave, an intractable existential tension, it insists that we attempt to transcend it. For R. Sacks, a life of faith—at its best—triumphs over the absurd and finds joy in the word of God; to live a life of faith, for R. Sacks, is to seek harmony, pursue happiness, and not bless but redeem solitude.

Notes

1. Rabbi Sacks himself explores various alternatives in his "Happiness: A Jewish Perspective." *Journal of Law and Religion* 29, no. 1 (2014): 30–47.
2. Jonathan Sacks, *Studies in Spirituality* (Israel: Toby Press, 2021), 258.

3. Joseph B. Soloveitchik, M. Krone, and S. Shmidt, *Divre Hashkafah* (Jerusalem: Sifriyat Eliner, 1992), 254 (translated from the Hebrew). The passage continues: "When man meets God, God demands self-sacrifice, which expresses itself in struggle with his primitive passions, in breaking his will, in accepting a transcendental "burden," in giving up exaggerated carnal desire, in occasional withdrawal from the sweet and pleasant, in dedication to the strangely bitter, in clash with secular rule, and in his yearning for a paradoxical world that is incomprehensible to others. Offer your sacrifice! This is the fundamental command given to the man of religion."
4. Albert Camus, *The Myth of Sisyphus* (United Kingdom: Knopf Doubleday Publishing Group, 2018), 123.
5. Jonathan Sacks, *The Great Partnership: Science, Religion, and the Search for Meaning* (United Kingdom: Knopf Doubleday Publishing Group, 2011), 192.
6. Ibid., 273.
7. Ibid., 285.
8. Ibid., 281.
9. Ibid., 280.
10. Ibid., 288.
11. Ibid., 193.
12. Jonathan Sacks, *Future Tense: Jews, Judaism, and Israel in the Twenty-First Century* (United States: Knopf Doubleday Publishing Group, 2012), 115.
13. Joseph B. Soloveitchik, *The Lonely Man of Faith* (United Kingdom: Doubleday, 2006), 4.
14. Joseph B. Soloveitchik, *Halakhic Man* (Israel: Jewish Publication Society of America, 1991), 142.
15. Jonathan Sacks, "Alienation and Faith," *Tradition: A Journal of Orthodox Jewish Thought* 13/14 (1973): 137–62; published later in his *Tradition in an Untraditional Age: Essays on Modern Jewish Thought* (United Kingdom: Vallentine, Mitchell, 1990), 222.
16. Ibid., 242.
17. Jonathan Sacks, *The Great Partnership*, 91.
18. Ibid.
19. Jonathan Sacks, *Tradition in an Untraditional Age*, 242.

CHAPTER 27

"I Will Tell You How Once They Were Joyous": On the Joy of the Baal Shem Tov's Hasidim and of R. Nahman of Bratslav

Biti Roi

At the beginning of the Hasidic movement, a new model of leadership was established: a charismatic zaddik focused on devotion to God developed a community to worship God with great religious and emotional fervor. Alongside awe and love, devotion and humility, some leaders of Hasidism promoted joy among the most important of religious emotions, making joy a central imperative.

Traditions in the name of the Baal Shem Tov (the Besht) emphasize the obligation to distance oneself from sadness and call instead to pursue joy actively. Statements that support this sentiment include: "Crying is very wrong; one should serve [God] with joy", and crying that is rooted in joy is very good,"[1] and, "Without joy, one cannot achieve intimacy with God."[2]

The Besht tradition offers a novel approach that opposed central concepts of Ashkenazic Hasidism, which posited asceticism as an excellent way

B. Roi (✉)
Schechter Institute, Jerusalem, Israel

Shalom Hartman Institute, Jerusalem, Israel

© The Author(s), under exclusive license to Springer Nature Switzerland AG 2023
E. Brown, S. Weiss (eds.), *An Ode to Joy*,
https://doi.org/10.1007/978-3-031-28229-4_27

to serve God. Sadness, the feeling of sin and filth rather than joy, was considered a central means of instilling the fear of heaven in Ashkenazic practice preceding R. Yisrael Baal Shem Tov; this was also practically manifest in widespread ascetic practices.[3]

In this literature, joy was identified for the most part with a minimum degree of trust and as an expression of the values of Ish Ben Gamzu.[4] And it was identified with the human ability to accept fully whatever happens, for better or for worse.[5]

At the same time, those who worshipped God fervently were generally assumed to suffer depression, anxiety, and even a certain sadness. If joy burst forth, it was regarded as an expression of pride or contempt for the fundamental condition of those who stand before God. In many Hasidic writings, moreover, the very opposite of joy in prayer was normative—namely, the lowering of the body enabled the raising of the spirit and vice versa. Physical manifestations of joy were considered on the margins of devotion to God, as the very opposite of it, or as an expression of a particularly diminished spiritual state.[6]

In contrast to these notions, the tradition of the Besht consciously opposed this path. The Besht was irritated by the "fearful" way in which his disciple and chief scribe, R. Jacob Joseph of Polnoye, leaned. He urged him to abandon the way of fasting and asceticism and to turn, instead, to a new way of religious awakening and devotion and warned him against sadness.[7]

It is further stated, in the name of the Besht, that serving through awe alone leads to chaos while the combination of joy with awe fills the world with light (according to the story of creation in Genesis);[8] joy is connected to special holy times.

According to the Besht, the Sabbath induces joy that has a special character above and beyond that which can be achieved during the rest of the week. Jewish tradition does not negate the significance of physical joy. Sabbath pleasures like food, sleep, rest, and conjugal intimacy demonstrate that, according to the Besht, it is impossible to reach spiritual joy without physical joy.[9]

Moreover, in the book of "In Praise of the Baal Shem Tov," which had a great influence on the shaping of Hasidic consciousness, joy emerges as a display of increased religious awakening. It carries a "burning fire" from heaven that is likened to a "mini" revelation akin to Mount Sinai or the story of the chariot.[10]

In contrast to fear-inducing Ashkenazic literature, many Hasidic writers offered a spiritual revolution of sorts on three levels:

1. Instead of resigning oneself to one's fate, one needs to acknowledge that joy is an essential force in human experience that must be actively cultivated.
2. Instead of equating sadness and guilt with fear of Heaven, one should regard joy as conducive to a transcendent religious state.[11]
3. In order to achieve spiritual fulfillment, one must not suppress joy. On the contrary, the body and its actions—dancing, singing, clapping and more—are a critical means of achieving joy and are evidence of its intensity.[12]

The Joy of R. Nahman of Bratslav

The great-grandson of the Besht, R. Nahman of Bratslav, addressed joy profoundly. His thought reveals an extensive preoccupation with the subtleties of joy, its virtue, and the challenges it poses.

At the same time, joy is sharpened by its opposite: sadness and the "black bitterness" (melancholy) of the soul. R. Nahman investigates the sources of sadness, studies its disadvantages, and offers ways to defeat different types of depression.[13]

He stated that, "It is a great mitzvah to be joyous always, and to overcome sadness and melancholy with all one's strength."[14]

The claim that a certain emotional behavior is a "great mitzvah [commandment]" is extremely interesting because it turns joy from a mode of fulfilling a commandment into a commandment in and of itself. The definition of joy as a "great mitzvah" is not superogatory to the commandments but rather positions joy as a central and foundational duty. It emphasizes joy as a significant life task that is comprehensive and unceasing. In this, R. Nahman continued the tradition of his rabbi and teacher—the Besht—by affirming joy as a religious duty while further developing it in his own original way.

Mitzvah [Commandment], Ritual and the Body

R. Nahman considers joy the very purpose of all the commandments and even their inner root, as he wrote:

> When one is joyous or dancing, one should make sure one is filled with joy from head to toe, because sometimes joy is only in the legs, or sometimes only in the heart or only in the brain [...] The essence of joy is to experi-

ence it completely, that is through all the levels of joy, and this requires the observance of many commandments, because the root of all the commandments is joy, as it says, "The commandments of God are upright and make the heart rejoice" (Psalms 19:8). Every commandment of the 613 commandments generates [will not let me eliminate has] has a corresponding physical manifestation of joy, every commandment according to its meaning.[15]

R. Nahman's thought is characterized by deep psychophysical insight; the profound connection between the body and the soul that produces joy is not a purely conscious matter. The fulfillment of a commandment brings joy to different bodily organs, thus awakening the whole body and making it whole.[16] If a *mitzvah* is an expression of happiness, then sin is the very negation of it. Sin expresses not only a violation of a person's moral integrity, or a rebellion against God's authority, but also, first and foremost, a violation of joy:

> If one transgresses a commandment, either positive or negative ... then the limb that violates that commandment, cannot experience joy in that same place because it transgressed the very commandment whose inherent purpose is joy, as described above; rather, one should be anxious that it is the opposite of joy, and this is the meaning of, "I am fearful over my sin" (Ps. 38:15).[17]

The anxiety is not the result of a particular sin but a response to the act of sin itself. Transgression produces a state of worry and distance from the natural vitality and serenity and joy of the body.

This integral connection between the mind and the body allows for two-way movement. The mind can awaken joy in the body, but the opposite is also true: physical action can awaken the mind. Since this is so, physical acts of joy can remove sadness, even if they are done unwillingly or even under duress:

> When it comes to joy, a parable is instructive: when people are joyous and dancing, and they encourage one person from the outside who is sad and bitter into the circle of dancers, they force him against his will to be joyous with them too—so, yes, there is joy in this.[18]

R. Nahman here notes "the superior value" of a deliberate intervention when it comes to a person overwhelmed by sadness in order to include them in an experience that promotes happiness. The parable of the dancers' circle teaches the value of dispelling sorrow through inclusion in the ring of joy; one need not succumb to the way of those who "stand outside." When encountering a person suffering from depression, one is commanded to help that individual overcome such depressive tendencies to the degree possible.

> It is supremely important to strive purposefully to embrace melancholy and to have it encounter happiness in such a way that the anguish itself will transform into joy [...] that then, from the surfeit of joy and happiness, one's worries, sadness, and melancholy will turn into happiness. Melancholy can be overtaken by force and brought into contact with joy, as in the above parable. This is the meaning of "They shall attain joy and gladness, while sorrow and sighing flee." At times of happiness, sorrow and sighing "stand aside" as above, but one needs to acknowledge them, embrace them and bring them into the joy as described above. This is the meaning of, "They shall attain joy and gladness;" they will achieve joy and gladness and overcome grief and sighing, which tend to flee and run away from joy, and bring them forcefully into a state of happiness.[19]

This parable beautifully expresses the Kabbalistic idea that one need not judge oneself harshly. It expresses the belief in the human power to turn the roots of sadness into joy and to create a profound change without denying the existence of misery. It also emphasizes how joy relies upon the body and its actions, namely dance in this example, to bring about this effect.

Joy in this World and the Next

The important status of joy is further strengthened by the description of joy as foundational for the post-Messianic future. Following from Zoharic literature, exile is seen not only the exile of the people from their country but also an exile of the heart. In accordance with this, and the verse, "You shall leave with joy" (Is. 52:12), R. Nahman describes the central element of redemption as great joy[20]:

> And in the future, joy will increase greatly, and that is why the Sages said[21] that the Almighty will lead the dance for the righteous in the End of Days, that is, He will make a dance for the righteous.[22]

The image of God dancing and joyous elevates dance to a divine act that we are obligated to imitate. R. Nahman describes the nature of the post-Messianic world. The Hebrew word "ḥolah," refers to both illness and to dance, emphasizing once again the transformation from sadness to joy and capacity of a kinesthetic activity to stimulate the healing of a depressive.[23]

The Ways to Achieve Joy

Whether from his own troubled personal life or out of recognition that the human condition is drawn to sadness, R. Nahman is aware of the challenges of achieving contentment. How then can joy be commanded at all? R. Nahman offers techniques to achieve joy, even if the person in question did not originally intend it:

> And the rule [is] that one has to marshal all one's strengths to be joyous always because it is human nature to be drawn into despair and despondency due to the adversities and exigencies of time … One, therefore, has to force oneself always with great strength to be joyous and to make oneself happy in whatever way one can, even with jokes and silly words.[24]

The claim that joy is achieved also through silly words[25] describes a didactic technique to aid learning, as stated in the Talmud BT *Shabbat* 30b. R. Nahman, however, sees joy as an end in itself. Like R. Nachman's suggestion about an intervention for someone else to be brought into the circle of dancers to overcome grief, he believes in "forcing oneself with great strength." Joy is a personal and conscious decision that one must make in the battle against melancholy.

R. Nahman begins the "Tale of the Seven Beggars" with a catastrophe that leaves a boy and a girl orphaned. They eventually get married in a mound of dirt and garbage. Every day of the seven days of their wedding feast, deformed beggars come to them and give them valuable gifts. The tale begins with the statement: "I will tell you how they were joyous," and emphasizes that happiness does not depend on external elements but rather on an internal state. In relation to God, any external shortcomings can be turned into great advantage. Blindness can sharpen spiritual sight. Stuttering can enable extraordinary singing and playing, and humpbacks can create spaces above themselves even though "there is no space at all." Every visible defect can be completely altered. Wealth and perfection are no replacement for true joy, for it is precisely at a shabby wedding with deformed guests that it is possible to achieve "great and wonderful" happiness.[26]

Another profound discussion of the difficulty of sustaining joy appears in "The Tale of the Sophisticate and the Simpleton," where R. Nahman sketches, with an artisan's hand, the figure of the sophisticate as someone who is not satisfied with reality, in accordance with an early verse from Ecclesiastes (1:18): "To increase learning is to increase heartache." The simpleton, the shoemaker who lacked everything, is described as someone who had joy in his heart wherever he turned. The simpleton is even joyous, creating a useless triangular shoe. When joy is identified with simplicity—that is, with a human's ability to accept the reality around him as it is—the fundamental relationship between sophistication and sadness is overturned. Worldliness and urbanity in the story is likened to swampy mud and clay in which one can drown. These humorous descriptions emphasize how joy can be achieved by those who embrace an imperfect and flawed reality. The simpleton says to his sophisticated friend, "I wish you would come to my level." One question remains: does R. Nahman believe that even those who are sophisticated can achieve a "second simplicity" and experience great joy?

Other examples of R. Nahman's novel exegesis and interpretation support his general approach that links happiness to spiritual states. For example, the verse, "I will sing praises to God while I exist" (Psalms 146:2) implies, according to R. Nahman, that one should, with the joy of his wisdom and erudition, somehow find in himself a place of positivity.

The human potential to achieve joy can be reinforced through specific techniques. One of them is guided imagination by which a person focuses on the "good points" in his life, and thereby achieves serenity. Since sadness is a barrier to serving God, a person must make an effort to "think positively." While the Mishna in Ethics of the Fathers calls on each person to judge his neighbor favorably (1:6), R. Nahman instructs people to judge themselves favorably as well. One must identify the goodness in oneself. The expression "point" emphasizes not only that in every person there is a positive inner source, a kind of "point" hidden within them, but also that in order to achieve joy, a person should not underestimate even the small inner treasures one possesses; one small point will join another good point and expand into great light and joy to the heart.

"By somehow finding in himself a good point, as explained in the verse, "I will sing praises to God while I exist," refers to one who can connect joy with his mind and his erudition."[27]

Beodi", in the verse, means both "while I exist" and also "with the abundance - "*od*" that I have, implies that one should find within himself ever increasing aspects of self-worth. Acknowledging one's own inner goodness is also a praise of God

True to his view that one must learn how to be joyous, R. Nahman offers another thought exercise. First, R Nahman describes the dissatisfaction of human nature and the challenge of experiencing true happiness. The expression "all" in the verse (Ex. 18:9), "And Jethro rejoiced over *all* the good," describes Jethro's expression of delight. In R. Nahman's opinion, it is possible to find a person who is sometimes joyous or a little joyous, but it is rare to find a person who is joyous all the time about everything:

And Jethro rejoiced over *all* the good: ordinary people rejoice over the collective good they experience. There are many subjective aspects to joy. For example, at a wedding, there are those who are joyous when they eat fish and meat and the like, and there are those who are joyous because of the music, and some who are joyous from other aspects. Some are joyous because of the wedding itself, such as the in-laws who ... are joyous from the wedding itself ... But there is no one who requires all the aspects of the wedding to be joyous to experience happiness ... There is also one who has no joy at all, not from eating, drinking or any other aspect, rather he experiences jealousy and sorrow, because he is envious of the match.

R. Nahman describes how one can climb the ranks of happiness to reach great joy from spiritual observation:

Because all kinds of happy occasions are only joyous at the moment when they occur, such as, for example, the joy of a wedding or a circumcision. The joy is only at that time. But if one looks beyond that, there is no joy in the world because of the end of human life (BT *Berakhot* 17). Yet if one past "the end of the end," then one is very joyous, because the end of all ends is the purpose, is very good. And this is the meaning of "And Jethro rejoiced over all the good." It was joyous even when he looked beyond the good of the moment.

The events that a person rejoices in, such as weddings and circumcisions, are only a momentary relief to an enduring difficult reality. The fact of one's death is a consciousness that fills one's life in the present and affects one's entire behavior in this world: "If one looks at the end, there is no joy in the world because it is the end of a person...." In the face of this fleeting joy, R. Nahman presents that true joy that will be achieved, not in the face of the bitter end, namely death and loss, but at a point beyond momentary joy. The preposition "over" in the term "rejoicing *over* the good" is interpreted not as "about" but rather "beyond," or from what there is above, from the ability to look "beyond the good" to what is beyond this world, which also gives the reality, here and now, its deeper meaning.

Later, R. Nahman explains that "to rejoice over everything" is a special virtue, which is only achieved by the one who reflects on the Divine Source of all things, where everything is "one":

> But the completeness and greatness of joy is that of the one who rejoices over *all* the good things together, and this is impossible, unless you look beyond all the good things, that is, at the [Divine] Source, from which all good things flow, and from which everything becomes one.... And this is the meaning of, "And Jethro rejoiced over *all* the good," that is, at the Source, where everything is one and where *all* joys exist together.

Summary

The image of Hasidim dancing in a forest and drinking strong wine, as disparagingly described by the *mitnagdim*, the *maskilim*, and even some of the first researchers of Hasidism, offer a superficial view of a complex and demanding emotional and spiritual discipline. The joy about which the Hassidim wrote, and its public expression in various Hasidic communities, takes on great depth in the writings of the Besht, and in particular in the writings of his student R. Nahman of Bratslav. Happiness is expressed and described as a general and comprehensive religious commandment in itself beyond the manner in which commandments are observed. True joy overcomes separation and alienation and supercedes a sense of the partiality and finality of life. It is achieved by the human ability to experience freedom from a foreboding sense of mortality that shadows human life and the capacity to look beyond it "at the Divine Source, where everything is one." The story "Silly Words" describes a physical awakening of simple joy from dance. Even an activity that begins with minimal intensity can develop into strong physical and emotional joy. Such a concept of joy recognizes rudimentary sadness and grief as a basic existential state. Practices of guided imagination, sublimation, elevation, and inversion, can be considered precursors to many psychophysical states that have been developed in the Western world in psychoanalysis and other therapeutic methods. All of this comes to teach us about the virtue of joy and its importance. Happiness is more than achieving personal wellbeing. It also helps achieve an exalted religious state.

Notes

1. *Tzavaat HaRivash* (Heb.), 46, 19.
2. *Ya'akov Yosef of Polnoye, Toldot Yacov Yosef, Tezave 64b.*
3. Yitzhak Be'er, *Sefer Hasidim* (Heb.).
4. On the attributes of Ish Ben Gamzu and the influence of stoic concepts as an attraction and a source of peace of mind, see Ephraim E. Urbach, *The Sages* (Jerusalem: Magnes Press, 1975).
5. See *Menorat HaMeor* (Heb.), chapter 14; Zeev Gries, *HaSimḥa BeHasidut* (Joy in Hasidism) (Heb.), Kabbalah 38 (5777), 171–84.
6. See *Menorat HaMeor*, chapter 14. R. Yona Megirandi in *Shaarei Teshuva LeMerirut Lev Leda'aga Ufaḥad* (Heb.), see 4, 14, 4:12: "To be joyous in his sufferings inasmuch as they have brought him sublime benefits," 2:4; to increase "sorrow in the heart," 1:11; "to be a responsive soul," 1:13; and more.
7. This is established, for example from the letter of the Besht to the Ba'al HaToldot (*Shivḥei HaBesht* [In Praise of the Besht] (Heb.), Rubenstein edition, 103–5). On the reliability of the letter, see Rosman, *Miḥtavei HaBesht*, 9–10. On the asceticism of the Maggid of Miedzyrzec before he met the Besht, idem Rubenstein, 16–129. On the "alternate" way of Hasidism that opposes asceticism, see also *Butzine Denohora*, page 15b (see also *Or HaNegoz*, 74). For further sources in the introduction of the *Sefer HaBesht*, 33–34. Margolin, *Mikdash Adam*, 242–44.
8. *Ya'akov Yosef of Polnoye* (Heb.), Ben Porat Yosef, Bereshit 10b.
9. Idem., Shelaḥ 137a.
10. *Shivḥei HaBesht* (Heb.), Mondstein edition, 125.
11. However, one should stress sadness as a valued attribute for Hasidim, and this is according to the Babylonian Talmud, Hagiga 14a, see that for whom "his heart worries inside" is someone who is deserving of high achievements.
12. On music as a source of joy, see *Likutei MoHaran*, part 2, 24. The types of music are related there to the blood pulsing through the arteries, and therefore to living. On Hasidic dance, see Yosef Panton, *Rikud HaKodesh*

BeRuhaniut HaYehudit: HaRikud Hahasidi (Heb.), Da'at 45 (5760), 135–45.
13. The second name of R. Nachman was Simḥa (Joy). On melancholy in Hasidut and in R. Nachman of Breslau, see Z. Marak, *Mistika Shigaon* (Heb.).
14. *Likutei Moharan*, part 2, 24. In fact, it was already mentioned by Rabbenu Behaye.
15. Likutey Mohara" n 178.
16. Moshe Idel, *The Executive Body*. While the Sages established the body as the site of the performance of the mitzvah, R. Nachman sees it as a space for joy and even for faith. See, for example, the claim of R. Nachman, that the body tells the soul, and reminds it of things, *Likutei Moharan*, part 1, 22. On these psychophysical precepts, see Roni Bar Lev, *Emunah Radikalit* (Heb).
17. Idem., see also *Likutei Moharan*, part 2, 48: "Because sadness is the other side [evil], and God hates it."
18. *Likutei Moharan*, part 2, 23.
19. Idem, idem.
20. *Likutei Moharan*, part 1, 24b.
21. Midrash Raba, Shmini, 9:11.
22. "When a person makes himself happy with the joy of a mitzvah, and the joy is so great that it touches his feet, that is, he is dancing because of joy, [...] we are directed to examine the heart by the joy in the heart, because the joy lifts people up, and this is the dance that lifts one's feet every time." *Likutei Moharan*, part 2, 81. On Hasidic dance, see above, fn. 13.
23. *Likutei Moharan*, part 2, idem. (The English translation is in the book by David Shulman, 33–36).
24. *Likutei Moharan*, part 2, 24.
25. Babylonian Talmud, Shabbat 30b, Pesaḥim 117a, Zohar, part 2, 107a.
26. Sipurey Maaasiyot, Jerusalem maase 13, Jerusalem 1985, 237–83.
27. *Likutei Moharan*, part 2, 34.

PART VI

Joy in Jewish History and Modernity

CHAPTER 28

Happy Alone or Happy Together? R. Jonathan Sacks, Contemporary Culture, and the Promise of Hope

Jonathan D. Sarna

"In Judaism," Rabbi Jonathan Sacks once wrote, "happiness is not something we find in solitude, still less in self-gratification. It is something we experience together."[1] To Rabbi Sacks, Judaism's "most original contribution to the understanding of human wellbeing" lay in its emphasis on the *shared* nature of happiness.[2] He demonstrated this by highlighting the word *simha*, the most common term for happiness in the Torah. "*Simha* in the Torah is never about individuals. It is always about something we share," he argued.[3] He explained that *simha* "is not a private emotion… It is a social state, a predicate of 'we,' not 'I.' There is no such thing as feeling *simha* alone."[4]

Both in his focus on the "essentially collective" nature of happiness in Judaism, and in his privileging of *simha* over *ashrei*, the better-known biblical term for happiness, Rabbi Sacks differed from others who have studied the Jewish view of happiness. Nahum Sarna, for example, pointed to

J. D. Sarna (✉)
Brandeis University, Waltham, MA, USA

Psalm 1 as the Bible's quintessential statement on happiness. He highlighted both the Psalm's individualistic focus ("Happy is the one") and its employment of the word *ashrei*." Happiness, according to Sarna's interpretation of the Psalm, contains the "seminal idea" that "the study of the sacred and revered text itself constitutes a pious act, a profoundly religious experience, and is an important mode of worship." For the Psalmist, he wrote, "the highest form of happiness results from the deliberate assumption of a commitment to a certain way of life, a course that is governed by God's Teaching (*Torah*)." The Psalmist focused on the individual—'*ish*— Sarna observed. Happiness in Psalm 1 entails conscious *withdrawal* from social situations likely to produce deleterious effects. The happy person whom the Psalm celebrates, instead of being part of a group as Rabbi Sacks would have led us to expect, actually "stands apart from the crowd."[5]

Hava Tirosh-Samuelson, in her exhaustive studies of "happiness in premodern Judaism" likewise argues that "the main biblical term to denote happiness is *ashrei*, a state of being that emerges from a certain pattern of life, precisely as the Greek philosophers held."[6] The ancient rabbis, she shows, "understood philosophy as a way of life that leads to happiness." They promoted *individual* character formation as the route to happiness. Based on Psalm 1, they linked happiness to personal conduct, and witnessed the ethics of the Fathers. Subsequent Jewish philosophy similarly focused on the individual. To Philo of Alexandria, for example, "the zenith of the happy life is an *individual* ecstatic and unmediated coming to know the transcendent and immaterial God." Abraham Ibn Daud, according to Tirosh-Samuelson, asserted that "happiness means perfection of the human soul attainable by those who cultivate the virtues through the observance of Torah and who also actualize their rational potential." For Jews who lived under Christianity, she found, discourse concerning happiness "was configured in the context of the interreligious debate about the salvation of the *individual* soul," which was also the arena of competition between Judaism and Christianity, and so forth. Since Jews followed Aristotle in linking happiness to the cultivation of virtues and the attainment of knowledge, it was the study of Torah and the pursuit of wisdom (variously defined) that dominated Jewish discourse concerning happiness prior to modernity, Tirosh-Samuelson concludes.[7] Interpersonal relationships, so critical to Jonathan Sacks' view of happiness in Judaism, go unmentioned here.[8]

They also go practically unmentioned in Michael Fishbane's lofty survey entitled, revealingly "The *Inwardness* of Joy in Jewish Spirituality." A lengthy discussion there of the sixteenth-century Rabbi Elijah de Vidas' spiritual-moral compendium entitled *Reshit Hokhmah* ("The Beginning of Wisdom"), with its important section on happiness, focuses on awakening joy through contemplation, Torah study, song, prayer, the fulfillment of the commandments, and—most significantly—"contemplation of the Name and Greatness of God in isolation (*hitboddedut*)." Contrary to R. Sacks, De Vidas, a mystic, *did* experience *simha* alone![9]

Of course, the world in Rabbi Sacks' day was entirely different from that of the Psalmist, the medieval Jewish philosopher, and the mystic. Rabbi Sacks' readers considered happiness not a reward granted to a fortunate few who stood apart from their peers and focused their lives around Torah study and the pursuit of wisdom, but rather "a natural condition, a law of our nature, and the way we were intended to be."[10] The American Declaration of Independence, in 1776, had declared it a self-evident truth that "the pursuit of happiness" was an "unalienable right" with which all humans were "endowed by their creator." In France, the Declaration of Rights of Man (1789) set forth principles that would "redound to the happiness of all." George Washington, writing to the Jews of Newport in 1790, prayed that God would make them and all Americans "in his own due time and way everlastingly happy."[11]

The problem, as Rabbi Sacks expressed it in *Celebrating Life* (2000), was that notwithstanding these lofty aspirations, "happiness has proved elusive." Indeed, "survey after survey shows that we are no happier than our parents were a generation ago, and our children are even less so."[12] His solution was to focus on relationships. In an Anglo-American world that privileged rugged individualism and freedom of self, he boldly spoke out in favor of families, neighborhoods, communities, voluntary organizations and religious groups.[13] In his approach to happiness, too, he focused on the collective. His, he explained, belonged "to a worldview that has already declared at the start of the human story that "[i]t is not good for man to be alone [Gen 2:18]."[14]

Rabbi Sacks quoted a remarkable story about the Lubavitcher Rebbe in support of his critique of individualism and its discontents:

> When I was an undergraduate student, I visited the great Jewish leader Rabbi Menahem Mendel Schneersohn, known as the Lubavitcher Rebbe. As I was waiting to meet him, one of his disciples told me the story of a man who had recently written a letter to the Rebbe that went something like this: "I need the Rebbe's help. I am deeply depressed. I pray and find no comfort.

I perform the commands but feel nothing. I find it hard to carry on." The Rebbe had sent a compelling reply without writing a single word. He simply ringed the first word in every sentence of the original letter, the word "I." It was, he was hinting, the man's preoccupation with himself that was at the root of his depression.[15]

The Rebbe's response to a single, depressed individual became for Rabbi Sacks a diagnosis of society's ills writ large. His prescription was *simha*, replacing "I" with "we"—joy experienced together.

Rabbi Sacks was well aware of alternative Jewish approaches to happiness that focused more on *ashrei*, philosophical happiness, mystical happiness, serving God, and the like.[16] It was, though, the "social vision" that he found particularly compelling because of "our condition now." Citing such cultural critics as Tony Judt, Alasdair C. MacIntyre, Robert Bellah, Robert Putnam, and Jean-Francois Lyotard, he asserted that "values and virtues were being eroded in the headlong pursuit of material gain." People "were getting richer but not measurably happier." They were "more preoccupied with self and less with society and community."[17]

Rabbi Sacks' vision of happiness, drawing upon Jewish sources, looked to reverse these doleful trends. In the name of happiness, he promoted a more conservative social agenda aimed at restoring society's central values and institutions:

> Social happiness requires a network of strong relationships, of which the family is the first and most basic. This requires an ethic of sexual fidelity as well as parental responsibility. Collective happiness also requires a sense of collective responsibility and a practical concern for the welfare and dignity of others. We need to cultivate the sense of gratitude, which in turn requires collective memory as well as the rituals of thanksgiving.[18]

Understood as cultural criticism, Rabbi Sacks' focus on social happiness to the exclusion of other Jewish approaches to the subject makes perfect sense. He was concerned above all with "what is at risk *in our present culture*."[19] The Psalmist, the philosopher, the mystic—they had lived in different times and settings. Rabbi Sacks, living as he did amid "the acquisitive individualism of our late capitalist, postmodern order," concluded that "the resilience of *simha*, the joy that exists in virtue of being shared," could provide Jews and non-Jews alike with "the ever-renewable promise of hope."[20]

NOTES

1. Jonathan Sacks, "Happiness: A Jewish Perspective," *Journal of Law and Religion* 29 (February 2014): 38.
2. Ibid., 45.
3. https://www.rabbisacks.org/covenant-conversation/ki-tavo/the-pursuit-of-joy/ (*Ki Tavo* 5775).
4. https://www.rabbisacks.org/archive/happiness-is-to-be-found-in-being-not-in-having/ (25 October 2008).
5. Nahum M. Sarna, *Songs of the Heart: An Introduction to the Book of Psalms* (New York: Schocken, 1993), 27–32.
6. Hava Tirosh-Samuelson, *Happiness in Premodern Judaism: Virtue, Knowledge and Well-being* (Cincinnati: Hebrew Union College Press, 2003); Hava Tirosh-Samuelson, "Virtue and Happiness," in *The Cambridge History of Jewish Philosophy: From Antiquity Through the Seventeenth Century*, eds. Steven Nadler and T.M. Rudavsky (Cambridge: Cambridge University Press, 2008), 707–67, quotes from 711, 763.
7. Tirosh-Samuelson, "Virtue and Happiness," 720,730, 738, 762 (italics added).
8. "It is the quality of our interpersonal relationships that more than anything else shape the nature of our happiness," Sacks, "Happiness: A Jewish Perspective," 41.
9. Michael Fishbane, "The Inwardness of Joy in Jewish Spirituality," in *In Pursuit of Happiness*, ed. Leroy S. Rounder (Notre Dame: University of Notre Dame Press, 1995), 71–88, esp.77–81. Later Hasidic masters like Rabbi Nahman of Bratslav placed greater emphasis on interpersonal expressions of *simcha*, especially through dance and pilgrimage to the sage; ibid., 83–85.
10. Darrin M. McMahon, *Happiness: A History* (New York: Atlantic Monthly Press, 2006), 201.
11. These documents may conveniently be found online: https://www.archives.gov/founding-docs/declaration-transcript; https://avalon.law.yale.edu/18th_century/rightsof.asp; https://founders.archives.gov/documents/Washington/05-06-02-0135.
12. Jonathan Sacks, *Celebrating Life: Finding Happiness in Unexpected Places* (London: HarperCollins, 2000), 1–2.
13. Jonathan Sacks, *The Politics of Hope* (London: Jonathan Cape, 1997).
14. Sacks, "Happiness: A Jewish Perspective," 39.
15. Ibid., 38; for other versions of this story see Sacks, *Celebrating Life*, 47–48, and https://www.rabbisacks.org/covenant-conversation/reeh/collective-joy/.

16. Ibid., 34–35, 45.
17. Ibid., 46.
18. Ibid.
19. Sacks, *Celebrating Life*, 51 (italics added).
20. Sacks, "Happiness: A Jewish Perspective," 46–47.

CHAPTER 29

Joy and Judaism at the Battle of Bunker Hill

Ari Lamm

"The capacity for joy," wrote our teacher Rabbi Lord Jonathan Sacks, "is what gives the Jewish people the strength to endure."[1] Over the course of millennia, there have been few more fundamentally joyous activities in Jewish life than Torah study. Classical rabbinic literature understood joy as so fundamental to the study of Torah that it rendered this activity incompatible with mourning on the ninth of Av.[2] Elsewhere, the rabbis debate which element of the learning experience brought true joy—is it the straightforward study of Mishnah, or the tumultuous analysis of Talmud?[3] Of greatest significance for our purposes, however, is Rabbi Zeira's conviction that the joy of Torah study lies in dialogue.[4] What could possibly compare to the delight one feels in studying with another person—in the give and take in pursuit of God's Will? It is precisely this sort of joy that typifies the revival of Torah learning upon American shores during the twentieth century. But how far back in the annals of this country can it be traced?

In fact, it first manifested in an unusual relationship between a prominent rabbi and a well-known figure from the Founding Era. In exploring

A. Lamm (✉)
Bnai Zion Foundation, New York, NY, USA

© The Author(s), under exclusive license to Springer Nature Switzerland AG 2023
E. Brown, S. Weiss (eds.), *An Ode to Joy*,
https://doi.org/10.1007/978-3-031-28229-4_29

217

this story, we can learn a great deal about the influence of learned Jews and Jewish ideas upon the early years of the American experiment.

In July of 1775, Ezra Stiles wrote to a friend about the "Civil War, which rages with unbounded Fury Horrors and Desolation especially in New England"—describing with special detail, even excitement, the recent Battle of Bunker Hill. At the time, Stiles was a congregationalist minister in Newport, Rhode Island. An influential theologian and man of letters—historian Edmund Morgan deemed him "one of the most learned men in America"—Stiles assumed the presidency of Yale during the Revolutionary War in 1778, and became one of the founders of Brown University.

Stiles' 1775 letter was addressed not to a statesman, nor a military officer, nor even a fellow Christian clergyman, but to none other than Rabbi Raphael Haim Isaac Carigal, scion of a rabbinic family in Hebron, who had traveled extensively across the Middle East, Europe, and the Americas. In 1773, his sojourns had taken him to Stiles' Newport, where he served for just under a year as the much-beloved rabbi of Congregation Yeshuat Israel, known today as the Touro Synagogue, before moving on to the Caribbean. For a short year, then, Stiles and Rabbi Carigal overlapped as spiritual leaders in one of the most prominent colonial towns in the New World. But shared geographical circumstances notwithstanding, why would the two have become more than passing acquaintances? Why, in fact, should Stiles have felt the need to write Rabbi Carigal about a revolution underway in a land where the latter had resided for only a few months?[5]

To make matters more interesting, consider another letter Stiles penned a few years earlier to an altogether better-known correspondent. On December 27, 1769, Stiles wrote to his friend Benjamin Franklin, then in London, asking him to procure a copy of "[The] Zohar. With the Latin Translation if to be had: else in Hebrew alone." Why would Stiles have been interested in this famously esoteric work of Jewish mysticism? And why on earth would he assume that Franklin, of all people, would know where to find it?[6]

In order to make sense of all this, we'll need to situate Stiles' America against the backdrop of European civilization during the sixteenth and seventeenth centuries. The rise of humanism during the Renaissance followed soon after by the Reformation forced individuals in the West—laypeople, diplomats, philosophers, and theologians alike—to rethink what constituted a righteous personal life and a virtuous society. If prior generations of Europeans had looked to Greco-Roman thought and scholastic philosophy, mediated by the church, as the basis for piety, major figures from Erasmus to Martin Luther challenged this approach as benighted—possibly even heretical. Those seeking to know what is good should instead look directly to the Bible, God's word, for guidance.

While this seemed simple enough in theory, the problem quickly arose that the Bible is famously quite difficult to interpret. So how should one know what the Bible actually meant in any given context? Europeans could no longer rely for help upon traditional scholarly commentaries and translations, whose many inaccuracies the humanists had exposed. And with the advent of the Reformation, Protestants were certainly unwilling to trust the biblical interpretations of the medieval church. The only available option, it seemed, was *ad fontes*—to go back to the original sources, per the Renaissance battle cry—and examine the Bible afresh in its original language. The subsequent explosion of Hebrew study and scholarship across Europe beginning in the sixteenth century led to another realization: the best way to understand the Bible might be to ask those who had been studying it for centuries, but whose insights had been uncorrupted by any association with the Roman church.

What body of literature could possibly fit this bill? The answer quickly became clear: Jewish interpretive tradition. The sixteenth and seventeenth centuries accordingly saw extraordinarily widespread interest in classical rabbinic works. By the end of this era, Europeans had translated into Latin the Mishnah, much of the Babylonian Talmud, numerous midrashic texts and Aramaic targumic works, the Zohar, the major publications of Maimonides, Judah Halevi, Ibn Ezra, Radak, and many more luminaries of the Jewish Middle Ages. Meanwhile, the rise of the printing press ensured that both scholarly and popular writings rooted in this new scholarship spread as widely as possible. The results for Western civilization were profound. "This explosion in the quantity of available Hebraica," wrote historian Eric Nelson, "affected virtually every aspect of European intellectual life," from medicine, to theology, to political philosophy.[7]

What did Europe's re-discovery of Jewish wisdom mean for actual, living Jews? It typically produced one of two outcomes. For some Renaissance scholars and clergymen, it resulted in even more virulent antisemitism. The more they needed to rely on *past* Jews, the more they felt the need to demonstrate correspondingly greater antipathy to Jews in the present. Perhaps the most notorious example is the father of the Reformation, Martin Luther himself. Even for his time, Luther voiced Christian antisemitism in the extreme. For other eminent minds of this period, by contrast, the new encounter with Jewish tradition yielded a philosemitism unprecedented in the history of the West. One such thinker, Johannes Reuchlin, was a German humanist and leading figure in the field of Hebrew studies; his work paved the way for the Hebraic revival in Europe. Reuchlin became best known for his indefatigable efforts to defend the Jewish community of the Holy Roman Empire from the notorious imperial mandate of 1509 that required the confiscation and burning of all Jewish books. Jewish history did not forget Reuchlin's support at such a critical moment. No less a rabbinic luminary than Rabbi Israel Lipschutz of Danzig, author of the celebrated mishnaic commentary *Tiferet Yisrael*, remembered him as one of the righteous among the nations (*hasidei ummot ha-olam*).[8]

Nevertheless, while sixteenth-century philosemitism represented an extraordinary civilizational achievement, particularly for its time, it had its cultural limits. When Reuchlin, for instance, used his defense of Jewish books to argue for the importance of providing Hebrew instruction in the empire's universities, he had an opportunity to propose that living Jews serve as teachers. Instead, he suggested that "Jews who are resident in our lands should be of assistance to us, out of good neighbourly relations and willingly loan their books, in return of course for a substantial deposit." Reuchlin understood that Europe's appetite for Jewish learning for the most part extended to learning *from* dead Jews, not *with* living ones. Reuchlin himself, to be sure, had no such compunction. During a 1498 stay in Rome, he spent about six months in daily study with none other than Rabbi Obadiah Sforno, for whom Reuchlin had deep admiration. But there were constraints on what one could or would wish to declaim in public with respect to learning with Jews.[9]

This brings us back to Stiles. He eventually procured a copy of the Zohar in 1772—the first such copy ever to reach the New World. Within a few short months, he met and became entranced by Rabbi Carigal. He attended synagogue services on numerous occasions to hear Rabbi Carigal speak. But even more significantly, he was able to exercise his fascination with rabbinic wisdom and Jewish mysticism in regular study with his Newport colleague. One afternoon in late April of 1773, for example, he recorded a visit by Rabbi Carigal who, "sat with me in my Study till Evening." The two engaged in a capacious discussion of everything from the books of Genesis and Exodus to a text from *Sefer Ha-Yetzirah*. On a personal level, Stiles—like Reuchlin—was perfectly comfortable learning not only *from* Jews past, but *with* Jews present.[10]

The difference, however, is the lengths to which Stiles went to ensure that this *ethos* would actually become part of American public life.

Stiles assumed the presidency of Yale just as the American Revolution was underway. Due to the war, the college had suspended commencement exercises since 1775, and would only resume them in September of 1781, just over two weeks before the Battle of Yorktown. On that occasion, Yale's first commencement since the beginning of the Revolution, President Stiles stepped to the podium to address the gathered crowd. The title of his remarks was "An Oration Upon the Hebrew Literature," in which he explored the stunning breadth of Jewish intellectual history from Ezra to rabbinic literature, to the great medieval writers. But Stiles' remarks—composed in Hebrew and delivered in English translation—are especially noteworthy for two further reasons. First, he proposed that the study of rabbinic literature serves as the foundation for a proper university education: "This kind of Learning is worthy to be sought after and transplanted into the Colleges of America"—in his words: *beitei midrash shel America [religious study halls of America]*—"With desire I have earnestly desired to see it illuminating the Scholars of Yale College." Second, and more importantly, Stiles illustrated to his students exactly how he felt such studies should ideally take place. In his stirring concluding passage, Stiles exclaimed: "I have never poured Water upon the hands of Elijah, nor sat at the Feet of Gamaliel; but I have been taught personally at the mouth of the Masters of Wisdom...But as Light expelleth Darkness, so far doth R. [C]arigal surpass & excel all the rest."[11]

At this formative moment in the history of American higher education, Stiles made clear that American life would—at its best—be an experiment not merely in learning *from* Jews, but *with* them. No wonder, then, that Stiles felt the need to relate to Rabbi Carigal all the details of the incipient Revolution. After all, Stiles understood that the colonists' war for liberty was just as much for Rabbi Carigal's Jewish community as it was for Stiles' own parishioners. And the nation Stiles hoped would arise as a result would be built on the very Jewish wisdom he had learned from his rabbinic friend and teacher.

Rabbi Carigal spent just a few short months in what would soon become the United States of America. But even in so short a time he was able to put into practice one of Rabbi Sacks' most penetrating observations, offered over two centuries later: "To defend a country you need an army.

But to defend a free society you need schools. You need families and an educational system in which ideals are passed on from one generation to the next, and never lost, or despaired of, or obscured. So Jews became the people whose passion was education, whose citadels were schools and whose heroes were teachers."[12]

Notes

1. Jonathan Sacks, "The Pursuit of Joy," Covenant and Conversation (blog), accessed November 29, 2022, https://www.rabbisacks.org/covenant-conversation/ki-tavo/the-pursuit-of-joy/.
2. See BT *Ta'anit* 30a.
3. See BT *Bava Batra* 145b, with Rashbam ad loc., and Rabbeinu Gershom ad loc.
4. See BT *Eruvin* 54a.
5. For Stiles' letter to Rabbi Carigal, see Beinecke Library, *Ezra Stiles Papers*, letter to Raphael Haim Isaac Carigal, July 7, 1775. On Stiles' learned reputation, see Edmund S. Morgan, *The Gentle Puritan: A Life of Ezra Stiles, 1727–1795* (New York: W. W. Norton & Company, 1962), 134. On his acceptance of the post at Yale, then called Yale College, see ibid., 307; on his founding role at Brown, then the College of Rhode Island, see ibid., 204–6.
6. For Stiles' letter to Franklin see "To Benjamin Franklin from Ezra Stiles, 27 December 1769," National Archives: Founders Online, accessed November 28, 2022, http://founders.archives.gov/documents/Franklin/01-16-02-0172.
7. On the rise of Hebraic scholarship during the sixteenth and seventeenth centuries, see Eric Nelson, *The Hebrew Republic: Jewish Sources and the Transformation of European Political Thought* (Cambridge: Harvard University Press, 2010), 7–16. On the role of the printing press in the Reformation, see Andrew Pettegree, *Brand Luther: 1517, Printing and the Making of the Reformation* (Penguin Books, 2016).
8. On Luther's antisemitism, see David H. Price, *Johannes Reuchlin and the Campaign to Destroy Jewish Books* (Oxford University Press, 2011), 213–20. On Reuchlin's campaign against the Jewish book pogrom, see ibid., 95–138. On Reuchlin as one of the *hasidei ummot ha-olam*, see Rabbi Israel Lipschutz, *Tiferet Yisrael* to Mishnah Avot 3:1.
9. For Reuchlin's proposal that Jews should loan their books to German universities for Hebrew instruction, see Daniel O'Callaghan, *The Preservation of Jewish Religious Books in Sixteenth-Century Germany: Johannes Reuchlin's*

Augenspiegel (Leiden: Brill, 2012), 197. On Reuchlin's study with the Sforno, see Price, *Johannes Reuchlin*, 66–67.

10. On Stiles' receipt of a copy of the Zohar, see Franklin Bowditch Dexter, ed., *The Literary Diary of Ezra Stiles* (New York: C. Scribner's sons, 1901), 370; and see Brian Ogren, *Kabbalah and the Founding of America: The Early Influence of Jewish Thought in the New World* (New York: New York University Press, 2021), 155. For Stiles' study session with Rabbi Carigal, see Beinecke Library, *Ezra Stiles Papers*, journal entry for April 26, 1773. On Stiles' warm relationship with several rabbis see Arthur A. Chiel, "The Rabbis and Ezra Stiles," *American Jewish Historical Quarterly* 61, no. 4 (1972): 294–312. In Stiles' view, however, none of his rabbinic interlocutors could match Rabbi Carigal's erudition; on which see below.
11. On Yale's suspension of commencement exercises during the American Revolution, see David Andrew Wilock, "Testing the Elite: Yale College in the Revolutionary Era, 1740–1815" (PhD diss., St. John's University, 2021), 110. For Stiles' commencement remarks, see Ogren, *Kabbalah and the Founding of America*, 246–47. For the Hebrew version, see ibid., 236.
12. See Jonathan Sacks, "Freedom's Defence," Covenant and Conversation (blog), accessed November 29, 2022, https://www.rabbisacks.org/covenant-conversation/bo/freedoms-defence/.

CHAPTER 30

Joy in the Interfaith Encounter

Malka Z. Simkovich

My husband and I are friendly with a couple who host occasional gatherings at their elegant home after Shabbat prayer services. At one such get-together some months ago, our host approached me and my husband as we were socializing with some friends in the couple's garden. After asking whether we needed refills on our hors d'oeuvres, he turned to me with an amicable smile. "Malka," he asked, "What do the Jews have to do to get you back?" I laughed and shrugged, assuming that my friend's question was a friendly way of suggesting that my position on a Catholic campus is far afield from the Jewish community, a world apart from the gatherings, prayer services, and Shabbat meals that shape our religious lives. On the walk home, however, I wondered whether I had correctly interpreted my friend's question. Perhaps he meant to challenge my acceptance of a position that was sponsored by a community of people whose ancestors had brought misery to the Jewish people. Like most observant Jews, my friend did not consider interfaith dialogue to be a source of spiritual nourishment for Jews. Instead, he viewed dialogue as an undesirable exercise whose Jewish participants are misguided or manipulated.

M. Z. Simkovich (✉)
Catholic Theological Union, Chicago, IL, USA

© The Author(s), under exclusive license to Springer Nature Switzerland AG 2023
E. Brown, S. Weiss (eds.), *An Ode to Joy*,
https://doi.org/10.1007/978-3-031-28229-4_30

Of all the religions practiced in North America and Israel, the Catholic Church boasts the oldest and most organized formal relationship with global Jewry. Yet this relationship was only established after 1965, when the Second Vatican Council retracted the Church's position that the Jews are guilty of deicide, or God-murder. Jews, for their part, have only just begun to publicly respond to these overtures, and the public statements they have produced pay little attention to the emotional benefits of interfaith encounters.[1] Instead, their statements treat Jewish-Christian dialogue as a pragmatic response to overtures that highlight values and scriptures which both faiths share. Emotions such as joy simply do not come into play.

Three major Jewish statements on Jewish-Christian relations have been produced over the past few decades that clarify the Jewish community's attitude toward Jewish-Christian dialogue. These statements unconsciously build on one another, moving from a focus on shared values and a call to ethical action, to mutual love, and finally, to joy. They can be used to establish a case that observant Jews may engage in interfaith dialogue not only on the basis of shared values (or political interests, a factor that goes unmentioned in these statements), but also on the basis of emotional and spiritual enrichment.

The first major Jewish statement on Jewish-Christian dialogue is *Dabru Emet*, a document commissioned by the Institute for Christian and Jewish Studies in Baltimore, which was composed by four Jewish academics: Peter Ochs, Tikva Frymer-Kensky, David Novak, and Michael Signer. The document was published in *The New York Times* in September of 2000, and signed by hundreds of academics. *Dabru Emet* lists ten shared beliefs that bond Jews and Christians to one another. Some examples are that "Jews and Christians worship the same God" and that "Jews and Christians accept the moral principles of Torah." The statement also controversially declares that "Nazism was not a Christian phenomenon," and that if the Nazis were permitted to continue their assault upon humanity, they would have turned to Christians after eliminating the Jews.[2]

Orthodox Jewish academics lambasted *Dabru Emet* on the basis that it overstates Jewish and Christian similarities and absolves Christians of culpability for the decimation of European Jewry.[3] The document's list of shared values, moreover, seemed to presume that these values alone demand mutual engagement. The focus on shared goals is embodied in the statement's closing lines, which cites a verse from Isaiah:

Separately and together, we must work to bring justice and peace to our world. In this enterprise, we are guided by the vision of the prophets of Israel: "It shall come to pass in the end of days that the mountain of the Lord's house shall be established at the top of the mountains and be exalted above the hills, and the nations shall flow unto it ... and many peoples shall go and say, "Come ye and let us go up to the mountain of the Lord to the house of the God of Jacob and He will teach us of His ways and we will walk in his paths." (Isaiah 2:2–3)

This statement suggests that Jewish-Christian dialogue marks a subtle but significant movement toward the messianic age, which will be characterized by universal recognition of the One God. There is no mention of the internal nourishment that interfaith dialogue can offer, perhaps because the statement's authors felt that such a claim would be considered frivolous or controversial. Still, the implication that Jews can fulfill Isaiah's prediction of movement toward the messianic era by engaging in dialogue raises its stakes.

Fifteen years after the publication of *Dabru Emet*, Orthodox rabbis affiliated with the Center for Jewish–Christian Understanding and Cooperation (CJCUC) produced a statement of their own. Entitled *To Do the Will of Our Father in Heaven*, this statement cites Orthodox rabbis of the modern era who expressed fraternal friendship toward Christianity, not on the basis of shared values, but on the basis of mutual love. Note the following passages:

> Both Jews and Christians have a common covenantal mission to perfect the world under the sovereignty of the Almighty, so that all humanity will call on His name and abominations will be removed from the earth. We understand the hesitation of both sides to affirm this truth and we call on our communities to overcome these fears in order to establish a relationship of trust and respect. Rabbi Hirsch also taught that the Talmud puts Christians "with regard to the duties between man and man on exactly the same level as Jews. They have a claim to the benefit of all the duties not only of justice but also of active human brotherly love." In the past relations between Christians and Jews were often seen through the adversarial relationship of Esau and Jacob, yet Rabbi Naftali Zvi Berliner (Netziv) already understood at the end of the nineteenth century that Jews and Christians are destined by God to be loving partners: "In the future when the children of Esau are moved by pure spirit to recognize the people of Israel and their virtues, then we will also be moved to recognize that Esau is our brother."

> We Jews and Christians have more in common than what divides us: the ethical monotheism of Abraham; the relationship with the One Creator of Heaven and Earth, Who loves and cares for all of us; Jewish Sacred Scriptures; a belief in a binding tradition; and the values of life, family, compassionate righteousness, justice, inalienable freedom, universal love, and ultimate world peace. ... In imitating G-d, Jews and Christians must offer models of service, unconditional love, and holiness. We are all created in G-d's Holy Image, and Jews and Christians will remain dedicated to the Covenant by playing an active role together in redeeming the world.[4]

On the surface, *To Do the Will of Our Father in Heaven* seems to be more conservative than *Dabru Emet*. It underscores key differences between Jews and Christians, and references the Church's dark history of Jew-hatred. And yet, the effort to establish firm lines between Judaism and Christianity frees the writers to go beyond *Dabru Emet* when it comes to the emotional bonds that Jews and Christians can forge. Whereas *Dabru Emet* argues for dialogue based on shared values, *To Do the Will of Our Father in Heaven* internalizes dialogue by emphasizing mutual love. The sources that this document cites, moreover, are not about common conviction, but about the idea that Jews and Christians can encounter one another in love.

Orthodox rabbis produced yet another statement on the Jewish-Christian relationship just two years later. Entitled *Between Jerusalem and Rome*, this statement was written collaboratively by rabbis representing the Conference of European Rabbis, the Rabbinical Council of America, and the Chief Rabbinate of Israel. This document goes further than *Dabru Emet* and *To Do the Will of Our Father in Heaven* by placing a heavier burden of responsibility on the Church for its history of anti-Judaism and its culpability for the atrocities of the Holocaust.[5] Again, however, this articulation of difference allows the writers to raise the emotional stakes of the Jewish-Christian relationship. Here the bond is not based on shared action, or even love, but on the desire to bring joy to humanity:

> We seek to deepen our dialogue and partnership with the Church in order to foster our mutual understanding and to advance the goals outlined above. We seek to find additional ways that will enable us, together, to improve the world: to go in God's ways, feed the hungry and dress the naked, give joy to widows and orphans, provide refuge to the persecuted and the oppressed, and thus merit His blessings.[6]

The possibility that Jewish-Christian dialogue can lead to joy remains unexplored. Perhaps this is because the idea that interaction with Christians can cause joy is considered to be insensitive and macabre in light of the suffering that Jews have experienced at the hands of Christians.

Rabbi Sacks, however, invited his readers to think about encountering the other as an opportunity for joy, without ignoring Christianity's intolerant past. He drew a simple equation. Where God is found, so is joy. Rabbi Joseph Dov Soloveitchik, Rabbi Aharon Lichtenstein, and other giants of the Orthodox community eloquently described how immersion in the Torah gives a Jew pleasure and delight.[7] Rabbi Sacks took the light that these figures shone upon the Torah and gently turned it around to illuminate God's other precious creations.[8] If God is in the Torah, Rabbi Sacks suggested, surely God lies in all creation.[9] And if God is in all creation, then the encounter with all people can lead to the same kind of joy: the joy of self-discovery, and the joy of God-discovery, that the Torah offers. This joy does not demand forgiveness for moral evils of the past. But it does demand a radical optimism about the future that so profoundly characterized Rabbi Sacks' life and work.

Notes

1. This paper will focus on the Jewish relationship with the Catholic Church. This is because the Protestant communities, whether mainline or evangelical, or too diversified to be subject to productive generalization. The relationships between Jews and Protestants vary widely and operate on a mostly local level. The Catholic Church, however, has a centralized body of policy decisors which, in theory, should impact the way every Catholic relates to Judaism. Of course, this does not work in practice, which is why this article treats documents produced by the elite and has little to say about what's happening "on the ground."
2. The text of *Dabru Emet* is accessible at https://www.ccjr.us/dialogika-resources/documents-and-statements/jewish/dabru-emet.
3. Jon D. Levenson, "Dual-Covenant Theology vs. Dual-Truth Theory: An Exchange on Catholic-Jewish Dialogue," *Commonweal*, February 10, 2014, https://www.commonwealmagazine.org/dual-covenant-theology-vs-dual-truth-theory. For another response to *Dabru Emet* which expresses similar concern, see David Berger's essay, available at https://www.ccjr.us/dialogika-resources/documents-and-statements/analyses/dabru-emet-berger.

4. *To Do the Will of Our Father in Heaven*, 4–5, 7. This text is accessible at https://www.ccjr.us/dialogika-resources/documents-and-statements/jewish/orthodox-2015dec4.
5. Malka Z. Simkovich, "The Changing *Mesorah:* Orthodoxy on Interreligious Dialogue and Women's Leadership," in *From Confrontation to Covenant: Jews and Christians Reflect on the Orthodox Rabbinic Statement of "To Do the Will of Our Father in Heaven,"* ed. Eugene Korn (Jerusalem: Urim Press, 2021).
6. *Between Jerusalem and Rome*, accessible at https://www.ccjr.us/dialogika-resources/documents-and-statements/jewish/cer-cri-rca-2017.
7. See, for instance, Joseph B. Soloveitchik, "Al Ahavat Ha-Torah veGeulat Nefesh haDor," in *Be-Sod haYahad vehaYahid*, ed. Pinchas Peli (Jerusalem, 1976), 410–11.
8. Rabbi Sacks made his case knowing Rav Soloveitchik's influential position that Jewish-Christian dialogue demanded a quid pro quo relationship in which concession on one side would demand concession on the other. For Soloveitchik, "the mere appraisal of the worth of one community in terms of the service it has rendered to another community, no matter how great and important this service was, constitutes an infringement of the sovereignty and dignity of even the smallest of faith communities." Joseph B. Soloveitchik, "Confrontation," *Tradition* 6, no. 2 (1964): 5–29. Sacks was willing to consider the possibility of personal transformation as part of the interreligious encounter, and in his first edition of *The Dignity of Difference*, touted this transformation as enriching and desirable. See Jonathan Sacks, *The Dignity of Difference: How to Avoid the Clash of Civilizations* (New York: Bloomsbury, 2003).
9. Sacks insists, for instance, that "We encounter God in the face of a stranger. That, I believe, is the Hebrew Bible's single greatest and most counterintuitive contribution to ethics. God creates difference; therefore it is in one-who-is-different that we meet God." *The Dignity of Difference: How to Avoid the Clash of Civilizations* (Revised ed.; New York: Bloomsbury, 2003), 51. Sacks' position that interfaith dialogue can and should transform the observant Jew changed over time and is too complex to discuss in detail here. His approach to interfaith encounters as internally enriching, however, and his insistence that the interfaith encounter was an ends in itself, remained consistent.

PART VII

Joy in Hebrew Literature and Prayer

CHAPTER 31

Joy, Sorrow, and Emotional Equilibrium in Agnon

Jeffrey Saks

Rabbi Jonathan Sacks' observation that, "It is easy to speak to God in tears; it is hard to serve God in joy," reflects his ability to communicate the deep truths of religious experience in elegant aphorisms.[1] It is equally challenging to capture the complexities of human life in the medium of literature when cast in a joyous hue. Literature portrays human existence, and it more often does it well when recalling Tolstoy's adage that "Happy families are all alike, every unhappy family is unhappy in its own way." To get at a literary portrait of the good life, and to do so in a compelling way, the outlines of joy are often cast in relief against unhappiness, tragedy, sorrow, and suffering. If literature can be used as a lens to look back at ourselves as thinking, feeling, and spiritual beings, many of its best and most effective exemplars do so as cautionary tales. This may be particularly true for literature that depicts religious experience—think Tolstoy, Dostoevsky, Flannery O'Conner, Graham Greene, Marilynne Robinson, and while we're at it, the Bible itself, with its own panoply of unhappy families. While the first impulse of an author is almost always aesthetic, literature, in the formulation of R. Aharon Lichtenstein, "generally help[s] to

J. Saks (✉)
ATID/WebYeshiva.org & Agnon House, Jerusalem, Israel

© The Author(s), under exclusive license to Springer Nature Switzerland AG 2023
E. Brown, S. Weiss (eds.), *An Ode to Joy*,
https://doi.org/10.1007/978-3-031-28229-4_31

develop our spiritual personality. Time and again, [it intensifies] our insight into basic problems of moral and religious thought.... [It] deepens our understanding of man: his nature, functions, and duties."[2]

If, as the witticism goes, "Jews are like everyone else, only more so," then certainly Jewish literature *not only* but *even* more so. From Yiddish literature's well-placed *bitterer gelechter* [bitter laugh] through even much of contemporary Hebrew writing, we are reminded that modern authors depicting the Jewish experience would often take their heroes "beyond comedy into madness...[asking] the readers' pardon for having been able to rescue the humor from its end in tragedy."[3]

In the works of S.Y. Agnon, Hebrew literature's only Nobel laureate, the tragic, even when foregrounded with humor, was the author's most often chosen register to best explore the Jewish condition in the transformations it underwent in the nineteenth and early twentieth centuries. This says as much about that millennia-old literary genre as it does about that Jewish condition. As Ariel Hirschfeld observed:

> For many generations tragedy was the most serious literary genre examining the existential human condition and the questions which emanate from it: what is man and for what is he destined, what is human evil and from whence does it spring—and to sketch a portrait of mankind evolving throughout history. More than that, tragedy connects identity and belonging; it is the active center which binds Western civilization as a continuum of culture and tradition, transcending nations, languages, and geography. Tragedy's status, despite all the many religious and political transformations in the West, remains on the artistic frontlines, unaffected by historical, religious, or philosophical transformations.[4]

It is not surprising, therefore, that Agnon rarely depicts scenes of unbridled joy. To demonstrate, we will survey a few central passages in two of his better-known works to experience his depiction of joy, harmony, and emotional equilibrium. As I have noted elsewhere, despite his distillation of the classic Jewish bookshelf into the mold of modern literature, the Hebrew master was not writing a contemporary *Guide of the Perplexed*. Nevertheless, reading his work offers insight into the life well-lived as part of the religious quest.

In his 1950 novella, *Tehilla*, Agnon introduces his readers to one of the greatest figures of modern Hebrew literature.[5] At age 104, the title character is an "old woman, as comely an old woman as you have seen in all your days. Righteous she was, and wise she was, and gracious and humble too: for kindness and mercy were the light of her eyes, and every wrinkle in her face told of blessing and peace." As the senior citizen par excellence of the *Yishuv HaYashan* in Jerusalem's Old City (the story is set in 1924–25), she is a model of virtue. As the story slowly unfolds, we come to learn of the many trials and tribulations, suffering and agony she has borne over her long life. As she dictates her autobiography of woe to the narrator, who is recording it for delivery to the next world, we come to understand something about the relationship of joy and sorrow.

> Even as she spoke, her face clouded over with grief.
> Your joy has passed away, I said.
> She was silent for a moment. Then she said: Yes, my son, I was joyful, and now it is not so.
> Yet even as she spoke, the light shone out again from her face. She raised her eyes and said: Blessed be He, Who has turned away my sorrow.
> Why, I asked, were you joyful, yet afterwards sad, and now, joyful again?
> She said, very gently: Since your words are not chosen with care, I must tell you, this was not the right way to ask. Rather should you have said, "How have you deserved that God should turn away your sorrow?" For in His blessed eyes, all is one, whether sorrow or joy.
> Perhaps in the future, said I, my words will be chosen with care, since you teach me how one must speak. "Happy is the man who does not forget Thee." It is a text of much meaning.
> She said: You are a good man, and it is a good verse you have told me; so I too shall not withhold good words. You asked why I was joyful, and why I was sad, and why I now rejoice.

She corrects the narrator's misunderstanding, despite one's outer demonstration of happiness, who is to say what her actual default emotional state truly is. If indeed he encounters her as joyful, he overlooks the effort which must be exerted by her to find balance against her inherent sorrowful existence. At this point, Tehilla explains at some length her custom to recite a daily portion of the Psalms. She measures out the passage of time and her long life through its daily recitation. That day, having unintentionally recited two days' worth of psalms she began to question if her time in this world was not speeding toward its end, and this was cause for sorrow. (Note her name, Tehilla, means a Psalm; the use of the given name Tehilla in Israel was clearly influenced by this story's wide and enduring popularity.)

I glanced at her, wondering to myself by what path one might come to a like submission. I thought of the men of ancient times, and their virtuous ways; I spoke to her of past generations. Then I said, You have seen with your own eyes more than I can describe in words.

She answered: When a person's life is prolonged for many days and years, it is granted him to see many things; good things, and yet better things.[6]

Tehilla's wisdom has been acquired from a long life well-lived, but one fraught with trauma and grief. She is wise, not learned. She can read from the Siddur and Psalms but requires the use of the narrator-scribe to compose her epistolary life story. Nevertheless, there is theological depth to her words. Surely, we hear echoes of Mishnah *Berakhot* (9:5):

One is obligated to recite a blessing for the bad that befalls him just as he recites a blessing for the good that befalls him, as it is stated: "And you shall love the Lord your God with all your heart, with all your soul, and with all your might" (Deuteronomy 6:5)… Some say, it may be explained that "with all your might" means with every measure that He metes out to you; whether it is good or troublesome, thank Him.

This quality of emotional harmony and equanimity, embodied by Tehilla, is often present in our lives, aspirationally, if not fully achieved in fact. We may locate an articulation of this ideal (and potential source of influence on Agnon) in the writings of Rabbi Abraham Isaac Kook.[7] Not only need we keep balance in our sense of how God's providence manifests itself in the world, for joy or sorrow as observed by us, but in all matters interpersonal as well. R. Kook identifies this emotional state with the quality of *hishtavut*, from the root *sh-v-h* (as in *shaveh*, equal)—a type of equanimity.[8] The Ba'al Shem Tov had rooted this trait in Psalms (16:8): "I have set the Lord (*shiviti*) before me always," a verse which serves as a motto for all service of God, identifying a sense of mindfulness of God's presence in all life situations, good and bad.

In all that befalls a person, whether others praise him or denigrate him…in all manner of things he should say 'This, too, comes from Him may he be exalted,' since it is proper in God's eyes that it should occur. Therefore, one's intentions in all things should be for the sake of Heaven, because in fact there is no difference [between good and bad, joy and sorrow]—indeed this is a very mighty level to achieve.[9]

A properly balanced spiritual-emotional keel, as depicted through Tehilla, is achieved when one is mindful that our *experience* of reality is filtered through subjective human emotions and values—but in fact from God's exalted perspective it appears quite differently. R. Kook amplifies these ideas, describing the state of inner balance he strives for in the face of the brutal attacks and withering criticisms to which he was subjected:

> As for myself, thank God, I do not derive pleasure from the praise of others, neither am I pained or pay heed when disparaged. Praised be His exalted name, ongoing engagement with moral study and the inner works of our holy Torah has brought about this good trait in me.[10]

In Agnon's writing, the worldview of Rabbi Kook may have been best captured in the character of Reb Menahem HaOmed, in that epic novel of the Second *Aliyah*, Agnon's magnum opus, *Temol Shilshom* (in English as *Only Yesterday*). The novel is a portrait of Isaac Kummer, a young immigrant to Palestine, struggling to obtain *hishtavut*, yet torn between different worlds. Against that main character the reader encounters Reb Menahem—a pious farmer, pitchfork in one hand, a Talmud in the other—as one of the few to obtain peace of mind and synthesis in personality, precisely through the actualization of the values of religious Zionism (of its day): a combination of settling the soil while maintaining traditional beliefs and lifestyle.[11]

Menahem is only one of a string of characters in the Agnonian canon pulled between different worlds. Among these figures, however, it is Menahem, who stands out as one of the very few to achieve balance, the often sought and rarely found value of *hishtavut*—the serenity that comes from equanimity. Menahem is contrasted with the novel's tragic anti-hero, Isaac, who remains trapped between secular Jaffa and pious Jerusalem, on a horizontal plane, but also between the imperfect realities of terrestrial Jerusalem (*shel matta*) and celestial Jerusalem (*shel ma'alah*), on the vertical plane. Unable to achieve the aspired-for equanimity, Isaac meets a tragic end, bound to a bed (reminiscent of his biblically bound eponym), ravaged by the rabid bite of the demonic dog Balak.

From the very way Menahem denies having reached the "state of equanimity" we can understand precisely how clearly he has obtained it, while Isaac is said to have achieved *hishtavut* upon settling in Jerusalem, particularly at the novel's central scene as he recites Kaddish for his mother at the Western Wall, the tragic conclusion belies this claim, and shows his achievement to have been fleeting. Most useful for our discussion here, compare R. Kook's description of *hishtavut*, to Menahem's response to Isaac's questioning about how one can live without regret—especially concerning decisions which distanced him from the pioneering (balanced) ideal:

> Said Isaac, When I look at myself, I'm sorry I didn't stand the test and didn't become a farmer. Said Menahem, No matter what, you would be sorry. Said Isaac, What reason do you have to say that? Said Menahem, Everyone who is sorry about the thing he didn't do will be sorry about every single thing. Isaac asked Menahem, And what could a person do not to be sorry? Said Menahem, You're asking me? I don't know what sorrow is. Said Isaac, That is, you are happy with your lot? Said Menahem, I don't know what happiness is. Said Isaac, That is, you have reached a state of equanimity [*hishtavut*]? Said Menahem, That state I haven't reached, but if a day passes and I'm not ashamed of it, I'm satisfied.[12]

Late in the novel, in a highly symbolic dream following immediately after this final encounter between Isaac and Menahem, Isaac sees himself

> in the street barefoot without shoes, his head bare. He heard the sound of prayer and followed the sound. He came to a two-story house, the bottom story in ruins and you climbed a ladder to the top story where they were praying. And the ladder stood straight. He leaned the ladder and ascended. When he put his head in, the door closed on him from inside and his body was outside.[13]

Literary critic Dan Miron interprets the dream as a symbol for the "tragic vision" of *Only Yesterday* (and, I would add, the tragedy of so many young people of the Second *Aliyah*): the unsuccessful attempt to combine the thesis and antithesis of Judaism—traditional observance and Zionism.[14] Perhaps Agnon had this in mind by juxtaposing Isaac's dream with his final encounter with Menahem: that the tragedy emanates from ignoring the "third harmonizing verse," the potential synthesis, which R. Kook had tried, often unsuccessfully, to communicate to that generation. Isaac is destroyed by the struggle between secular Zionism and a particularly fanatical ultra-Orthodoxy; he is unable to actualize a lifestyle where tradition and modernity, religion and Zionism, and the old world and the new can coexist—the precise value of *hishtavut* as a type of religious life that R. Kook had hoped for.

In the Jewish worldview, as transmitted by the figures discussed here (admittedly, there are other views both within the *beit midrash* and the literary canon), joy is achieved through *hishtavut*—the peace of mind that comes about through a balanced sense of priorities and commitments. Otherwise, like Isaac suspended out of the window, we become entangled, and sacrificed on the altar of conflict. In 1966, near career's end, Agnon stood on the Stockholm stage to accept his Nobel Prize in Literature. Delivering a curious acceptance speech he reminded the assembled that he "belong[s] to the Tribe of Levi; my forebears and I are of the minstrels that were in the Temple." Had it not been for the "historic catastrophe in which Titus of Rome destroyed Jerusalem and Israel was exiled from its land," resulting in the fact that he "was born in one of the cities of the Exile," he would have stood with his

> brother-Levites in the Holy Temple, singing with them the songs of David, King of Israel, melodies such as no ear has heard since the day our city was destroyed and its people went into exile. I suspect that the angels in charge of the Shrine of Music, fearful lest I sing in wakefulness what I had sung in dream, made me forget by day what I had sung at night; for if my brethren, the sons of my people, were to hear, they would be unable to bear their grief over the happiness they have lost. To console me for having prevented me from singing with my mouth, they enable me to compose songs in writing.[15]

Aside from its curiosity as a piece of rhetoric (surely no similar speech has ever been delivered before the crowned heads of Europe), Agnon was articulating something about his craft as an artist and the Jewish response to tragedy and "historic catastrophe." Perhaps the opposite of trauma is not joy, but rather creativity. Because of the unhappiness which was the lot of Jewish Exile, he imagines his life's work as compensation—to compose in prose that which was formerly sung in praise.

If, indeed, we reconceive the scope and sources of Jewish joy in this way, and look back on our individual, communal, and national achievements as creative responses to the vicissitudes of history and individual existence, we may discover that, to paraphrase the musical iteration of Jewish literature's most famous milkman, we have something to be joyful for—even when our hearts lie panting on the floor.

Notes

1. Jonathan Sacks, *Covenant and Conversation: Deuteronomy* (Maggid Books, 2019), 127.
2. Aharon Lichtenstein, "A Consideration of Synthesis from a Torah Point of View," in *Leaves of Faith*, vol. 1 (Ktav, 2003), 63. I have discussed R. Lichtenstein's championing of the value of the humanities in general, and literature in particular, to achieve and advance a variety of goals advantageous to the religious personality in my "The Best That Has Been Thought and Said by Rabbi Lichtenstein About the Role of Literature in Religious Life," *Tradition* 47, no. 4 (Winter 2015): 240–49.
3. Ruth R. Wisse, *No Joke: Making Jewish Humor* (Princeton: Princeton University Press, 2013), 25–26, stated specifically in the context of Sholem Aleichem, but relevant in general for our larger conversation.
4. Ariel Hirschfeld, *Likro et Sh.Y. Agnon* (Ahuzat Bayit, 2011), 167.
5. In English as "Tehilla," trans. Walter Lever in S.Y. Agnon, *Two Scholars Who Were in Our Town and Other Novellas*, ed. and annotated by Jeffrey Saks (Jerusalem: Toby Press, 2014), 223–63.
6. "Tehilla," *Two Scholars*, 231–32; note: "good things, and yet better things," *not* "good things and bad things."
7. For background on the influence of R. Kook on Agnon and the presence of his teachings in the latter's writing, see my "A Portrait of Two Artists at the Crossroads: Between Rav Kook and S.Y. Agnon," *Tradition* 49, no. 2 (Summer 2016): 32–52.
8. R. Kook did not coin the term nor was he the first to discuss it, but I choose to situate our discussion on his writings because of their proximity and likely influence on Agnon.

    The earliest source may be the eleventh-century *Hovot HaLevavot* (*Sha'ar Yihud Hama'aseh*, ch. 5). For background on earlier sources and the development of the idea, see Moshe Halamish, *Mevo le-Kabbala* (Elinor/WZO, 1992), 50; and Ohad Teharlev, "*Mateh, Nes, ve-Shurah: Iyyunim be-Middat ha-Hishtavut,*" *Akdamot* 1 (1997): 1–8, on its presence in the writings of *Sefat Emet*.
9. Ba'al Shem Tov, *Tzava'at HaRivash*, #2.
10. *Iggerot HaRa'ayah*, vol. I, #43 (p. 42), and cf. *Orot HaKodesh*, vol. 3, #18 (p. 246).
11. S.Y. Agnon, *Only Yesterday*, trans. Barbara Harshav (Princeton: Princeton University Press, 2000).
12. *Only Yesterday*, 571; for Isaac's scene at the Western Wall, 368–69.
13. *Only Yesterday*, 573. The symbols of hats and shoes appear throughout the novel, and may likely be pointing to "that which is above and that which is below" (cf. *Hagiga* 2:1). Isaac being barefoot and bareheaded in the

dream telegraphs his disconnect from both terrestrial and celestial Jerusalem.
14. Dan Miron, "*Bein Shtei Neshamot*," in *Mi-Vilna le-Yerushalayim: Mehkarim Mugashim le-Professor Shmuel Werses*, ed. David Assaf (Jerusalem: Magnes Press, 2002), 549–608; see at 604.
15. "Shmuel Agnon Banquet Speech" (December 10, 1966), available at: www.NobelPrize.org/prizes/literature/1966/agnon/speech. I have written on this in "Always I Regarded Myself As One Who Was Born in Jerusalem," in *Agnon's Tales of the Land of Israel*, ed. Jeffrey Saks and Shalom Carmy (Pickwick, 2021), 125–34.

CHAPTER 32

The Joy of Ordinary Living

Yael Ziegler

The Book of Psalms has always been a widely loved book, presenting a broad array of human experiences. Its authentic portrayal of the human perspective charts a unique path among biblical books. The psalms are essentially prayers, affording humans the opportunity to express their thoughts and emotions before God.

Open the Book of Psalms and you are confronted with the pitiful state of the human condition, laced with despair, confusion, sorrow, fear, regret, and yearning. The psalms unleash a torrent of human grievances. Addressing God from their pain, humans pour out their hearts in a bid to comprehend the world, to exist, and to prevail. Other psalms offer a more agreeable portrait of the human experience. These psalms fill the reader's heart with joy or tranquility, expressing various states of harmony, faith, confidence, and jubilation.

Remarkably, many psalms are erratic, moving fluidly from despair to joy, or the opposite, from abiding trust in God's presence to fearful insecurity. An accurate reflection of human passions, emotions flow and collide in dizzying displays of volatility. Consider, for example, Psalm 13, which opens with a series of rhetorical questions that express despair:

"Until when God will you forget me for eternity? Until when will You hide Your face from me?" In its final verse, the psalm pivots abruptly, concluding on a confident, triumphant note (13:6): "And I, trust in Your loyalty; my heart delights in Your salvation, I will sing to the Lord for He has been benevolent to me!" Psalm 27 moves in the opposite direction—from confidence and joy in God's closeness: "He will keep me safe in His shelter in times of terror... Now my head is held high above the enemies around me... I will sing and chant praises to the Lord!" (Ps. 27:5–6) to uncertainty, fraught with loneliness and fear: "Hear my voice, Lord, when I call... Do not hide Your face from me... Do not reject or forsake me God, my savior... Do not abandon me to the wills of my foes!" (Ps. 27:7–12). These rapid shifts, especially in reflecting upon one's relationship with God, may be as intrinsic to the religious experience as it is to the emotional one.

It is not just the internal cohesiveness of the psalms that seems erratic. Looking at the Book of Psalms as a whole, one may easily conclude that there is no order to the book, that the different chapters loosely cohere together to render an impressionistic portrait of human emotions, a motley, unmediated jumble of experiences. One *midrash* suggests otherwise; some rabbis sensed that the Book of Psalms maintains some kind of structure, even if it is not the usual sort of narrative, with a sequential plot or an identifiable cast of characters.

> R. Joshua ben Levi wanted to order this book [Psalms]. A heavenly voice emerged and said, "Do not awaken the sleeping."[1] R. Ishmael wished to order this book in the presence of his teacher. He cited (Psalms 111:8): "They are juxtaposed for eternity, formed in truth and righteousness."[2]

By citing the above verse, R. Ishmael implies that he has found order in the Book of Psalms, and that it is deliberate, both worthy and true. While this essay cannot properly examine that claim, one thing seems fairly clear; the Book of Psalms moves gradually, inexorably toward joy. Not unvarying joy—the volatility of human passions precludes any immutable disposition—but nevertheless, an identifiable rise and swell, a marked tendency to depict a state of contentment, sometimes even elation. The fifth—and final—"book" in Psalms (consisting of Psalms 107–150)[3] contains three different groups of psalms dubbed "*hallel*" or "praise" collections.[4] Jubilation mixes with gratitude as humans rejoice in the good world that God has provided, the celebratory events in Israel's history, the blissful joy of being alive.[5] The Book of Psalms charts the desired trajectory of human existence, a mercurial but steady movement toward joyous existence.[6]

In its resounding finale, the book tenders a cohesive collection of five psalms (146–150), each of which is framed by the word, "*hallelu-ya*," "Praise God."[7] These exhortative psalms conclude with a symphony of acclaim, a jubilant tribute to God's surpassing greatness (Psalm 150:3–6): "Praise Him with the harp and the lyre; praise Him with timbral and dance; praise Him with strings and flute; praise Him with resounding cymbals; praise Him with cymbals that blast! Let all that breathe praise the Lord! Praise God!" The joy is palpable, all creatures sing in harmony to God. An exultant conclusion for this book of human yearning, Jews recite this collection of praises, along with Psalm 145 (the psalm colloquially known as "*Ashrei*"), daily. These final psalms form an integral part of the morning prayers, launching each new day with optimism and song.

One is well-advised to adopt this practice. Indeed, studies of positive psychology have consistently concluded that daily expressions of gratitude and optimism can be transformative behavior, which is regularly associated with greater happiness. Yet, an intriguing exchange in BT *Shabbat* 118b casts doubt on this practice. R. Yosi appears to acknowledge the benefit and importance of daily recitations of praise, proclaiming his desire to join those who recite *hallel* every day. The Talmud, however, records resistance to this notion, brandishing the severe assertion that, "One who recites the *Hallel* every day is a blasphemer and a scoffer!"[8] The Talmud quickly resolves this difficulty, however, explaining that R. Yosi is not referring to the psalms colloquially known as *hallel*—namely, Psalms 113–118—but rather, to the concluding psalms of the book, known as the *pesukei d'zimra*, or stanzas of song (145–150).

What is the difference between daily recitation of the *hallel*, which the Talmud deems blasphemous, and the daily recitation of the *pesukei d'zimra*, to which R. Yosi aspires? R. Shmuel Eidels, the Maharsha, notes that the collection of psalms known as *hallel* (Psalms 113–118) is recited to commemorate God's miracles, affirming God's ability to transform nature and save His nation from catastrophe. These psalms sing of deliverance from Egypt, of death that swirls around, of eyes that weep and feet that stumble. They depict the silencing of the blasphemous idolaters, who delightedly mock God's power during the period of Israel's adversity, gleefully querying, "Where is their God?" Raising the cup of salvation, the *hallel* psalms celebrate God, who has rescued His nation from enemies. Gratitude spawns action as the psalmist pledges to spread the tale of God's dramatic deeds (Ps. 118:17): "I will not die but live, and I will tell the tale of God's deeds!" The *hallel* psalms sing of the faith that carries humans through their suffering and of the God who answers them from the depths of despair. These psalms, explains Maharsha, should be recited only on special days, on "this day that God has made," a day of deliverance and rejoicing. No one should aspire to experience the jubilation of salvation from destruction on a daily basis!

The *pesukei d'zimra* psalms that conclude the book—the ones that we wish to recite daily—bear witness to the routine gifts of everyday life; they express delight in God's ongoing commitment to deliver humans from the burdens associated with the exigencies of our quotidian existence. In these psalms, we praise God every day (*be'khol yom*, 145:2) for the mundane gifts that He bestows upon His creatures: for sufficient food and for supporting those who fall, for protecting the stranger and providing courage to the humble, the orphan, and the widow, for healing the brokenhearted and for blessing the children of Zion. We thank God for nature, for snow and for frost, for wind and for water.

Above all, we express gratitude to God for His abiding presence amongst us, for His greatness and His beneficence, for His statutes and His laws, for His height in the heavens and for His interactions with the earth, for His distant majesty and for His close intimacy. We sing and rejoice with timbral and harp for God's imposition of a moral order and the promise of retribution against evildoers. We invite all God's creatures—angels, heavenly bodies, sea creatures, mountains, trees, animals, and humans—to join in this crescendo of daily praise, in the hopes that all of God's creations will join together in gratitude for the opportunity to live a good life, one that celebrates God.

The Book of Psalms takes us on a true-to-life journey through the vicissitudes of human existence; anguish and grievances intersperse with moments of elation and revelation. Psalms' supreme quest is not to hold on to moments of euphoria—as blessed as they may be—but rather, to strive for a contented life, for *ashrei*, a word that opens both the book (Ps. 1:1) and its magnificent finale (Ps. 145:1). One does not achieve *ashrei* by relying upon the fleeting elation of momentary victories and divine salvation. Nor does one attain *ashrei* by hoping—in vain—for a permanent state of unmitigated joy. To obtain *ashrei*, one must develop a fine-tuned appreciation of daily life, of each day's small triumphs. Rabbi Sacks describes the attainment of true joy as, "the grateful acceptance and celebration of today. We are here; we are alive; we are among others who share our sense of jubilation. We are living in God's land, enjoying His blessing, eating the produce of His earth, watered by His rain, brought to fruition under His sun, breathing the air He breathed into us, living the life He renews in us each day."[9] And yes, writes Rabbi Sacks elsewhere, "Life is full of grief and disappointments, problems and pains, but beneath it all is the wonder that we are here, in a universe filled with beauty, among people each of whom carries within them a trace of the face of God."[10]

The Book of Psalms presents this type of conscious living as its conclusion, in a bid to cultivate consciously, amid "an assembly of the devoted," an appreciation of God for the commonplace gifts of daily life. This daily paean leads to a satisfied and blessed life, one that is laced not with drama, but rather with serenity and tranquility, with the joy of ordinary living.

Notes

1. This is a reference to an earlier part of this Midrash, which explains that God withheld knowledge of the correct sequencing of the Torah because it contains the secrets to great wonders, including how to revive the dead. The Midrash equates the secret of the order of the Torah to the secret of the order of the Book of Psalms. A heavenly voice prevents R. Yehoshua ben Levi from exploring the order of the Book of Psalms so that he does not learn the secret to reviving the dead (termed here, awakening the sleeping).
2. Midrash Tehillim 3.
3. According to Midrash Tehillim (Buber) 1:2, the Book of Psalms is subdivided into five books. This division is based on the concluding doxology of each book, aside from the last, which ends with a paean of praise.
4. *Hallel haGadol* (The Great *Hallel*) is the term used for Psalm 136 (and perhaps some other psalms along with it; for more on this, see BT *Pesahim* 118a). *Hallel hamitzri* (The Egyptian *Hallel*) consists of Psalms 113–118 and is often simply referred to as *Hallel*. The final five psalms of the Book (146–150) contain many repetitions of the root *hallel* and is dubbed by some scholars, *Hallel Hakatan* (The Little *Hallel*). The group of psalms (120–134) that begin with *Shir HaMaalot*, (Songs of Ascent), also tends toward expressions of gratitude and joy. Other individual psalms join these collections to add their voice to the growing symphony of festive acclaim of God (e.g., 107, 138).
5. It must be noted that some of these collections contain moments of pain or confusion; they convey realistic portrayals of the complexity of human existence. Nevertheless, the overriding tone remains a joyous one.

6. According to many modern scholars, the Book of Psalms loosely represents the forward movement of Israel's history, progressing from the disappointment of the collapse of Jerusalem and the Davidic dynasty (Book 3) to a representation of Israel's coping mechanisms in exile (Book 4), and finally to the redemption and return to Jerusalem and the Davidic covenant (Book 5). This approach explains the movement of the book within a national context, accounting in its own way for the concentration of expressions of gratitude and praise of God as the book draws to its felicitous conclusion. For a recent overview of this approach (including an up-to-date bibliography), see Peter C. W. Ho, *The Design of the Psalter: A Macrostructural Analysis (Eugene, OR: Pickwick Publications, 2019)*.
7. The word *hallel* (along with its variation *tehilla*) appears 42 times in the final six psalms of the book. This is not simply a large number, but it is also a multiple of seven, which Umberto Cassuto regarded as the key to identifying the leading word of a biblical section. See, for example, *A Commentary on the Book of Exodus* (Jerusalem: Magnes Press, 1967), 75, 91 ff.
8. BT *Sabbath* 118b.
9. Jonathan Sacks, *Essays on Ethics* (Jerusalem: Maggid Books, 2016), 314.
10. Jonathan Sacks, *Studies in Spirituality* (Jerusalem: Maggid Books, 2021), 258.

CHAPTER 33

Celebrating the Good Through the *Sheheheyanu* Blessing

Johnny Solomon

How often have you received a message letting you know that someone in your community is unwell and asking you to pray for their *refuah* [healing]? And how often have you received a message that someone you have been praying for has actually recovered? Sadly, when it comes to questions like these, I receive far more of the former than the latter. In newspapers and on television, the quantity of bad or negative news almost always eclipses good and positive news. There are days when one genuinely wonders whether there is any good news at all!

Social scientists have examined this phenomenon, and according to Roy Baumeister, Ellen Bratslavsky, and Catrin Finkenauer, "Bad events are on average five times as powerful as good ones."[1] Hearing bad news, in other words, leaves a significantly greater impression on us than hearing good news. As Rabbi Sacks, who was keenly interested in this topic, explained: "We are genetically predisposed to paying more attention to the bad than the good. For sound biological reasons, we are hyper-alert to potential threats and dangers."[2]

J. Solomon (✉)
Matan; Midreshet Lindenbaum, Jerusalem, Israel

© The Author(s), under exclusive license to Springer Nature Switzerland AG 2023
E. Brown, S. Weiss (eds.), *An Ode to Joy*,
https://doi.org/10.1007/978-3-031-28229-4_33

If this is so, how can we lead a life that isn't perpetually overshadowed by mistakes, misconduct, tragedy, grief, and loss? Is it even possible to live a vibrant, optimistic, and hopeful life if the bad always leaves a greater impression upon us than the good?

Having thought about this question for some time, my conclusion is that notwithstanding our predispositions, we can live an upbeat life if we train ourselves to seek out opportunities to celebrate the good. And in terms of Judaism, I strongly believe that we are duty bound to foster habits that celebrate the good. Once we do, we will find—as Rabbi Sacks further observes—that, "The more we celebrate the good, the more good we discover that is worthy of celebration."[3] But where does Judaism teach us that we should train ourselves to seek out the good?

Seek Out the Good

Mishna *Brachot* 9:2 states that we should recite the *HaTov VeHaMeitiv*[4] blessing ["Blessed are You, Lord our God, King of the Universe who is good and does good"] upon hearing *Besorot Tovot* [good news] which benefits multiple people, while the *Sheheheyanu* blessing ["Blessed are You, Lord our God, King of the Universe who has given us life, sustained us, and brought us to this day"][5] should be recited upon hearing good news that is personally beneficial. Paralleling this, we recite the blessing *Dayan HaEmet* ["Blessed are You, Lord our God, King of the Universe, the true judge"] upon hearing *Shmu'ot Ra'ot* ([bad news)].

Having introduced these blessings, the Mishna (*Brachot* 9:5) then states that, "A person is obligated to recite a blessing on the bad just as they do on the good," which Rava explains in *Brachot* 60b to mean that just as someone accepts the good *b'simha* [with joy], so should he or she accept the bad *b'simha* [with joy]. According to this explanation, the equivalence made by our Sages is not about making sure that both blessings are recited in equal number, but instead, that when each are recited, each should be recited with an equal measure of joy.

Rabbi Yosef Shaul Nathanson, however, explains that there is a simpler and more literal way to interpret this teaching that asks us to celebrate the good just as we acknowledge the bad since everything ultimately comes from God.[6] Still, as Rabbi Nathanson observes, "It is generally harder for someone on a festive day to direct their attention to God than to do so when experiencing physical pain."[7] Rabbi Sacks similarly expressed this sentiment when he said: "It is easy to speak to God in tears. It is hard to serve God in joy."⁸ Although the Mishna above encourages us to engage with the bad with the same measure of recognition of God's role in the universe as our recognition of the good, practically speaking, we often struggle to connect to God in the good times. This is precisely why the Mishna instructs us to recite the *HaTov VeHaMeitiv* and the *Sheheheyanu* blessings: if we seek and seize the manifold opportunities to recite these blessings in the good times, we can foster the habits that will help us serve God in joy.

HaTov VeHaMeitiv and *Sheheheyanu*

The problem, however, is not just that "We are genetically predisposed to paying more attention to the bad than the good," but when the good does come along, we ignore the clear statements in the Mishna, Talmud, and *Shulhan Aruch* concerning the recitation of *HaTov VeHaMeitiv* and *Sheheheyanu*. Many Jews simply do not recite these blessings, thereby resulting in a community where *Dayan HaEmet* is recited far more often than *HaTov VeHaMeitiv* and *Sheheheyanu*. It is hard to imagine why this is so, even in religiously observant communities, especially given the unambiguous texts which encourage us to recite these beautiful blessings on good occasions.

One suggestion could be that dwelling more on the bad than the good will make us more reflective and productive human beings, in the spirit of the words of King Solomon: "It is better to frequent a house of mourning than a house of feasting" (Eccl. 7:2). He follows this thought by emphasizing it again: "A wise man's heart is in the house of mourning, and a fool's in the house of celebration" (Eccl. 7:4). This moral advice applies to someone who has the option of either going to a house of mourning or joining a house of celebration. Make the choice, Ecclesiastes advises, that will have a better, more pious outcome for the individual. Still, such verses do not negate the importance of seeking opportunities to celebrate and praise God for the good.

It seems that one compelling answer to our question stems from our instinctive trust that we can recognize the bad, whereas we may not trust our instincts to recognize the good. While we may feel confident that we can recognize *Shmu'ot Ra'ot*, to which we respond with the *Dayan HaEmet* blessing, we feel less sure that we can recognize *Besorot Tovot*, for which the *HaTov VeHaMeitiv* or the *Sheheheyanu* blessing would be recited. While numerous *Aharonim*, rabbinic commentators, have made such a claim, this idea is most pointedly expressed by Rabbi Simcha Rabinovitch in his *Piskei Teshuvot*,[9] where he writes that, "[The reason that] many people are *meikil* (lenient) [about the recitation of the *Sheheheyanu* blessing] is that they are worried that perhaps they have not achieved a sufficient level of joy in their heart in order to recite *Sheheheyanu*."

This suggests that many observant Jews do not recite *HaTov VeHaMeitiv* and *Sheheheyanu* on good news because they don't feel confident that they have reached the necessary level of positive emotions to do so, whereas Jews often recite *Dayan HaEmet* on bad news because they do experience sufficient sadness to warrant the blessing. Bad news, in other words, leaves a significantly greater impression on us than good news. Yet it is precisely because of this that our Sages established the *HaTov VeHaMeitiv* and *Sheheheyanu* blessings so that we acknowledge the good and train ourselves to seek out the good!

It therefore seems that to help ourselves experience God's blessing and the emotional fullness of the world, we should be *machmir* [strict] about the recitation of our positive blessings and, thereby, grasp every opportunity to celebrate all the good that comes our way. And were we to say these blessings more frequently, it would not only help generate greater joy which, as Rabbi Sacks teaches, "is the supreme religious emotion,"[10] it would also help us foster a happier and healthier Jewish community since, "Joy helps heal some of the wounds of our injured, troubled world."[11]

Blessing God for the Good

Rabbi Sacks encouraged us "to equal the score by celebrating the good"[12] and this brings me to a recent personal experience where I had to internalize this message.

My wife Donna was diagnosed with breast cancer in July 2021. When we received the terrible news, she and I sent a handful of messages to our family and closest friends to let them know about our situation. Within hours, our news had been forwarded to others, and within a day, a global network of women and men committed themselves to prayer, Psalms recital, and acts of kindness in the merit of Donna's recovery. Over the ensuing nine months, my phone would regularly ping with texts informing me that someone had said a prayer or performed a good deed in the merit of Donna's recovery.

Thankfully, between God's grace and the excellent medical treatment that she received, Donna is now cancer free. When we got the all-clear, we decided to write a note telling people about our good news and thanking them profusely for all that they had done. And when we did so, not only did all those who saw this message express their great relief, but they also expressed their great appreciation that we had shared this good news with them. People who were with us in our pain should be with us in our celebration and gratitude. Our response should be self-evident. But it is oftentimes not the case, and while many of us share our problems, we often don't share their resolution.

True, it may be easier to speak to God in tears and harder to serve God in joy. Still, if we choose to recite the *HaTov VeHaMeitiv* and *Sheheheyanu* blessings for the good more frequently, we might just be able to equal the score.[13]

Notes

1. Roy Baumeister, Ellen Bratslavsky, and Catrin Finkenauer, "Bad is Stronger than Good," *Review of General Psychology* 5, no. 4 (2001): 329.
2. Jonathan Sacks, *Judaism's Life Changing Ideas* (Jerusalem: Maggid Books, 2020), 136.
3. Ibid.
4. *HaTov VeHaMeitiv* is generally understood to be the pluralized version of the *Sheheheyanu* blessing.
5. Note that though it says "us" it is generally personalized.
6. *Chiddushei Rabbeinu Yosef Shaul HaLevi* on *Brachot* 54a, quoting from *Shoel UMeishiv* III Vol. 3 No. 51.
7. While quoting from Rabbi Shmelke of Nikolsburg's commentary to the Akeida as cited in *Divrei Emet*, Parshat Vayera.
8. Jonathan Sacks, *Covenant and Conversation: Deuteronomy* (Jerusalem: Maggid Books, 2019), 127.
9. *Piskei Teshuvot* Vol. 2 *Orach Chaim* 225:1.
10. Jonathan Sacks, *Studies in Spirituality* (Jerusalem: Maggid Books, 2021), 258.
11. Ibid., 259.
12. Jonathan Sacks, "It's Love that Guides Our Feet Along the Path of Joy," Moral Voice recording, 2020, https://rabbisacks.org/its-love-that-guides-our-feet-along-the-path-to-joy-thought-for-the-day/.
13. "Dedicated to Rabbi Sacks who guided me through his words of encouragement, through his remarkable leadership, through his profound teachings, and especially during the toughest of days, to equal the score by celebrating the good."

PART VIII

Joy in the Arts

CHAPTER 34

Ashrei Yoshvei Veitekha: Joy in the Ancient Synagogue

Steven Fine

Strolling down a street in one Israeli city or another around dusk, I have occasionally heard a voice calling out repeatedly *Ashrei yoshvei veitekha*, Joyful are those who dwell in your house, they will again praise you! (Psalm 84:6). Sometimes the voice is directed at me. The caller is invariably an older man trying to make a minyan, a prayer quorum of ten men, calling out of the door of some old synagogue. Sometimes his voice is plaintive, almost desperate, at other times, joyful and welcoming. More than once I have stopped, smiled to myself, and entered the shul to make the *minyan*. This repeat experience, this literal call to prayer, has long lingered in my imagination. To this day it influences my vision of the synagogue—both those of our own day and the distant, ancient synagogues that I study and write about.

The synagogue, together with the "study house," is the place where Jewish communities assemble to conduct weddings and circumcisions, bar and bat mitzvah celebrations, and funerals. Here we come to pray and to learn Torah, to navigate and to cultivate human relationships.[1] Here we

S. Fine (✉)
Yeshiva University Center for Israel Studies, New York, NY, USA

experience the joy of Simhat Torah and the discomfort that comes of fasting and self-reflection. We are hopeful that God is present, for, as the Sages have it, "God [*Elohim*] is present in the congregation of God [*El*]" (Ps. 82:1), joining His people in the synagogues and study houses.² In what follows, I focus on the synagogue as a stage created by our ancestors upon which to live the life of Torah—a place of joy, to meet God, and to be "called."

The synagogue is the creation of the Jews themselves. It has no heavenly prototype, unlike the Jerusalem Temple, and was not ordained by God, unlike the biblical Tabernacle. We, each and every Jewish community, have created it over millennia. The first synagogues appeared sometime during the latter Second Temple period as houses of assembly—which is what both the Greek *synagogue* and the Hebrew *beit ha-knesset* mean. It began as a place to come together for the reading and exposition of Scripture. Today, a synagogue building may be as simple as a "house synagogue," a *stiebel*, with a build-it-yourself cabinet as its "holy ark" and a folding table as its *bima*, or as ornate as any of the great nineteenth- and twentieth-century edifices—and everything in between.

By the Tannaitic period (ca. 70–220 CE), the essential contours were set: a Torah shrine (then called just "chest," *teva*), placed on the Jerusalem-aligned wall, a place to read the Torah, and seating for the congregation.³ Neither the *Mishneh Torah* nor the *Shulhan Arukh* adds appreciably in their discussions of synagogue buildings.⁴ With this flexible skeletal set of instructions, communities throughout the generations have created their own synagogues—with startling variety. In the time of the Amoraim (third to fifth centuries), these "places of assembly" came to be called "holy places." These were the spaces where the holy people carry on holy tasks in the presence of the holy Torah. This sanctity was expressed explicitly through metaphors derived from the Tabernacle and the Temple. While the Tannaim originated from this nascent connection, it reached full and explicit bloom in the third and fourth centuries. By then, the Torah shrine was called an "ark," after the ark of the covenant; its curtain called a *parokhta*, after the temple veil or curtain, and, with time, the synagogue and study house buildings were each called a *mikdash me'at*, a "small sanctuary" reminiscent of the Temple.⁵

Hazal, the Talmudic sages, conceived the inner space as divided between the "sanctity of the synagogue" and "the higher "sanctity of the *aron*," reminiscent of the graded holiness of the tabernacle/Temple.⁶ At the focal point of the room was the Torah shrine. Local communities seemed to agree. Large synagogues of the fourth through the seventh centuries typically include *bimot* with shrines on their Jerusalem-aligned wall. With each renovation, the *bima* grew. Eventually many were enclosed by low stone, wooden, or reed fences (*gedarim*), sometimes with huge Torah shrines flanked by metal or stone menorahs with flickering oil lamps set atop each branch and glass hanging lamps acting as spotlights for the Ark and accentuating its holiness.[7]

From early on, our ancestors associated "joy" with the act of entering synagogues and study houses. Thrice each day we recite the *Ashrei* prayer. In our *siddurim*, our prayer books, this text is most prominent at *Minha*, the afternoon prayer service, where it literally introduces the proceedings.[8] It is a kind of call to prayer. Two related biblical verses introduce Psalm 145. The verse that concludes, Psalm 115:18, frames this Psalm.[9] *Ashrei* opens with Psalm 84:6 and Psalm 144:15, "Joyful are the people for whom this is so, joyful (*ashrei*) are the people whose God is the Lord." This unit dates to Amoraic times, when synagogue prayer blossomed.[10]

In his *Siddur*, Rabbi Jonathan Sacks translates the verse from Psalm 84:6 as, "Happy are those who dwell in your house, they shall continue to praise you, Selah." My preferred translation for the Hebrew *ashrei* is "joyful." According to the *Oxford English Dictionary*, joy is "A vivid emotion of pleasure arising from a sense of well-being or satisfaction; the feeling or state of being highly pleased or delighted; exultation of spirit; gladness, delight." Rabbi Sacks' "happy," standard in Jewish translations into English, is quite similar—though at least in contemporary English "happy" has the potential to be less exalted than joy.[11] The Septuagint translated *ashrei* as *makárioi* [blessed]. This Greek translation focuses on the source of the happiness, thus those who "sit in your house" are "blessed" for their efforts. A. J. Berkowitz charts a median course, translating *ashrei* as "fortunate."[12]

Our liturgy lifts this verse from its Temple pilgrimage context and sets it at the start of Psalm 144. This block of texts is an introductory formula that ushers in the afternoon prayer service. Psalm 84:6 instructs the faithful to join in—and sets the mood. For this reason, I translate *od yehalelukha* in a rather stilted way that assumes a continuing liturgical practice: "They will [once] again praise you." The Sages promise that whoever enters the synagogue will "again" praise God in the heavenly synagogues and study houses.[13] The synagogue has become a cosmic institution. Psalm 84 is a pilgrimage psalm, expressing the longing of the pious to enter God's house. The Psalmist describes both physical and spiritual transition from the mundane into the Temple. "How lovely is thy dwelling place, O Lord of hosts" (Ps. 84:2), he exclaims. A bit later our pilgrim describes his physical response to entering the Temple. "My heart and flesh sing for joy to the living God" (verse 3). He extolls the path of the pilgrim, "They go from rampart to rampart [or perhaps, strength to strength], appearing before God in Zion" (verse 8).[14] This sense of movement and transformation, of physically and spiritually crossing a gateway in liminal time and space is essential to Psalm 84. The pilgrim's search for joy is applied by our liturgy to each Jew who enters her local "holy place," the *mikdash me'at*.

This verse is further fitted to the synagogue/study house context through a transvaluation of "your house" to refer to not only the Temple, but to include "synagogues and study houses." Thus, those commendable people who "dwell/sit in your house," the Temple or a synagogue, achieve joy/fulfillment/happiness. This expansion of meaning appeared already in the *Sifra* on Leviticus 26:31, "I will destroy your sanctuaries:" "Temple, temples, your temples, these [derivatives of the word "temple"] are the synagogues and the study houses," *Mikdash, mikdashim, mikdashtem, mikdashi, elu batei knisiot u'midrashot.*[15] This process, which I have called "imitatio templi" and "templization" continued through late antiquity and continues to modern times. *Beit ha-Knesset/ bei knisha* [house of assembly] in Hebrew and Aramaic, sometimes just *beta*, "house" were standard designations in antiquity, as was the Greek *oikos*, "house." Midrash Psalms 84:3 (ed. S. Buber, and parallels) connects "your house" in Psalm 84:6 explicitly to "the synagogues and study houses."

This parallels the Sages' transvaluation of the "curse" of Balaam (Numbers 24:5), "How goodly are your tents, O Jacob, your dwelling places, O Israel," to refer to "synagogues and study houses."[16] Above a portal of a fifth-century synagogue at Meroth, in the Upper Galilee, is inscribed an explicit welcome and promise: "Blessed are you in your coming, and blessed are you in your going (Deuteronomy 28:6)." Midrash Tanhuma directs this toward those who enter and depart from "synagogues and study houses."[17] A talmudic exhortation urges congregants to walk quickly to the synagogue, but to depart slowly (JT *Berakhot* 5:1, 9a).[18] A bit earlier in the Jerusalem Talmud, Psalm 84:6 is interpreted to regulate bodily movements once the congregant enters the synagogue and prepares to recite the *Amidah*, the rabbinic "standing prayer":[19] "Said Rabbi Joshua b. Levi: He who enters the synagogue to stand and pray must sit twice, once before he prays [the "Eighteen Benedictions"] and once after he prays [them]. Before he prays, [as it says in Scripture]:

"Joyous are those who sit in your house." *Yoshvei*, conventionally translated "dwell," is taken simply as "sit": joyous are those who sit in your synagogues before and after reciting the standing prayer.

Our liturgy adds the final verse of Psalm 144 before Psalm 145, and immediately after 84:6: "Joyful (*ashrei*) are the people for whom this is so, joyful (*ashrei*) are the people whose God is the Lord." This artful liturgical unit asserts joy/happiness/fulfilment three times—once for those who "dwell in your house," once for those who behave "thusly," and finally identifies the temple dwellers in the verse as Israel, the people for whom "the Lord is their God." This assembly of verses addresses the congregant in the second person plural, a deliberate choice when we consider the individual focus of the psalms cited.

Three, a plurality, is a particularly stable and roundly inclusive number in Jewish thought—from the "A threefold cord is not quickly broken" of Ecclesiastes 4:2 to the three "things" upon which the world rests of *Mishnah Avot* 1:2, and the three patriarchs, Abraham, Isaac, and Jacob. I could suggest many others. In some medieval manuscripts the name of God was signified by three *yuds*. Most significantly, the three appearances of the *Ashrei* in our versions framing verses of Psalm 145 responds to a tradition preserved in BT *Berakhot* 4b, which promises that whoever recites Psalm 145 three times a day "is assured his place in the world to come." Berkowitz argues that in Talmudic times, though, *Ashrei* was recited but once, and that this talmudic text was altered from "one time" to "three times" to conform with the expanded recitation of this *Ashrei* known from later Gaonic period.[20]

What joy awaits inside the synagogue? Psalm 145 is a series of praises of God, set out alphabetically from *alef* to *tav* (minus *nun*), epitomizing Torah from A to Z. Appended at the conclusion is Psalm 115:18: "We will bless the Lord now and forever, Halleluya!." The choice of this verse continues the theme of "blessing" in the actual final verse Psalm 145, broadening the personal exclamation there to include the experience of community. At *shacharit*, morning prayers, it connects *Ashrei* to the subsequent five Psalms (145–150), all of which begin and conclude "Halleluya." At *minha* this choice presages the task before those enter the sacred realm—where prayer, learning, fellowship, and celebration are enacted and await. Here the block of texts that make up the *Ashrei* prayer expresses a liminal transition from outside the "house" of God to its all-inclusive core and then transition into the next phases of the liturgy and synagogue/study house life.

What did the Jew see once "inside"? Generations have decorated synagogues ornately and lovingly as the "stage" for these events, generally explaining this within a rubric that medieval rabbis called *hiddur mitzvah*, the "beautification of a commandment."[21] Through design and sometimes artistry, they transformed mundane spaces into "holy places." At other times, communities constructed large purpose-built spaces. They decorated the ark, the interior walls, textiles, Torah appurtenances, tables, and the sacred books. They inscribed themselves on the walls and columns and furnishings through donor inscriptions that were visible for generations—each adding their own. They wrote in their vernacular, whether Aramaic or Greek or Latin—or English. Sometimes they wrote in the sacred tongue and script, Hebrew. Jews approached the Torah shrine with awe. As the actors on this "stage" they also "decorated" themselves with fine garments, exquisite dresses, and well-woven, prayer shawls, *talitot* (sometimes with glistening silver collars, *atarot*). Some medieval (and modern) rabbis found much of this distracting. Their responsa survive, and over time their opinions set a limiting frame for synagogue decoration.[22] Communities and their sages that created lively and deeply visual environments, however, expressed their attitudes in stone and mortar, silks and silver. Satisfied with their work, they seldom wrote about what they made. The Roman rite acknowledges the artisans responsible for "the beauty of holiness" at the high point of the Torah service: "He who blessed our (mothers) Sarah, Rebecca, Rachel and Leah, He will bless every daughter of Israel who makes a wrapping or a cloth to honor the Torah, or sets up a lamp to honor the Torah."[23]

Sheer joy is how I, for one, often perceive a visually rich *beit ha-knesset*. My senses full, I begin praying and learning with a deeper sense of focus, of *kavannah*. This sense was just as true in the distant past as it is of the present. In my research, I never cease to marvel at the great "double stoa," the synagogue of Alexandria, remembered as huge and lavish, peopled with craftsmen who surely must have appreciated fine workmanship. There were goldsmiths, silversmiths, common weavers, Tarsian (that is, fine) weavers, and blacksmiths, each trade arrayed separately within the building.[24] Seventy-one thrones for the communal elders were made of heavy gold: "each one made from twenty-five talents." The Jerusalem Talmud (*Sukkah* 5:1, 55a–b) adds that each was studded with fine stones and pearls. What a joy!

Let us consider just one early synagogue that elicits this response. The deep reds, greens, browns, and yellows of the ancient Dura Europos synagogue (completed 244/5 CE) never cease to enthrall me.[25] The walls of this local synagogue on the Euphrates River in Syria are covered with a panoply of biblical characters—each declaring in her or his own way the greatness of God and the truth of Torah. Whether it be Esther with Ahasuerus or Aaron in the Tabernacle, Elijah resuscitating the son of the Shunamite or Moses himself crossing the sea, or holding up a Torah scroll, this ancient *shtiebel* is literally inhabited by the heroes of our people. Illuminated by small oil lamps, as this building certainly was in antiquity, I imagine the endless grades of light and changing experience as our ancestors' shadows within this rather dark room became one with images of Abraham and Moses and Esther and so many others as they—dressed in garments not unlike those imagined for our culture heroes—moved about this small room. Just writing about Dura, I find myself smiling with joy.

The environment of the synagogue is more than just lamps and furniture and even textiles, of course. The community spoke in a cacophony of Aramaic and Greek and Persian, as fits a border town between Rome and Persia. The community responded to the paintings by adding evocative comments, so we know some of what they thought. Below the miracle of the Shunamite, a Persian speaker scratched: "When Hormazd the scribe came and by him this [picture] was looked at: 'Living the child (?) who had been dead.'" One Jew proclaimed in Aramaic across the face of the Torah shrine for all to see, "I, Uzi donated the house of the Ark, and a leader named Samuel sat beneath the image of 'Samuel when he anointed David.'" They prayed in Hebrew, the text preserved on a surviving parchment is amazingly close to the prayers of the Sages.

The sounds of our liturgy—both artfully performed and otherwise—fill every synagogue—as do the petty conversations, arguments, and crying children that have always accompanied the official prayer and learning of the place. Smells create environments like no others, as in North African and Asian communities—where the scent of rose water and fragrant flowers often fill the air. Ashkenazim experience this on Shavuot, when the synagogue is blanketed with flowers—as Mt. Sinai was, tradition has it, at the moment of theophany (not to mention the savory scent of *cholent* cooking in the kitchen of a *stiebel*). The *beit ha-knesset* is, then, a complete sensual experience, where sight and smell and sound and touch are activated. Through ritual, communities across the world create an environment where Israel might encounter its Maker. It is a holy place of our own.

Our synagogues and study houses are the training ground for our joyful interaction with Torah, the very "stages" upon which it is acted out publicly. Often, we take for granted the carefully designed decor of our synagogues and the ways that these spaces, lighting choices, and even the typeface in our prayer books can enhance and be activated by the liturgy itself. All of these developed over centuries and are ever refreshed. They are the triggers that are baked into the experience of those who call synagogues and study houses "home." By focusing on the spatial and experiential aspects of synagogue life, recognizing their power and holistic holiness, we can deepen our attachments to our own very local "holy places." May we all achieve such "joy" as we enter our own synagogues and study houses: "Joyful is the people for whom this is so."

Notes

1. On the synagogue as liturgical space, see S. Fine, *Art and Judaism in the Greco-Roman World: Toward a New "Jewish Archaeology"* (Cambridge, rev. ed. 2010), 167–173.
2. JT Berakhot 5:1, 8d 9a.
3. Megilla 2:21-22 (ed. S. Lieberman). See Steven Fine, *This Holy Place: On the Sanctity of the Synagogue during the Greco-Roman period* (Notre Dame, 1997).
4. *Mishneh Torah, Hilkhot Tefillah* 11 and *Shulhan Arukh*, O.H. Hilkhot Beit ha-Knesset 150.
5. BT Megilla 29a, manuscript traditions.
6. JT Megilla 3:1-3, 73d-74a.
7. Steven Fine, *Art, History and the Historiography of Judaism in Roman Antiquity* (Boston: Brill, 2014), 139–160.
8. For other occasions where *Ashrei* is recited, see Eliezer Levi, *Yesodot ha-Tefillah* (Tel Aviv, 1955), 131–132, 317; Elbogen, *Jewish Liturgy*, 71, 182, 214.
9. Ezra Fleischer, *Prayer and Prayer Customs of Palestinian Jews during the Times of the Genizah* (Jerusalem, 1988), 283 (Hebrew). For example, *Mahzor Vitry* (ed. S. L. Horowitz [Nurnberg, 1923], 1: 63–64 precedes Ps. 84:6 with Psalms 119:1, 2; 84:6; 112:1; 89:16. See: Abraham Jacob Berkowitz, *The Life of Psalms in Late Antiquity*, PhD dissertation (Princeton, 2018), 193–194, 247.
10. Berkowitz, *The Life of Psalms*, 182–184.
11. See the *Oxford English Dictionary*, s.v. happy, and *The American Heritage Dictionary of the English Language*, www.ahdictionary.com, s.v. "joy" and "happy."
12. Berkowitz, *The Life of Psalms*, 182.

13. JT Berakhot 5:1, 8d; Deuteronomy Rabba 3:1 and parallels; Fine, *This Holy Place* 65–66.
14. Following NJPS.
15. See also m. Megilla 3:1–3.
16. See Steven Fine, "'Their Faces Shine with the Brightness of the Firmament:' Study Houses and Synagogues in the *Targumim* to the Pentateuch," *Biblical Translation in Context*, ed. F. W. Knobloch (Bethesda, 2002), 63–92.
17. *Midrash Tanhuma* (Jerusalem, 1953), *Ki Tavo* 4 (p. 120).
18. JT Berakhot 5:1, 9a, b. Berakhot 6b and parallels.
19. See BT Berakhot 32b.
20. Berkowitz, *The Life of Psalms*, 183–184, 247–248.
21. Fine, *Art and Judaism*, 108–110.
22. Steven Fine, "Lernen To See: 'Modernity,' Torah and the Study of Jewish 'Art,'" *Milin Havivin* 7 (2013–2014), 24–35.
23. *Siddur di rito Italiano secondo l'uso di Gerusalemme*, ed. A. Piattelli (Jerusalem, 2016), 194.
24. BT Sukkah 4:5.
25. See Fine, *Art, History*, 101–122.

CHAPTER 35

The Music Beneath the Noise: Faith and Joy in the Writings of Rabbi Sacks

Meir Soloveichik

It was a celebrated journalistic experiment, memorably described in an article that won the Pulitzer Prize. *The Washington Post*'s Gene Weingarten asked Joshua Bell, one of the most gifted violinists alive, to stand at a Washington, DC, Metro station in the midst of rush hour, playing one of Bach's most beautiful compositions on his Stradivarius. Today, one can watch the results on YouTube.[1] A crowd never gathered; almost everyone rushed by, utterly oblivious to the fact that they had a free front row to an experience that at this proximity would usually cost thousands of dollars.

Weingarten reports that the letters poured in by people deeply affected by his piece, who cried after they read it; not, presumably, because they were classical music aficionados, but rather, as Weingarten put it, the experiment prompted a question: "If we can't take the time out of our lives to stay a moment and listen to one of the best musicians on Earth

---

M. Soloveichik (✉)
Straus Center for Torah and Western Thought, Yeshiva University, New York, NY, USA

Congregation Shearith Israel, New York, NY, USA

© The Author(s), under exclusive license to Springer Nature Switzerland AG 2023
E. Brown, S. Weiss (eds.), *An Ode to Joy*,
https://doi.org/10.1007/978-3-031-28229-4_35

play some of the best music ever written; if the surge of modern life so overpowers us that we are deaf and blind to something like that—then what else are we missing?"[2]

The image of the passers-by ignoring exquisite music, ensconced in the cacophonous cocoon of modern life, of countless commuters failing to listen to the music evident in their own lives, inspires us to ponder the nature of faith itself. In one of his most beautiful essays on the weekly Torah reading, Rabbi Sacks contemplated what is, for the Talmud, the final commandment in the Torah:[3] "Now therefore write this song for you and teach it to the children of Israel; put it in their mouths, that this song may be a witness for Me" (Deut. 31:19). Read simply, the verse refers here to the song exultantly sung by Moses at the end of his life; but as the rabbis understand it, this is a command that actually obligates us to write a Torah scroll, which is itself the song of which scripture speaks. Seen this way, all of Judaism is compared to Moses' joyful song: the Torah, for the Rabbis, is not a turgid technical text, it is sheet music. But how exactly is the observance of the Jewish faith, which applies its observances to all aspects of life, like unto an exultant musical performance?

The question has occupied countless commentators throughout the centuries, and in asking it, Rabbi Sacks cites another insightful author with his own name, who was, as he reflected, "No relative, alas": Oliver Sacks, whose book *Musicophilia* tells of the musicologist Clive Wearing, who, afflicted with a terrible brain infection, experienced an amnesia of the most profound kind, instantly forgetting any knowledge acquired. Time, for Wearing, lacked any continuity. And yet, in midst of this utter inability to connect most moments together, struck with a disease that made everything ephemeral, Wearing nevertheless retained his ability to play music. This, for Sacks, reveals how music, in the most elemental manner, creates a bone-deep, ineradicable sense of continuity unlike anything else. Oliver Sacks' analysis of this heartbreaking story quotes the philosopher of music Victor Zuckerkandl: "Hearing a melody is hearing, having heard, and being about to hear, all at once. Every melody declares to us that the past can be there without being remembered, the future without being foreknown."[4]

Inspired by this reflection, Rabbi Sacks proceeded to explain the rabbinic equation between the embrace of faith and exultant song. The metaphor of music, he argued, is meant to tell us something profound about continuity, and its connection to belief. And as we read Rabbi Sacks' words, it is hard not to think of the experiment of Weingarten at the Washington Metro:

> Music is a form of sensed continuity that can sometimes break through the most overpowering disconnections in our experience of time...
> Faith is more like music than science. Science analyses, music integrates. And as music connects note to note, so faith connects episode to episode, life to life, age to age in a timeless melody that breaks into time. God is the composer and librettist. We are each called on to be voices in the choir, singers of God's song. *Faith is the ability to hear the music beneath the noise.*[5]

If this is the case, then the joy of Judaism—and the inextricable connection between joy and faith—lies in our finding our place in the larger whole, in the symphony of generations. It is in a similar sense that my grandfather, Rabbi Ahron Soloveichik, interpreted the enigmatic statement of Hillel uttered at the Temple Festival of the Water Drawing, once the most joyous moment of the Jewish year: "*Im ani ka'an, ha-kol ka'an, ve-im ein ani ka'an, mi ka'an*; if I am here, then all is here, and if I am not here, then who is here?" The seeming self-centeredness of this utterance cannot reflect its true meaning, as Hillel was known for his humility. In my grandfather's profoundly psychological reading, Hillel, at this exultantly joyous occasion, was wondering about the nature of joy itself: his reference to *ani*, or "I", was meant to describe the internal I, the essence of our identity. Most forms of purported rejoicing are in no way connected to our covenantal calling, to the essence of who we are; and this, for Judaism, is not genuine joy, but mere escapism. This is the point Hillel was making: he was not narcissistically describing himself, but making a universal claim, at a joyous moment in the Temple, the locus of Jewish religious life. *Im ani ka'an*, if one's "I" is here, if one's pursuit of joy places one's identity within a larger whole, endowing it with resplendent meaning, then *ha-kol ka'an*, all is here, and the rejoicing is justified. But if not, if what is occurring is not an extension of one's truest self, but rather a defiance of it, then the joy is not genuine.

And so again: faith is the ability to hear the music beneath the noise, to connect moment to moment, life to life, generation to generation. This, of course, does not mean that what is required of us by faith is collective sameness: quite the contrary. Thus, the nineteenth-century Rabbi Yechiel Mikhel Epstein, observed that the Talmudic comparison between Torah and song, reflected that "The grandeur of a song is found when the voices are different from one another, for that is the essence of its beauty." Rabbi Epstein parallels here Rabbi Sacks' own elaboration on the rabbinic musical metaphor:

> To make the Torah live anew, it is not enough to hand it on cognitively - as mere history and law. It must speak to us affectively, emotionally ... The 613th command, to make the Torah new in every generation, symbolizes the fact that though the Torah was given only once, it must be received many times, as each of us, through our study and practice, strives to recapture the pristine voice heard at Mount Sinai. That requires emotion, not just intellect. It means treating Torah not just as words read, but also as a melody sung. The Torah is God's libretto, the Jewish people, are His choir, the performers of His choral symphony - and a song becomes more beautiful when scored for many voices interwoven in complex harmonies.[6]

Faith, in other words, like a joyous response to a song, is not only cognitive. Here, too, Weingarten's piece provides a powerful metaphor. If one carefully watches the entire video of Weingarten's experiment, one will observe, amid all the oblivious passers-by, a woman and her small child step into the scene. In Weingarten's words,

> The woman is walking briskly and, therefore, so is the child. She's got his hand. You can see the child clearly on the video. He's the cute kid in the parka who keeps twisting around to look at Joshua Bell, as he is being propelled toward the door. So his mom does what she has to do. She deftly moves her body between her boy and Bell, cutting off her son's line of sight. As they exit the arcade, the little boy can still be seen craning to look. On that day in DC, the behavior of one demographic remained absolutely consistent. Every single time a child walked past, he or she tried to stop and watch. And every single time, a parent scooted the kid away.

Weingarten once interviewed the poet Billy Collins, who once quipped that "we're born as poets. The heartbeat you hear in the womb is iambic-dah-DUM, dah-DUM. So we've already taken a course in meter when we come out of the womb. Then we have the poetry beaten out of us by teachers."[7] This, Weingarten comments, "may be true with music, too." His words remind one of the Talmud passages that parallels Plato's *Crito*, that every Jewish baby is taught the entire Torah by an angel in the womb, only to forget it upon emerging into the world. The point, perhaps, is that for the Jewish child the song of Judaism is never foreign: it is a haunting melody that touches the very depth of the soul, one that naturally entrances, but one which we, in our adulthood, we all too often ignore. And the greatest joy, for Judaism, lies in understanding our inner *ani*, our essential "I," the essence of who each of us is and our place in the larger whole.

Yet like the adults rushing blindly by Joshua Bell, wholly engaged in modern life but unaware of the performance unfolding before them, all too many today ignore the symphony of generations calling out to us. "Several centuries of Western thought," Rabbi Sacks ruefully reflected,

> have left us with the idea that when we choose how to live, we are on our own. Nothing in the past binds us Jewish life, in today's day and age, is a sustained countervoice. To be a Jew is to know that this cannot be the full story of who I am. A melody is more than a sequence of disconnected notes…The part has meaning in terms of its place within the whole.[8]

Rabbi Sacks was the maestro who could make those rushing through life pauseand truly appreciate Judaism for the resplendent symphony that it is, calling each Jew to find his or her place within it. The world is less musical without him; and that is one of many reasons that he is so missed today.

Notes

1. https://www.youtube.com/watch?v=hnOPu0_YWhw.
2. Gene Weingarten, "Pearls Before Breakfast: Can One of the Nation's Great Musicians Cut Through the Fog of a D.C. Rush Hour? Let's Find Out," *The Washington Post Magazine*, April 8, 2007.
3. Jonathan Sacks, "The Spirituality of Song," Covenant and Conversation (*Ha'azeinu*, 5776). https://www.rabbisacks.org/covenant-conversation/haazinu/the-spirituality-of-song/
4. Oliver Sacks, *Musicophilia: Tales of Music and the Brain* (Vintage, 2008), 228.
5. Sacks, "The Spirituality of Song."
6. Rabbi Sacks cites Rabbi Epstein in "The Torah as God's Song," Covenant and Conversation (*Vayelekh*, 5779). https://www.rabbisacks.org/covenant-conversation-family-edition/vayelech/the-torah-as-gods-song/
7. Gene Weingarten, "Below the Beltway," *The Washington Post*, July 7, 2002.
8. Jonathan Sacks, *Radical Then, Radical Now* (Continuum, 2004), 41.

CHAPTER 36

Expressing the Inexpressible: Rabbi Sacks on Music and the Search for a Religious Aesthetic

Harris Bor

INTRODUCTION

Music and song are constant themes in Rabbi Sacks' teachings. He saw music as capturing the inexpressible joy which underlies faith and signaling the transcendent in ways that philosophy cannot.

Rabbi Sacks discussed music with his family, collated music, engaged with musicians, and even performed.[1] In 1991, he appeared on BBC Radio Four's Desert Island Discs, a program in which famous personalities listen to and discuss the soundtracks of their lives.[2] It is evident how much music meant to him. He did not read or play music but told the London *Financial Times* in 2020 that "I love it with a completely untutored joy."[3]

Music is important to many of us too, whether as an expression of our inner worlds, a means to connect, or a shaper of memory. And so, we can ask, what is music's connection to the spiritual? What role should it play in religion?

H. Bor (✉)
London School of Jewish Studies, London, UK

To answer these questions, I would like to consider some of Rabbi Sacks' statements on music and to place them into philosophical context. Not all of Rabbi Sacks' ideas on the topic are fully developed, but there are certainly nuggets to be extracted and ideas worthy of further exploration.

Torah as Song

Rabbi Sacks was attracted to the idea, found in the Talmud, that Torah is song.[4] The Talmud learns this from the verse in Deuteronomy 31:19: "And now write for yourselves this song and teach it to the children of Israel, put it in their mouths, that this song may be a witness for Me among the children of Israel." According to the sages, "this song" is not a reference to *Ha'azinu* (the song that follows) but to the Torah as a whole.[5]

Rabbi Sacks riffs on this theme: "The Torah is God's libretto, and we, the Jewish people, are His choir." Only through song can the words of Torah penetrate the heart: "music is the affective dimension of communication, the medium through which we express, evoke and share emotion."[6] Without such dimension, Torah will find it hard to reach the next generation. And so, writes Rabbi Sacks, Judaism "modulates into song" whenever it aspires to the spiritual; when we read from the Torah, pray, and learn yeshiva-style.

For Rabbi Sacks, the idea of Torah as song signals the appropriate relationship between the individual and community. Torah is a "choral symphony scored for many voices, the written text its melody, and the oral tradition its polyphony."[7] Rabbi Sacks, it seems, wants us to find our voices, but urges us to do so within a community and remain faithful to the dominant melody.

This is a lovely idea, but a choral symphony is just one type of music. What about jazz, punk, reggae, rap, grunge, or grime? Many of us feel that we need some improvisation or a solo act or two. There should be room in our choir also for those whose voices are faint or discordant. In short, we need greater sonic diversity (while still avoiding cacophony). Rabbi Sacks has set us on a course, but his ideas have further mileage.[8]

Judaism as Aural Culture

Rabbi Sacks frequently observed that Judaism promotes listening over seeing.[9] For example, the Torah prohibits the making of visual images of the Divine, and instead commands us to listen and hear.[10]

What is the difference between sight and sound? Rabbi Sacks answers, based on an observation of Rabbi Yaakov Leiner, the son of the Ishbitzer Rebbe (Rabbi Mordechai Leiner) that: "Seeing tells us about the surfaces, the externalities, of things. Listening tells us about internalities, depths (*omek kol davar*)."[11] Sound penetrates and so, says Rabbi Sacks drawing on the thinker Walter J Ong, through speaking and listening "we are present to one another as subjects rather than objects."[12] The notion of Torah as song might be joined to this idea. Sound is about relationship, and the Torah sings because it too is about relationship; the relationship between God and humankind.[13]

The musicologist and theologian, Jeremy Begbie, provides us with an additional dimension when he explores similar themes to Rabbi Sacks, albeit in a Christian context. Begbie writes that, in the case of seeing, "distinct objects in our visual field occupy bounded locations, discrete zones, such that they cannot overlap without their integrity being threatened."[14] Thus we see either red or yellow, or orange if the two are merged. In contrast, two sounds, such as notes played on a piano, can occupy the same heard space in its entirety while remaining distinct.[15] They "interpenetrate" each other without either driving the other away.[16]

This has theological relevance because we speak of God as being transcendent, above the world and separate from us, or immanent, in the world.[17] Both are problematic—transcendence suggests distance and immanence a lack of freedom. Theologians also struggle to reconcile the two. But, argues Begbie, the dichotomy is rooted in our visual perception, the world of concrete edges, of either/or. Sound space offers us an alternative way to perceive God. A note can be higher than another but resonate alongside it: "The transcendence of one tone or chord over another, say, of a fundamental over its first overtone, is the transcendence of irreducible difference, certainly, but a difference that brings life, abundance, fullness to the other tones."[18] Music shows how God can be both transcendent and immanent at the same time.

Feeling Over Philosophy

Although Rabbi Sacks did not explore these theological possibilities, he did enlist music in his discussions on belief. In *A Letter in the Scroll* (*Radical Then, Radical Now* in the UK), Rabbi Sacks acknowledges Hume, Kant, and Nietzsche's efforts to show that the existence of God cannot be proven, but thought little of them. He was adamant that belief is not to be founded in philosophy, but an aesthetic sensibility:

> Of course it is possible to live a life without God, just as it is possible to live a life without humor, or music, or love; and one can no more prove that God exists than one can prove these other things exist to those who lack a sense of humor, or to whom Shubert is mere noise, or love a figment of the romantic imagination.[19]

Rabbi Sacks continues that those who hear the "call" understand that Judaism is "not a metaphysical wager" but the "courage to see the world as it is without the comfort of myth or the self-pity of despair" and to take on "human responsibility."[20]

Music therefore sits alongside humor and love, as an aspect of life that cannot be proven and which it makes no sense to deny. Rabbi Sacks writes: "Jewish faith is false only if we are wrong to believe in the objective reality of all that is personal."[21] Religion, like music (and humor and love), is personal and objectively real. God in this context is "the music beneath the noise,"[22] and faith the attempt to hear such music.[23]

The difficulty with this idea is that not everyone hears God's call, and, many who do, certainly do not hear it in the same way as Rabbi Sacks does. What then? While Rabbi Sacks will admit that God speaks in different voices or is heard differently by different people, he has little option but to say that those who do not hear God clearly or at all are tone deaf. He refers to a conversation he had with Sir Isaiah Berlin, the philosopher, about music and faith. Sir Isaiah ended it by stating "Chief Rabbi, don't talk to me about faith. When it comes to God, I'm tone deaf." Rabbi Sacks says he regrets not arguing the point with him.[24] Rabbi Sacks later tried the same argument on the well-known scientist and atheist, Richard Dawkins, who was similarly unimpressed—with good reason.[25] One can't impose one's own preferences on someone, and in most areas of life we don't try.[26]

A more productive outcome might have been achieved by explaining that understanding Torah as song or religion as music is not about imposing taste on another, but about teaching another to sing, to find his or her own voice so they can join with others in an act of creation and supernal beauty. Religion is a mode of human flourishing.[27] What follows is that if a choir wants to attract singers, it must make itself more attractive, a point which Rabbi Sacks well knew.

Toward a Jewish Aesthetic

Rabbi Sacks made it his life's work to beautify Judaism. In so doing, he acknowledged that many resist the idea that religion should be outwardly attractive—Judaism after all did not build great cathedrals or inspire great orchestral works. But Rabbi Sacks defends his position using the Torah's elaborate and detailed description of the grandeur of the *Mishkan* (desert tabernacle) and priestly vestments. He claims there has always been a place for aesthetics within Judaism.

Rabbi Sacks understood that for this reason we need creators to make works of art that inspire religion, and notes scientific research that shows how important emotions are to motivating action, a point we have seen before.[28] He agreed with Michael Wyschogrod's assessment that:

> The imagination of the poet is a reflection of his spiritual life. Myth and metaphor are the currency both of religion and poetry. Poetry is one of the most powerful domains in which religious expression takes place. And the same is true of music, drama, painting, and dance.[29]

Rabbi Sacks, however, did not spell out the limits that should be placed on the artist's endeavors or what happens when imagination conflicts with tradition, perhaps appreciating that the creative urge cannot be easily curtailed and must be allowed to find expression before being judged.

Music as Educational Tool

Rabbi Sacks' desire to develop a religious aesthetic was manifest in how he employed music in his teachings. He often referenced well-known music in his writings. These serve almost as a sound-track for his words, themselves expressed with musical beauty and power. In one place, Rabbi Sacks tells the story of Beethoven's Ninth Symphony, containing the famous musical setting of Schiller's poem, Ode to Joy.[30] Masterfully linking the Jewish ability to overcome suffering to Beethoven's courage in writing this work while deaf, Rabbi Sacks describes Judaism as an "Ode to Joy." We almost hear Schiller's words—"All men will emerge as brothers"—and Beethoven's famous melody, as we read this piece, feeling that sense of connectedness and hope which music brings.

Rabbi Sacks also understood the power of having his words interspersed with music. Anyone who attended one of the many packed midnight *Selihot* services with the Shabbaton Choir at which he spoke will attest to the emotional impact of those religious experiences: uplifting song and penetrating insight combined.

In 2008, Rabbi Sacks, compiled a double album—*Israel: Home of Hope*—that used the power of words and music to tell the story of the modern state of Israel. The album featured film music, and traditional and modern compositions including *Jerusalem* sung by Matisyahu, who at that time was making his name in the music world as a Hasidic rapper.[31]

In his introduction to the video of *Oseh Shalom* (a song from the album), which later appeared on YouTube, Rabbi Sacks tells the accompanying children's choir that, "When we're really excited that something great has happened, we have to sing to Hashem. And the best song that we can possibly sing is *Oseh Shalom Olenu*. We want one thing above all for Israel, for the Jewish people, for the world, [that] there should be peace."[32]

But not all music is joyful.

On the morning of 16 November 2016, Rabbi Sacks, looking bereft, delivered from his hotel room in New York a eulogy for Leonard Cohen, the Jewish singer-songwriter, who had just died. It was based on *Vayera*, that week's Torah portion. In it, Rabbi Sacks describes in a hushed tone (as if he did not want to wake the neighbors) Cohen's last song, *You Want It Darker*, as a "song for our times" and "a precise commentary" on the story of the binding of Isaac contained in the portion. Rabbi Sacks explains how Cohen tracks the biblical narrative by using the Hebrew word *Hineini*, "Here I am," three times and draws on other phraseology found in the biblical text.

According to Rabbi Sacks, Cohen, like Abraham, was appalled by the darkness of God's world ("I want out of the game"), but still loved God. Rabbi Sacks ends by thanking Cohen for teaching us how to "find God in the midst of darkness" and calls on us to "sing a song to God and find love and redemption in this broken world." The video shows Rabbi Sacks at his most authentic. We see in it an instinctive outpouring of grief, and the sense of kinship that he, an Orthodox leader, felt for Leonard Cohen, the secular Jew who sang in *Hallelujah* of the "Lord of Song" and whose last song, *Hineini*, incorporates the words of Kaddish.

And finally, in April 2020, during the height of the COVID pandemic and not long before Rabbi Sacks died, he participated with Ishay Ribo, the Israeli singer, in an online event entitled "Spirituality and Song" moderated by the Israeli journalist and educator Sivan Rahav Meir. Toward the start of the discussion, Rabbi Sacks makes a distinction between his role as rabbi and Ribo's as musician. He said: "I try at times like this to find words that bring people comfort and hope, but words alone are not enough because the mind speaks, but the soul sings."[33] Ribo followed with a performance of his exquisitely haunting lock-down song, *Keter Melukha* (Royal Crown), which demands that God explain "*Mah Atah Rotseh Shenavin Mizeh?*"—"What are we to make of this"?[34] Following the performance, Rabbi Sacks said humorously that Ribo, as a singer could ask such questions. If he asked the same question no one would listen.[35] The mind speaks, but the soul sings.

Reclaiming Romanticism

Rabbi Sacks' approach to music draws on traditional Jewish texts and contemporary writings[36] but has much in common with early German romanticism of the late eighteenth and early nineteenth centuries, particularly when he associates music with emotion and the divine. Romanticism sought to distance itself from the rationalism of the Enlightenment period and to create a synthesis between philosophy, science, and the arts. It also gave rise to a new age of instrumental music in which music was regarded as a source of contemplation in its own right, rather than merely an accompaniment for social or religious occasions. The result of such contemplation was an increased association between music, religion, and the non-rational.

In 1810, for example, Beethoven's Symphony No. 5 went viral after the music critic, Ernst Theodor Amadeus Hoffmann (1776–1882), enthused over the piece, describing how it drew the listener into the "spirit-realm of the infinite."[37] Hoffman explained that "music discloses to man an unknown realm, a world that has nothing in common with the external sensual world that surrounds him, a world in which he leaves behind him all definite feelings to surrender himself to an inexpressible longing."[38]

Friedrich Schleiermacher (1768–1834), a theologian who also played the piano and sang, more directly associated music with religion, by which he meant the "seeking of the Infinite in all temporal things in and through the Eternal" and finding it "in all growth and change, in all doing and suffering."[39] For Schleiermacher, both religion and music aspire to create order from the chaos: "A man's special calling is the melody of his life, and it remains a simple, meagre series of notes unless religion, with its endlessly rich variety, accompanies it with all notes, and raises the simple song to a full-voiced, glorious harmony."[40]

Schleiermacher further explained how music, especially when accompanied with words, has a greater power to convey messages than language alone: "In sacred hymns and choruses to which the world of the poet are but loosely and airily appended, there are breathed out things that definite speech cannot grasp."[41] Rabbi Sacks' ideas about music in many respects reflect the above sentiments.[42]

In the nineteenth and then twentieth centuries, however, with the rise of pop and rock, sentiments like the ones above were expressed without reference to the infinite, God, or religion. Instead, romantic love became a religion in its own right, and music became a consolation for the apparent death of God, and a secular means to access the transcendent.[43]

Rabbi Sacks' project was driven by an acute awareness of the void left by the retreat of religion, and desire to fill that gap not with dry argument, but a vibrant covenantal faith, which speaks to the heart as much as the head. In this sense, he was a romantic, and music was part of his romantic vision. Rabbi Sacks believed that music can bring people back to religion, just as it had moved them away. He also showed us that the Torah's song can be identified in many genres. His legacy then might inspire us to develop a more imaginative Jewish aesthetic in which the musician is given a seat alongside the king, prophet, and priest, and to sing our hearts out with joy, much the way the Levites did in the Temple. Music heals, as Rabbi Sacks reminded us: "Unlike happiness, joy is not conditional on things going well... Like music, it gives expression to the inexpressible."[44]

Notes

1. Most notably, *Oseh Shalom*, sung with Jonny Turgel and the Shabbaton Choir in 2008. See https://www.youtube.com/watch?v=qVM6x4BechI and the public performance at https://www.youtube.com/

watch?v=apMbinSz8RU. Alan Sacks, Rabbi Sacks' brother, tells me that Rabbi Sacks corresponded with him on songs by such artists as Leonard Cohen, Bob Dylan, Queen, Elton John, Paul McCartney, Bruce Springsteen, Eminem, and Sia, and that he had an overwhelming admiration for Lin-Manuel Miranda's hit musical, Hamilton. Indeed, in 2020 Rabbi Sacks posted a video on the subject of Pesach and Hamilton. See https://www.youtube.com/watch?v=7L7gFCPD-8M. (I am grateful to Alan for sharing his recollections and correspondence). In *Morality*, Rabbi Sacks refers to another musical, *Come from Away*, when describing the kindness showed by strangers in Newfoundland following the 9/11 attacks. *Morality* (London: Hodder & Stoughton, 2020), 307.
2. See https://www.bbc.co.uk/programmes/p0093z8b. In addition to traditional Jewish music, his choice for Desert Island Discs included Mahler, Beethoven, Brahms, and Ravel.
3. Ludovic Hunter-Tilney, "Out of Office: Jonathan Sacks," *Financial Times*, April 4, 2020.
4. The following section is based on *Covenant & Conversation*, Vayelech, 5775, https://www.rabbisacks.org/covenant-conversation/vayelech/torah-as-song/; and Vayelech, 5779, https://www.rabbisacks.org/covenant-conversation/vayelech/the-torah-as-gods-song/.
5. BT Nedarim 38a.
6. Referring to Antonio R. Damasio, *Descartes' Error: Emotion, Reason and the Human Brain* (Penguin, 2006).
7. Drawing on an idea of Rabbi Yechiel Michel Epstein (1829–1908) found in his introduction to *Choshen Mishpat* in the *Aruch ha-Shulchan*. Rabbi Epstein lived during the romantic era of music in which the symphony reached new heights following the likes of Beethoven who died two years before Rabbi Epstein was born.
8. In *The Home We Build Together*, Rabbi Sacks notes that devotees of a particular genre of music tend to listen to that genre exclusively, and are reluctant to explore further afield. The comment is made when discussing the disintegration of national cultures and the division of society into non-intercommunicating rooms (*The Home We Build Together: Recreating Society* (London: Continuum, 2007), 69). I would suggest that, even within a single tradition, we should have many rooms with interconnecting doors, each leading into the shared space of a national amphitheater.
9. As in *Covenant & Conversation*, Ki Tavo, 5780 https://www.rabbisacks.org/covenant-conversation/ki-tavo/be-silent-and-listen/ on which this section is based.
10. Examples of the demand to listen are: "Hear Israel. The Lord is our God. The Lord is One" (Deuteronomy 6:4) and "Be Silent and Listen, Israel.

You Have Now Become the People of the Lord Your God" (Deuteronomy 27:9).
11. The observation is made in *Beit Yaakov*, a collection of Rabbi Leiner's essays, vol. 4, *Torah u-moadim, Rosh Chodesh Menachem Av*, 131.
12. See Walter J. Ong, *Orality and Literacy: The Technologizing of the Word* (Routledge, 1982), 71.
13. In describing faith as a form of listening, Rabbi Sacks writes: "*Listening is an existential act of encounter, a way of hearing the person beneath the words, the music beneath the noise. Freud, who disliked religion and abandoned his Judaism, was nonetheless Jewish enough to invent, in psychoanalysis, the 'listening cure': listening as the healing of the soul*" (*The Great Partnership: God, Science and the Search for Meaning* (Hodder & Stoughton, Kindle Edition, 74)).
14. Jeremy Begbie, *Music, Modernity, and God: Essays in Listening* (Oxford: Oxford University Press, 2015), 143.
15. Begbie, *Music*, 155.
16. Begbie, *Music*, 159.
17. I have taken up these themes in the context of AI in my book *Staying Human: A Jewish Theology for the Age of Artificial Intelligence* (Eugene, Oregon: Cascade Books, 2021).
18. Begbie, *Music*, 165.
19. Jonathan Sacks, *Radical Then, Radical Now: The Legacy of the World's Oldest Religion* (London: Harper Collins, 2001), 214.
20. Sacks, *Radical Then*, 214.
21. Sacks, *Radical Then*, 214.
22. *Great Partnership*, 291.
23. *Ceremony & Celebration: Introduction to the Holidays* (Toby Press, 2017), 113.
24. Sacks, *Radical Then*, 214.
25. In *Covenant & Conversation*, Ha'azinu, 5776, fn 5, Rabbi Sacks relates: "*I once said to the well-known atheist Richard Dawkins, in the course of a radio conversation, "Richard, religion is music, and you are tone deaf." He replied, "Yes, it's true, I am tone deaf, but there is no music.*" https://www.rabbisacks.org/covenant-conversation/haazinu/the-spirituality-of-song/. The conversation is described in more detail in *Morality*, 254. There Rabbi Sacks comments, "*How, if you are tone deaf, can you know that there is no music?*" The theme of the tone deafness is found elsewhere in Rabbi Sacks' writings, particularly in *The Great Partnership*. Rav Sacks views literary critics of the Bible are "*tone deaf to the music of the Bible*" when they wrongly explain the two creation stories as the joining of two separate documents. Further, in a discussion of New Atheism, Rav Sacks relates a story of the Bal Shem Tov who compared atheists to a deaf man observing people

dancing to a violin, and believed the people to be mad. Rabbi Sacks sees the atheists of earlier times as being more attuned to religion, despite their rejection (*Great Partnership*, 10–11 and 204 on Nietzsche's understanding that a purely scientific interpretation of life would overlook "*the music*" in it). On similar lines, Rabbi Sacks later cites Leo Tolstoy who compares secular morality to a person conducting an orchestra ignorant of music (*Great Partnership*, 146).

26. As above, Rabbi Sacks appreciated that not everyone considers belief in God to be essential to life. Elsewhere, Rabbi Sacks further acknowledged that: "*There is no reason to expect everyone to believe in God or the soul or the music of the universe as it sings the improbability of its existence*" (*Great Partnership*, 94).
27. The point is that each person desires to thrive in all areas of life, including musically, if given the opportunity, so those opportunities should be given. As Rabbi Sacks writes in his essay "The Art of asking Questions," "*we learn by living and understand by doing. We learn to understand music by listening to music. We learn to appreciate literature by reading literature*" (*The Chief Rabbi's Haggadah: Hebrew and English Text with New Essays and Commentary* (London: HarperCollins, 2003), 108.)
28. *Covenant & Conversation*, Tetzaveh, 5772, https://www.rabbisacks.org/covenant-conversation/tetzaveh/the-aesthetic-in-judaism/.
29. Michael Wyschogrod, *The Body of Faith: God in the People Israel* (New York; London: Harper & Row, 1989). In *Future Tense*, Rabbi Sacks references the growth of educational and cultural activities, such as art, music, and film festivals, as part of a Jewish renaissance, although later warns that religion cannot be translated into the language of culture. Judaism is first and foremost a faith, and so Jewish art must first and foremost address that faith. Sacks, *Future Tense*, 52, 63, and 69.
30. *Covenant & Conversation*, Ki Tavo, 5775, https://www.rabbisacks.org/covenant-conversation/ki-tavo/the-pursuit-of-joy/. Beethoven's symphony and Schiller's poem are also given a mention in *Not in God's Name*, when discussing the West's failed attempt to replace religion with universalist values *Not in God's Name: Confronting Religious Violence* (London: Hodder & Stoughton, 2015), 40.
31. See https://www.rabbisacks.org/archive/israel-home-of-hope/. Rabbi Sacks appeared to take pride in Matisyahu's success as a Hasidic rapper. It aligned with his desire to see Jews contribute to global culture as Jews. In *Future Tense*, Rav Sacks quotes the British journalist, Andrew Marr who wrote that: "*Outside painting, Morris dancing, and rap music it's hard to think of many areas of Western endeavour where Jews haven't been disproportionality successful*" (*Future Tense: A Vision for Jews and Judaism in the Global Culture* (London: Hodder & Stoughton, 2010), 61). I recall that

Rabbi Sacks once quipped that Matisyahu had ticked the last one off the list. A tweet from Rabbi Sacks of 21 Dec 2012 (12.38pm) shows him meeting with Matisyahu, who looks somewhat less Hasidic than he once did. See https://twitter.com/rabbisacks/status/282102629029515264.
32. See https://www.youtube.com/watch?v=qVM6x4BechI, 0–30 seconds. Rabbi Sacks expresses the same sentiment when explaining why we recite Hallel at the Seder but not on Purim. Purim is about memory. Passover is about reliving the exodus. Hallel at the Seder therefore is a spontaneous expression of praise. It "*arises out of the emotions we feel having lived through the event again. It is a 'new song'.*" *Haggadah*, 48. The spontaneity of song and its inner connection to spirit is explored also in *Covenant & Conversation*, Beshallach, 5772, https://www.rabbisacks.org/covenant-conversation/beshallach/music-language-of-the-soul/.
33. https://www.youtube.com/watch?v=xClZGyj3Cx0, 4.14–4.22.
34. For a clearer version of the song, see https://www.youtube.com/watch?v=RVKoNZloRvQ. The Royal Crown represents God's sovereignty as well as the tell-tale crown of the COVID virus.
35. https://www.youtube.com/watch?v=xClZGyj3Cx0, 10.45–10.55.
36. For example, in addition to other works mentioned in this chapter, Rabbi Sacks references Arnold Bennett, Johann Richter, and Johann Goethe, and works by Oliver Sacks (*Musicophilia* (London: Picador, 2018)) and Roger Scruton (*An Intelligent Person's Guide to Philosophy* (London: Duckworth, 2002). See *Covenant & Conversation*, Beshallach, 5772 and *Ha-azinu*, 5776 (see links above). Roger Scruton has delved deeply into music in other of his philosophical works. See Roger Scruton, *The Aesthetics of Music* (Oxford: Oxford University Press, 1999) and Roger Scruton, *Understanding Music: Philosophy and Interpretation* (NY: Continuum, 2009). On the essential connection between music and the human species, see also Philip Ball, *The Music Instinct: How Music Works and Why We Can't Do Without It* (London: Vintage Digital, 2011) and Michael Spitzer, *The Musical Human: A History of Life on Earth* (London: Bloomsbury, 2021).
37. T. A. Ernst Hoffmann, "Review of Beethoven's Fifth Symphony, *Allgemeine usikalische Zeitung*," in *E. T. A. Hoffmann's Musical Writings: Kreisleriana, The Poet and the Composer, Music, Criticism*, ed. David Charlton and trans. Martyn Clarke (Cambridge: Cambridge University Press, 1989), 239. Quoted in Begbie, *Music*, 108.
38. Oliver W. Strunk, *Source Readings in Music History: the Romantic Era*, 5 vols, col. V (London: Faber & Faber, 1981), 35–36. Quoted in Begbie, *Music*, 107.

39. Friedrich Schleiermacher, *On Religion: Speeches to Its Cultured Despisers* (London: K. Paul, Trench, Trubner & Co, 1893), reprinted online Grand Rapids, MI: Christian Classics Ethereal Library, Second Speech, 31–32.
40. Schleiermacher, Friedrich. *On Religion*, Second Speech, 70.
41. Schleiermacher, Friedrich. *On Religion*, Fourth Speech, 106. Such views about the limitations of language to depict both the external world and its more nebulous aspects were common in the period. See Begbie, Music, 112–16.
42. For example, when he writes: "*Science practises detachment. Religion is the art of attachment, self to self, soul to soul. Science sees the underlying order of the physical world. Religion hears the music beneath the noise. Science is the conquest of ignorance. Religion is the redemption of solitude.*" *Great Partnership*, 6–7.
43. Andrew Bowie, *Music, Philosophy, and Modernity. Modern European Philosophy* (Cambridge: Cambridge University Press, 2007), 36–39; and Begbie, *Music*, 129–32. See also Sacks, *The Home We Build*, 34–35.
44. *Ceremony & Celebration*, 127–29.

PART IX

Joy in Psychology and Human Agency

CHAPTER 37

Agency in the Bible: Humans Wrestling with God

Martin Seligman, Noah Love, and Philip Maymin

I had the privilege of meeting with Rabbi Jonathan Sacks in my home in Philadelphia just after he had written his book, *Future Tense*.[1] I was particularly impressed with his contention that Judaism was the first religion to view history as linear and forward-looking, rather than circular. Rabbi Sacks also pointed out that the burning bush story was commonly mistranslated as God saying, "I am what am," but the correct translation is "I will be what will be." We subsequently met and corresponded about the kind of agency human beings have when contemplating how to act to influence their own future. I was intrigued by Rabbi Sacks' interest in happiness as conceived by the field of positive psychology. His thinking intersected with my own study of the Hebrew Bible and with some careful linguistic work I was doing in conjunction, eventually, with my colleagues,

---

M. Seligman (✉) • N. Love
University of Pennsylvania, Philadelphia, PA, USA

P. Maymin
Dolan School of Business, Fairfield University, Fairfield, CT, USA

© The Author(s), under exclusive license to Springer Nature Switzerland AG 2023
E. Brown, S. Weiss (eds.), *An Ode to Joy*,
https://doi.org/10.1007/978-3-031-28229-4_37

Noah Love and Philip Maymin, and with the broad theoretical framework we conceived about agency in this ancient Jewish text. Our central hypothesis is that when people believe in their own agency, progress occurs. In contrast, when they believe that God or fate or other external or collective force is primarily agentic and individual people are not, stagnation occurs.

Agency, the belief that I can influence the world, is made up of three components: efficacy, optimism, and imagination. Efficacy is the expectation that I can achieve a specific goal now. Optimism is how long into the future I believe I can achieve that goal. Imagination is the range of goals that I believe I can achieve. Efficacy stimulates hard work; optimism causes persistence, and imagination causes innovation. These are the mechanisms by which Agency causes progress.

We content-analyzed the entire Hebrew Bible for words that correlate with agency and its components. We used the most frequent 50 words from the dictionary of agentic words developed by Pietraszkiewicz et al.[2] These authors identified an extensive lexicon of agency words over a wide range of texts. Of those 50 top words, 40 occurred at least once in the Bible. In addition, for more nuanced analysis, we created subcategories with a smaller set of words for efficacy, optimism, and imagination, based on our judgment of their face validity. To calculate the frequency of agency words in Genesis, for example, we divided the total number of agency words in Genesis by the total number of words in Genesis. The Table below lists these categories and the words.

Category	Words
Agency	tried, victory, knowing, wit, pride, obtain, willing, choice, thinking, purposes, freedom, resolved, needs, opportunity, easy, determined, doing, success, obtained, established, sure, taking, liberty, need, knowledge, making, purpose, able, self, took, known, think, thought, know, take, make, your, do, should, made
Efficacy	able, many, some, which, have, having, but, also, these, those
Optimism	things, good, joy, yet, hope (but not "no hope")
Imagination	desire, new, truth, true, false, ask, asked, know, known

Our first finding was a much higher frequency of such words in the later books of the Hebrew Bible than in the Pentateuch.

More importantly, however, we needed to separate God's agency from human agency. The essence of humans wrestling with God is the very balance between divine agency and human agency. So, to compare human versus Godly agency, we computed the ratio of human agency word frequencies to frequencies of Godly agency. To compute human agency, we eliminated all uses of the target words that had God or Lord in the same verse. We also eliminated all verses in which human agency is merely obeying God's commands and demands. We eliminated verses with command/commanded and shall/shalt. These "command" verses were added to the category of God's agency verses.

Our next finding was that the Torah has much more Godly agency than human agency compared to the rest of the Hebrew Bible. This can be seen, for example, in the binding of Isaac story in Genesis 22.

> **2** "Take your son," God said, "your only son, Isaac, whom you love so much, and go to the land of Moriah. There on a mountain that I will show you, offer him as a sacrifice to me."
>
> **3** Early the next morning Abraham cut some wood for the sacrifice, loaded his donkey, and took Isaac and two servants with him. They started out for the place that God had told him about. **4** On the third day Abraham saw the place in the distance...
>
> **9** When they came to the place which God had told him about, Abraham built an altar and arranged the wood on it. He tied up his son and placed him on the altar, on top of the wood.
>
> **10** Then he picked up the knife to kill him. **11** But the angel of the LORD called to him from heaven, "Abraham, Abraham!"
>
> He answered, "Yes, here I am."
>
> **12** "Don't hurt the boy or do anything to him," he said. "Now I know that you honor and obey God, because you have not kept back your only son from him."

Notice how non-agentic Abraham is. God commands and Abraham acts. No whining, no weighing of outcomes, no demurral. He makes no choices (lack of efficacy). He does not reflect on the future (lack of optimism), and he does not think of alternatives (lack of imagination). Notice also how non-introspective Abraham is. He just behaves; he does not appear to think or plan or emote.

It is crucial to appreciate that we did a flat, literal reading of the words themselves. We bent over backwards not to interpret the words with modern sensibility and not to fill in the blanks with mental events that are not explicitly stated. Agency in the full form requires deliberation, choice, and the weighing of alternatives. To infer full agency, we need explicit mention of such mental events. So, it is the very scarcity of choice and deliberation of words in the Torah that is so striking.

But it must be said that Abraham is not totally passive. Earlier, Abraham negotiates at length with God on behalf of possible righteous inhabitants of Sodom.[3] In this instance, Abraham shows much more agency than when commanded to sacrifice Isaac. The agency Abraham demonstrates when interceding on behalf of Sodom, however, is more the exception than the rule. For the most part in the Torah, God commands and the people obey, albeit often with some grumbling, protesting, complaining, and questioning.

The quintessence of this type of conflict between God's agency and human agency occurs when Jacob wrestles with God, and God changes Jacob's name to Israel.[4] Here, by nature of the fact that Jacob will not release God until God blesses him, the wrestling itself implicitly acknowledges that the source of all agency is God: "I will not let you go unless you bless me."[5] Jacob's success here is certainly agentic, but, like Abraham when called upon to sacrifice Isaac, his agency is passive; Jacob is only agentic in as much as God allows him to be. Jacob is allowed to live, and a blessing is extended to him. His striving is for God's recognition, not to accomplish anything of his own. Ultimately, his goals, ambitions, and prospections are still fully dependent on God.

It is difficult to ignore the passivity of the pre-monarchic Israelites in exodus particularly compared to the activity of their omnipotent God. The escape from Egypt is illustrative. God does all the heavy-lifting ("with a mighty hand and an outstretched arm") and the Israelites (and of course the Egyptians) fall into line. Exodus 13:15–18 recounts God's leading Israel out of Egypt:

> And it came to pass, when Pharaoh would hardly let us go that the Lord slew all the firstborn in the land of Egypt, both the first-born of man, and the first-born of beast; therefore I sacrifice to the Lord all that opens the womb, being males; but all the first-born of my sons I redeem. And it shall be for a sign upon your hand, and for frontlets between your eyes; for by strength of hand the Lord brought us forth out of Egypt. And it came to pass, when Pharaoh had let the people go, that God led them not by the way of the land of the Philistines, although that was near; for God said: 'Lest peradventure the people repent when they see war, and they return to Egypt.' But God led the people about, by the way of the wilderness by the Red Sea; and the children of Israel went up armed out of the land of Egypt.

Quantitatively, there are many fewer expressions of positive human agency and much more divine agency in the Torah than in the later books of the Bible. Unsurprisingly, we find that Leviticus also has the highest shall/shalt occurrence: 243 mentions.

The Torah's omnipotent God, whose powers dwarf and can even negate human agency is not without consequence for the faithful. The God of the Torah is such a force. The book of Job, which depicts an omnipotent God, is excruciatingly non-agentic for humans: God suddenly destroys everything that Job holds dear,[6] and Job does not protest or do anything to better his condition.[7] Note that some scholars contend that the book of Job was composed even earlier than the Torah.[8] If this is the case, the book of Job strengthens the case that agency is related to progress, being, potentially, the oldest book of the Bible. God's omnipotence ("you can do all things; no purpose of yours can be thwarted") should not be glossed over. Omnipotence tilts the balance between God's agency and human agency way over to God's.

What predictions follow from the Torah's depiction of God's omnipotence and a relative lack of human agency for the believers?

The first is a lack of human progress: stagnation in thought, in technology and science, in the arts and literature, in the quality of life, and in political freedom.[9] Is such stagnation true of the Israelites of the early Hebrew Bible? The Torah narrates events from Abraham, roughly 1850 BCE to the epoch of Moses, roughly 1400 BCE then down to about 1200 BCE. The later books of the Hebrew Bible narrate the period of the Judges (c.1100 BCE), then the Monarchic period, of Saul (c. 1020 BCE), David (c.1000 BCE), and Solomon (c. 970 BCE), and then the prophets. It continues with the narration of the Babylonia Exile (587 BCE) and it concludes with the Persian Exile and the return of the Israelites to Jerusalem in 445 BCE.

We cannot say with any certainty how society advanced during the Torah period because of the sparse historical record. But we cannot point to any known advance in technology, medicine, science, the arts and literature, the quality of life, or political freedom from 1850 BCE to 1200 BCE among the Israelites. Some might argue that there *was* one major intellectual advance: the consolidation of many gods into a monotheism.

We know much more about human progress from 1000 BCE to the end of the Bible, when Nehemiah and the first Judeans returned from the Persian Exile to Jerusalem in 445 BCE. This is just the period over which, as our empirical analyses demonstrate, the balance between human agency and God's agency has shifted drastically toward humans, as expressed in the words of the Hebrew Bible. This 500-year period was certainly a time of enormous human progress. Labor moved from small farming and herding in the hill country to fixed settlements and cities with populations in the tens of thousands. This was a time of great economic growth and of the commercialization of agriculture. This was a time of monumental architecture, including the building and rebuilding of the Temple in Jerusalem, palaces, and the construction of sewage systems. This was a time of coinage and of literacy, with engraved writing in silver. This was a time of increasingly sophisticated warfare and fortresses, and of the diplomacy needed to deal (however unsuccessfully) with the conquering Assyrians and then the Babylonians.[10]

Why did such an increase in the belief in human agency occur just then?

From about 800 BCE to 500 BCE, all over the world, a new psychological epoch dawned. It dawned in Greece, and it also dawned in China, Egypt, Sumeria, and India, as well as in Israel. Jaspers (2014) called this the "First Axial Age." Buddha, Confucius, Solon, Zarathustra, the Kings, and the Prophets all share a new approach to the human condition. Materially, this is a time when people become "rich," where rich means living in a society that crosses a threshold of 20,000 kilocalories available per person, per day.[11] This affluence allows humans to sit and think, and we suggest that what they now think about is their own agency. We believe that this increase in belief in human agency is the psychological fulcrum of the First Axial Age. All modern religions and philosophy stem from this efflorescence. This is a new psychological epoch teeming with a pageant of choices, with optimism, and with imagination.

During the Babylonian Exile (587–538 BCE), when the Hebrew Bible was canonized, the exiled Israelites encountered people who thought and behaved very differently from themselves. They believed in different gods, and they spoke a different language. They saw the world differently. Those who could mentally put themselves in the place of their Babylonian masters, who had efficacious, optimistic, and imaginative cognitions, would survive, and out-reproduce their fellow, less agentic Israelites. Similarly, for the Hellenes who survived the Dorian invasions, the encounters with people from "across the sea." As Jaynes (1976) sees it, population pressures and encounters with peoples who have vastly different beliefs drive the development of such an elaborated self. As we see it, these encounters strongly selected for the more agentic mental life found in the post-Torah books of the Bible.

We should mention, nevertheless, that we are not completely convinced about our own findings of an increasingly agentic mental life across the Bible. Unlike the rich tradition of religious biblical scholarship, we did a flat, agnostic, and literal reading of the Bible. We treated the text as a quasi-historical document whose words mirror the thinking of people during the times depicted. This could be mistaken because the canonical compilation of the Hebrew Bible did not take place until long after the events narrated. Unlike our literal reading, biblical scholarship[12] is often much more imaginative and belief-driven about these matters, treating the words as metaphors or poetry, and interpreting the Bible as a living document that is best understood when re-interpreted and fleshed out in keeping with modernity. While we respect such treatments, we chose the literal path.

One hazard of the literal path is that our results might be mere artifacts of "stylistic" differences between the Torah, which tends to be sparse stylistically, and the later Hebrew Bible's narrative style. Consider the words themselves. In Homeric Greek, for example, there are not even words for the mental psychology of human agency. Rather there are only bodily words that over the centuries evolve into mental words. *Thumos* (breath), for example, becomes *psyche* (soul, which then evolves into mind) over the course of 500 years. It is possible that in the days of the Torah, as for the Bronze Age Greeks, words for the mental states of human agency did not yet exist. So mere stylistic change, rather than any underlying mental change, remains a real possibility.

Disentangling style from substance requires looking at the behavioral sequelae of such styles. To the extent these different styles correlate with, and even cause, changes in human progress, this suggests that there is mental substance at issue and not just stylistic difference. So, if changes in progress actually follow the "style," the way of talking actually is their way of thinking, and not just a stylistic epiphenomenon.

Another limitation of our work is that we might be wrong about the amount of human progress in each epoch. The data about human progress during these epochs are impressionistic and not at all quantitative. A fuller, more rigorous account of advances in thought, technology, science, medicine, the arts, quality of life, and political freedom over biblical time would add a great deal to our hypothesis that progress advances when the balance of agency tilts away from God toward humans.

It is also possible that obedience to God deserves a more special place for human agency than the lesser place we assign it. Obedience can be, under certain circumstances, highly agentic. Unlike matter, which "obeys" the law of gravity, human obedience sometimes entails choice. So, the decision to obey God may sometimes be a lesser form of agency. In contrast, at other times, such as martyrdom, obedience might indeed be a very active struggle, a wrestling.

Our final reservation about our findings is that we treat God's agency as competitive with human agency. This does violence to a common, theological interpretation that treats them as "collaborative" or "cooperative."[13] Our driving hypothesis is that when the balance is tilted away from humans and toward God (or toward fate or chance) human progress is stifled. When it tilts toward human powers, human progress is spurred.

Perhaps the Hebrew Bible demonstrates, as we have argued, that greater human agency has a positive, linear relationship with societal progress. Perhaps, however, the Hebrew Bible traces a relationship between God and humanity, initially God-saturated at the expense of human agency, which trends toward an increasing sense of partnership with human beings, allowing them the agency to act *b'tzelem Elokim*, in God's likeness, as they steward the future.

Notes

1. Jonathan Sacks, *Future Tense: Jews, Judaism, and Israel in the Twenty-first Century* (Schocken, 2012).
2. A. Pietraszkiewicz, M. Formanowicz, S. M. Gustafsson, R. Boyd, S. Sikström, and S. Sczesny, "The Big Two Dictionaries: Capturing Agency and Communion in Natural Language," *European Journal of Social Psychology* 49, no. 5 (2018), https://doi.org/10.1002/ejsp.256.
3. Gen. 18:23-33.
4. Gen. 32:24-30.
5. Gen. 32:26.
6. Job 1:13-19.
7. Job 1:20-22.
8. Anderson, F. I., *Job* (England: Inter-Varsity Press, 1976).
9. Martin Seligman, "Agency in Greco-Roman Philosophy," *The Journal of Positive Psychology* 16, no. 1 (2021): 1–10, https://doi.org/10.1080/17439760.2020.1832250.
10. R. N. Bellah, *Religion in Human Evolution: From the Paleolithic to the Axial Age* (Belknap Press, 2011).

11. N. Baumard, A. Hyafil, I. Morris, and P. Boyer, "Increased Affluence Explains the Emergence of Ascetic Wisdoms and Moralizing Religions," *Current Biology*, 25 (2015): 10–15.
12. A. Hart, *Coping with Depression in the Ministry and Other Helping Professions* (Waco: Word Books, 1984); J. Abelson, *The Immanence of God in Rabbinical Literature* (N.Y.: Hermon Press, 1969); A. Davison, *Participation in God: A Study in Christian Doctrine and Metaphysics* (Cambridge: Cambridge University Press, 2019).
13. A. Hart, *Coping with Depression in the Ministry and Other Helping Professions* (Waco: Word Books, 1984); J. Abelson, *The Immanence of God in Rabbinical Literature* (N.Y.: Hermon Press, 1969); A. Davison, *Participation in God: A Study in Christian Doctrine and Metaphysics* (Cambridge: Cambridge University Press, 2019); K. Pargament, J. Kennell, W. Hathaway, N. Grevengoed, J. Newman, and W. Jones, "Religion and the Problem-Solving Process: Three Styles of Coping," *Journal of the Scientific Study of Religion* 27 (1988): 90–104; J. Tillotson, Works of the Most Reverend Dr. John Tillotson, Late Lord Archbishop of Canterbury. Volume 5 (1772) Sermon CVI https://ccel.org/ccel/tillotson/works05/works05.iii.xxi.html.

CHAPTER 38

Serve God with Joy (and Self-Actualization): Positive Psychology and the Thought of Rabbi Sacks

Tamra Wright

Looking back 35 years, to my first encounters with R. Jonathan Sacks, I find myself surprised to say that what I have learned from him over the decades is, above all else, a philosophy of happiness. To be more precise, it is a twenty-first-century Jewish philosophy based on a classical Greek idea, *Eudaimonia* (sometimes translated as "happiness," but a more accurate translation is "flourishing"). And it is surprising to me because, as a student in his Jewish Ethics course at Jews' College in the 1980s, and early in my career teaching at the same institution, it would not have occurred to me to describe R. Sacks as "happy." To be fair, as a PhD student writing on post-Holocaust philosophy, joy and happiness were not high on my academic agenda either!

I have written elsewhere about R. Sacks' suggestion that a "new Musar" could be constructed based on Jewish teaching and contemporary

T. Wright (✉)
Bernard Revel Graduate School of Jewish Studies, Yeshiva University, New York, NY, USA

© The Author(s), under exclusive license to Springer Nature Switzerland AG 2023
E. Brown, S. Weiss (eds.), *An Ode to Joy*,
https://doi.org/10.1007/978-3-031-28229-4_38

psychology.[1] The first few times I heard him speak about this idea, the psychology in question was Aaron Beck's cognitive behavior therapy (CBT). As his thinking on this theme evolved, he brought in positive psychology, particularly the work of Martin Seligman, a co-founder of the movement. He often also mentioned a third Jewish psychologist, Victor Frankl, and pointed out that all three shared key assumptions: it is not events themselves that cause emotions, but our interpretation of those events, and we are free to choose from among competing interpretations. More broadly, R. Sacks emphasized the difference between these thinkers' approaches and Freudian psychology.[2] Inspired by the work of Israeli psychologist Mordechai Rotenberg, R. Sacks pointed out that Freud's work is ultimately more "Greek" than Jewish because it assumes a tragic, deterministic worldview.[3]

Beck created CBT after recognizing that his depressed patients exhibited common patterns in the way they thought about their experiences. By training them to dispute their own thinking and substitute more empowering explanations of events and experiences, he was able to help them overcome their depression. Under his leadership, CBT subsequently developed into a widely accepted, evidence-based therapy for a range of psychological disorders.[4]

Building on the work of Beck, Seligman shifted his focus from removing the disabling conditions of life to exploring the components of happiness and developing interventions that help people flourish. This focus on practical interventions, both in CBT and in positive psychology, is one of the features that makes them good candidates to form part of a "new Musar." Rather than always relying directly on a therapist, patients who use the approaches of CBT and positive psychology benefit from evidence-based exercises that can be performed independently. To take a simple example, one of the most popular positive psychology exercises is keeping a gratitude journal where patients write down at least three things they are grateful for at the end of each day. Research shows that people who do exercises of this nature experience several benefits. One study showed that participants who kept a gratitude journal, either weekly for ten weeks or daily for two weeks, experienced an increase in positive moods and optimism about the future, as well as better sleep.[5]

There are three main components of Seligman's approach which, I believe, are germane to R. Sacks' thought and could form part of a "new Musar": his analysis of the elements of flourishing, the idea of "signature strengths," and the focus on future-oriented thinking.[6]

Flourishing with PERMA

In his 2011 book *Flourish*, Seligman outlines the key elements of positive psychology. [7] Replacing an earlier framework in which the goal of positive psychology was to increase "happiness" as measured by life satisfaction surveys, the 2011 theory sees the goal of positive psychology as increasing "well-being," a construct comprising five distinct elements, each of which is sought for its own sake and can be measured independently. Seligman uses the acronym PERMA for these elements:

- Positive emotions
- Engagement (also known as "flow")
- Relationships
- Meaning
- Accomplishment

Positive emotions are the aspect of well-being that most people immediately associate with "happiness." Feelings of joy, cheerfulness, hope, as well as a sunny, upbeat disposition, come to mind. Philosophers (and philosophy professors, in my experience) are not generally known for these qualities.

Fortunately, there are four other aspects of flourishing in which even those not blessed with a genetic predisposition toward cheerfulness can excel. "Engagement" is one that is particularly suited to scholars. In the terminology of creativity researcher Mihaly Csikszentmihalyi, engagement is known as "flow," a state of mind in which one becomes completely engrossed in an activity to the extent that one may lose awareness of the passing of time and of bodily sensations such as hunger and thirst.[8] Often referred to by athletes as being "in the zone," the flow state is one in which the challenges presented by an activity are optimally matched to one's ability: too easy and we quickly become bored, too difficult and we soon become frustrated. Flow states can occur in a wide range of activities, from programming a computer to learning the steps of a new dance, from thinking about a problem to baking a cake. My favorite anecdote about a philosopher in flow comes via Professor Howard Wettstein. In the days before individual screens were installed on airplanes, Wettstein's colleague was on a long flight with his wife. He was staring in silence at the seat in front of him when his wife asked him a question. "Shhh," he admonished her, "Can't you see I'm working?"

That conversation might not have done much to boost another aspect of flourishing for this couple: positive relationships. Vast scholarship shows how crucial relationships are to well-being. George Vaillant, former director of the Harvard Study of Adult Development, remarked, "When the study began, nobody cared about empathy or attachment. But the key to healthy aging is relationships, relationships, relationships." [9]

The fourth aspect of flourishing, meaning, is potentially double-edged for those of a philosophical bent. Being able to see one's life and activities as contributing to something beyond the self is an important part of flourishing. At the same time, philosophers are perhaps more inclined than most to flirt with the idea that human existence itself is meaningless. I will address this issue, as it relates to R. Sacks' thinking about happiness.

The final element of flourishing is accomplishment. People often pursue goals, not because they are ultimately meaningful, nor because they will enhance relationships, provide flow, or even generate positive emotions, but simply for the sake of the goal itself.

Signature Strengths: A Contemporary Approach to "Virtue"

To maximize our eudaimonia or flourishing, Seligman teaches, we should aim to optimize each of the five elements of PERMA. In addition, we need to employ our "signature strengths" daily. The idea of signature strengths is one that Seligman and his colleagues developed in the early days of the positive psychology movement. They identified 24 virtues or "character strengths" that have been admired across cultures and throughout history. They then arranged the individual virtues under six main headings (wisdom, courage, temperance, humanity, justice, and transcendence) and devised a questionnaire to enable people to rank their individual strengths.[10] Rather than suggesting that people "work on themselves" by trying to improve their weakest virtues, Seligman's team encouraged them to exercise their strengths because deploying signature strengths enables people to enter flow states more easily. Subsequent research showed that regularly drawing on one's top character strengths supports all five aspects of PERMA, not just engagement.[11] Further research has also revealed that there are five key virtues that are strongly correlated with high levels of subjective well-being or happiness: zest, hope, gratitude, curiosity, and love.[12]

Future Focus: "Homo Prospectus"

A third, crucial aspect of Seligman's approach to psychology is the emphasis on future-oriented thinking. Although there are many voices in our culture that encourage us to live "in the moment," Seligman argues that the ability to envision alternative futures is so key to human flourishing that we should be known as "homo prospectus." R. Sacks was thoroughly taken with this idea, viewing it as one of the motifs of the Bible and Jewish thought. With the concept of a Messianic age, he writes, Judaism "became the only civilization whose golden age is in the future. And throughout the Torah, the promised land lies in the future. [...] Even Moses, who spends forty years leading the people there, does not get to enter it. It is always just beyond." [13]

R. Sacks related this future focus to Seligman's approach to psychology. Seligman, he explained, had concluded that "the people with a positive psychology tended to be future-oriented, whereas those with a negative mindset [...] were often fixated on the past." Humans, R. Sacks writes, "are the future-oriented animal." He continues:

> I wish this were more deeply understood, because it is fundamental. [...] Human action is always oriented to the future. I put the kettle on because I want a cup of coffee. I work hard because I want to pass the exam. I act to bring about a future that is not yet. Science cannot account for the future because something that hasn't happened yet cannot be a cause. Therefore there will always be something about intentional human action that science cannot fully explain. [...] I believe that we must honour the past but not live in it. Faith is a revolutionary force. God is calling to us as once He called to Moses, asking us to have faith in the future and then, with His help, to build it.[14]

Twenty-First-Century Musar: A Jewish Guide to Flourishing

R. Sacks' vast corpus of talks and publications contains a wealth of insights and inspiring ideas about leading a joyful, satisfying, and meaningful life—in other words, about how to flourish. In his 2017 TED talk, R. Sacks related that, as a younger man, his focus had not been on joyful flourishing but on the then fashionable pleasures of existential angst: "Once upon a time, a very long time ago, I was a 20 year-old undergraduate studying philosophy. I was into Nietzsche, and Schopenhauer, and Sartre, and

Camus. I was full of ontological uncertainty and existential angst. It was terrific." [15]

The story he told in the Ted talk was about encountering another person, someone thoroughly unlike himself, who challenged him and made him grow:

> I was self-obsessed and thoroughly unpleasant to know until one day I saw across the courtyard a girl who was everything that I wasn't. She radiated sunshine. She emanated joy. I found out her name was Elaine. We met, we talked, we married, and 47 years, three children, and eight grandchildren later, I can safely say it was the best decision I ever took in my life because it's the people not like us that make us grow.[16]

At the same time, his intellectual journey traced a path away from fashionable trends in continental philosophy, including existentialism, poststructuralism, and deconstruction, and from the moral relativism of much Anglo-American philosophy. Even the philosophy of R. Joseph Soloveitchik, with its loneliness and dialectical tensions, was not immune to criticism from the young R. Sacks.[17]

Within the Jewish corpus, the book that appears to be most aligned with existentialist angst is Kohelet. Yet R. Sacks was able to detect in it a refrain that is more of an ode to joy than a meditation on despair.[18] The word root s-m-h (*simha*), which R. Sacks translates as "joy," occurs 17 times in Kohelet—more than in all the books of the Torah combined. Although Ecclesiastes is best known for the phrase "Vanity, vanity, all is vanity" (King James Bible 1:2), R. Sacks points out that "After every one of his meditations on the pointlessness of life, Kohelet ends with an exhortation to joy." The key to understanding this is choosing the appropriate translation of another *leitwort* of the book: *hevel*—often translated as "meaningless," "pointless," "futile," or, with King James, "vanity"—should instead be understood as "a shallow breath." Kohelet, R. Sacks explains, is a meditation on mortality: "However long we live, we know we will one day die. Our lives are a mere microsecond in the history of the universe. The cosmos lasts forever while we, living, breathing mortals, are a mere fleeting breath."[19]

Of course, any existentialist could have told us that. What Kohelet uniquely offers, in R. Sacks' reading, is an alternative to despair. Without denying our own mortality and human finitude, we can choose to rejoice in the good we do in this world, in our work, in our pleasures, and in the lifespan we are granted, however long or short.[20]

Given R. Sacks' focus on the future and his endorsement of Seligman's view of humans as *homo prospectus*, it might seem surprising that he emphasizes the importance of *simha* which, he explains, is a momentary emotion, whereas happiness is "an attitude to life as a whole." He distinguishes between the biblical usage of the word *ashrei*, which he translates as "happy," and the word *simha*. In addition to the difference in meaning between the two terms, which seems to roughly correlate with the contemporary psychological distinction between the "remembering self" (happiness as an evaluation or attitude toward one's life) and "the experiencing self" (joy in the moment),[21] R. Sacks emphasizes that *ashrei* is used to describe individuals, whereas joy is always collective. "*Simha* is joy shared. It is not something we experience in solitude."[22]

Ultimately, R. Sacks argues, rejoicing with others is the key to the Jewish people's survival, and Judaism itself is "an ode to joy."

> Toward the end of his life, having been deaf for twenty years, Beethoven composed one of the greatest pieces of music ever written, his Ninth Symphony. […] The words he set to music were Schiller's Ode to Joy. I think of Judaism as an ode to joy. Like Beethoven, Jews have known suffering, isolation, hardship and rejection, yet they never lacked the religious courage to rejoice. A people that can know insecurity and still feel joy is one that can never be defeated, for its spirit can never be broken nor its hope destroyed.[23]

In his reading of Kohelet, and throughout R. Sacks' corpus, we can see an approach to Judaism that is aligned with some of the key ideas of positive psychology: a future-oriented focus; a balanced approach to positive emotions of the moment (such as joy) with an emphasis on the "more serious" concerns with engagement, relationships, meaning, and accomplishment; and frequent references to at least four of the five virtues that are most highly correlated with well-being (curiosity, gratitude, hope, and love).

Hope, gratitude, and love are frequently recurring themes in R. Sacks' work, and his promotion of *Torah v'chochmah* (Torah with secular wisdom) and his wide reading are in themselves a testament to his own prodigious curiosity. His rejection of angst and despair can also be seen as embracing, or at least enabling, the strength of zest, which is the virtue that is most highly correlated with well-being. Zest is defined by positive psychologists as "approaching a situation, or life in general, with excitement and energy." [24]

What, though, of positive psychology's counsel that we identify and deliberately deploy our signature strengths? Although I haven't found a direct discussion of this theme in R. Sacks' work, I think it is implicit in his general embrace of Seligman's approach to positive psychology and, above all, in his belief that each of us has a divinely given role or task to perform in this world. This is not simply a question of individual flourishing, but of understanding that an adult morality deals not just in universal rules, but in particulars. To lead a truly good life, R. Sacks explains in *To Heal a Fractured World*, we must learn to discern God's call:

> God commands in generalities but calls in particulars. He knows our gifts and he knows the needs of the world. That is why we are here. There is an act only we can do, and only at this time, and that is our task. The sum of these tasks is the meaning of our life, the purpose of our existence, the story we are called upon to write… There is no life without a task; no person without a talent; no place without a fragment of God's light waiting to be discovered and redeemed; no situation without its possibility of sanctification; no moment without its call.[25]

To flourish under the guidance of R. Sacks' thought would be to strive for self-actualization, aiming to become the best version of ourselves, attuned to our calling, and serving God with joy.

Throughout his writings, R. Sacks articulated a novel, modern, yet profoundly Jewish philosophy of happiness, synthesizing the insights of modern psychology with the ancient wisdom of Jewish texts. Though he made countless contributions to Jewish thought, laying the conceptual framework for this "new Musar" may one day rank among the most significant. Younger scholars are already following his lead, combining Torah sources and contemporary psychological approaches to help others flourish.[26] I like to think that the angst-filled young man described in R. Sacks' TED talk would be pleased with that outcome—or at the very least, that he would appreciate the irony.[27]

Notes

1. See my "Afterword: A New Musar?" in *Radical Responsibility: Celebrating the thought of Jonathan Sacks*, ed. Michael J. Harris, Daniel Rynhold and Tamra Wright (Jerusalem: Maggid Books, London School of Jewish Studies and Yeshiva University Press, 2012), 245–58; "The BEST: Tiny Habits by B. J. Fogg", *Tradition: A Journal of Orthodox Jewish Thought*, December 17, 2020, https://traditiononline.org/the-best-tiny-habits/; and "Little steps can make a big difference to our well-being", *Jewish Chronicle*, January 24, 2022, https://www.thejc.com/judaism/all/little-steps-can-help-make-a-big-difference-to-our-wellbeing-OGOfOn2BKDfUNxZkiAu03.
2. Rabbi Sacks refers to these psychologists several times in his "Covenant and Conversation" pieces and other writings.
3. Rotenberg emphasizes both Christian and Greek aspects of western psychology and has developed "Jewish Psychology" as an alternative approach. The Rotenberg Institute of Jewish Psychology, established in 2005, aims to counter contemporary western society's "egocentric, individualistic and self-assertive approach" via a "mutual-responsibility model that reclaims the psychological principles found in Midrashic and Hassidic literature." ("Jewish Psychology"), Rotenberg Institute, accessed June 30, 2022, https://www.jewishpsychology.org/jewish_psychology_e.php).
4. Suma P. Chand, Daniel P. Kuckel, and Martin R. Huecker, "Cognitive Behavior Therapy", *National Library of Medicine*, May 8, 2022, https://www.ncbi.nlm.nih.gov/books/NBK470241/.
5. R. A. Emmons and M. E. McCullough, "Counting Blessings Versus Burdens: An Experimental Investigation of Gratitude and Subjective Well-Being in Daily Life," *Journal of Personality and Social Psychology*, 84 no. 2 (2003), 377–89.
6. As we will see below, R. Sacks argued that, in Judaism, *simcha* or joy is an even higher value than happiness or eudaimonia. However, in what follows, my focus is on the potential that he saw for positive psychology, with its focus on flourishing, to form part of a "new Musar."
7. Martin Seligman, *Flourish: A New Understanding of Happiness and Well-Being—and How to Achieve Them* (London: Nicolas Brealey, 2011).
8. Mihaly Csikszentmihalyi, *Finding Flow: The Psychology of Engagement with Everyday Life* (New York: Basic Books, 1998), 31.
9. Liz Mineo, "Good Genes Are Nice, But Joy Is Better," *The Harvard Gazette*, April 11, 2017, https://news.harvard.edu/gazette/story/2017/04/over-nearly-80-years-harvard-study-has-been-showing-how-to-live-a-healthy-and-happy-life/.

10. The VIA Character Strengths questionnaire and other assessments can be accessed for free on Seligman's website https://www.authentichappiness.sas.upenn.edu/testcenter.
11. Signature strengths are one of the most researched areas of positive psychology. A selection of academic studies on the effects of interventions to help people identify and deploy their strengths can be found on the Values In Action (VIA) website: https://www.viacharacter.org/research/findings/signature-strengths.
12. Ryan N. Niemiec, "The 5 Happiness Strengths", *Psychology Today*, November 27, 2013, https://www.psychologytoday.com/us/blog/what-matters-most/201311/the-5-happiness-strengths. I will discuss these virtues as they relate to R. Sacks' thought below.
13. Jonathan Sacks, "Faith in the Future: Shemot 5780", *Covenant and Conversation*, https://www.rabbisacks.org/covenant-conversation/shemot/faith-in-the-future/.
14. Jonathan Sacks, "Faith in the Future: Shemot 5780", *Covenant and Conversation*, https://www.rabbisacks.org/covenant-conversation/shemot/faith-in-the-future/.
15. Jonathan Sacks, "How We Can Face the Future without Fear, Together", https://www.ted.com/talks/rabbi_lord_jonathan_sacks_how_we_can_face_the_future_without_fear_together.
16. Jonathan Sacks, "How We Can Face the Future without Fear, Together", https://www.ted.com/talks/rabbi_lord_jonathan_sacks_how_we_can_face_the_future_without_fear_together.
17. In "Alienation and Faith," his first published essay (1973), R. Sacks critiqued R. Solovetichik's essay "The Lonely Man of Faith". "Alienation and Faith" was re-printed in R. Sacks' first book, *Tradition in an Untraditional Age* (London: Vallentine Mitchell, 1990), 219–44. More recently, he wrote, "I still take the view that Rav Soloveitchik's account in that essay flowed from the specifics of his life and times. It remains a classic of the genre, but it is not the only way Jewish spirituality has been understood through the ages." ("Faith and Friendship: Beha'alotecha 5778," *Covenant and Conversation*, https://www.rabbisacks.org/covenant-conversation/behaalotecha/faith-and-friendship/).
18. Jonathan Sacks, "The Pursuit of Joy: Ki Tavo 5775", *Covenant and Conversation*, accessed 30 June, 2022, https://www.rabbisacks.org/covenant-conversation/ki-tavo/the-pursuit-of-joy/.
19. Sacks, "The Pursuit of Joy".
20. Kohelet 3:12, 22, 8:15, 11:8.
21. Daniel Kahneman, *Thinking Fast and Slow* (London: Penguin Books, 2011), 14.
22. Sacks, "The Pursuit of Joy".

23. Sacks, "The Pursuit of Joy".
24. "Zest", VIA Institute on Character, accessed June 29, 2022, https://www.viacharacter.org/character-strengths/zest.
25. Jonathan Sacks, *To Heal a Fractured World* (London: Continuum, 2006), 262. The reference to divinely given gifts and talents leads me to see his approach as sympathetic both to the emphasis on "signature strengths" in positive psychology and, potentially, to Maslow's idea of "self-actualization", the penultimate stage in Maslow's hierarchy of needs, superseded only by "self-transcendence."
26. See, for example, Mordechai's Schiffman's recent book *Psyched for Torah* (New York: Kodesh Press, 2022).
27. I am grateful to Erica Brown, Shira Weiss, and Joe Gamse for helpful comments on an earlier draft of this article.

CHAPTER 39

Joy Stick: Judaism, Video Games, and the Pursuit of Happiness

Liel Leibovitz

It was a few hours to Yom Kippur, sometime in the late 1980s, and I was feeling a sense of existential dread.

Not, mind you, because of the approaching day of fast—I was a child then, and not obligated by the commandments that bind adults. Nor was I particularly fearful of that whole business of being inscribed in the Book of Life, nor jittery about asking those I might've wronged for forgiveness. Any awe I was feeling, in fact, had nothing to do with the Almighty and everything to do with Sid Meier.

Does the name ring a bell? If you spent even one lazy afternoon playing video games at any point in the past four decades, you've likely come across Meier's work. Having gotten his start developing cash register systems for department stores, Meier soon realized computers could be used for an even higher purpose than commerce: fun. He created a few silly shoot-'em-ups, but before too long stumbled into simulators, the genre that quickly won him the adoration of tens of millions of nerds worldwide. His first efforts allowed players to pretend they were manning the cockpit of a World War II *Supermarine Spitfire*, going head-to-head with Nazi

L. Leibovitz (✉)
Tablet Magazine, New York, NY, USA

© The Author(s), under exclusive license to Springer Nature Switzerland AG 2023
E. Brown, S. Weiss (eds.), *An Ode to Joy*,
https://doi.org/10.1007/978-3-031-28229-4_39

warplanes during the London Blitz. From there it was on to bigger and better jets. By 1987, even the F-15 couldn't hold Meier's attention. He was looking for more demanding challenges, and he settled on, well, just about the entire known world. Within a few years, he released a slew of games that allowed players to manage the warp and woof of complete civilizations, allowing every pre-pubescent child to unleash her inner Napoleon and charge the Russian steppes without ever leaving her bedroom.

Me, I spent my afternoons sailing the azure waters of the Caribbean, plundering gold and stabbing scallywags with my dagger. The game that allowed me these pleasures was *Sid Meier's Pirates!*, and for a few months in 1987—and, if I'm being honest, a good chunk of 1988 as well—it was more real to me than my friends, my family, or my school. So when my mother appeared one fall day, all dressed in white, and demanded that I shut off the computer already and hurry up to go hear Kol Nidre, I was devastated.

It wasn't just that I was well on my way to acquiring wealth and social rank in the bustling island of Tortuga, the Manhattan of seventeenth-century piracy. It was that, by then, I'd come to develop a distinct theology that put video games on one end of the scale and Judaism on the other. Echoing St. Paul's nasty old zinger, I argued—loudly, to anyone who'd listen—that Judaism was merely about laws while video games were about a higher order of feeling, about possibilities and self-discovery and self-expression. Video games allowed you to shake off the accidents of your birth and the contours of your physical body and be reborn as an avatar, free to be whomever you wanted and explore whatever you wished. Video games did not prescribe rigid rituals for life's every occurrence, telling you what to eat and when to pray, and how to wash your hands. Video games just wanted you to have a good time, and what, given the brevity of our stay here on earth, could be more meaningful than that?

I spent that Yom Kippur in shul, begrudgingly listening to the prayers, and it wasn't long before I embarked on the short and furious path to shedding many of the religious observances of my childhood. As I became a teenager, I began drifting away from the faith of my fathers and toward my newfound digital obsession. I stopped keeping, and while some well-meaning cousins suggested that this yeshiva or that would be just my speed, I concluded my army service, decamped for New York, enrolled in Columbia University, and began working on my PhD. The subject? Video games.

For years, and with the help of everything from classical ethnographic methods to the latest in eye-tracking technology, I researched what I now realized was the seminal question of my field, namely why did people spend so much of their time playing video games. Was it sheer escapism? A mild addiction? Something else? Diligently, I designed experiments, took notes, and watched as volunteers joined me in my lab and played away for hours.

As is so often the case, I stumbled on my biggest insight almost by accident. Looking at my research assistants one day, I noticed that those of them who'd been playing for longer—three hours, say, or even five—seemed much more immersed in the game than those who'd only been playing for a few minutes, even if the latter happened to be engaging in a dramatic fight, say, and the former simply milling about. Put simply, the game's actual stimulation—the images on the screen, the challenges presented, the story line—barely registered; the only variable that seemed to matter to gamers was the time they had already invested in playing. The more hours they'd clocked, the harder it was for them to shift their attention away from the game.

Fascinated, I tested this hypothesis again and again and found it correct each time. Gamers, my research soon demonstrated, were in something approaching a trance-like state when they played. Unlike television watchers, say, or book readers, they weren't discerning subjects, interacting with their medium of choice at a critical distance, and offering their perspectives and analyses as they watched or read. Instead, they were completely steeped in the game, experiencing it not only with their eyes and brains but also with their thumbs and their bodies, rocking to and fro as they clutched their controllers in their hands, lost in an alternate reality.

Great, I thought to myself. I left one set of people who swayed as they prayed only to end up with another who behaved more or less the same way. Furious, but also curious, I started interviewing gamers in depth. What they told me wouldn't have surprised my great-great-grandfather, Rabbi Yosef Chaim Sonnenfeld, a prominent Haredi leader who, after an education in a good European university, decided to shun modernity and double down on tradition. Video games, my subjects confessed, were appealing because their basic premise was so innately familiar. They required stepping into a universe whose logic you didn't quite understand, interacting with a creator you'll never meet, and following a simple set of rules in order not only to survive but also to thrive. Put differently, they required ... faith.

With this jagged realization prickling my mind, I had no choice, of course, but to inquire precisely what, if anything, was this faith all about. I should've realized it at the time—researchers rarely do when the terrain they're studying is more intimate than they care to admit—but the subject I was soon pondering was my own soul. If these gamers of mine were having something that felt like a religious experience, what, precisely, was its nature? Was it merely about escaping reality, or was something deeper afoot? And if I, too, greatly enjoyed playing video games, what, if anything, did it say about my own faith?

I grabbed a game controller, turned on the machine, and began meditating on these existential questions. As I wandered here and there in a splendid, pixelated universe, I stopped to appreciate the glories of its creation. Behold, for example, that adorable little orc over there, the one clad in mummy-like shrouds with beady red eyes. Feast your eyes upon the giant man-eating plant with its goofy red tongue. All these marvelous creations, I realized as I smashed buttons and fought my way through the game's magical kingdom, were put here strictly for my pleasure, for me to discover and enjoy. Sure, the game had strict rules—even the most complex algorithms are, after all, little more than if/then propositions. Algorithms require you to do precisely what the game's developer intended you to do and in precisely the right order, too. But these rules were never intended as restrictions. They were the guardrails on my journey, making sure that I get to see and feel and appreciate the full scope of surprises the game's creator had in store for me. And what precisely did I feel while prancing through this digital cornucopia? My hands told me what my brain couldn't; looking down, I observed the slick, black game controller I was holding, and was struck by its very apt name—joystick, an instrument designed to deliver joy.

I wish I could say that I dropped that controller on the floor, thanked HaShem and Nintendo, and rushed to put on a pair of tefillin. In life, Hallelu-ya, spiritual growth happens at a slower, more contemplative pace, and it took years for this insight into joy in gaming to ripen into a personal understanding of—and commitment to—religious observance and practice. As was so often the case on my own Jewish journey and that of so many others, it was the wisdom of Rabbi Sacks that crystalized it all so beautifully. "I am moved," he wrote in one of his commentaries on the Torah, by the way Jews, who know what it is to walk through the valley of the shadow of death, still see joy as the supreme religious emotion. Every day we begin our morning prayers with a litany of thanks, that we are here, with a world to live in, family and friends to love and be loved by, about to start a day full of possibilities, in which, by acts of loving kindness, we allow God's presence to flow through us into the lives of others. Joy helps heal some of the wounds of our injured, troubled world.

Here was a potent reminder: Judaism isn't about joy; it *is* joy. This is often easy to forget. We rush to pray *Shacharit*, say, and we think of that swelling inbox awaiting us at work and not about the fact that we're about to step outside of the boundaries of our well-regimented lives and commune with the Maker of all things. Or we dash to make all the necessary arrangements for Shabbat and focus more on our list of chores than on the transcendent idea that we're about to step out of time itself for 25 hours and experience a taste of the World to Come. Sure, Judaism can be arduous, and yes, it does have a lot of rules. But if you come to it, like I did, from playing video games, you understand that games, for all their apparent frivolity, are trying to capture precisely the reality that observant Jews live in real life. Video games, again, are worlds in which many complicated things, not always explained or understood, have to be done at precisely the right order and at just the right time, or else risk the wrath of the game's creator, who will smite you in a host of vengeful ways. And they're about learning that mastering this kind of practice—playing for hours and hours until it becomes reflexive, innate, embodied rather than merely considered—brings with it something that transcends mere fun, which is a fleeting and frivolous feeling. It brings joy, the feeling Rabbi Sacks so wisely understood lies at the heart of any activity that gives you some glimpse into the world of possibilities that lies at your feet if you only choose to see it.

Let us, then, rejoice. According to the Entertainment Software Association, the video game industry's umbrella organization, there are 227 million gamers in America, which means that even if the number is slightly bloated, still well over two thirds of our fellow citizens spend at least a few hours every week yearning to have the same connection—to others, to the unknown, to themselves—we cultivate when we daven. It is here, to paraphrase another great teacher, Reb Leonard Cohen, that we have the spiritual thirst. Never mind, then, the empty pews and the bleak surveys that inform us that fewer and fewer people choose to identify as "religious," whatever that means. Peak only into living rooms and dens across the nation, and you'll see that the central emotion required to jumpstart millions of small, personal great awakenings is right there, alive in our hearts and our thumbs. It's morning in America, and it's a good thing, too. Weeping may endure for a night or two, but joy, as us Jews and gamers know, always cometh in the morning.

CHAPTER 40

Rabbi Sacks' Psychology of Individual and Collective Well-Being

Eli Gottlieb

Happiness isn't perhaps the first topic one would associate with Rabbi Sacks.[1] Relative to other topics he tackled, such as faith, modernity, and pluralism, happiness might seem a little lightweight. Nevertheless, he spoke and wrote extensively about happiness—and with the same combination of erudition and analytic clarity that he treated seemingly weightier themes. He believed that we are, "searching for happiness in the wrong places. We may even be searching for the wrong thing entirely."[2]

In what follows, I summarize Rabbi Sacks' psychology of individual and collective well-being—how to look for happiness in the right places—and show how he uses it, first to critique consumer culture and then to promote the virtues of community as an antidote. After laying out his argument, I then ask if it works. In particular, I consider four reasons to suspect that the antidote he proposes may be inadequate to the severity of the disease. Finally, I suggest that, despite his argument's possible weakness,

---

E. Gottlieb (✉)
Institut Interdisciplinaire de l'Innovation i3—CNRS & Télécom, Paris, France

Graduate School of Education and Human Development, The George Washington University, Washington, DC, USA

© The Author(s), under exclusive license to Springer Nature Switzerland AG 2023
E. Brown, S. Weiss (eds.), *An Ode to Joy*,
https://doi.org/10.1007/978-3-031-28229-4_40

Rabbi Sacks' own practices as a teacher and religious leader make a strong case of their own for how balancing the "I" and the "we" can contribute to individual and collective well-being.

Rabbi Sacks had a distinctive style as an author and speaker. A key element of this style was the coining of dichotomies to draw out nuances of difference and similarity. His writing on happiness is no exception. Four dichotomies appear time and again in his writings on the topic: individual versus collective happiness; happiness versus joy; happiness as pleasure versus happiness as life well lived; and pursuit of happiness versus pursuit of meaning.

Rabbi Sacks often contrasted the Bible's conception of happiness with modern, individualistic, conceptions. The idea of individual happiness is present in the Bible. But it takes second place to what Sacks calls "joy shared"[3] or "social happiness":[4]

> Biblical Hebrew has two key words for happiness ... Asher is the happiness we feel. Simha is the happiness we make. Asher is the happiness we can experience on our own, but Simha is the happiness that only exists in virtue of being shared ... Simha is the happiness we make when we come together to give collective thanks for the miracle and the gift of simply being alive. It's something exuberant, joyous, celebratory, and it is something we only feel when we leave behind the separatenesses of each of us and become a part of a "We", an "Us", a community.[5]

Rabbi Sacks viewed Simha as being different from other kinds of happiness, not only in virtue of its being shared, but also in virtue of a particular palette of emotion with which it is associated. In particular, while considering Simha to be "untranslatable in English," [6] "joy" was the word he used most often to paraphrase it: "Happiness is about a lifetime but joy lives in the moment. Happiness tends to be a cool emotion, but joy makes you want to dance and sing. It's hard to feel happy in the midst of uncertainty. But you can still feel joy."[7]

Rabbi Sacks distinguished between happiness as pleasure and happiness as a life well lived to describe a historical shift in which our conception of happiness became divorced from morality and social responsibility.

> It was Aristotle who gave the West its most influential analysis of happiness ... Happiness is, he said, an activity of the soul in accordance with virtue ... It was only in the late seventeenth century that happiness began to be thought of in terms of feelings, of private experience ... This was an

important shift, from *eudaemonia*, happiness as a state of being-and-doing, to *hedonia*, a state of feeling, the pursuit of pleasure.[8]

To drive home the above distinction, and spell out its contemporary implications, Rabbi Sacks contrasted the pursuit of happiness with the pursuit of meaning:

> The American Declaration of Independence speaks of the inalienable rights of life, liberty and the pursuit of happiness. There have been hundreds of books written on happiness and how to achieve it. Yet there is something more fundamental still to the sense of a life well-lived, namely, meaning. The two seem similar. It's easy to suppose that people who find meaning are happy, and people who are happy have found meaning. But the two are not the same, nor do they always overlap. Happiness is largely a matter of satisfying needs and wants. Meaning, by contrast, is about a sense of purpose in life, especially by making positive contributions to the lives of others. Happiness is largely about how you feel in the present. Meaning is about how you judge your life as a whole: past, present and future. Happiness is associated with taking, meaning with giving.[9]

When brought together, these four dichotomies comprise an implicit characterization of true, lasting happiness. It is social, not individual; it involves sharing and gratitude; and it includes striving toward a higher purpose.

Sacks uses this characterization of individual and collective well-being to critique contemporary consumer culture. Specifically, he argues that our focus on achieving individual happiness is self-defeating. The more we seek it, the further it recedes from our grasp. Consumer culture, argues Sacks, cultivates the "I" at the expense of the "We." But is only through the "we" that we can achieve true happiness:

> A consumer society, in short, encourages us to spend money we don't have, on products we don't need, for a happiness that won't last. The reason such happiness does not last lies in the fundamental difference between hedonic happiness, a momentary feeling of pleasurable sensation, and eudaemonic happiness, which is the lasting feeling brought by having lived a good, meaningful, and worthy life.[10]

We who live in affluent, consumer societies, are subject to all the social forces Rabbi Sacks argues are detrimental to our happiness. How, then, are we to live happily, despite them? Rabbi Sacks' answer is to participate, actively, in a community. Ideally, that community should be one with institutions and practices that foster gratitude, sharing, and service to some higher purpose. It should be a community that is proud of, and thoroughly committed to, its particular traditions but seeks to contribute positively to society more generally. For Sacks himself, the answer was Jewish community. He encouraged people, regardless of background or religion, to consider joining a religious congregation.

> Happiness, like friendship, trust, altruism, virtue, enduring values and real relationships, is most readily achieved in community, and in an age when face-to-face communities are elsewhere in steep decline, in houses of worship they are still strong. So ignore the world of brands and bling, and consider joining a religious congregation. Unlike the culture of glossy surfaces and glittering superficiality, it's the real thing.[11]

In support of this solution, Sacks marshalled and synthesized a large body of social scientific findings, gleaned from recent books on the causes and effects of happiness. As he put it, "the new "science of happiness" ... has confirmed some very ancient truths indeed."[12] One such ancient truth is the power of the Sabbath to serve as a counterforce to the market mindset and as an opportunity to engage in the kinds of practice that bring lasting joy. Citing findings that expressing gratitude weekly led to better well-being outcomes than did expressing it more frequently, Sacks comments:

> This is a powerful scientific finding that explains why the Sabbath, which I mentioned in connection to smartphones and social media, has had such a powerful effect on cultures that have adopted it. The Sabbath is a focused, one-day-a-week antidote to the market mindset. It is dedicated to the things that have a value but not a price. It is the supremely nonmarket day. We can't sell or buy. We can't work or pay others to work for us. It's a day when we celebrate relationships ... In the synagogue we renew our sense of community. People share their joys.[13]

This is an interesting, and intuitively plausible, argument. And, as the literature Rabbi Sacks cites attests, he was not alone in making it. Long is the list of "cyberpessimists" who warn that the internet and social media are bad for society and detrimental to our well-being.[14] A shorter, but still substantial, group of authors, acknowledges that things look bad but proposes we can make them less so by strengthening institutions, communities, and relationships that call us to a higher purpose.[15]

Rabbi Sacks' version of the argument is a particularly Jewish one, synthesizing ideas from the Bible and rabbinic literature with Western philosophy and contemporary social science to illustrate the protective power of "We" and the joy of togetherness. But, like other versions, one can't help wondering if there's something a little too neat and nostalgic about it, as if Rabbi Sacks' question—How to live meaningfully in a world of infinite choice?—may be stronger than his answer: community.

To be fair, there is considerable evidence that members of religious communities are healthier and happier than their non-religious peers.[16] It is one thing, however, to note a positive correlation and quite another to propose that joining a religious community will make you happier. Rabbi Sacks never went quite that far, but he got close. Nevertheless, by proposing participation in religious community as an antidote to the anxieties and loneliness of consumer culture, he suggested implicitly that such participation would indeed increase well-being.

There are at least four reasons to suspect that the proposed antidote may not be strong enough to counter the forces against which it is applied. First, as sociologists regularly cited by Rabbi Sacks pointed out, religious communities are often the market mindset's first casualties.[17] Indeed, as Rabbi Sacks himself noted, contemporary consumer culture is one in which, "Religion itself is transformed from salvation to a branch of the leisure industry, and we are transformed, as one writer put it, 'from pilgrim to tourist.'"[18] When this happens, religion loses much of its power as a potential counterforce to consumerism, becoming just one more leisure activity or lifestyle choice, and one that increasing numbers of young people see as demanding too much of them for too little payoff.

Second, the research findings on which Rabbi Sacks bases his arguments are not as reliable as perhaps he thought. Positive psychology is a relatively young branch of psychological research and practice. Many of its key findings are still highly controversial, especially with respect to interventions that seek proactively to apply its principles to improve participant outcomes.[19] Results of the most recent and rigorous metastudies are mixed.[20] To generalize from such findings to the claims about the prophylactic power of religious community is therefore risky at best.

Third, Rabbi Sacks' call for community involvement may sound compelling to people of his own generation and those slightly younger, but it is less likely to inspire younger generations. Gen Z is arguably the most secular generation ever to have walked the planet.[21] Fewer of them believe in God or attend religious services than any other cohort studied.[22] And, as Jean Twenge showed, their low levels of participation in face-to-face community are not limited to religion. On almost every measure of communal participation, Gen Z scores lower than previous cohorts, and in inverse proportion to the amount of time they spend online. [23] It appears that smartphones have disrupted how young people believe and belong even more radically than Sacks supposed—perhaps to the extent that, even if they could be persuaded to view his TED talk on the value of community,[24] much of his argument would sound to them alien and out of touch.

Fourth, the very synagogues that Sacks paints as idylls of *communitas* are often themselves dominated by consumer culture. Wealthy donors exert disproportionate influence; congregants compete to lay on the most lavish family celebrations or attend services in the latest fashions; and so on. The potential may be there to turn synagogues into bases from which to launch what Pete Davis called, "a counterculture of commitment."[25] But many congregations are themselves bastions of consumer culture, where, in spite of elevated rhetoric and the efforts of a committed few, the market mindset has already taken over.

Do these weaknesses in Rabbi Sacks' argument mean that he was wrong? Not necessarily.

First, Rabbi Sacks himself recognized his argument's limitations. He does not portray religious community as some kind of panacea for the ills of consumerism but rather as an example of the kinds of social structure and habits of heart needed to balance "I" and "we" in our era of I-worship. The Sabbath is "one way of setting limits to the market and its mindset … there are other ways, too."[26] Moreover, although he focused much of his critique on the inflated "I," he saw the dangers of overcompensating with too much "we:" "Now you have too much we, you get China and you lose freedom. You have too much I, and you get the States and Britain today, which have just gone a little too far. Maintaining the balance between I and we is not easy. It's a constant challenge."[27]

Perhaps the strongest argument in support of his belief in the power of active communal participation to promote well-being was his own personal example. For much of his life, Rabbi Sacks lived a very "we" existence—working daily in the service of others as a rabbi, a teacher, and a religious leader. Yet, even during his most intensely public and busy years as Chief Rabbi, he continued to publish approximately one book each year. And not just any books but wide-ranging books replete with up-to-date references to recent literature, politics, and empirical research, and new perspectives on hot social topics.

How did he manage it? Each year he'd find the "I" time to retreat into his writing shed and find the solitude required. Like an inhabitant of Plato's cave, or a biblical prophet returning after 40 days and nights, he invariably emerged to share with the "we" world his new insights and calls to action.

By dedicating his professional life to strengthening Jewish community and using his powers of synthesis and expression to promote values undervalued in modern life, it seems that Rabbi Sacks found a balance between the "I" and the "we" in his own life, where what he wanted to do met what needed to be done. And that, as he told Yeshiva University students in 2014, is the first step to achieving inner happiness: "Where what you want to do meets what needs to be done, that is where Hashem wants us to be."[28]

Of course, not all of us are blessed with the talent and resources to balance "I" and "we" in precisely the ways that Rabbi Sacks did. However, there are at least two lessons from his personal example that anyone can learn. The first is that we are more likely to find true happiness if we devote at least as much attention to what needs to be done—for others, for what matters most, for what will leave the world better for our having lived—as to what makes us feel good right now. The second is that, a key to doing this well is to identify your unique blend of talents and opportunities, and to place yourself in situations[29]—be that a pulpit, a shed, a clinic, a classroom, or a boardroom—likely to maximize their impact.

Notes

1. Gila Sacks, "Gila Sacks Surprises Her Father." Presented at The Templeton Prize, 2016.
2. Jonathan Sacks, *Morality: Restoring the Common Good in Divided Times*, First US edition (New York: Basic Books, 2020).
3. Jonathan Sacks, "Interfaith Summit on Happiness with the Dalai Lama." Emory University, October 28, 2010, https://www.rabbisacks.org/videos/interfaith-summit-on-happiness-with-the-dalai-lama/.
4. Jonathan Sacks, "Beneath Glossy Surface Lies the Real Thing." *The Times*, November 11, 2013, https://www.rabbisacks.org/archive/beneath-glossy-surface-lies-the-real-thing/.

5. Jonathan Sacks, "Interfaith Summit on Happiness with the Dalai Lama." Emory University, October 28, 2010, https://www.rabbisacks.org/videos/interfaith-summit-on-happiness-with-the-dalai-lama/.
6. Jonathan Sacks, "Re'eh—Collective Joy." in *Covenant and Conversation—Family Edition* (2019), https://www.rabbisacks.org/covenant-conversation-family-edition/reeh/collective-joy/.
7. Jonathan Sacks, "Re'eh—The Deep Power of Joy." in *Covenant and Conversation* (2016), https://www.rabbisacks.org/covenant-conversation/reeh/deep-power-of-joy/.
8. Jonathan Sacks, *Morality: Restoring the Common Good in Divided Times*, First US edition (New York: Basic Books, 2020).
9. Jonathan Sacks, "Vayikra—The Pursuit of Meaning." In *Covenant and Conversation—Family Edition* (2019), https://www.rabbisacks.org/covenant-conversation-family-edition/vayikra/the-pursuit-of-meaning/.
10. Jonathan Sacks, *Morality: Restoring the Common Good in Divided Times*, First US edition (New York: Basic Books, 2020).
11. Jonathan Sacks, "Beneath Glossy Surface Lies the Real Thing." *The Times*, November, 11, 2013, https://www.rabbisacks.org/archive/beneath-glossy-surface-lies-the-real-thing/.
12. Jonathan Sacks, "Holy Days Are an Annual Check to Mission Drift." *The Times*, September 25, 2009, https://www.rabbisacks.org/archive/holy-days-annual-check-mission-drift/.
13. Jonathan Sacks, *Morality: Restoring the Common Good in Divided Times*, First US edition (New York: Basic Books, 2020), pp. 116–17.
14. Nicholas Carr, *The Shallows: How the Internet Is Changing the Way We Think, Read and Remember* (New York: W.W. Norton & Co. Turkle, 2011); Sherry. *Alone Together: Why We Expect More from Technology and Less from Each Other* (London: Hachette UK, 2011). Twenge, Jean M. *IGEN: Why Today's Super-Connected Kids Are Growing up Less Rebellious, More Tolerant, Less Happy—And Completely Unprepared for Adulthood and (What This Means for the Rest of Us)*. (New York: Atria Books, 2017).
15. David Brooks, *The Second Mountain: The Quest for a Moral Life*. (New York: Random House, 2019). Yuval *A Time to Build: From Family and Community to Congress and the Campus, How Recommitting to Our Institutions Can Revive the American Dream*. (New York: Basic Books, 2020). Robert D. Putnam and Shaylyn Romney Garrett. *The Upswing: How America Came Together a Century Ago and How We Can Do It Again*. (New York: Simon & Schuster, 2020). Pete Davis, *Dedicated: The Case for Commitment in an Age of Infinite Browsing*. (New York: Avid Reader Press/Simon & Schuster, 2021).

16. Morgan Green and Marta Elliott, "Religion, Health, and Psychological Well-Being." *Journal of Religion and Health* 49, no. 2 (2010): 149–63, https://doi.org/10.1007/s10943-009-9242-1.
17. Peter L. Berger, *The Sacred Canopy: Elements of a Sociological Theory of Religion.* (New York: Anchor Books, 1990). Zygmunt Bauman. "From Pilgrim to Tourist—or a Short History of Identity," in *Questions of Cultural Identity*, ed. Stuart Hall and Paul du Gay (London: Thousand Oaks, Calif: Sage, 1996), pp. 18–36.
18. Jonathan Sacks, "Markets and Morals—The 1998 Hayek Lecture." Institute of Economic Affairs at the London School of Economics, June 2, 1998, https://www.rabbisacks.org/archive/markets-and-morals-the-1998-hayek-lecture/.
19. Jesse Singal. "Positive Psychology Goes to War: How the Army Adopted an Untested, Evidence-Free Approach to fighting PTSD," *Chronicle of Higher Education,* June, 2021, https://www.chronicle.com/article/positive-psychology-goes-to-war.
20. Jesse Singal, "Magical Thinking on Positive Psychology: The Field's Founder Can't See Past His Own Hype." *Chronicle of Higher Education,* July, 2021, https://www.chronicle.com/article/magical-thinking-on-positive-psychology.
21. Barna Group and Impact 360 Institute. 2018. *Gen Z: The Culture, Beliefs and Motivations Shaping the next Generation,* https://shop.barna.com/products/gen-z.
22. Eli Gottlieb, "Analog Faith in a Digital Age." *Religion & Politics,* March, 2021, https://religionandpolitics.org/2021/03/17/analog-faith-in-a-digital-age/.
23. Jean M. Twenge, *IGEN: Why Today's Super-Connected Kids Are Growing up Less Rebellious, More Tolerant, Less Happy—and Completely Unprepared for Adulthood and (What This Means for the Rest of Us)* (New York: Atria Books, 2017).
24. Jonathan Sacks, "How We Can Face the Future without Fear, Together." April 25, 2017, https://www.ted.com/talks/rabbi_lord_jonathan_sacks_how_we_can_face_the_future_without_fear_together/transcript?language=en.
25. Pete Davis, *Dedicated: The Case for Commitment in an Age of Infinite Browsing* (New York: Avid Reader Press/Simon & Schuster, 2021).
26. Jonathan Sacks, *Morality: Restoring the Common Good in Divided Times,* First US Edition (New York: Basic Books, 2020).
27. Tim Ferriss, Rabbi Lord Jonathan Sacks on Powerful Books, Mystics, Richard Dawkins, and the Dangers of Safe Spaces (#455) (2020), https://tim.blog/2020/08/29/rabbi-lord-jonathan-sacks-transcript/.

28. Jonathan Sacks. "The Seven Principles to Inner Happiness." Yeshiva University, January 28, 2014, https://www.rabbisacks.org/archive/the-seven-principles-to-inner-happiness/.
29. As Menachem Mendel Schneerson, the late Lubavitcher Rebbe, told the young Jonathan Sacks, "Nobody finds themselves in a situation; you put yourself in a situation," https://www.chabad.org/news/article_cdo/aid/1691120/jewish/Transcript-Chief-Rabbi-Sacks-Highlights-Rebbes-Inspiring-Charge.htm.

CHAPTER 41

Becoming Whole: The Positive Value of Negative Emotions

Marc Eichenbaum

INTRODUCTION

The study of joy has been an increasingly popular area of research in the field of psychology in recent years. While, traditionally, psychology focused primarily on the treatment of mental disorders and abnormal psychological functioning, a shift began in the late 1980s when Dr. Martin Seligman and his colleagues founded the field of positive psychology that sought to systematically research how to increase happiness and subjective well-being in healthy populations. With its focus on the cultivation of positive emotions, positive psychology succeeded in developing constructive tools to help people achieve greater overall happiness. Decades after its inception, however, the time is ripe to evaluate whether positive psychology tells the full story of happiness in light of recent psychological studies and ancient Torah wisdom.

M. Eichenbaum (✉)
Ferkauf School of Psychology, New York, NY, USA

© The Author(s), under exclusive license to Springer Nature Switzerland AG 2023
E. Brown, S. Weiss (eds.), *An Ode to Joy*,
https://doi.org/10.1007/978-3-031-28229-4_41

The Effects of Focusing Solely on Positive Emotions

The value of developing positive emotions—such as joy, happiness, gratitude, hope, and awe—cannot be overstated. Among many other benefits, positive emotions play a vital role in building important social, physical, and cognitive resources. They also enhance social affiliations, strengthen cognitive flexibility, and are associated with improved overall health.[1] Converging research has also shown that decreasing negative emotions is highly beneficial to one's overall psychological[2] and physical health.[3] The importance of cultivating positive emotions and decreasing those that are unhealthy is especially important in light of the fact that we possess a strong negativity bias,[4] causing us to see the glass half-empty when it would be psychologically beneficial for us to see it half-full.

At the same time, researchers have argued that positive psychology's heavy focus on positive emotions has unwittingly created a false and polarizing dichotomy that sees positive emotions as inherently good and negative emotions as inherently bad.[5] While this was neither Seligman's nor his colleagues' intention, their emphasis on positive emotions nonetheless created the unintended consequence of skewing our view of human emotions. In reality, human emotions are complex and multifaceted. To believe one should only experience positive emotions runs the risk of pathologizing normal human emotions such as guilt, shame, regret, disappointment, sadness, and anger. While these negative emotions can escalate to the level of abnormality and become pathological, for most people they are part and parcel of ordinary living and expressions of the human condition. Rather than recognizing their ubiquitous presence, researchers in one study found that one-third of us judge ourselves and others poorly for having healthy levels of negative emotions, leading to adverse psychological effects.[6]

This focus on positive emotions has contributed to a "good vibes only" culture in which people eschew even a modicum of negative energy, confrontation, and anxiety. It has also contributed to what Harvard psychologist Susan David calls a "tyranny of positivity," in which we are expected to appear perfectly jovial in the public eye, despite the difficult disappointments we all know occur behind closed doors.[7] Showing our vulnerability, let alone speaking about it, has become taboo in the workplace and other social spheres. Many have similarly decried the existence of "toxic positivity," the phenomenon in which people deny their own or others' negative emotions, often resulting in adverse consequences. Indeed, research has demonstrated that when emotions are suppressed instead of being expressed in a healthy manner, they are actually amplified, causing adverse health effects.[8] Unfortunately, it turns out that wearing a "Don't Worry be Happy" T-shirt won't actually alleviate our stress.

What these studies demonstrate, while counterintuitive, is that focusing too much on personal happiness can also be detrimental to one's health. In one study, researchers found that those who read fictitious articles extolling the benefits of happiness reported feeling lonelier than those who did not read the articles.[9] Despite, or perhaps partly because of,[10] the proliferation of self-help books in the last decades, anxiety and depression levels continue to rise dramatically. It seems that somewhere along the path to happiness, we have lost our compass.

The Value of Negative Emotions

Recalibrating our compasses might have something to do with deepening our understanding of negative emotions. Just as positive emotions are not all good, negative emotions are not all bad, and when experienced in proper quantity and proportion, are both adaptive and healthy. After all, it is fear that propels us to look both ways before we cross the street; disgust that triggers us to avoid toxic substances and immoral behavior; anger that sharpens our sense of right and wrong and causes us to repudiate injustice. Regret has been shown to help us avoid past mistakes and motivate us to perform better in the future.[11] Research has demonstrated that a certain amount of anxiety is necessary for peak performance.[12] While many of us would like to live a stress-free life, most people who face hardships go on to experience post-traumatic growth, not post-traumatic stress.[13] Even healthy amounts of sadness, which in the field of psychology has been all too often mistaken for clinical depression, has been shown to be associated with increased creativity and attention.[14] Sadness and melancholy can also cultivate empathy,[15] as artistically exemplified in Pixar's *Inside Out*.[16] Further research demonstrates that merely accepting our negative emotions, as opposed to judging ourselves for having them, leads to long-term psychological health benefits.[17]

Wholeness

All These studies show that true and realistic happiness does not necessitate the complete abolition of negative emotions. Human beings are complex and, consequently, negotiate a cacophony of different emotions simultaneously. Instead of trying to mute the volume of those very real aspects of our psyches, we need to learn to contend with our complexity and celebrate each emotion in its proper proportion. This new understanding of the scientific study of happiness has been labeled "the second wave of positive psychology" by Dr. Paul Wong and Tim Lomas,[18] "Bittersweet" by Susan Cain in her recent book of that title,[19] and "Wholeness" by Todd Kashdan and Robert Biswas-Diener in their *The Upside of Your Darkside*.[20] Regardless of what we call it, recent research has shown that to be authentically happy we need to live *with* our negative emotions and sometimes even *through* our negative emotions. "To open your heart to pain is to open your heart to joy," wrote Dr. Steven Hayes, the founder of Acceptance and Commitment Therapy (ACT) which seeks to help clients accept, rather than avoid and struggle with, their negative emotions.[21] We can be happy while holding onto sadness, cheerful while harboring some anger, have a deep sense of meaning while feeling guilt, and content even when anxious. While this conception of mixed emotions may seem far from the popular connotation of joy, it is more realistic and more integrative, as it combines all the parts of ourselves into a whole unit.

WHOLENESS IN JUDAISM

This perspective of joy can be found in Jewish sources as well. Jeremiah famously sent a letter to the devastated exile in Babylon to "build houses and live in them, plant gardens and eat their fruit. Take wives and beget sons and daughters; and take wives for your sons, and give your daughters to husbands, that they may bear sons and daughters. Multiply there, do not decrease" (Jeremiah, 29:5–6). Jeremiah revealed Judaism's greatest survival mechanism: to cherish life and move forward, even in the midst of destruction and despair. More than a century later, Ezra the Scribe stood upon a wooden platform and read the Torah, causing the nation to weep due to their realized spiritual shortcomings. Nehemiah then instructed the nation to "go, eat choice foods and drink sweet drinks and send portions to whoever has nothing prepared, for the day is holy to our Lord. Do not be sad, for your rejoicing in the Lord is the source of your strength" (Nehemiah, 8:10). According to Rabbi Jonathan Sacks,[22] Jeremiah and Nehemiah were not encouraging the Jewish people to disassociate from their real-life sorrows, but were instructing them to have a more expansive emotional worldview.

The truth is, unlike certain philosophers who saw religion as an escape from pain and suffering, many thinkers argued that Judaism recognizes and contends with the reality of the human condition. According to Rabbi Joseph B. Soloveitchik, "Religion is not, at the outset, a refuge of grace and mercy for the despondent and desperate, an enchanted stream for crushed spirits, but a raging, clamorous torrent of man's consciousness with all its crises, pangs, and torments."[23] Rather than serving as an escape from the pains of the world, Judaism encourages us to embrace struggle. Judaism does not "anaesthetize us to the pains and apparent injustices of life. It does not reconcile us to suffering," argued Rabbi Jonathan Sacks.[24] Judaism encourages wholeness. It teaches us to embrace joy, even while being gripped tightly by suffering.

The Hebrew language itself may point to this idea. There are many Hebrew words for happiness,[25] perhaps each one reflecting a different facet of this complex emotion. Rabbi Elijah Kramer, the Vilna Gaon, contrasts two of these words: *simha* and *sasson*. *Simha*, says the Gaon, expresses pure unadulterated happiness. *Sasson*, on the other hand, describes happiness when it is accompanied with a degree of broken-heartedness.[26] This insight suggests that one type of happiness is not inherently better than the other, but that each one is appropriate for differing circumstances and times. "There is nothing more whole than a broken heart," said the Kotzker Rebbe,[27] and that wholeness is reflected in our language.

It is not only humans who contend with contradictory emotions, but so does God Himself, so to speak. The Talmud discusses the complexities of God's emotions based on the verse in Jeremiah, "but if you will not hear it, my soul shall weep in secret [*bemistarim*] for your pride" (13:17):

> R. Shmuel bar Inya said in the name of Rav: The Holy One, Blessed be He, has a place where He cries, and its name is *Mistarim*... [The Talmud asks]: But is there crying before the Holy One, Blessed be He? Didn't R. Pappa say: There is no sadness before the Holy One, Blessed be He, as it is stated: "Honor and majesty are before Him; strength and gladness are in His place" (I Chronicles 16:27)? [The Talmud responds]: This is not difficult. This statement, [that God cries] is referring to the innermost chambers, whereas this statement, [that He contains strength and gladness], is referring to the outer chambers.[28]

Just as humans contain multiple "chambers" housing different emotions, apparently God too, as it were, contains these multiple chambers.

Similarly, the Zohar[29] states that, "weeping is lodged in one side of my [God's] heart, and joy is lodged in the other." Identifying and honoring our negative is beneficial for our mental health and cuts to the heart of the Jewish conception of a full life. It is, according to one view in the Talmud and Zohar, deeply divine.

Conclusion

Rabbi Jonathan Sacks was a living exemplar of what it means to be whole. With the burdens of world Jewry on his shoulders while suffering multiple bouts of cancer, Rabbi Sacks managed to remain remarkably joyful. He frequently preached messages of hope, the celebration of life, and the value of finding happiness in unexpected places. He taught us to confront hardship and suffering while still living a happy life. Rabbi Sacks left behind a wealth of Torah for us to study, but we have an equal amount to learn from the way he spent his days. To live with joy, we need to live with both our positive and negative emotions, with *simha* as well as with *sasson*. To live contentedly with a range of emotions, we need to become whole.[30]

Notes

1. June Gruber, Iris B. Mauss, and Maya Tamir, "A Dark Side of Happiness? How, When, and Why Happiness Is Not Always Good," *Perspectives on Psychological Science* 6, no. 3 (May 2011): 222–33.
2. June Gruber, Iris B. Mauss, and Maya Tamir, "A Dark Side of Happiness? How, When, and Why Happiness Is Not Always Good," *Perspectives on Psychological Science* 6, no. 3 (May 2011): 222–33.
3. Laura D. Kubzansky and Ichiro Kawachi, "Going to the Heart of the Matter," *Journal of Psychosomatic Research* 48, no. 4–5 (2000): 323–37, https://doi.org/10.1016/s0022-3999(99)00091-4.
4. Catherine J. Norris, "The Negativity Bias, Revisited: Evidence from Neuroscience Measures and an Individual Differences Approach," *Social Neuroscience* 16, no. 1 (February 2021): 68–82.
5. Tim Lomas, "Positive Psychology—The Second Wave," *The Psychologist* 29 (2016): 536–39. Although numerous advocates for positive psychology wrote explicitly about the importance of negative emotions, their relative lack of integrating them into their studies has caused them to be forgotten and disconnected to happiness. See Joseph, Stephen. Positive Psychology in Practice: Promoting Human Flourishing in Work, Health, Education, and Everyday Life. Stephen Joseph and Brian G. Pauwels, "The Uneasy-

and Necessary-Role of Negative in Positive Psychology," in *Positive Psychology in Practice: Promoting Human Flourishing in Work, Health, Education, and Everyday Life* (London: Routledge, 2015), pp. 807–822.
6. Susan David, *The Gift and Power of Emotional Courage* | TED Talk, 2017, https://www.ted.com/talks/susan_david_the_gift_and_power_of_emotional_courage?language=en.
7. Ibid.
8. Benjamin P. Chapman, Kevin Fiscella, Ichiro Kawachi, Paul Duberstein, and Peter Muennig, "Emotion Suppression and Mortality Risk over a 12-Year Follow-Up," *Journal of Psychosomatic Research* 75, no. 4 (2013): 381–85, https://doi.org/10.1016/j.jpsychores.2013.07.014.
9. Iris B. Mauss, Maya Tamir, Craig L. Anderson, and Nicole S. Savino, "Can Seeking Happiness Make People Unhappy? Paradoxical Effects of Valuing Happiness," *Emotion* 11, no. 4 (2011): 807–15, https://doi.org/10.1037/a0022010.
10. Raymond, Catherine, Marie-France Marin, Anne Hand, Shireen Sindi, Robert-Paul Juster, and Sonia J. Lupien, "Salivary Cortisol Levels and Depressive Symptomatology in Consumers and Nonconsumers of Self-Help Books: A Pilot Study," *Neural Plasticity* 2016 (December 29, 2015): 1–12, https://doi.org/10.1155/2016/3136743. See also the popular works, Marianne Power, *Help Me!: One Woman's Quest to Find out If Self-Help Really Can Change Her Life* (New York: Grove Press, 2019), and Svend Brikmann, *Stand Firm Resisting the Self-Improvement Craze* (Cambridge: Polity, 2017).
11. Marcel Zeelenberg, "The Use of Crying over Spilled Milk: A Note on the Rationality and Functionality of Regret," *Philosophical Psychology* 12, no. 3 (1999): 325–40, https://doi.org/10.1080/095150899105800. See also Daniel H. Pink, *The Power of Regret: How Looking Backward Moves Us Forward* (Edinburgh, UK: Canongate, 2022).
12. Karl Halvor Teigen, "Yerkes-Dodson: A Law for All Seasons," *Theory & Psychology* 4, no. 4 (1994): 525–47, https://doi.org/10.1177/0959354394044004. See also, See Tracy Dennis-Tiwary, *Future Tense: Why Anxiety Is Good for You (Even Though It Feels Bad)* (Harper Wave, 2022).
13. Tal Ben-Shahar, "Introduction," in *Happier, No Matter What: Cultivating Hope, Resilience, and Purpose in Hard Times* (New York, NY: The Experiment, LLC, 2021), 4–5.
14. Christina Ting Fong, "The Effects of Emotional Ambivalence on Creativity." *The Academy of Management Journal* 49, no. 5 (2006): 1016–30, http://www.jstor.org/stable/20159814.
15. Yuan Cao, Genevieve Dingle, Gary C. Chan, and Ross Cunnington, "Low Mood Leads to Increased Empathic Distress at Seeing Others' Pain,"

Frontiers in Psychology 8 (2017), https://doi.org/10.3389/fpsyg.2017.02024.
16. *Inside Out*. Film. United States: Walt Disney studios home entertainment, 2015.
17. Brett Q. Ford, Phoebe Lam, Oliver P. John, and Iris B. Mauss, "The Psychological Health Benefits of Accepting Negative Emotions and Thoughts: Laboratory, Diary, and Longitudinal Evidence." *Journal of Personality and Social Psychology* 115, no. 6 (2018): 1075–92, https://doi.org/10.1037/pspp0000157.
18. Tim Lomas, "Positive Psychology—The Second Wave," *The Psychologist* 29 (2016): 536–39.
19. Susan Cain, *Bittersweet: How Sorrow and Longing Make Us Whole* (New York, NY: Crown Publishing Group (NY), 2022).
20. Todd B. Kashdan and Robert Biswas-Diener, *Upside of Your Dark Side: Why Being Your Whole Self—Not Just Your "Good" Self—Drives Success and Fulfillment* (NY, NY: Plume, an imprint of Penguin Random House LLC, 2015).
21. Steven C. Hayes, "From Loss to Love," *Psychology Today*. Sussex Publishers, June 18, 2018, https://www.psychologytoday.com/us/articles/201806/loss-love.
22. Jonathan Sacks, "Happiness: A Jewish Perspective," *Journal of Law and Religion* 29, no. 1 (2014): 30–47. http://www.jstor.org/stable/24739084.
23. Joseph B. Soloveitchik, *Halakhic Man*, trans. Lawrence Kaplan. (Jerusalem: Sefer Ve Sefel Publishing, 2005), 142.
24. Jonathan Sacks, "Essay," in *Covenant & Conversation: Genesis, The Book of Beginnings* (New Milford, CT: Maggid Books & The Orthodox Union, 2009), 240.
25. Avot D' Rebbe Natan (34:10) lists ten.
26. Elijah Kramer, *Divrei Eliyahu*. Psalms 119.
27. See, for example, https://aish.com/gems-of-wisdom-of-the-kotzker-rebbe/.
28. *Sotah* 5b.
29. Lev. 75a.
30. I would like to thank my wife Sonny, as well as my friends and colleagues Rabbi Effie Wagner, Yehuda Fogel, and Rabbi Dr. Mordechai Schiffman for their editorial help and insights in crafting this essay.

PART X

Joy in Jewish Education

CHAPTER 42

Positive Psychology and Jewish Wisdom in the Classroom: A Synergic Effect

Mordechai Schiffman

INTRODUCTION

In her afterword to *Radical Responsibility*, Dr. Tamra Wright points to Rabbi Jonathan Sacks' affinity for the fields of positive psychology and cognitive behavioral therapy. She calls on leaders and educators to create what she terms a "new *Musar*," which incorporates the findings from those disciplines with Torah content in order to "best help ourselves and each other to change negative behaviours and to develop the *midot* the Torah demands of us."[1] Following her lead, I will provide a brief overview of the field of positive psychology and its application in the school setting, with a particular focus on positive emotions in the classroom. Next, I will compare the psychological literature to the lessons gleaned from classical Jewish texts and commentaries. I will close with a practical application demonstrating the integration of Torah ideas and positive psychology with an overview of the literature on the use of humor in the classroom.

M. Schiffman (✉)
Azrieli Graduate School of Jewish Education and Administration, Yeshiva University, New York, NY, USA

© The Author(s), under exclusive license to Springer Nature Switzerland AG 2023
E. Brown, S. Weiss (eds.), *An Ode to Joy*,
https://doi.org/10.1007/978-3-031-28229-4_42

Positive Psychology

Positive psychology is a relatively new sub-discipline within psychology which focuses on how to encourage, promote, and sustain the good life. For too long, Martin Seligman argued, psychology has focused on deficiencies; in the early twenty-first century, he encouraged the field to also focus on helping people flourish. Using a numeric metaphor, he writes that instead of just finding ways to help someone who is functioning at a minus five get to a minus three, we should encourage someone at a plus two to function at a plus seven.[2]

Positive psychology, in its nascent development, had an individualist bent that predominantly stressed the hedonic elements of happiness, such as feeling pleasure and increasing positive emotions. To counter this bias, Seligman later accentuated the importance of eudemonic well-being, or the broader idea of a flourishing life which includes engagement and meaning, rather than just happiness. Additionally, the field started to move away from its individualistic orientation to include enhancing the flourishing of institutions and broader society. To help promote this new vision, Seligman proposed the PERMA framework, which is an acronym for five key elements of flourishing, namely, positive emotions, engagement, relationships, meaning, and achievement.[3]

To promote institutional flourishing, an emphasis was made to try and integrate positive psychology within a school framework. Theoretical calls stressed that school should be a place where the goal is to cultivate student well-being. According to Noddings, "Happiness and education are, properly, intimately related: Happiness should be an aim of education and a good education should contribute significantly to personal and collective happiness."[4]

In a seminal article, Seligman and colleagues explained the value of integrating positive psychology into the classroom, concluding that, "Well-being should be taught in school on three grounds: as an antidote to depression, as a vehicle for increasing life satisfaction, and as an aid to better learning and more creative thinking."[5] Many aspects of the PERMA framework are pertinent for schools and work is being done in some schools to incorporate elements of positive psychology both in the classroom and as a part of the school culture.[6]

In line with the theme of joy we will narrow our focus primarily on the first element of PERMA, namely, positive emotions, and how they relate and function within a classroom setting. While distinction among different positive emotions is an important endeavor, for our present purposes, we will assume an expansive definition of positive emotions to include joy, hope, gratitude, awe, and love.[7]

Joy in the Classroom

Until recently, emotions were not considered an important part of the classroom experience. This may trace back to the philosophical notion that intellect and emotion are distinct spheres, and schools should, therefore, focus on intellect and neglect emotion. Rabbi Sacks, however, has noted several times[8] that recent advances in neuroscience and psychology demonstrate how crucial emotions are to the cognitive process.[9] Consequently, over the last 25 years there has been an increase in research related to both positive and negative emotions and their respective function in the learning environment. This is particularly true as it relates to students' motivation, memory, overall learning, and development of interpersonal resources.[10] While acknowledging that there can be beneficial outcomes from negative emotions, [11] as well as maladaptive manifestations of positive emotions, [12] for the purpose of this chapter, we will focus on the robust benefits that emerge from positive emotions.

Early theories assumed that positive emotions would inhibit effective learning as they can "induce unrealistic appraisals, lead to shallow, superficial processing of information, and reduce motivation to become more deeply involved with the pursuit of challenging goals."[13] Aspinwall summarizes the pre-existing twentieth-century literature as assuming that "feeling good makes us lazy thinkers who are oblivious to potentially useful negative information."[14] Building on the early work of Alice Isen, Barbara Fredrickson, and others, positive psychologists, the field has evolved to demonstrate that positive emotions can provide several essential benefits including more resilience,[15] social connectedness,[16] and more optimal psychological functioning.[17] Particular within a learning context, a positive mood helps divergent, creative, and flexible thinking, allowing for increased problem solving.[18] Studies also show that positive emotions lead people to make more word associations, have a more global visual processing style, and become more flexible in object categorization.[19]

In order to explain the benefits of positive emotions, Fredrickson developed what she deemed the "broaden and build" model of positive emotions. Unlike negative emotions that tend to narrow and restrict a person's focus, positive emotions expand a person's thoughts and actions, which allows them to solve problems more effectively and build resources more efficiently, leading to enhanced health and fulfillment. This, in turn, leads to more positive emotions, resulting in a continual upward spiral of well-being.[20]

But positive emotions do not only have an intellectual benefit; they also enhance other important educational factors. For instance, positive emotions help with both intrinsic and extrinsic motivation, build interest in learning, and increase the possibility that students will reengage with the content later, influencing students to become lifelong learners.[21] Emotions such as joy, hope, and pride impact students' overall achievement by building their academic self-efficacy, academic interest, and effort.[22] Broadly speaking, positive emotions have been associated with higher student engagement.[23] Finally, positive emotions may impact achievement levels as they are associated with higher quality relationships with friends and teachers, which can enhance social and academic support.[24]

JOY WHILE LEARNING TORAH

Joy is an essential aspect of Torah learning. Several statements in the Talmud highlight the importance of learning with joy,[25] and later rabbinic works accentuate the importance of joy in learning Torah.[26] While joy can be seen as an outgrowth of learning Torah, we will frame the discussion as it relates to how joy can enhance the learning process itself. To do so, we will use the sixth *Baraita* in the sixth chapter of *Ethics of the Fathers* as our starting point. The *baraita* lists 48 dispositions that facilitate the acquisition of Torah; one of them is *simḥa* (joy). While much of *Ethics of the Fathers* can be assumed to promote various traits that are generally beneficial for the religious personality, the context of these 48 as part of the acquisition of Torah leads commentaries to make direct connections between these qualities and the learning process. A brief survey of the commentaries as they relate to the trait of *simḥa* highlights and foreshadows much of the research on positive psychology in the learning context.

Starting with the negative consequences of learning without joy, the fifteenth-century Spanish Kabbalist, Shem Tov ibn Shem Tov, writes that if one is not happy with his learning, it will not endure. Several other fifteenth-century commentators including Rabbis Yosef Alashkar, Matityahu ha-Yizhari, and Isaac Abarbanel all focus on how other negative emotions, such as worry, distract from effective learning. Rabbi Shmuel de Uceda (sixteenth century, Safed) adds a motivational component, that if the Torah is not learned with joy, but as a burden, the learner will eventually just stop learning. In contrast, learning done with joy will lead to more motivation to learn. Focusing on the cognitive ramifications of joy, Rabbi Yaakov Emden (eighteenth century, Germany) writes that through happiness, one's memory is enhanced, one's mind is widened, and one's intelligence is sharpened. He cautions, however, that this is only true for joy that is related to learning. A frivolous type of joy will distract and ruin the learning process. Also highlighting the cognitive benefits of joy, Rabbi Israel Lipschitz (nineteenth century, Germany) explains that concepts will be better grasped in one's mind if accompanied with joy. Finally, as it relates to efficiency of learning, Rabbi Chaim of Volozhin (d. 1821) contends that one who learns one hour with joy accomplishes much more than one who learns several hours while being sad.[27]

Practical Application: The Use of Humor

The Talmud relates that Rabah began his lessons with a joke.[28] Rashi (eleventh century, France), foreshadowing Fredrickson's broaden-and-build model, explains that the joke provided the positive emotion that helped "open their minds" to better facilitate the subsequent learning. Research on the use of humor in the classroom indicates that it enables quicker and more effective learning, promotes student participation, interest, motivation, and enjoyment of the content.[29] Noble and McGrath outline other contexts that humor can be used effectively in the classroom, including as

> a style of interaction, an approach to teaching and learning (e.g. using cartoons or humorous images in a slide presentation or playing educational games), a curriculum activity (e.g. conducting a class survey to identify the most amusing of four different jokes or cartoons, the reading and analysis of funny books, or the writing of funny stories or poems) and, when used appropriately, it can also be an effective coping skill (e.g. laughing at your own silly mistake can help to keep things in perspective).[30]

However, two caveats are important.[31] First, the humor should be positive and non-aggressive. Second, the research indicates that humor can also be overused, and, at a certain point, become a distraction from learning. After conducting a meta-analysis of humor research, Rod Martin, perhaps echoing Rabah's sentiment, recommends that humor is useful for engaging students at the beginning of a lesson but should not be overly used throughout.[32] Future research should investigate how best to synthesize educational psychological literature that aims to find the right balance between positive emotions and more serious moods during the learning context with the related balance in Torah learning between the value of *simha* as stated above, and the necessity to incorporate other emotions essential to learning Torah such as "reverence, fear, quaking, and trembling."[33]

Conclusion

Analyzing the concept of joy in the learning context provides a fitting example of the possibility of "a new *mussar*," where the findings of positive psychology and the wisdom of the Torah literature converge. Research in positive psychology provides new insight, modern language, and innovative application to the concepts embedded within our millennia old laws and traditions. Utilized in tandem, they can enhance the efficacy of the transmission of Torah within our sacred learning institutions.

Notes

1. Tamra Wright, "Afterward: A New Musar," in *Radical Responsibility: Celebrating the Thought of Chief Rabbi Lord Jonathan Sacks*, eds. Michael J. Harris, Daniel Rynhold, and Tamra Wright (New Milford: Maggid Books, 2012), 247.
2. Martin E. Seligman, *Authentic Happiness: Using the New Positive Psychology to Realize Your Potential for Lasting Fulfillment* (New York: Free Press, 2002), ix.
3. Martin E. Seligman. *Flourish: A Visionary New Understanding of Happiness and Well-being* (New York: Free Press, 2012).
    For variations, see Margaret L. Kern, K. A. Allen, M. Furlong, S. Vella-Brodrick, and S. Suldo. "PERMAH: A Useful Model for Focusing on Wellbeing in Schools." *Handbook of Positive Psychology in Schools, Third Edition* (New York: Routledge, 2021) and Tal Ben-Shahar, *Happier, No Matter What: Cultivating Hope, Resilience, and Purpose in Hard Times* (New York: The Experiment, 2021).
4. Nel Noddings, *Happiness and Education* (Cambridge: Cambridge University Press, 2003).
5. Martin E. Seligman, Randal M. Ernst, Jane Gillham, Karen Reivich, and Mark Linkins. "Positive Education: Positive Psychology and Classroom Interventions," *Oxford Review of Education* 35, no. 3 (2009): 293–311.
6. Kelly-Ann Allen, Michael J. Furlong, Dianne Vella-Brodrick, and Shannon M. Suldo, *Handbook of Positive Psychology in Schools: Supporting Process and Practice* (New York: Routledge, 2022).

7. Barbara L. Fredrickson, "Positive Emotions Broaden and Build," in *Advances in Experimental Social Psychology*, vol. 47, (Cambridge: Academic Press, 2013), 1–53.
8. Jonathan Sacks, "Descartes Error," accessed June 30, 2022, https://www.rabbisacks.org/covenant-conversation/chukat/descartes-error/.
   Jonathan Sacks, "Thinking Fast and Slow," accessed June 30, 2022, https://www.rabbisacks.org/covenant-conversation/acharei-mot/thinking-fast-and-slow/.
   Jonathan Sacks, "Torah as Song," accessed June 30, 2022, https://www.rabbisacks.org/covenant-conversation/vayelech/torah-as-song/.
9. Lisa Feldman Barrett, Michael Lewis, and Jeannette M. Haviland-Jones, eds. *Handbook of emotions* (New York: Guilford Publications, 2016).
10. Carlos Valiente, Jodi Swanson, and Nancy Eisenberg. "Linking Students' Emotions and Academic Achievement: When and Why Emotions Matter," *Child Development Perspectives* 6, no. 2 (2012): 129–135.
11. Laura McInerney. "Applying Happiness and Well-being Research to the Teaching and Learning Process," in *Oxford Handbook of Happiness*, ed. Susan A. David, Ilona Boniwell, Amanda Conley Ayers (Oxford: Oxford University Press, 2013), 592–608.
12. Carlos Valiente, Jodi Swanson, and Nancy Eisenberg. "Linking Students' Emotions And Academic Achievement: When and Why Emotions Matter." *Child Development Perspectives* 6, no. 2 (2012): 129–135.
13. Reinhard Pekrun, Thomas Goetz, Wolfram Titz, and Raymond P. Perry, "Positive Emotions in Education," in *Beyond Coping: Meeting Goals, Visions, and Challenges*, ed. Erica Frydenberg (Oxford: Oxford University Press, 2002), 149–173.
14. Lisa G. Aspinwall, "Rethinking the Role of Positive Affect in Self-Regulation," *Motivation and Emotion* 22, no. 1 (1998): 7.
15. Michele M. Tugade, and Barbara L. Fredrickson. "Resilient Individuals Use Positive Emotions to Bounce Back from Negative Emotional Experiences," *Journal of Personality and Social Psychology* 86, no. 2 (2004): 320–333.
16. Iris B. Mauss, Amanda J. Shallcross, Allison S. Troy, Oliver P. John, Emilio Ferrer, Frank H. Wilhelm, and James J. Gross, "Don't Hide your Happiness! Positive Emotion Dissociation, Social Connectedness, and Psychological Functioning," *Journal of Personality and Social Psychology* 100, no. 4 (2011): 738–48.
17. Barbara L. Fredrickson, and Marcial F. Losada, "Positive Affect and the Complex Dynamics of Human Flourishing," *American Psychologist* 60, no. 7 (2005): 678–86.
18. Alice M. Isen, "On the Relationship Between Affect and Creative Problem Solving," *Affect, Creative Experience, and Psychological Adjustment* 3, no. 17 (1999): 3–17.

19. Laura McInerney. "Applying Happiness and Well-being Research to the Teaching and Learning Process," in *Oxford Handbook of Happiness*, ed. Susan A. David, Ilona Boniwell, and Amanda Conley Ayers (Oxford: Oxford University Press, 2013), 592–608.
20. Barbara L. Fredrickson, "Positive Emotions Broaden and Build," *Advances in Experimental Social Psychology*, vol. 47 (Cambridge: Academic Press, 2013): 1–53.
21. Anne C. Frenzel, Thomas Goetz, Oliver Lüdtke, Reinhard Pekrun, and Rosemary E. Sutton. "Emotional Transmission in the Classroom: Exploring the Relationship Between Teacher and Student Enjoyment." *Journal of Educational Psychology* 101, no. 3 (2009): 705–16.
22. Reinhard Pekrun, Thomas Goetz, Raymond P. Perry, Klaudia Kramer, Michaela Hochstadt, and Stefan Molfenter. "Beyond Test Anxiety: Development and Validation of the Test Emotions Questionnaire (TEQ)." *Anxiety, Stress & Coping* 17, no. 3 (2004): 287–316.
23. Amy L. Reschly, E. Scott Huebner, James J. Appleton, and Susan Antaramian. "Engagement as Flourishing: The Contribution of Positive Emotions and Coping to Adolescents' Engagement at School and with learning." *Psychology in the Schools* 45, no. 5 (2008): 419–431.
24. Carlos Valiente, Jodi Swanson, and Nancy Eisenberg. "Linking students' emotions and academic achievement: When and why emotions matter." *Child Development Perspectives* 6, no. 2 (2012): 129–135.
25. See Berakhot 63b, Eruvin 54a, Taanit 30a, and Avoda Zara 19a.
26. See *Pachad Yitzchak, Chanuka*, no. 6, and *Pachad Yitzchak Iggerot U-Ketavim*, no. 2.
27. For other interesting perspectives, see Rabbi Yosef Nahmias, Rabbi Yitzchak MiToledo, and Maharal.
28. BT Shabbat 30b.
29. Toni Noble and Helen McGrath. *The PROSPER school pathways for student wellbeing: Policy and practices* (New York: Springer, 2015).
30. Toni Noble and Helen McGrath. *The PROSPER school pathways for student wellbeing: Policy and practices* (New York: Springer, 2015), 6.
31. Laura McInerney, "Applying Happiness and Well-being Research to the Teaching and Learning Process," in *Oxford Handbook of Happiness*, ed. Susan A. David, Ilona Boniwell, Amanda Conley Ayers (Oxford: Oxford University Press, 2013) 592–608.
32. Rod A. Martin & Thomas Ford, *The Psychology of Humor: An Integrative Approach* (United Kingdom: Elsevier Science, 2018).
33. BT Berakhot 22a.

CHAPTER 43

The Jewish Value of Joy and Positive Education

Daniel Rose

What redeems life and etches it with the charisma of grace is joy[1]

In 1993 the head teacher of a failing school in London reached out to Rabbi Sacks. She had heard several of his broadcasts and connected to his messages, so she reached out to him to hear his perspective on the challenges she was facing. He invited her and two members of her senior leadership team to meet with him at his home. She described a school with morale at an all-time low. Parents had been withdrawing their children; examination results were unacceptably poor, and teachers felt desperate and frustrated. The school faced the real possibility of closure.

During the ensuing discussion, Rabbi Sacks spoke with them about education in general, including building school community and how to develop a school ethos. But then he changed tact and took a more practical direction. He urged them to create opportunities for joyful celebrations of achievement in the school, even when it seemed hard to find anything to celebrate. Some years later, the same head of school wrote to

D. Rose (✉)
The Rabbi Sacks Legacy, London, UK

© The Author(s), under exclusive license to Springer Nature Switzerland AG 2023
E. Brown, S. Weiss (eds.), *An Ode to Joy*,
https://doi.org/10.1007/978-3-031-28229-4_43

Rabbi Sacks to describe the impact of that conversation on their school. General morale was vastly better, and examination results and enrollment had improved exponentially. She was proud to tell him she had since been made a Dame of the British Empire in recognition of her contribution to education.

What role did making space for joy in this school have and what impact can it play in education in general? In this essay, we will explore joy in the thought of Rabbi Sacks, and how the school of Positive Psychology, and specifically Positive Education, which integrates its central theses in educational frameworks, can be a practical expression of joy as a Jewish value.

Positive Education

Research in the field of Positive Psychology, which can be defined as the scientific study of what makes life most worth living,[2] has identified that the pursuit of meaning and engagement are more predictive of life satisfaction than the pursuit of pleasure.[3] Positive Education, a branch of Positive Psychology, focuses on creating a synergy between learning and positive emotion, arguing that the skills for happiness and well-being should be taught in school. There is strong evidence that the teaching of life skills that increase resilience, positive emotion, engagement, and meaning in schools leads to increased well-being.[4]

Martin Seligman, one of the founders of positive psychology, applied Positive Psychology into educational frameworks as a way to enhance the well-being of young people. By using his PERMA model[5] in schools, educators and practitioners aim to promote positive mental health among students and teachers. The PERMA model encompasses five main elements critical for long-term well-being:

1. Feeling *positive emotions* such as joy, gratitude, and hope
2. *Engagement* in the present moment, being fully absorbed in activities
3. Having *positive relationships*
4. Finding *meaning* in life, and belonging to and serving something bigger than yourself
5. Pursuing success and *achievement*

We will argue here that these five elements in particular, and this general approach to education in general, can inform our understanding of the articulation of joy as a Jewish value in the writings of Rabbi Sacks, and how to integrate joy as a value into Jewish education.

JOY VERSUS HAPPINESS

Happiness (*osher*) is clearly a value in Judaism. Both the first chapter of the Book of Psalms, and the prayer said three times each day called *Ashrei* begins with this word. Yet Rabbi Sacks argues this is not a supreme value in Judaism. *Simha*, joy, is. "Happiness in the classic sense, *eudaemonia* in Greek, *felicitas* in Latin, and *ashrei* in Hebrew, means doing well and faring well. The good person acts morally and is blessed with a life well lived."[6]

But happiness depends on a secure and stable society where there are shared values, where morality is central, and those who are blessed share their blessings with the vulnerable. In this context, happiness can be achieved. But in the radical insecurity of our world, where injustice and oppression diminish the possibility of happiness for the weak in our society, it is *simha* that is the antidote to suffering. In the words of Kierkegaard, "The one whose joy is dependent on certain conditions is not joy itself."[7]

In his exquisite exploration of the Book of Ecclesiastes, Rabbi Sacks understands Kohelet's angst and search for elusive joy, despite his obvious material wealth and success, as an absence of meaning. "Kohelet is speaking about how he acquired houses, vineyards, orchards, male and female servants, silver, gold, wives and concubines. He had everything. Except meaning. Except purpose. Except joy."[8] What more important goal is there for educators today than to provide opportunities for children to explore and find a sense of meaning in their lives beyond the prevalent values of consumerism and materialism in society?

Seligman included *meaning* in his PERMA model. He expressed meaning as belonging and the service of something greater than ourselves. Finding purpose in life helps us focus on what is really important in the face of significant challenge or adversity, such as adolescence.[9] Adolescence is a turbulent time of enhanced growth and the search for identity. Adolescents need to have a sense of belonging; they need to feel valued and respected, while finding a way to make a contribution to their community and society. This is tied to adolescents' search for meaning and larger purpose.[10] Helping students find joy in life beyond materialism and the pursuit of wealth, despite the challenges and difficulties that life throws their way, can be an integral part of meaning-making in life. This is the time to develop the necessary skills and thinking to achieve joy through finding meaning in life.

COLLECTIVE JOY

Rabbi Sacks explores joy as a central value in biblical Judaism in many places. Happiness, he highlights, is something that can be experienced on one's own. But joy is a social emotion that must be experienced in community:

> Joy in the Hebrew Bible is essentially shared. It is a phenomenon of 'We.' A husband must make his wife rejoice (Deut. 24:5). Festivals are to be occasions of collective rejoicing, 'you, your sons and daughters, your male and female servants, the Levites in your towns, and the strangers, the fatherless and the widows living among you' (Deut. 16:11). Bringing first fruits to the Temple involved collective celebration: 'you and the Levites and the strangers in your midst shall rejoice in all the good things the Lord your God has given to you and your household' (Deut. 26:11). Joy is happiness shared.[11]

The word *simha* appears once only in every book of the Torah, except for Deuteronomy, where it appears 12 times, as we can see from the verses just cited. Why is joy specifically emphasized in the book of Deuteronomy? Having overcome many challenges and hardships, from slavery in Egypt, through the wandering in the wilderness, the Israelites had reached the border of the Promised Land. About to enter, charged with the task of building a Jewish nation, Moses feared the greatest challenge of all that lay ahead. Living with security and contentment. In his speeches in Deuteronomy, Moses was "giving prophetic expression to the great paradox of faith: *It is easy to speak to God in tears. It is hard to serve God in joy.*"[12]

This idea of *simha* as communal, social, and national rejoicing, is a ubiquitous theme in biblical Judaism. Not just by crisis, catastrophe, or war would the people experience unity, but also through collective celebration in the presence of God. And unity is an expansive term here, where the celebration itself was to be deeply moral. "Not only was this a religious act of thanksgiving; it was also to be a form of social inclusion. No one was to be left out: not the stranger, or the servant, or the lonely (the orphan and widow)."[13]

In a later biblical book, Kohelet's dissatisfaction with material wealth and success is found in the double use of the first person singular. "I built for myself...I planted for myself...I collected for myself...I acquired for myself..." (Eccl. 2:4–8). This is the key to understanding Kohelet's despair. He lacked the sense of responsibility for the collective joy of others that is central to Deuteronomy.

Collective joy and community are expressions of *positive relationships* of Seligman's PERMA model in Positive Education. Schools are models of community, built on the central values of their parent communities. Joy can play an important role here. Children are socialized into their parent communities where community living can be experienced as a model for adult Jewish life. Community is an educational end in itself. It is an outcome of schooling, a commitment to a life lived together with others and with others' interests, needs, and dignity in mind.[14] School community not only models the parent community, but can also set the ideal for society. In the words of Rabbi Yitz Greenberg, "Day schools give educators the opportunity to create a world which can embody the holistic holy community which is our dream for the world."[15] Schools can become "covenantal communities" where commitments to these values are expressed "in the way the adults listen to a child, in the way students are respected, in the way each person is helped to develop his/her *tselem elokim*, image of God... and forge an ideal society for the Jewish people and for humanity."[16]

Joy as Religious Courage

Joyful religious service is a testament of faith. In the midst of the curses in Deuteronomy 28, Moses says that travesties will befall the nation not because they served idols or abandoned God but "Because you did not serve the Lord your God with joy and gladness out of the abundance of all things" (28:47). Why does the Torah attribute national disaster to a lack of joy?

Kierkegaard wrote: "It takes moral courage to grieve. It takes religious courage to rejoice."[17] The capacity for joy is what gives the Jewish people the strength to endure suffering. Without it, we become vulnerable to the multiple disasters set out in the curses in Deuteronomy 28. On the capacity of Jews to see joy as the supreme religious emotion despite the travails of Jewish history, Rabbi Sacks writes:

> Every day we begin our morning prayers with a litany of thanks, that we are here, with a world to live in, family and friends to love and be loved by,

about to start a day full of possibilities, in which, by acts of loving kindness, we allow God's presence to flow through us into the lives of others. Joy helps heal some of the wounds of our injured, troubled world.[18]

This approach is expressed in the practical rabbinic requirement to increase joy from the beginning of the month of Adar (*Mishe-nichnas Adar marbim be-simha*).[19] Rabbi Sacks termed this *therapeutic joy*:

> The Jewish response to trauma is counterintuitive and extraordinary. You defeat fear by joy. You conquer terror by collective celebration… Precisely because the threat was so serious, you refuse to be serious—and in that refusal you are doing something very serious indeed. You are denying your enemies a victory. You are declaring that *you will not be intimidated*. As the date of the scheduled destruction approaches, you surround yourself with the single most effective antidote to fear: joy in life itself.[20]

Joy is a form of thanksgiving. If we can find joy in the face of fear and suffering, we acknowledge life is a gift—and if it is a gift, there must be a Giver. Seeking meaning in life can form a powerful pedagogic approach to managing the experience of periods of suffering, whether national historical (and in the Jewish calendarial cycle) such as educational approaches to Holocaust and Israel education, or current experiences of national or communal tragedy. Helping young people find joy and gratitude in the face of suffering and misfortune is a vital spiritual skill they will benefit from as they navigate their search for spiritual maturity and independence and engage in lifelong meaning-making.

Joy Celebrates the Power of Now

Kierkegaard said, "Joy is the present time, with the whole emphasis on *the present time*."[21] As opposed to happiness, joy involves no judgment about life as a whole. Joy lives in the moment. It asks no questions about tomorrow. It celebrates the power of now. While admittedly life is sometimes unfair and the world unjust, life is precious, and all too fleeting, so with joy we celebrate each moment. Joy in the moment prevents obsessing about tomorrow and instead celebrates today. In joy, we bless God day-by-day and celebrate our very existence, in this eternity-in-a-moment that was not before and will not be again.

Joy embraces the contingency of life. It knows that yesterday has gone and tomorrow is unknown. It does not ask what was or will be. It makes no calculations. It is a state of radical thankfulness for the gift of being. Even in an age too fraught for happiness, there can still be joy.[22]

Engagement in the moment is a fundamental tenet of the aims of Positive Education, often achieved by exercises in mindfulness and gratitude.[23] Finding a state of flow, and focusing on this as a significant goal, is an "Engaged Life." This consists in a loss of self-consciousness, time stopping for you, being "one with the music."[24] Engagement in the moment enriches life and paves the way for meaning-making and must be a core educational goal for institutions with the well-being of students at their heart.

Conclusions

Well-being as a psychological state, can be divided into three very different realms, each of which is skill-based and can be taught to children.[25] The first is "positive emotion," such as joy, love, contentment, etc. A life led around having as much of this as possible is the "Pleasant Life."[26] This corresponds to the general definition of joy derived here from the writings of Rabbi Sacks. The second is the "Engaged Life," termed flow by positive psychologists, and is being present and engaged in the moment.[27] This is articulated by Rabbi Sacks as "Joy as the power of now."[28] The third realm of well-being is the "Meaningful Life." From a Positive Psychology perspective, meaning consists in knowing what your strengths are, and then using them to belong to and serve something you believe is larger than the self.[29] Intrinsic to this is the moral and social elements of community and how Rabbi Sacks understood collective joy as foundational to the moral and social elements of a healthy community. He believed in and taught the religious courage of joy in the face of suffering. This joy is a testament of gratitude and acknowledgment of blessing that also leads to mindfulness and engagement in the present. The symbiosis between the definition and exploration of the value of joy in the thought of Rabbi Sacks, the theory of Positive Psychology and specifically Positive Education, forms a powerful and practical approach to Jewish education in our schools.

I would like to end with a personal reflection on how we in Anglo-Jewry watched first-hand, time and again, as Rabbi Sacks modeled the Jewish value of joy for us, especially in the context of Jewish education.

Rabbi Sacks rarely seemed more joyful than when he was conversing with Jewish educators in his home which was always open to us or visiting Jewish schools in-person. The image of him sitting on the floor engaged in deep conversation with pre-school students will forever be an inspiration to the Jewish educational community in Britain and beyond. But for me, the experience that will stay with me forever, was watching Rabbi Sacks, a peer in the House of Lords, personal friend to royalty and prime ministers, at Bnei Akiva National weekend standing on his chair, leading close to a thousand young people, parents, and grandparents, in a gleeful rendition of *kol ha-olam kulo gesher tzar meod, ve-haikar lo lefakhed klal*—the whole world is a very narrow bridge, but the main thing is to have no fear at all. How fitting, and vital, to take this message, together with his articulation of the value of joy, and how he modeled this in his life, into our work as Jewish educators.

Notes

1. Jonathan Sacks, *Ceremony & Celebration* (Jerusalem: Maggid, 2017), 126.
2. Christopher Peterson, "What is Positive Psychology, and What Is It Not?," *Psychology Today*, 2008. Retrieved from https://www.psychologytoday.com/us/blog/the-good-life/200805/what-is-positive-psychology-and-what-is-it-not.
3. Christopher Peterson, Nansook Park, and Martin Seligman, "Orientations to Happiness and Life Satisfaction: The Full Life Versus the Empty Life," *Journal of Happiness Studies* 6 (2005): 25–41.
4. Martin E. P. Seligman, Randal M. Ernstb, Jane Gillhamc, Karen Reivicha, and Mark Linkinsd, "Positive Education: Positive Psychology and Classroom Interventions," *Oxford Review of Education* 35, no. 3 (2009): 293–311.
5. Martin E. P. Seligman, *Flourish: A Visionary New Understanding of Happiness and Well-Being* (New York: Atria Paperback, 2012)
6. Jonathan Sacks, *Ceremony & Celebration* (Jerusalem: Maggid, 2017), 126.
7. Soren Kierkegaard, *Without Authority* (Princeton University Press, 1997), 37.
8. Sacks, *Ceremony & Celebration* (Jerusalem: Maggid, 2017), 129.
9. Martin E. P. Seligman, *Flourish: A Visionary New Understanding of Happiness and Well-Being* (2012).
10. Ronald E. Dahl, Nicholas B. Allen, Linda Wilbrecht, and Ahna Ballonoff Suleiman, "Importance of Investing in Adolescence from a Developmental Science Perspective," *Nature* 554, no. 7693 (2018): 441–50.

11. Jonathan Sacks, *Morality* (New York: Basic Books, 2020), 113.
12. Jonathan Sacks, *Covenant & Conversation: Deuteronomy: Renewal of the Sinai Covenant* (Jerusalem: Maggid, 2019), 127.
13. Ibid., 128.
14. Alex Pomson and Howard Deitcher, *Jewish Day Schools, Jewish Communities* (The Littman Library of Jewish Civilization, 2009), 18.
15. Yitzchak Greenberg, *Judaism and Modernity* (Jerusalem: Targum Shlishi, 2006), 35–36.
16. Ibid.
17. Søren Kierkegaard, *Journals and Papers* (Indiana Press, 1975), 2179.
18. Jonathan Sacks, *Studies in Spirituality* (Jerusalem: Maggid, 2021), 259.
19. Babylonian Talmud Taanit 29a.
20. Jonathan Sacks, The Therapeutic Joy of Purim, 2015, Retrieved from https://www.rabbisacks.org/archive/therapeutic-joy-purim/.
21. Søren Kierkegaard, *Without Authority* (Princeton University Press, 1997), 39.
22. Sacks, *Ceremony & Celebration* (Jerusalem: Maggid, 2017), 127.
23. Martin E. P. Seligman, Randal M. Ernstb, Jane Gillhamc, Karen Reivicha, and Mark Linkinsd, "Positive Education: Positive Psychology and Classroom Interventions," *Oxford Review of Education* 35, no. 3 (2009): 293–311.
24. Mihaly Csikszentmihalyi, *Flow: The Psychology of Optimal Experience* (New York: Harper & Row, 1990).
25. Martin E.P. Seligman, *Authentic Happiness: Using the New Positive Psychology to Realize Your Potential for Lasting Fulfillment* (New York: Free Press, 2002)
26. Martin E. P. Seligman, Randal M. Ernstb, Jane Gillhamc, Karen Reivicha, and Mark Linkinsd, "Positive Education: Positive Psychology and Classroom Interventions," *Oxford Review of Education* 35, no. 3 (2009): 293–311.
27. Mihaly Csikszentmihalyi, *Flow: The Psychology of Optimal Experience* (New York: Harper & Row, 1990).
28. Jonathan Sacks, *Ceremony & Celebration* (Jerusalem: Maggid, 2017), 127.
29. Martin E. P. Seligman, *Authentic Happiness: Using the New Positive Psychology to Realize Your Potential for Lasting Fulfillment* (New York: Free Press, 2002)

CHAPTER 44

Joy and Parenting: Partners or Paradox?

Rona Milch Novick

Parents trying to calm a colicky baby at 3:00 a.m., anxiously awaiting a teen's return home at midnight, or meeting with a principal to discuss a child's learning challenges or behavior, would not likely describe their emotional state as joyful. Yet, parents who have heard their infant giggle, watched their toddler's first steps, seen their child sing at a *siddur* play, or walked their child down the aisle will describe being overwhelmed with joy. Some authors, such as Daniel Gilbert in his 2006 book *Stumbling on Happiness*, discuss common casualties of parenthood, including dips in self-reported marital satisfaction and overall happiness.[1] Others, such as Stertz and Weisz, exploring child-related bliss, present data and arguments suggesting that parenting increases happiness.[2] By exploring the psychological research on parenting and happiness, the wisdom of Torah sages, and the synergy across these two perspectives, we may begin to understand how one of life's most demanding challenges can bring us both unrivaled stress and unbridled joy.

Studies have found women report engaging in activities with their children as less enjoyable than engaging in most other daily activities.[3] Other

R. M. Novick (✉)
Azrieli Graduate School of Jewish Education and Administration,
Yeshiva University, New York, NY, USA

© The Author(s), under exclusive license to Springer Nature Switzerland AG 2023
E. Brown, S. Weiss (eds.), *An Ode to Joy*,
https://doi.org/10.1007/978-3-031-28229-4_44

research compares parents to non-parents and finds enduring decreases in happiness[4] and marital satisfaction.[5] Many acknowledge that the parenting-happiness relationship is more complex, noting that levels of happiness vary across demographics (single parents report lower levels, fathers may have higher ratings) and geographic location, with United States parents experiencing the greatest degree of unhappiness.

Parents' struggles are not for lack of information. An Amazon search for parenting books results in over 60,000 items, and googling "parent advice blog" reveals over 85 million options. Might this plethora of information designed to help actually create a roadblock to parental happiness? "Expert wisdom" suggests childrearing has a singular right and wrong approach, and unless parents follow the correct guidance, and optimize "job performance" they risk raising imperfect children. Add to the advice overload media portrayals of parenting, and you have a powerful set of unreasonable, happiness-jeopardizing expectations. As a single mother lamented, "From baby-lotion commercials that make motherhood look happy and well rested, to commercials for Disney World where you're supposed to feel like a kid because you're there with your kids, we've made parenthood out to be one blissful moment after another, and it's disappointing when you find out it's not."[6]

Long before Amazon, the Torah and Jewish wisdom offered considerable guidance, including how to educate one's children (*hanoch l'na'ar al pi darcho*—one should educate according to the child's unique way), what to teach (*limadata l'bincha*—teach your child, included in daily prayers), how to discipline (push away with the left hand, draw closer with the right),[7] and much more. Like the modern parenting advice literature, Torah advice focuses on the child's needs. Discovering how to parent with joy may require a deeper exploration of psychological research and Torah wisdom.

Experiencing joyful parenting requires reasonable expectations about *both* parenting and happiness. Rabbi Sacks explains, "Happiness is about a lifetime but joy lives in the moment. Happiness tends to be a cool emotion, but joy makes you want to dance and sing. It's hard to feel happy in the midst of uncertainty. But you can still feel joy." [8] This distinction is reflected in the somewhat conflicting findings in two research approaches: measuring parental happiness vs. assessing parental bliss. Parental bliss is conceptualized as a pleasant and emotionally rewarding experience involving feelings of fulfillment and subjective meaning.[9] As such, researchers document the regular presence of bliss by asking parents if they feel completely absorbed in their new role, if interaction with their baby gives them great pleasure, if it is fulfilling to be there for their child, and whether being parents gives deeper meaning to their life. Parental happiness evaluations, in contrast tend to ask parents to rate their subjective level of happiness when they engage in daily tasks. When measuring in the moment of diaper changing or bedtime, parents may seem less than happy. Asking parents about the joy they experience in their role and with their child, focusing them on the purpose and meaning being a parent offers, provides a different picture.

A review by Nelson, Kushlev, and Lyobumirsky challenges the notion that parents do not experience ongoing happiness aside from blissful moments of parental joy.[10] They explain that there are four elements of parenting which contribute to happiness; parenting provides meaning and purpose, parenting satisfies a basic human need, parenting engenders positive emotions, and parenting expands parents' social roles. I explore psychological and Torah wisdom regarding these parenting happiness contributors below.

Pursuing Goals/Purpose in Life

In their research using multiple measurement techniques including comparing parents to non-parents, exploring changes in the transition to parenthood or having parents sample meaningful moments in their day, Nelson, Kushlev, and Lyoburmirsky found that parents routinely report a greater sense of purpose and meaning in their lives.

Living with purpose is strongly endorsed in Jewish sources. Rabbi Moshe Chaim Luzatto's eighteenth-century *Path of the Just* argued: "The foundation of life is for a person to have clarity as to what he is living for." Rabbi Tarfon famously reminds us that even when a task is difficult, we "are not free to avoid it."[11] The Torah, directly through its commandments, and indirectly through the examples of the patriarchs and *matriarchs*, provides us with a comprehensive guide of *mitzvot*, or commandments, for living with meaning and purpose.

Having a child forces a focus on goals and purpose. For Jewish parents who observe Jewish law, added to the support of children's general growth and learning is the goal of raising *b'nei u'b'not* Torah, children who respect and observe the laws of the Torah, who will themselves live with meaning and purpose. This is voiced when lighting Shabbat candles and praying to be "granted the privilege to raise children and grandchildren who are wise, love God and will illuminate the world with Torah and good deeds."[12]

SATISFYING A BASIC HUMAN NEED

Nelson and colleagues argue that psychological research identifies three basic human needs: autonomy, connectedness, and competence. It is through the fulfillment of these needs that optimal well-being is achieved. Parenting, Nelson and colleagues argue, provides all three. They postulate that parenting is among the highest human needs, hardwired into our species and evolutionarily adaptive. Consequently, raising children to adulthood should result in greater well-being. Since the daily demands of raising children may not be immediately rewarding, parents must regard the goal of raising successful children as a long-term objective. This is accomplished as children reach developmental milestones such as first words, learning to read, graduation, etc.

The human need to have children is strongly supported in Jewish texts. The Torah views this *mitzvah* as a central command for all Jews, and an opportunity to both emulate and partner with God, *pru urvu*, to be fruitful and multiply.[13] Rabbi Shimshon Raphael Hirsch, a German Orthodox rabbi and Torah scholar who lived in the 1800s explains, "Perpetuate your race, plant in the garden of God new human shoots, to whom you are everything and whom you train up for God."[14] It is, R. Hirsch explains, not birth alone, but the parental care that contributes to "human increase."[15] The Torah poignantly portrays the yearning for children, with Rachel, Hannah, and others expressing the longing to become parents. Abraham, Jacob, Rachel, and others demonstrate, as Hirsch expounds, that having a child is just the beginning; the drive to parent, to connect, to dedicate, and to educate, is an ongoing process.

Rabbi Sacks describes this basic human drive through a Jewish lens. "Judaism takes what is natural and sanctifies it; what is physical and invests it with spirituality; what is elsewhere considered normal and sees it as a miracle. What Darwin saw as the urge to reproduce and what Richard Dawkins calls "the selfish gene," is for Judaism high religious art, full of drama and beauty. Abraham the father, and Sarah the mother, are our enduring role models of parenthood as God's gift and our highest vocation".[16]

Infusing Positive Emotions

In the 1960s Art Linkletter's TV show, *Children Say the Darndest Things* demonstrated how amusing and entertaining children can be. Children can infuse adult emotional experiences with powerful doses of fun, laughter, and novelty. As well as broadening our emotional diet, our behavioral repertoire is enhanced as well. Since children are constantly changing, parents are constantly exposed to new experiences and adventures. It is unlikely that I would have bundled into four layers of clothing and headed down a local hill on a sled, were I not sharing the experience with my children. There is much knowledge and learning I would not have been exposed to had I not needed to support my children's mastery. If I feel a tinge of sadness, a video of my grandchildren's antics will make me smile, and an in-person visit is sure to include giggles.

Rabbi Aaron Lichtenstein, the head of Yeshivat Har Etzion and a noted authority in Jewish law and thought in the twenty-first century, shared a personal example of this broadening of experience and the joy it engenders. When a student quoted him as saying parents should be prepared to both learn *and* play ball with their children, he offered an important clarification:

> I did not play ball with my children as a trick, as a tactic. I did not think, "Today I'll play basketball with him, and in a year, we will learn *Minchat Chinuch*." I don't think one should approach it that way. There is joy, there is wonder, in the ability to play with one's children; it is not simply a tool, not just instrumental. It is a joy in its own right, and one of the joys which I think God fully permits us and wants us to participate in.[17]

For a Torah giant, a master of learning, to recognize, resonate with and reinforce the joy of parenting, and describe it as a holy gift is powerful encouragement for all parents to engage with and enjoy their children.

Boosting Parents' Identity with Multiple Social Roles

Holding multiple roles means that one can acknowledge success in one role to mitigate disappointments in another, resulting in greater levels of happiness. When roles are intrinsically driven, experienced as a calling, rather than an externally assigned chore, the happiness boost is greatest.

Modern parents routinely endorse wearing multiple hats, an experience made more acute by COVID, which put parents in roles as teachers, chefs, and home health aides.

A view in the Babylonian Talmud (BT Kiddushin 29a) explains: "The Sages taught: A father is obligated with regard to his son to circumcise him, to redeem him, and to teach him Torah, and to marry him to a woman, and to teach him a trade. And some say: A father is also obligated to teach his son to swim." Each of these obligations derive from biblical sources and make clear that parents serve multiple care-giving roles, complementing other roles they play in their community, family, and career.

Perhaps the most central and well-known role of Jewish parents is that of educator and spiritual guide, elucidated in the words of the Torah that are recited three times daily in the central *Shema* prayer: *v'shinantam l'vanekha,* and you shall teach your children. This spiritual teaching, beyond imparting knowledge, aims to establish belief and foster practice. Rabbi Sacks, considering this educational role of Jewish parents in building future generations, considers the initial father of the Jewish faith. In the one verse in which the Bible explains why Abraham was chosen as the father of a new faith it says, "For I have chosen him, so that he will direct his children and his household after him to keep the way of the Lord by doing what is right and just." Abraham was chosen to be both a parent and an educator.[18]

Finding Joy Outside Parenting

Our communities are particularly focused around families and children. In public rituals, such as the *Simhat Torah kol hanearim* prayer (a prayer for all the children), gathering the community's children under a large *tallit* [prayer shawl], and in personal mommy-and-me outings, carpools, and playdates, Jewish communal life is often child-centric. We need to exercise sensitivity to the pain and longing of couples with fertility and other challenges. As we consider the above discussion of parenting fostering happiness, it is imperative to acknowledge that those not able to pursue parenthood can discover other equally valid and valuable pathways to meaning, fulfillment, and joy.

Welcoming Joy into Parenting

Translating theory and research into practice can help open the door to joy in our parenting. I offer the ideas below as possibilities, not panaceas, as contributors, not cure-alls.

Connecting to Meaning

While much of parenting involves mundane actions, making lunches, sorting laundry, supporting homework, what we think while we engage in those actions can elevate them. We can consciously choose to recognize that whatever seemingly simple parenting actions occupy us, we are engaged in a sacred partnership of creation.

As Rabbi Sacks wrote, "Stephen Hawking famously wrote at the end of *A Brief History of Time* that if we had a Unified Field Theory, a scientific theory of everything, we would know the mind of God. We believe otherwise. To know the mind of God we do not need theoretical physics. We simply need to know what it is to be a parent. The miracle of childbirth is as close as we come to understanding the-love-that-brings-new-life-into-the-world that is God's creativity."[19] Our challenge is to stay connected to that feeling of joy and creation even as we go through the daily motions of parenting.

Finding Fulfillment Along the Way

When a three-and-a-half-year-old is not toilet trained, a four-year-old still sucks her thumb, or a second-grader struggles on playdates, invariably someone offers the pithy parenting wisdom that "no one walks down the aisle in diapers." This exhortation to be patient and reminder that children are works in progress is important, but it is only part of joyful parenting. Parents and children will be so much happier if, while working toward and waiting for large accomplishments, we appreciate and celebrate incremental goals.

Going a step further, we need to embrace mistakes and failure as a critical part of the journey. I experienced the joyful moment of letting go of my youngest's bicycle and having him ride independently, only after I thought to tell him, despondent and frustrated by his falling, that he *needed* to fall at least five times on each ride to the corner. This transformed every fall from a tragedy to a critical part of the learning. It turned failure to success.

Embracing Novelty, Spontaneity, Learning, and Laughter

Your children will open doors to new worlds. Even when it feels uncomfortable or out of character, go through those doors! The novelty children bring will stretch and challenge you, but it will also fuel your happiness.

When you follow your child's lead into new experiences, you not only expand your horizons, but you also build the all-important parent-child relationship. Psychologists, Russel Barkley and Carol Webster Stratton, begin their evidence-based parenting programs with some version of a fully child-driven activity.[20] They encourage parents to offer children a routine 10 or 15-minute opportunity to select an activity to do together, and to suspend typical parent-direction for the duration. Instead of correcting, adjusting, or teaching, parents are told to be positive and simply enjoy their child. Imagine how liberating and joyful it is for a parent and how empowering for a child when "you should color in the lines" is replaced by "what amazing scribbling you made." These special times support both parent and child happiness and build a child's sense of connectedness.

Welcoming Roles and Opportunities

As a complement to embracing novelty, wear with pride and pleasure the new roles that parenting entails. During COVID lockdown, one parent shared feeling like a teacher, chef, supply chain manager, conflict mediator, security officer, and medical advisor. Pandemic aside, that could be a typical parent resume! Rather than bemoan added job titles, see them as an opportunity to apply your skills broadly and to cultivate new talents and connections. Often parents create meaningful and lasting social connections through carpool or little league coaching.

Being Spiritual

Spirituality, a sense of awe, and feeling part of something grander than oneself is perfectly engendered by parenting. From the moment we meet them, our children amaze us, and if we are open to it, allow us to witness miracles daily. As a parent, you feel the enormous power of being a creator, bringing life into the world. Concurrently, you are humbled. You feel tiny compared to the endless responsibility you negotiate, the depths of worry you experience, and the heartfelt hopes you harbor for their healthy growth and happiness. Find and embrace moments of wonder. Learn to live with chronic uncertainty. Pray—for your children's well-being, but also for your own. Prayer provides an opportunity to connect to the Divine. Through personal prayer you connect to the Ultimate Parent, who is, every step of the way, ready to share your joy.

Conclusion

Rabbi Aharon Lichtenstein's summary of parental economics, its costs, and its dividends is the most fitting conclusion to this article. If you do the math and consider parenting through a non-spiritual, pragmatic lens, it makes little sense. Rabbi Lichtenstein reminds us:

> You have to be willing to give, and willing to receive. Family life is all about giving and receiving reciprocally, to children, to parents, to a spouse, in all areas of life. Superficially regarded, raising children is massive giving. But I tell you that it is massive receiving, but massive! The joy and *nachas* are beyond words.[21]

As a parent, I have known moments of panic and pride, of worry and wonder. The rollercoaster never stops, and the thrills keep coming. I have been blessed with more moments of joy than I can count and I'm counting still. When I was joyful at their first steps, I could not have imagined how happy I would feel when they walked down the aisle to marry the mates of their dreams. When I reveled in their happiness and their accomplishments, I had no idea what expansive joy I would feel when I saw them build their own homes and lives and hold their children in their arms, beaming with a happiness like no other.

Notes

1. Daniel Gilbert, *Stumbling on Happiness* (New York: A.A. Knopf, 2006).
2. Anna M. Stertz and Bettina S. Wiese, "Child-related Bliss and Couples' Partnership Satisfaction in the Early Parenthood Period: A Longitudinal Dyadic Perspective," *Journal of Family Psychology* 34, no, 8 (2020): 1046–57.
3. Daniel Kahneman, Alan Krueger, David Schkade, Norbert Schwarz, and Arthur Stone, "A Survey Method for Characterizing Daily Life Experience: The Day Reconstruction Method," *Science* 306, no. 5702 (December 3, 2004): 1776–80. https://doi.org/10.1126/science.1103572. PMID: 15576620.
4. Maike Luhmann, et al., "Subjective Well-Being and Adaptation to Life Events: A Meta-Analysis," *Journal of Personality and Social Psychology* 102, no. 3 (2012): 592–615. https://doi.org/10.1037/a0025948.
5. Jean M. Twenge, et al., "Parenthood and Marital Satisfaction: A Meta-Analytic Review," *Journal of Marriage and Family* 65, no. 3 (2004): 574–83. https://doi.org/10.1111/j.1741-3737.2003.00574.x
6. Newsweek Staff, "Does Having Children Make You Happy?" *Newsweek*, June 6, 2008, accessed, https://www.newsweek.com/does-having-children-make-you-happy-91157.
7. BT Sota 47a.
8. Jonathan Sacks, "The Deep Power of Joy," *Covenant and Conversation*, Re'eh 5776, https://www.rabbisacks.org/covenant-conversation/reeh/deep-power-of-joy/
9. Anna M. Stertz and Bettina S. Wiese, "Child-Related Bliss and Couples' Partnership Satisfaction in the Early Parenthood Period: A Longitudinal Dyadic Perspective," *Journal of Family Psychology* 34, no. 8 (2020): 1046–57. ISSN: 0893-3200, https://doi.org/10.1037/fam0000717.
10. Katherine S. Nelson, et al., "The Pains and Pleasures of Parenting: When, Why, and How is Parenthood Associated with More or Less Well-Being?," *Psychological Bulletin* 140, no. 3 (2014): 846–95, https://doi.org/10.1037/a0035444.
11. *Ethics of the Fathers* 2:16.
12. Nosson Scherman, *The Complete ArtScroll Siddur* (New York: Mesorah Publications, Ltd, 1984), 297, Kindling Sabbath and Festival Lights.
13. Gen. 1:28.
14. Samson Raphael Hirsch, *Horeb: A Philosophy of Jewish Laws and Observances* (London: Soncino Press, 1962) Chapter 80.
15. Samson Raphael Hirsch, Commentary on Gen. 1:28.
16. Jonathan Sacks, "On Being a Jewish Parent", accessed, https://outorah.org/p/32137/.

17. Aharon Lichtenstein, "On Raising Children: A Torah Perspective," *Journal of Jewish Day School Leadership* (November 2018), accessed, https://www.cojds.org/2018/11/28/on-raising-children-a-torah-perspective/.
18. Jonathan Sacks, "On Parents and Teachers," *Covenant and Conversation*, Pinchas, 5767, 5773, accessed, https://www.rabbisacks.org/covenant-conversation/pinchas/on-parents-and-teachers/.
19. Jonathan Sacks, "On Being a Jewish Parent," accessed, https://outorah.org/p/32137/.
20. Russel Barkley, *Defiant Children* (New York: Guilford Publications, 1997); Carolyn Webster-Stratton, *The Incredible Years: A Trouble-Shooting Guide for Parents of Children Aged 2–8 Years*, 3rd ed. (Seattle: The Incredible Years, 2019).
21. Aharon Lichtenstein, "On Raising Children: A Torah Perspective," *Journal of Jewish Day School Leadership* (November 2018), accessed, https://www.cojds.org/2018/11/28/on-raising-children-a-torah-perspective/

CHAPTER 45

Building the Joyful Classroom

Jeremy Bruce

In recent years, there have been troubling indications that all is not well within our schools, with significant challenges affecting students of all ages, especially our teenagers. In a 2019 study of over 20,000 American high school students, the words most often used to describe their school experience were "tired," "stressed," and "bored."[1] While students also reported positive feelings associated with school, the authors of this study highlighted some concerning responses that reflect children's negative experiences. Unfortunately, the COVID-19 pandemic has created further challenges for adolescents, with a report using data collected in 2021 suggesting that the pandemic has caused a mental health crisis in schools, with 44% of respondents reporting persistent feelings of sadness or hopelessness with a troubling 20% of students said that they had seriously considered attempting suicide.[2]

While the studies above are representative of students in the United States as a whole, a similar story is emerging from the Jewish day-school world. While, to date, there has been little research on the mental health and well-being of Jewish day school students, the evidence available paints

J. Bruce (✉)
Rabbi Sacks Legacy, North America, Cleveland, OH, USA

© The Author(s), under exclusive license to Springer Nature Switzerland AG 2023
E. Brown, S. Weiss (eds.), *An Ode to Joy*,
https://doi.org/10.1007/978-3-031-28229-4_45

a concerning picture. One recent study by the Blue Dove Foundation in Atlanta, Georgia, surveyed 154 Jewish teens, the majority of whom attended Jewish day schools. Researchers found that many students were experiencing significant emotional distress. For example, 89% reported feeling stressed, 79.2% experienced anxiety and nervousness that interfered with normal activities, and just over half of the respondents reported experiencing depression defined as elongated periods of hopelessness and intense sadness.[3] This research has been confirmed by anecdotal evidence provided by experts in the field of mental health in Jewish day schools. For example, Rabbi Noam Stein, the executive director of *Refuat HaNefesh*, a U.S. based Jewish mental health organization, has noted a sharp increase in the need for psychological support due to the trauma and disruption caused by the pandemic. This is a pattern mirrored across the country with increased reports of stress and social isolation.[4] Marc Fein,[5] a mental health advocate, and educator who has lectured on well-being in numerous Jewish day schools, has noted an increased sense of isolation and loss among our teenagers.

Yet there is also much to celebrate. Our Jewish day schools are institutions that can best facilitate the growth of a new generation of committed and knowledgeable Jewish adults. Educators transmit Jewish cultural norms and ways of thinking to our young people. According to current research, Jewish days schools have an impressive record of educating knowledgeable and committed graduates who form strong Jewish social bonds, are academically successful, well-prepared for college, and contribute to society.[6] A recent study of Jewish communal leaders demonstrates that Jewish day schools, along with Jewish overnight camps and youth groups, play an important role in forming the next cadre of Jewish leaders and provide a sense of purpose, knowledge, and skills that far exceed the narrower success criteria of college and career preparation that are typical goals for secondary education.[7]

For Rabbi Sacks, Jewish schools are the foundation of Jewish civilization. He wrote that "Jews knew that to defend a country you need an army, but to defend a civilization you need schools."[8] Jewish day schools are called upon to inspire students with a sense of purpose and meaning that are "essential to human dignity."[9] To do so, schools must look beyond narrow academic goals and bring a palpable sense of joy to the learning process. According to Rabbi Sacks this can be achieved by helping students to appreciate the world of beauty and meaning that surrounds them.[10] Jewish day schools take this responsibility seriously and work to create a meaningful and joyful environment for their students. Their efforts to do so have only increased in importance as we emerge from the COVID-19 pandemic.

In response to the challenges presented by the pandemic, Jewish day schools have undertaken a variety of initiatives to improve students' mental health. These include increased funding for mental health professionals embedded within schools, teen mental health clubs, as well as creating more opportunities for students to connect through informal programming.[11] Further, during the pandemic, COVID-safe policies allowed students to attend school in person earlier and more frequently than the general school population in the United States. This not only positively impacted students' mental health but also led to an increase in day school enrollment.[12]

While many of these responses take place in a general school setting, it is worth noting that students spend the majority of their time at school in a classroom. Therefore, it is imperative that schools pay even more attention to what happens within the classroom if they wish to address these worrying mental health trends. I would like to suggest two approaches that administrators and educators might consider within the classroom setting to create what I will term the "joyful classroom."

RELATIONSHIPS

Education is more than the transmission of knowledge and skills. John C. Maxwell, the leadership and management expert, stated that "Students don't care what you know until they know that you care." This simple aphorism contains an important truth about education and reminds us that the classroom is at its core a relational space. The physical isolation caused by the pandemic placed a strain on interpersonal connections between students and their peers, and between students and teachers. In a post-pandemic world teachers should consider how they enhance their relationships and inter-personal connections with their students.

Rabbi Sacks suggests that direct, open, and deeply focused interactions with each other are essential to realize our humanity. "To be fully human, we need direct encounters with other human beings. We have to be in their presence, open to their otherness, alert to their hopes and fears, engaged in the minuet of conversation, the delicate back-and-forth of speaking and listening."[13] Creating spaces where students and teachers feel comfortable speaking and listening to one another respectfully and honestly is perhaps the most important aspect of the joyful classroom.

Nel Noddings, the late Stanford University philosopher, believed that teachers should foster what she terms the "caring relation in teaching." For Noddings, it is not sufficient to tell students that their teacher cares for his or her students, since this does not guarantee that students feel cared for.[14] To create the caring relation, the teacher must be attentive in a way that Noddings terms "engrossment." This type of listening allows the teacher to understand the expressed needs of the student more fully. This approach requires teachers to put aside any assumptions or prior expectations they may have about what a student needs. This, in turn, leads to what Noddings calls "motivational displacement," a desire to respond and help in some way. There are times when a teacher may not agree with a student's request. For example, a student may be struggling to submit assignments in a timely fashion. The teacher could approach this in a formal bureaucratic manner by referring to school policies and expectations. Alternatively, the teacher can acknowledge the student's struggle but at the same time convey the expectation that the assignment is completed. This approach acknowledges the challenges that this student may be experiencing while still maintaining the caring relationship.[15]

While teachers are often well-placed to engage in these types of interactions with their students, the demands of the curriculum can sometimes act as a barrier to these relationships. An interesting example of an approach that intentionally facilitates deeper relationships between teachers and students and between students and their peers is the *Lifnei V'lifnim* program created by Rabbi Dov Singer at Yeshivat Mekor Chaim in Israel. Over the past five years, this program has been introduced first as a pilot project at Fuchs Mizrachi School in Cleveland, Ohio, and has now expanded to other schools in North America.

The program's goal is to first engage educators in their own process of personal religious growth that will, in turn, enable them to create spaces for students to build a deeper relationship with God. This work is achieved by practicing the core skills of being present, building trust, facilitating authentic dialogue, and encouraging self-awareness.[16] At least once a week, teachers set aside a dedicated time in the Judaic Studies classroom for students to engage in reflective conversations that emphasize relationship and dialogue over any content or skills. During these sessions students are able to connect with each other and their teacher to explore issues of religious and personal growth in a supportive environment that allows students and teachers to bring their more authentic selves to the learning. This relationship-building experience is a powerful way to create a joyful classroom. As Rabbi Sacks explains, joy is achieved when individuals join together and share moments a part of a group. It is a "redemption of solitude."[17]

These shared experiences of camaraderie build deep relationships within the classroom, sparking moments of joy that positively impact every other aspect of the learning experience.

While the *Lifnai V'lifnim* program is most applicable within the Judaic studies classroom, the principles that create this joyful classroom climate can also be applied to other disciplines.

Relevance

A second approach is to examine the content of the curriculum. Creating learning experiences that students find meaningful and relevant is a constant challenge. Students do not always appreciate the necessity of a topic or unit and can find it hard to understand its importance. This can lead to feelings of boredom and disengagement. While there is no practical way to remove all feelings of boredom at school, research suggests presenting the material that connects to young peoples' life goals, and real-world problems, or taking a more project-based approach can lead to more motivated students.[18]

Project-based learning (PBL) is defined as a model that organizes learning around challenging questions, problem-solving tasks, or investigative activities. It allows students the opportunity to work in a semi-autonomous manner to create some form of final presentation or product.[19] The defining feature of this model is giving students more ownership over their work which encourages intrinsic motivation. When students find a task more relevant and personally meaningful, deeper and long-lasting learning is more likely to occur.[20]

Like all aspects of teaching, getting PBL right requires training and planning. It is essential that the teacher moves away from a more frontal teaching modality and, instead, acts as a facilitator and guide to allow the students to encounter challenges and work with their peers to arrive at possible solutions. As such, PBL is essentially collaborative, and to be successful all students need to contribute to the final product. This is no simple matter, and teachers need to spend time guiding students in effective group work protocols, scaffolding instruction so that students achieve growth just beyond their reach, and encouraging them when challenges arise.²¹ Another essential element of effective PBL is a clear framework of assessment and achievement. While this model emphasizes student independence, it is still important that students are aware of how their work will be evaluated. Ron Berger, a veteran American educator, has promoted this model as one that can transform students' experiences at school.²²

This model can work equally well in Judaic studies as it does in general studies and has been demonstrated to address boredom and increase student motivation²³ PBL can also be an excellent model for integrating Judaic and general studies in Rabbi Sacks' concept of Torah *V'Chochmah*, ensuring that there is a genuine conversation between Jewish and worldly knowledge. Furthermore, PBL has been linked to better mental health outcomes, increased well-being, and greater civic engagement.²⁴

Conclusion

Rabbi Sacks taught us that joy is the result of a communally focused effort—moving away from the "I" to the "We." When teachers build deep trusting relationships with students and model attentive listening, and they craft relevant, collaborative learning modalities, they create a classroom environment that encourages all participants to work together to create meaningful, engaging, and joyful educational experiences.

For Rabbi Sacks, facilitating educational moments that are full of joy and meaning is one of the most important acts one generation performs for the next, for as he so eloquently explained in a House of Lords debate in 2017, "Schools are about more than what we know and what we can do. They are about who we are and what we must do to help others become what they might be. The world our children will inherit tomorrow is born in the schools we build today."²⁵

Notes

1. Julia Moeller, Marc A. Brackett, Zorana Ivcevic, and Arielle E. White. "High School Students' Feelings: Discoveries from a Large National Survey and an Experience Sampling Study," *Learning and Instruction* 66 (2020): 101301.
2. Sherry Everett Jones, Kathleen A. Ethier, Marci Hertz, Sarah DeGue, Vi Donna Le, Jemekia Thornton, Connie Lim, Patricia J. Dittus, and Sindhura Geda. "Mental Health, Suicidality, and Connectedness Among High

School Students during the COVID-19 pandemic—Adolescent Behaviors and Experiences Survey, United States, January–June 2021," *MMWR supplements* 71, no. 3 (2022): 16.
3. See the summary of the study and accompanying survey data at https://thebluedovefoundation.org/persevering-with-my-peers-insight-into-teen-mental-health/.
4. Rabbi Noam Stein, Personal communication to the author. See https://www.refuathanefesh.org/about/ for further details of this organization.
5. Marc Fein, personal communication to author.
6. Fern Chertok, Charles Kadushin, Annette Koren, Graham Wright, Leonard Saxe, and Aron Klein. *What Difference Does Day School Make? The Impact of Day School: A Comparative Analysis of Jewish College Students* (Boston, MA: The Partnership for Excellence in Jewish Education, 2007).
7. *The Jewish Education of Today's Jewish Leadership: Day Schools, Overnight Camps, &Other Educational Experiences among Lay & Professional Jewish Communal Leaders* (Keren Keshet and Research Success Technologies Ltd, November 2021), https://www.jewishdatabank.org/content/upload/bjdb/2021_Jewish_Education_of_Today's_Jewish_Leaders_(ReST)_DB.pdf.
8. Jonathan Sacks, *Future Tense: Jews, Judaism, and Israel in the Twenty-First Century* (New York, Schocken Books, 2009), 176.
9. Jonathan Sacks, *The Dignity of Difference: How to Avoid the Clash of Civilizations* (London and New York, Continuum, 2002), 137.
10. Jonathan Sacks, *Studies in Spirituality* (Jerusalem, Koren, 2021), 258.
11. "Mental Health. Prizmah Knowledge Center", accessed June 10, 2022, https://prizmah.org/knowledge/search?know_cntr_search%5B0%5D=knowledge_topics%3A15771.
12. Jack Wertheimer and Alex Pomson, "Jewish Education and the Pandemic: The Surprising Success of Day Schools in a Time of Crisis", Commentary, January 2021, accessed June 10, 2022, https://www.commentary.org/articles/jack-wertheimer/jewish-education-pandemic/.
13. Jonathan Sacks, *Morality: Restoring the Common Good in Divided Times* (New York, Basic Books, 2020), 58–59.
14. Nel Noddings, "Caring in Education," accessed July 7, 2022, https://infed.org/mobi/caring-in-education/.
15. Nel Noddings." The Caring Relation in Teaching" *Oxford Review of Education* 38, no. 6 (2012): 771–81.
16. "Mekor Chaim: Lifnai V'lifnim Global Educators' Development," accessed July 11, 2022, https://makorchaim.org/us-educators-training-program/.
17. Jonathan Sacks, Covenant & Conversation, The Pursuit of Joy, Ki Tavo, 5775, 5782, accessed July 12, 2022, https://www.rabbisacks.org/covenant-conversation/ki-tavo/the-pursuit-of-joy/.

18. Ann Bainbridge Frymier and Gary M. Shulman. "What's In It for Me?": Increasing Content Relevance to Enhance Students' Motivation." *Communication Education* 44, no. 1 (1995): 40–50; Michael Furlong, Douglas C. Smith, Tina Springer, and Erin Dowdy. "Bored with School! Bored with Life? Well-being Characteristics Associated with a School Boredom Mindset." *Journal of Positive School Psychology* 5, no. 1 (2021): 42–64.
19. Bill Lucas, Guy Claxton, and Ellen Spencer. *Expansive Education: Teaching Learners for the Real World*. (Camberwell, Victoria, ACER Press, 2013), 83.
20. James M. Lang. *Small Teaching: Everyday Lessons from the Science of Learning*, (San Francisco, Jossey-Bass, 2016), 169.
21. Dimitra Kokotsaki, Victoria Menzies, and Andy Wiggins. "Project-Based Learning: A Review of the Literature." *Improving Schools* 19, no. 3 (November 2016): 267–77.
22. Ron Berger, Leah Rugen, and Libby Wooden, *Leaders of Their Own Learning*, (San Francisco, Jossey-Bass, 2014).
23. Phyllis C. Blumenfeld, Elliot Soloway, Ronald W. Marx, Joseph S. Krajcik, Mark Guzdial, and Annemarie Palincsar. "Motivating Project-Based Learning: Sustaining the Doing, Supporting the Learning." *Educational Psychologist* 26, no. 3–4 (1991): 369–398.
24. Lynn E. Swaner, "Linking Engaged Learning, Student Mental Health and Well-being, and Civic Development: A Review of the Literature." *Liberal Education* 93, no. 1 (2007): 16–25.
25. Jonathan Sacks, "The House of Lords Debate on Education", December 7, 2017, accessed July 13, 2022, https://youtu.be/1yupkG7NB8w.

CHAPTER 46

Three Paths to Joy: *Noble Sacrifice, Inner Peace, and Covenantal Community*

Benji Levy

Joy, according to Rabbi Sacks, is a road with multiple lanes. In his unique address on the topic of happiness at Emory University in 2010, Rabbi Sacks identified three key pathways to happiness: sacrificing for a cause, seeking inner peace, and building covenantal communities.[1] As with many intertwined paradoxes, "Happiness is inflected differently in these several modes of being."[2] Rabbi Sacks was able to isolate and analyze each of these, and expound upon their interplay, providing a framework by which to approach this most elusive of pursuits. Rabbi Sacks' presentation highlights that no one has a monopoly on happiness and there is no one approach to achieve it. Each of the three paths he outlines, therefore, is an effective way to find joy and perhaps one needs all three *in combination* to achieve a complete sense of happiness.

B. Levy (✉)
Israel Impact Partners, Jerusalem, Israel

© The Author(s), under exclusive license to Springer Nature Switzerland AG 2023
E. Brown, S. Weiss (eds.), *An Ode to Joy*,
https://doi.org/10.1007/978-3-031-28229-4_46

Noble Sacrifice

The first type of joy is born from struggle for a noble cause, a sacrifice for higher ideals. One prime example that Rabbi Sacks identifies is the sacrifice a person makes for their home, as is evident in many biblical characters and legendary tales of Jewish tradition—beginning with the father of ethical monotheism: Abraham. Abraham's life was ridden with setbacks and difficulties: famine, leaving his father's home, the kidnapping of his wife and nephew, repeated fertility crises, the banishment of Ishmael, and then the binding of Isaac. Despite these trials, tribulations, and travails, the Torah tells us that Abraham died old and satisfied with life. As Rabbi Sacks puts it: "One of the most serene deaths in the bible. There is a kind of happiness in all of this."[3] Following God's direction, Abraham ultimately found joy within his sacrifice for the noblest of causes, the establishment of a people with a home to call their own. The patriarch of the Jewish people discovers the first kind of happiness. According to Rabbi Sacks:

It is the happiness, not of being at peace in the universe, but the happiness that comes from challenge, struggle, and sometimes sacrifice for high ideals. A life that has its setbacks and its moments of despair… from having taken part in the struggle, knowing that you took part in a noble cause.

Setting up this paradigm, Rabbi Sacks establishes the precedent to trace this countercultural strand of happiness throughout Jewish history. Jumping to the modern period, for example, one can observe great joy emanating from painful sacrifice during the early Zionist settlement of the Land of Israel, which echoes Abraham's struggles. Arriving at desolate lands and malaria-infested swamps, early pioneers labored under torturously onerous conditions to realize the vision for a Jewish state. As per the prophetic vision of the Psalmist, when the return to Zion happens: "those who sow in tears, reap in joy."[4]

Rabbi Shlomo Goren, who founded the Israel Defense Forces' military rabbinate and became the State's third Ashkenazi Chief Rabbi, arrived in the Land of Israel in 1925 from Poland with his family and went straight to a barren hill in the north of the country. They lived in tents until huts were built through a particularly brutal winter. In his autobiography, Goren recalls a storm that raged through the settlement one night and "carried away everything in their path, including our tents…we were left without shelter, exposed to the wind and rain, shivering from the cold and soaked to the bone."[5] And yet, he writes:

In the middle of the night, we wrapped ourselves in blankets and all sorts of rags, gathered together in a circle, and danced with extraordinary enthusiasm and Hasidic fervor until sunrise. Then the men gathered for morning prayers. I will remember that night as long as I live—how the joy never departed from the hearts of the Hasidim, despite the cold, the rain, and the storm, even though they had left all they owned in Warsaw, along with the good life there. [6]

What Abraham, the ancient *oleh*, and the early Zionist *olim* had in common was an undying faith, vision, and commitment to a cause beyond themselves.

Paradoxically, those who achieve great success, especially those that are dedicating themselves to a cause, often do not seek it. It seeks them in the long term, as an offshoot of their sacrifice in the short-term. Happiness shares this feature, as Viktor Frankl (whose writings had a profound influence on Rabbi Sacks) observed:

> Success, like happiness, cannot be pursued; it must ensue, and it only does so as the unintended side effect of one's personal dedication to a cause greater than oneself or as the by-product of one's surrender to a person other than oneself. Happiness must happen, and the same holds for success: you have to let it happen by not caring about it. [7]

Dr. Frankl's wisdom, born in the tragedy and destruction of the Holocaust, had a philosophical antecedent from a different era. Rabbi Sacks located this idea through Maimonides in the Laws of Repentance declaring that: "You do not arrive at happiness by pursuing it directly."

This is the first version of Rabbi Sacks' understanding of happiness: the joy that ensues from struggling for a noble cause, fueled by faith in a better future.

Inner Peace

The second type of joy in Judaism derives from harmony or peace within oneself. There is tension between this path to happiness and the first path just described, but since Rabbi Sacks' overall thesis suggests all paths as legitimate, perhaps one needs to balance or oscillate between both.

Rabbi Sacks quotes the opening of Psalms in framing this more universal conception: "Happy is the one…whose delight is in the law of the Lord, and who meditates on His law, day and night."[8] He calls this:

A happiness of balance, of virtue, of compassion, of living well and faring well. The happiness of one who is good, who does good, who has been blessed in life, and who has been held in high regard... Happiness as rootedness.

As the rabbinic adage professes: "There is no happiness like the resolution of doubts."[9] This understanding of joy is not just about resolving *doubt*. It is about resolution in general. Peace (*shalom*) and wholeness (*shlemut*) share the same etymological root in Hebrew. In this sense, happiness results from arriving at a sense of completion.

Rabbi Sacks dedicated the least time to this path in his presentation, perhaps because it is the most universally accepted. While pointing out that serenity and resolution lead one to happiness may not be unique, Rabbi Sacks' brilliance lies in observing the plurality of legitimate paths within and across traditions:

> Happiness takes many forms. There is the happiness of one who is at peace with the world, and the happiness of one who challenges and changes the world. There is the happiness of Mozart, as sweet and natural as a spring breeze, and there is the happiness of the late Beethoven string quartets, carved from the rock by struggle and pain.[10]

COVENANTAL COMMUNITY

Elements of the first two paths to happiness can be achieved either alone or with others. When Abraham was enjoined to go forth from his land, his birthplace and the house of his father to a place that God would show him, this injunction was all conveyed to him in singular form: "go for yourself"[11] not the plural "go for yourselves" (even if Abraham did travel with Sarai, his wife, and Lot, his nephew). The consequence of that sacrifice was also explained in singular form: "I will make you a great nation and I will bless you."[12] Sacrifice can of course be unilateral and lonely. Similarly, one may resolve one's doubts internally without the involvement of any other person. But the third path outlined can only be found in the context of community, as Rabbi Sacks states: "In Judaism, happiness is not something we find in solitude, still less, in self-gratification. It is something we experience together... essentially collective[ly]. It only exists in virtue of being shared."[13]

Rabbi Sacks traces this through the Book of Deuteronomy in connection with sources of joy that are outside of ourselves. He cites verses relating to the interaction between spouses,[14] expressed at festivals or on bringing first fruits to Jerusalem,[15] and with people who are often more vulnerable.[16] All examples require engagement with others. This is so critical to a functional society that, as he says, "the failure to experience happiness is identified as a cause of national disintegration and the curses of division and defeat."[17] The converse could be inferred as well, that is, the disintegration of community and the curse of division are causes of a failure to find happiness.

Rabbi Sacks describes this as:

> Covenantal happiness, the happiness of an entire people as it gives thanks to God for its land, its freedom, its harvests, and its crops. It is communal, something we only experience when we leave our separate-nesses behind and become part of a covenanted community... Happiness is part of the tenor and texture of our relationships... It belongs to a worldview that has already declared at the start of the human story that "[i]t is not good for man to be alone."[18]

According to Martin Buber, one way to discover the "inner rhythm" of the biblical text is by identifying a *leitwort* or principal word repeated throughout.[19] Indeed, forms of "covenant" are found no fewer than 289 times in the Hebrew Bible and one also finds this *leitmotif* reappearing frequently through the writings and addresses of Rabbi Sacks. His series of essays on the weekly *parasha* was entitled "Covenant and Conversation" and it makes great sense that Rabbi Sacks sees this third type of happiness as the most unique of the three and representing "Judaism's most original contribution to the understanding of human wellbeing."[20]

"Social happiness comes from the idea of covenant," says Rabbi Sacks, which he defines as: "a moral commitment, in which two individuals or more, each respecting the dignity and independence of the other, come together in a bond of love and trust to do together what neither can do alone."

Two of the most defining covenants Rabbi Sacks often discussed were coined by a rabbinic leader for whom he had tremendous respect and admiration, Rabbi Soloveitchik, namely: the Covenant of Fate and the Covenant of Destiny.[21] Rabbi Soloveitchik points to the oppressive experience of slavery in Egypt as the birth-pangs of Israel as a nation and the Covenant of Fate, while he would refer to the receiving of the Torah at Sinai as the inception of the Covenant of Destiny. In Egypt, the Jewish people were bound by common suffering and mutual responsibility, and in this covenant, "the individual is subject and subjugated against his will to the national fate existence, and it is impossible for him to avoid it."[22] In contrast, the Sinaitic covenant is an expression of "the covenant of destiny," and is entered into by choice rather than imposed by historical happenstance. Whereas fate is inevitable, passive, and created by circumstance, the covenant of destiny is "an active experience full of purpose, movement, ascension, aspirations and fulfillment."[23] Rabbi Sacks based his development of covenants on Rabbi Soloveitchik's conceptual framing, outlining the need for both types and extending their communal applications into other areas such as this notion of covenantal happiness.[24]

It was this third path to happiness, anchored in the fabric that bound the Jewish people, that Rabbi Sacks felt was most lacking in society: "Something is wrong with an economy predicated on spending money, we do not have to buy things we do not need for the sake of a happiness that will not last."[25] Especially toward the end of his life, Rabbi Sacks expressed deep concern that covenantal faith communities and a general sense of shared identity in the West were receding. Titles of chapters from his final published book, *Morality*, include "Loneliness," "Unsocial Media," "The Solitary Self," and "From We to I."[26] He was fond of quoting Harvard sociologist Robert Putnam's landmark 2000 study, *Bowling Alone*, to demonstrate the drastic decline in social, faith, and civic group participation in the second half of the twenty-first century. Although he was also hopeful in referencing one of Putnam's later works, a sweeping study on religious life in America, that presented an optimistic view toward the United States' remaining faith communities.[27]

Difficult moments—as arduous, agonizing, and distressing as they may be—can also lead individuals to a heightened sense of meaning, purpose, and peace. After all, for there to be resolution there will have had to be conflict. Nevertheless, while modern society appears to be familiar with the first and second paths to happiness, it is forgetting the ancient message of Jewish tradition: that communal or covenantal happiness is a crucial element of a joyous life.

Rabbi Sacks declared:

> Three strands in a very complex picture in Judaism. Happiness as struggle—prophetic happiness. Happiness as peace—wisdom happiness. Happiness as the thing we share—covenantal happiness. That is enough at least to begin a conversation… Let us have this conversation, because it matters.

Commemorating Rabbi Sacks through an anthology like this serves as a reminder—especially in these divisive times—that this conversation is truly important. However, a conversation is not enough and it should happen early on through the formative development of students. When a more superficial view of happiness is often centered around celebrity culture/social media mimesis and even schadenfreude, this multilayered analysis of Rabbi Sacks should be converted into curricula and taught to the next generation. Different approaches will resonate with different students at different ages and stages, however, throughout their life, they should ideally be sensitive to and aim for a combination of all three. More than anything else, they should all need to be reminded that complete happiness depends, also, on the assembly of humans among their communities, their congregations, schools, families, workplaces to share each other's experiences and joy and investing in this space can yield the greatest results.

Notes

1. Rabbi Jonathan Sacks, "Rabbi Lord Jonathan Sacks: Happiness in the Jewish Perspective," Center for the Study of Law and Religion at Emory, (Nov. 13, 2020): https://www.youtube.com/watch?v=2S_rqcJnvpE. All quotes without attribution from this presentation.
2. Rabbi Lord Jonathan Sacks, "Happiness: A Jewish Perspective." *Journal of Law and Religion* 29, no. 1 (2014), 31. This essay seems to be a further development of his address at Emory University. While different thinkers, including Rabbi Sacks, ascribe nuanced difference to the terms "happiness" and "joy," for the purposes of this chapter, I will use them interchangeably and while Rabbi Sacks explores other happiness paths, I focus on the key three pathways underlying his thesis.
3. Rabbi Sacks based on *Genesis* 25:8 and surrounding verses.
4. *Psalms* 126:5.
5. Shlomo Goren, *With Might and Strength* (Maggid, 2016), Kindle version, locations 396–404.
6. Ibid.
7. Viktor Frankl, *Man's Search for Meaning* (New York: Washington Square Press, 1963), 16.
8. *Psalms* 1:1.
9. For an example of this expression, see R. David Altschuler, *Metzudat David* on *Proverbs* 15:30.

10. Sacks, "Happiness: A Jewish Perspective," *Journal of Law and Religion* 29, 31.
11. *Genesis* 12:1.
12. Ibid, 12:2.
13. Ibid., 37.
14. *Deuteronomy* 24:5.
15. *Deuteronomy* 26:11.
16. *Deuteronomy* 16:11.
17. Sacks, "Happiness: A Jewish Perspective." *Journal of Law and Religion* 29, 40, based on *Deuteronomy* 28: 47–48.
18. *Genesis* 2:18, Sacks, "Happiness: A Jewish Perspective." *Journal of Law and Religion* 29, 39.
19. Martin Buber, *The Art of Biblical Narrative*, trans. Robert Alter (New York: Basic Books, 2011), 93.
20. Sacks, "Happiness: A Jewish Perspective." *Journal of Law and Religion* 29, 45.
21. Joseph Dov Soloveitchik, *Kol Dodi Dofek: Listen-My Beloved Knocks*, trans. David Z Gordon (New York: Yeshiva University, 2006).
22. Soloveitchik, *Kol Dodi Dofek*, p. 57.
23. Ibid., *Kol Dodi Dofek*, p. 65.
24. Rabbi Sacks later adapted the term "destiny" to "faith," see for example, Jonathan Sacks, *Radical Then, Radical Now: On Being Jewish* (London, Continuum, 2008), 116. For an exploration of this framing and its implications of Jewish identity, see Benji Levy, *Covenant and the Jewish Conversion Question* (Springer Nature, 2021).
25. Sacks, "Happiness: A Jewish Perspective," *Journal of Law and Religion* 29, 46–47.
26. Jonathan Sacks, Morality: *Restoring the Common Good in Divided Times* (London: Hodder & Stoughton, 2021).
27. Robert D. Putnam and David Campbell, *American Grace: How Religion Divides and Unites Us* (Simon & Schuster, 2012).

Index[1]

A
Aaron, 16, 56n16, 60, 61, 64, 136, 263
Abraham, 171, 176, 212, 228, 261, 263, 278, 291–293, 358, 360, 376–378
Agency, 289
Agnon, S.Y., 234, 236–239, 240n7, 240n8
Akiva, R., 66, 83–89, 128, 132n7
Albo, Joseph, 169–172
Anger, 104, 141, 328–330
Aquinas, 160
Aristotle, 50, 83, 91, 148–154, 159, 160, 172, 175, 178, 179, 212, 318
Ashrei, 3, 50, 53, 54, 65, 149, 150, 157n16, 164, 165, 167n25, 184, 211, 212, 214, 245, 246, 259, 261, 305, 347
Athens, 147–156

B
Baal Shem Tov, 197–206
Beck, Aaron, 300
Beethoven, 21–24, 83, 277–279, 281n7, 283n30, 305, 378
Bell, Joshua, 267–271
Blessing, 10, 11, 19, 23, 43, 85, 97–100, 105, 106, 113, 136, 163, 167n26, 185, 228, 235, 236, 246, 247, 249–253, 261, 292, 347, 351
Bunker Hill, 217–222

C
Carigal, Raphael, 218, 220, 221, 222n5, 223n10
Cognitive behavior therapy (CBT), 300
Cover, Robert, 128–131, 132n14
Crescas, Hasdai, 159–166

[1] Note: Page numbers followed by 'n' refer to notes.

D

David, King, 49, 51, 53, 55, 102n8, 170, 239, 263, 293
Deuteronomy, 1, 9, 10, 61, 65, 111, 112, 115, 117n14, 134, 136, 150, 184, 236, 260, 274, 348, 349, 378

E

Ecclesiastes, Kohelet, 3, 36–41, 63, 65, 70, 83, 104, 110, 120, 164, 180, 185, 203, 251, 261, 304, 347
Education, 3, 104, 191, 221, 222, 313, 338, 345–352, 368, 369
Empathy, 140, 141, 194, 195, 302, 329
Esther, 43–46, 61, 62, 65, 263
Ethics of the Fathers, 97, 102n7, 212, 340
Eudomonia, 94
Exodus, 56n16, 60, 68, 172, 220, 284n32, 292

F

Fear, 46, 49, 52, 66, 70–72, 79, 80, 106, 141, 169–173, 186, 198, 199, 227, 243, 244, 329, 342, 350, 352, 369
Four Species, 68
Frankl, Viktor, 300, 377
Freud, Sigmund, 42n20, 121, 282n13, 300

G

Genesis, 98, 100, 102n7, 194, 198, 220, 290, 291
Gersonides, 160
Guide of the Perplexed, 151, 152, 178, 234

H

Halevi, Judah, 219
Hallel, 22, 68, 79, 244–246, 247n4, 248n7, 284n32
Haman, 43–45, 61–63
Hasidism, 197, 205, 206n7
Hedonia, 3, 93, 94, 178, 319
Hirsch, R. S.R., 147, 227, 358
Holiday, festival, 26, 45, 69, 70, 92–93, 114, 119, 120, 130, 134, 153, 186

I

Ibn Ezra, Abraham, 219
Imitatio Dei, 101
Isaac, 171, 237–239, 240n13, 261, 278, 291, 292, 340, 376
Israel, 22, 23, 28, 29, 51, 53, 54, 67, 71, 79, 80, 98, 99, 105, 106, 134, 136, 169, 172, 226–228, 235, 239, 244, 245, 248n6, 261–263, 268, 274, 278, 292, 294, 350, 370, 376, 379

J

Jacob, 60, 61, 64, 97, 98, 105, 106, 227, 260, 261, 292, 358
Jerusalem, 9, 10, 59, 65–66, 69, 71, 81n8, 92, 95n8, 122, 147–156, 196n3, 235, 237, 239, 241n13, 248n6, 258, 293, 294, 379
Jonah, 61, 62
Judah, 97–99, 102n7

K

Kabbalah, 206n5
Karo, Joseph, 78
Kierkegaard, 347, 349, 350

INDEX 385

Kook, Abraham, 71, 72, 112, 236–238, 240n7, 240n8
Korah, 16

L
Laban, 60, 61, 64
Leibowitz, Yeshayahu, 176, 177
Leviticus, 134, 184, 260, 293
Lichtenstein, Aharon/Aaron, 229, 233, 240n2, 359, 363
Lulav, 68–69

M
Maimonides, 10, 63, 78–80, 91–94, 95n8, 111, 112, 114, 151–154, 157n28, 159–162, 171, 172, 175, 178, 179, 181n14, 219, 377
Megilla, 44, 46, 62
Mishneh Torah, 78, 80, 94, 95n8, 258
Mordecai, 43–46
Moses, 10, 16, 56n16, 60, 61, 64, 134, 151, 154, 176, 263, 268, 293, 303, 348, 349
Music, 9, 21–23, 25–30, 55, 60, 63, 69, 72, 167n27, 204, 206n12, 273–280, 305, 351

N
Nahmanides, 121
Nahman of Bratslav, 109, 197–206, 215n9
Nicomachean Ethics, 148, 151–153, 156n7
Nietzsche, Friedrich, 183–187, 276, 283n25, 303
Numbers, 2, 3, 8, 14, 15, 27, 28, 62, 67, 78, 84, 116n5, 117n9, 163, 186, 188n3, 248n7, 250, 260, 261, 290, 315, 321

P
Plato, 51, 151, 152, 270, 323
Poetry, poem, 51, 52, 55, 56n15, 270, 277, 295
Positive psychology, 3, 53, 245, 289, 299–306, 321, 327, 328, 330, 332n5, 337–342, 346, 351
Prayer, 3, 9, 22, 25–28, 65, 68, 69, 73n25, 79, 80, 110, 111, 150, 157n16, 193, 213, 225, 238, 243, 245, 252, 257, 259–264, 312, 315, 347, 349, 356, 360, 363, 377
Psalms, *Tehillim*, 49, 50, 52, 53, 55
Purim, 10, 43, 45, 46, 62, 92, 153, 284n32

R
Rachel, 60, 262, 358
Radak, 219
Rashbam, 67
Rashi, 37, 41n9, 111, 341
Redemption, 8, 9, 43, 54, 55, 85, 194, 201, 248n6, 278, 371
Rosh Hashana, 79, 80

S
Sabbath, 9, 91, 93–94, 95n7, 95n8, 111, 112, 117n14, 151, 177, 198, 320, 322
Sarna, Nahum, 211, 212
Schneersohn, M.M., 213
Second Vatican Council, 226
Seligman, Martin, 158n46, 300–303, 305, 306, 308n10, 327, 328, 338, 346, 347, 349
Sforno, Obadiah, 220, 223n9
Shakespeare, 35, 51, 55
Shavuot, 129, 263
Shavuoth, 60
Sheheheyanu, 249–253

Simhat Torah, 132n19, 135, 258
Sinai, Mt., 172, 198, 263, 270
Sisyphus, 191–195
Solomon, 114, 251, 293
Soloveitchik, Joseph, 36, 79, 81n8, 93, 169, 176, 177, 181n7, 189n17, 191, 192, 194, 195, 196n3, 229, 230n8, 304, 331, 379, 380
Song of Songs, 99, 114
Stiles, Ezra, 218, 220, 221, 222n5, 223n10, 223n11
Sukkot, sukka, 60, 66–70, 73n15, 73n22, 111, 119–122, 153, 187
Synagogue, 22, 26, 68, 97, 218, 220, 257–264, 320, 322

T
Temple, 9, 10, 59, 70, 71, 73n15, 77–79, 99, 100, 128, 135, 164, 239, 258–261, 269, 280, 294, 348

Y
Yom Kippur, 22, 26, 79, 80, 311, 312

Z
Zeresh, 44, 45, 62
Zion, 53, 246, 260, 376
Zohar, 218–220, 223n10, 332

Printed by Printforce, United Kingdom